SAMUEL TAYLOR COLERIDGE

A Biographical Study

Oxford University Press, Amen House, London E.C. 4

GLASGOW NEW YORK TORONTO MELBOURNE WELLINGTON
BOMBAY CALCUTTA MADRAS CAPE TOWN

Geoffrey Cumberlege, Publisher to the University

FIRST PUBLISHED 1938
Reprinted lithographically in Great Britain
at the UNIVERSITY PRESS, OXFORD, 1950
from corrected sheets of the first edition

SAMUEL TAYLOR
COLERIDGE

A BIOGRAPHICAL STUDY

BY

E. K. CHAMBERS

OXFORD
AT THE CLARENDON PRESS

To

N. C.

PREFACE

EVERY writer about Coleridge must be conscious of his debt to the *Narrative* of James Dykes Campbell, which took its final form in 1894, and must regret that the full biography, so long contemplated by the poet's grandson, Ernest Hartley Coleridge, was destined to remain a fragment. Some intrepid scholar will, no doubt, one day take up that task. My own survey, like Campbell's, is a comparatively brief one, but it is able to draw upon a good deal of material which has accumulated during the last half-century, and some which, although probably known to him, he did not, in 1894, think it discreet to use. And, like Campbell, I have confined myself, in the main, to the limits of a narrative. One does not, indeed, get the full picture of Coleridge from a bare chronicle of his questing and self-tortured pilgrimage through life. But I do not think that it would have been wise to break the continuity of the book by any attempt at a detailed appreciation of his poetry, or of his Shakespearean criticism, or of his contribution to aesthetic theory, or of his political development, or of his final endeavour to provide a metaphysical basis for Trinitarian Christianity. These are tempting themes, but, although their student must take account of chronology, they can hardly be presented under its limitations.

Much of the purely biographical interest lies, I think, in the rise and fall of Coleridge's many friendships. Into these he was apt to enter lightly. He was not unaware of the tendency; there was little, indeed, in his own psychology, or in the whole sphere of things, which he was unable, by flashes, to illumine. He had the gift of good companionship, could both feel and inspire strong affections, and was ready, at times, to take considerable trouble for others. But in friendship, as in all else, he lacked staying-power. His 'Estese' was the most pathetic of his dreams. The ultimate breach with the Wordsworths amounted, of course, to a major tragedy. But the same quality which determined it is traceable enough elsewhere. The chequered relations, throughout life, with Southey make a curious study. So, in a less degree, do those with Thomas Poole, George Coleridge, Daniel Stuart, Godwin, Davy, Charles Lloyd, Estlin, Mrs. Clarkson. Even with Charles Lamb, the tolerant and faithful, there was at least once a coolness. In this respect, it is possible to draw too sharp a distinction between the wander-years and those at Highgate. There, too, although Coleridge seems, except on one occasion, to have been happy with the Gillmans, resentments often flared up or lay smouldering in embers. It was not until the very end of life, when ill health and a premature old age had dulled his sensibilities, that he really became the serene philosopher of a legend. He who walks with Coleridge must tread thorny ways and pass through valleys of humiliation. Let him remember that Charles Lamb would never hear of 'poor Coleridge', and that to Wordsworth, in retrospect, Coleridge remained 'the most *wonderful* man that he had ever known'.

It is a pleasure to record my gratitude to the Rev. G. H. B. Coleridge for allowing me to use Coleridge material of which the copyright is vested in him, to the Harvard College Library and the Trustees of the Wordsworth Museum at Dove Cottage, Grasmere, for the letters printed in Chapter V and the Appendix, and to Professor de Selincourt for the opportunity of consulting in advance the sheets of his forthcoming final instalment of *The Letters of William and Dorothy Wordsworth*, which contains, among other things, an interesting contemporary notice by Wordsworth of his first meeting with Coleridge. I am indebted also to the recent collections of letters from Coleridge and members of his family by Mr. and Mrs. E. L. Griggs and Mr. Stephen Potter, to the 'anniversary' volume on Coleridge edited by Mr. Edmund Blunden and Mr. Griggs, to Mr. T. M. Raysor's *Coleridge and* '*Asra*', and his studies of Coleridge's lectures and literary criticism; and for personal help on special points to the Rev. G. H. B. Coleridge himself, Lord Coleridge, Mrs. Rennell Coleridge, Dr. R. W. Chapman, Miss K. H. Coburn, Mrs. Griggs, Captain R. B. Haselden, Miss Enid Hill, Mr. E. Lobel, Professor John Livingston Lowes, the late Mr. E. V. Lucas, Miss Winifred Parry, the Rev. L. B. Stallard, Professor H. C. Wyld, and the Registrar of Cambridge University.

E. K. C.

September 1938.

CONTENTS

TABLE OF REFERENCES

Note. *Letters are cited by serial numbers or, if there are none, by the pages on which they begin.*

A.   Letters, Conversations and Recollections of S. T. C. Edited by Thomas Allsop. 1836, 1858 (cited), 1864.

Aids.   Aids to Reflection in the Formation of a Manly Character. . . . By S. T. C. 1825, 1831, 1836, 1839, 1843 (cited).

Allston.   The Life and Letters of Washington Allston. By J. B. Flagg. 1892.

Annus Mirabilis.   Some Dates in Coleridge's Annus Mirabilis. By E. K. Chambers. 1934. (*Essays and Studies*, xix.)

A.P.   Anima Poetae. From the Unpublished Note-Books of S. T. C. Edited by E. H. Coleridge. 1895.

Archiv.   Herrig's Archiv für das Studium der neueren Sprachen und Literaturen.

Asra.   C. and 'Asra'. By T. M. Raysor. 1929. (*Studies in Philology*, xxvi, 305.)

B.   Memorials of Coleorton . . . Letters to Sir George and Lady Beaumont. Edited by W. Knight. 1887.

Batho.   The Later Wordsworth. By E. C. Batho. 1933.

B.L.   Biographia Literaria. By S. T. C. Edited by J. Shawcross. 1907.

Bowles.   A Wiltshire Parson and his Friends: the Correspondence of W. L. Bowles. By G. Greever. 1926.

Brandl.   S. T. C. and the English Romantic School. 1887.

Byron.   Letters and Journals of Lord Byron. Edited by R. E. Prothero. 1898–1901.

C.   Letters of S. T. C. Edited by E. H. Coleridge. 1895.

Campbell.   S. T. C. A Narrative. . . . By J. Dykes Campbell. 1894, 1896.

Campbell, *Poems.*   The Poetical Works of S. T. C. Edited by J. Dykes Campbell. 1893.

Campbell-White.   Coleridge's Poems. A Facsimile Reproduction of Proofs and MSS. Edited by J. Dykes Campbell and W. Hale White. 1899.

Carlyon.   Early Years and Late Reflections. By C. Carlyon. 1836–58.

Church and State.   On the Constitution of the Church and State. By S. T. C. 1830 (cited) 1830, 1839, 1852.

Collins.   Memoirs of the Life of William Collins. By his Son. 1848.

I

THE BLUE-COAT BOY

October 1772—October 1791

SAMUEL TAYLOR COLERIDGE was born, according to his father's entry in the register of Ottery St. Mary, about 11 o'clock in the forenoon of 21 October 1772. It was one of the facts of life which he could never accept. He habitually treated 20 October as his birthday, and in later life came to add two years to his real age. The discrepancies are hardly explained by a belief that his mother had told his wife of some error either in the baptismal register or in a transcript sent to Christ's Hospital. In fact there is complete agreement between the Ottery record and the Hospital documents, one of which, incidentally, is signed by a Samuel Taylor of Ottery, whom we know to have been Coleridge's godfather. There is, indeed, much evidence that Coleridge's capacious and retentive memory for things which had happened to him, and still more for things which he had read, was qualified, not only by an easy oblivion of his own past sentiments, but also by a marked lack of precision in chronological detail. His retrospective datings for his early poems are inconsistent and unreliable.[1] Nor can we rely with implicit confidence on all the statements made in a series of biographical letters which he began to write to Thomas Poole in 1797, but of course never finished, or in his similar communications to James Gillman at Highgate.[2]

So far as these relate to the origin and history of his family, they are admittedly based upon 'dim traditions' received from his mother and an aunt, and can to some extent be corrected. Colrige, Coldridge, Coleridge—there are several other spellings—is a place-name in more than one part of Devonshire, and would easily give rise to a

[1] C. 1, 2, 37, 226; G. 89, 101, 184; A. 22; *A.P.* 19, 295; A. W. Lockhart, *Ch. H. Exhibitioners*, 36; R. B. Johnson, *Ch. H.* 69; cf. Lowes, 415, 584.
[2] C. 1–5, 249 (misdated 1830 for 1821); *Addl. MS.* 35343, f. 382; P. ii. 258, 279; Gillman 1–39.

family name. There is a Hundred of Coleridge, with a manor-house of the same name, in the extreme south, from which the poet himself believed his grandfather to have come. There is a northern Coleridge in the Hundred of Roborough. And between the two, in the Hundred of North Tawton, comes a Coldridge.[1] It is a little south of this that Coleridge families have been traced in a group of villages, Drewsteignton, Dunsford, Doddiscombsleigh, and Ashton, which lie along the Teign valley, to the south-west of Exeter and Crediton. A John Coleridge, who married a Sarah Ealeb at Dunsford in 1694, may have been the poet's great-grandfather, and another John, who married Mary Wills at Drewsteignton, may fairly be taken as his grandfather. This John became a weaver or woollen draper (*textor*) at Crediton, not, as the poet thought, South Molton, and here his son, a third John, was born early in 1719. A daughter Susannah still kept an 'everything shop' at Crediton about 1777.[2] Coleridge's accent struck a girl from the midlands disagreeably. Joseph Farington, in 1804, describes his dialect, particularly in reading, as 'what I should call *broad Devonshire*, for a gentleman'. He prolonged 'cow' into 'kee-ow', and sounded the *l* in 'talk', 'would', and 'should'. Carlyle also dwells on the 'tawlk' in 1824.[3] When Coleridge came to Stowey in 1794 the inhabitants caught his name as Coldridge. At Keswick, too, his wife became 'auld Mrs Cauldridge'. Variants from other sources are Coltridge, Coledridge, Colrige, Colredge, Coloridge. Leigh Hunt says that his schoolmaster called him Cŏlĕrĭdge, 'pronouncing the word like a dactyl'. Coleridge himself found 'a peculiar indescribable Beauty of the lofty kind in Cōlĕrīdge'.

For it is one of the vilest Beelzebubberies of Detraction to pronounce it Col-ridge, or Cŏllĕridge, or even Cōle-ridge. It is and must be to all honest and honorable men, a Trisyllabic Amphimacron – ◡ – !

In humorous verse he rhymed it with both 'Polar ridge' and 'scholarage'.[4]

[1] *Devon Place-Names* (P.N. Soc.), 50, 227, 313, 332, 365.
[2] C. 1, 3; *D.H.* 11; *Studies*, 5.
[3] Litchfield, 139; Farington, ii. 210; Leslie, i. 44; 2 *Gent. Mag.* x. 27; Froude, *Carlyle*, i. 222, 292; cf. pp. 167, 183, 321.
[4] G. 251; P. i. 95, 124, 139, 146, 244; *P.W.* 972, 981; *Studies*, 82; Sara Coleridge, *Memoir*, ii. 233; Leigh Hunt, ch. iii; Lowes, 354, 583, 604ˢ.

One of the 'traditions' tells that, when Coleridge's father was 15, the weaving business failed, and he was sent into the world, with half a crown and a blessing, to seek his fortune. A kind gentleman found him weeping by the side of the road, and settled him in a neighbouring town as a schoolmaster. He married, and at 20 had scraped up enough money to walk to Cambridge and enter as a student at Sidney Sussex College. There is a Dick Whittington air about this. A version by Southey, itself not quite accurate, identifies the kind gentleman with James Buller of Downes, near Crediton. In fact John Coleridge was educated at Crediton Grammar School, where he had an exhibition. About 1745 he became master of a small endowed school at Clyst Hydon, and married Mary Lendon of Crediton. In 1747, being then not 20, but 28, he matriculated at Sidney Sussex. In 1749 he became master of Squire's Grammar School at South Molton, and was ordained with a title as curate of Mariansleigh. In 1751 his first wife died. By her he had four daughters, of whom only the youngest, Elizabeth, who married Jacob Phillips of Exeter, figures in the poet's biography. In 1753 John Coleridge became lecturer at Molland near South Molton, and here found a second wife in Ann Bowdon, a member of a good tenant-farmer family. In 1760 he became master of the Grammar School of Ottery St. Mary and chaplain priest of the collegiate church, and James Buller gave him also the vicarship of Ottery. He added to his income by taking boarders, of whom Francis Buller, the son of James, later a judge and Sir Francis, was one.[1]

John Coleridge, not perhaps without some help from the mythopoeic genius of his son, comes before us as something of a 'character'. He was a competent scholar, a mathematician, and a Hebraist as well as a classic; contributed to the *Gentleman's Magazine*, helped Benjamin Kennicott in his work on the text of the Old Testament, and published *Miscellaneous Dissertations* (1768) on the Book of Judges. When his successor came, the parishioners of Ottery missed the relish of those moments when he would break the thread of his discourse to give them a few words in what, if

[1] C. 1; *D.H.* 12; *Studies*, 6.

De Quincey can be trusted, he called 'the immediate language of the Holy Ghost'. Of several school-books which he compiled, the most important was a *Critical Latin Grammar* (1772), prefaced by a logical analysis of the case-forms, wherein he defined the ablative—I do not know why De Quincey says the accusative—as the 'Quale-quare-quidditive' case. His son's 'Quippe-quare-quale-quia-quidditive' is an exaggeration. He did not in fact propose to adopt this nomenclature for teaching practice, since 'Antiquity pleads for the present names of the cases in opposition to Reason and prevails'. But, oddly enough, his 'possessive' for 'genitive' has since become common usage. In his lighter moments he wrote English verses, and even accomplished a translation of the *Phormio* of Terence as *The Fair Barbadian*, which he sent to Garrick as suited to the English stage. His private life was marked by simplicity and an extreme absent-mindedness, especially in matters of personal appearance. To Gillman, as to Poole and De Quincey before him, Coleridge would call him 'a perfect Parson Adams' and 'an Israelite without guile', and tell tales of his peculiarities until the tears ran down his face. They were told, says Gillman, of another clergyman in the neighbourhood as well. Withal, wrote Coleridge in more serious mood, though not a first-rate genius, he was a first-rate Christian. He recalls 'that venerable countenance and name which form my earliest recollections and *make them religious*'. He was proud and tender to be told that he strongly resembled his father in person and mind. He thought that he had inherited from him a tendency to gout. And although 'one of the most temperate men alive in his ordinary practice' the vicar was sometimes affected by wine 'under the stimulus of society and eager conversation'. There is material for the student of heredity in all this.[1]

Samuel Taylor came at the end of a long family. John and Ann Coleridge had nine sons and one daughter. The simplicity of the vicar was such that he would have apprenticed his boys to traders, with the exception of Samuel him-

---

[1] C. 2, 4, 240; G. 184, 327; Gillman, 2; *Studies*, 8; *D.H.* 13; De Q. ii. 164; *L.P.* 87; *R.E.S.* x. 451.

self, whom he always intended for a parson. But here his
wife's 'maternal ambition' intervened.[1] One son, William,
died in infancy. Of the rest, John (n. 1754) and Francis
Syndercombe (1770) went early into the Indian Army. A
second William (1758), Edward (1760), and George (1764)
passed through Oxford into Holy Orders and schoolmaster-
ing. James (1759) joined the English Army. Luke Herman
(1765) became a doctor.[2] I do not know how De Quincey
came to think that Samuel had been 'almost an object of
persecution to his mother'. It is true that in 1804 Coleridge,
who was always inclined to see himself in a dramatic light,
wrote to Sir George Beaumont, 'I was hardly used from
infancy to boyhood, and from boyhood to youth most, MOST
cruelly'. But it is clear from his narratives to Poole and
Gillman that, in so far as this refers to his nursery rather than
his school days, it was not upon his parents that he laid any
blame. 'My father was very fond of me, and I was my
mother's darling: in consequence I was very miserable.'
The trouble was with a nurse Molly, who was jealous for
his next brother Frank, of whom she made a pet at Samuel's
expense. Frank himself 'had a violent love of beating me',
but in the intervals was affectionate, 'with a strange mixture
of admiration and contempt'. There was also some tor-
menting by his father's boarders.[3] As a result, Coleridge
thought, he became 'fretful and timorous, and a tell-tale',
took no pleasure in boyish sports, but read incessantly, of
Robinson Crusoe and the Seven Champions of Christendom,
acting over the stories by himself in the docks and nettles
and rank grass of the churchyard. A particular favourite
was the *Arabian Nights*, which he found at once repellent
and attractive, so that he would watch the window in which
the book lay, and whenever the sun lay upon it, would seize
it, carry it to a corner by the wall, and there bask and read.

So I became a *dreamer*, and acquired an indisposition to all bodily
activity; and I was fretful, and inordinately passionate, and as I could
not play at anything, and was slothful, I was despised and hated by the
boys; and because I could read and spell and had, I may truly say, a

---

[1] C. 4; G. 367.   [2] C. 2; Gillman, 9; *D.H. passim*.
[3] C. 3, 4; Gillman, 10; B. i. 44; De Q. ii. 164.

memory and understanding forced into almost an unnatural ripeness, I was flattered and wondered at by all the old women. And so I became very vain, and despised most of the boys that were at all near my own age, and before I was eight years old I was a *character*. Sensibility, imagination, vanity, sloth, and feelings of deep and bitter contempt for all who traversed the orbit of my understanding, were even then prominent and manifest.

Thus our present colours our past. Coleridge was even capable of regarding himself as a philosopher from the egg onwards. When his father explained to him the motions of the heavenly bodies at the age of 8, he listened without wonder or incredulity.

For from my early reading of fairy tales and genii, etc., etc., my mind had been habituated *to the Vast*, and I never regarded *my senses* in any way as the criteria of my belief. I regulated all my creeds by my conceptions, not by my *sight*, even at that age.

Children, he thought, should be brought up on romance. 'I know no other way of giving the mind a love of the Great and the Whole.'[1] One may comment that the *Arabian Nights* were also the favourite early reading of John Stuart Mill.

Incidents of Coleridge's childhood may have helped to sow the seeds of that ill health which pursued him to the end of his life. He had a putrid fever at the age of 6, and later, after a quarrel with Frank, ran into the fields beside the Otter, and lay asleep there in a stormy night, until he was found, wet through, on the brink of the river in the morning. A long period of intermittent ague followed. Long after, when a calf bellowed in the night at Keswick, he recalled the same sound as it came across those river fields.[2] One other reminiscence, perhaps his earliest, is also auditory, for at Ottery the future poet heard—

> Our old Musician, blind and grey,
> (Whom stretching from my nurse's arms I kissed,)
> His Scottish tunes and warlike marches play.[3]

Coleridge's father died suddenly in October 1781. Sir Francis Buller offered to provide for the boy's future, and obtained a nomination for him to Christ's Hospital from one

[1] C. 3, 4; Gillman, 10; *Fr.* i. 197.
[2] C. 3, 4; Gillman, 10; *A.P.* 29.   [3] *P.W.* 324.

John Way. The mother, who had hoped for Charterhouse,
was disappointed, thinking the blue coat a degradation.
However, he was sent to London, where he stayed for some
weeks with his uncle John Bowdon, who spoilt him by
treating him as a prodigy, and letting him talk and drink at
coffee-houses and taverns beyond his years. In July 1782 he
went to the preparatory school at Hertford, where he says
he was happy and had plenty to eat, and in September passed
to the main establishment in London.[1] Here he would have
been for two or three years in the Lower Grammar School,
under the Rev. Matthew Field. To this period must be
ascribed any cruelty which in fact accompanied Coleridge's
youth. The trouble was not in school-hours. Field, something of a scholar, but an idle and fashionable man, was no
stern disciplinarian. He carried his cane 'like a dancer', and
did not use the rod. James Boyer, the Upper Master, would
occasionally send to borrow it, and observe grimly 'how
neat and fresh the twigs looked'. Often enough, the boys
were left to their own devices, while Field retired to his
private room, and in all they learnt little, and 'lived a life
as careless as birds'. It was, otherwise out of school. Here
the Christ's Hospital life was undoubtedly a hard one for a
young and sensitive boy. Lamb, who gives the account of
Field, describes it in his Elia essay, written at the beginning
in the assumed person of Coleridge, although that affectation
is dropped half-way. So, even more fully, does Leigh Hunt
in his *Autobiography*. Lamb dwells on the scanty, ill-cooked,
and unvaried food, the peculation of the servants, the cold
in winter, the brutality of the monitors, the antiquated
penalties of solitary confinement. Coleridge had a delicate
stomach which suffered from the food. The clumsy shoes,
provided for the boys in bulk, hurt his tender feet. He
caught the itch, and the sulphur ointment used to cure it
was worse still. Compulsory 'whole-day-leaves' were only
an added trial for those who were without friends in London.

O the cruelty of separating a poor lad from his early homestead!
The yearnings which I used to have towards it in those unfledged
years! How, in my dreams, would my native town (far in the west)

[1] C. 4, 5; Gillman, 11; *D.H.* 20; Morley, 60.

come back, with its church, and trees, and faces! How I would wake weeping, and in the anguish of my heart exclaim upon sweet Calne in Wiltshire!

For Lamb's 'Calne' we must of course read Ottery.[1] Here come in the well-known lines of *Frost at Midnight*:

> I was reared
> In the great city, pent 'mid cloisters dim,
> And saw nought lovely but the sky and stars.

and those of *Dejection*:

> At eve, sky-gazing in 'ecstatic fit'
> (Alas! for cloister'd in a city School
> The Sky was all, I knew, of Beautiful)
> At the barr'd window often did I sit,
> And oft upon the leaded School-roof lay.

and the amplification of the theme in Wordsworth's *Prelude*:

> Of Rivers, Fields,
> And Groves, I speak to Thee, my Friend; to Thee,
> Who, yet a liveried School-Boy, in the depths
> Of the huge City, on the leaded Roof
> Of that wide Edifice, thy Home and School,
> Wast used to lie and gaze upon the clouds
> Moving in Heaven; or haply, tired of this,
> To shut thine eyes, and by internal light
> See trees, and meadows, and thy native Stream
> Far distant, thus beheld from year to year
> Of thy long exile.[2]

Perhaps Coleridge was not quite so friendless as Lamb thought. Sir Francis Buller invited him to his house on Sundays, but on one occasion, when there was company, he was sent to dine at the second table, and the silly boy would not go again. His brothers are said to have refused to see him in his school dress and he to visit them in any other. It is not clear, however, what brother can have been in London during these early days. William had been a master in Newcome's School at Hackney, but he died in 1780. There were, however, John Bowdon and his daughter Betsy, and a Miss Cabriere, who lived with her, and apparently also

[1] C. 5; Gillman, 13; Lamb, *Works*, ii. 13; Leigh Hunt, ch. iii; *Studies*, 55.
[2] *P.W.* 242, *Essays and Studies* (English Association), xxii. 17; *Prelude*, vi. 274.

a married sister of Bowdon, one Mrs. Short, with a family
of children.[1] But no doubt the boy was often lonely enough.
He became, he says, 'a playless day-dreamer, a *helluo librorum*'.
Access to a circulating library was given him by a kindly
stranger, with whom he collided as he thrust his way down
the Strand in the character of Leander swimming the Helle-
spont, and who at first took him for a pickpocket. He had
soon exhausted the limited curriculum of the Lower Grammar School, without impressing Field, who thought him
dull and inapt, and inclined to explain a construction in his
own words, instead of repeating the syntactical rule. His
emancipation came through the insight of a senior boy,
Thomas Fanshawe Middleton, who had observed him sitting in the cloister, slovenly in his attire and poring over a
book. On inquiry it proved to be Vergil, an author beyond
his years, whom he was studying 'for pleasure'. Middleton
spoke of him to Boyer, whose interest was aroused.[2] Presumably Coleridge was now taken into the Upper Grammar
School. The interest of Boyer was not, however, without
its disadvantages. His was not the easy-going rule of Field.
He wielded all the 'terrors of the rod.' A 'plagose Orbilius,'
Coleridge calls him, and complains that he always got an
extra cut, because 'you are such an ugly fellow'. In after
life, the severities of Boyer were still wont to mingle with
his distempered dreams. Lamb and Leigh Hunt, too, dwell
upon them. They were intermittent, indeed. You could
judge by his wig in the morning what the weather was
likely to be. One was 'serene, smiling, fresh powdered, be-
tokening a mild day'. The other was 'an old discoloured,
unkempt, angry caxon, denoting frequent and bloody
execution'.[3] Nevertheless, both Lamb and Coleridge pay
full credit to Boyer's ability and strong common sense as a
teacher. 'Under him were many good and sound scholars
bred', says Lamb. Coleridge, in the *Biographia Literaria*,
gives a fairly full acount of his methods, which 'sent us to

[1] Morley, 60; *Studies*, 7; *D.H.* 52; *I.L.N.* 'Calerica' (Campbell, 11) must be a misreading of 'Cabriere'.

[2] Gillman, 17, 19.

[3] C. 41; *B.L.* i. 4; *P.W.* 3; *T.T.* 83, 196; Leigh Hunt, ch. iii; Lamb, *Works*, i. 144; ii. 19, 20; Robinson, *Diary*, ii. 36.

the University excellent Latin and Greek scholars, and tolerable Hebraists'. By him the poet's taste was early moulded to the preference of the better classical writers, of Demosthenes to Cicero, of Homer and Theocritus to Vergil, of Vergil to Ovid, of Lucretius, Terence, and Catullus to the poets even of the Augustan era. Nor did he neglect the English writers. Shakespeare and Milton were to be studied as seriously as the Greek tragedians.

I learnt from him, that Poetry, even that of the loftiest, and, seemingly, that of the wildest odes, had a logic of its own, as severe as that of science; and more difficult, because more subtle, more complex, and dependent on more, and more fugitive causes. In the truly great poets, he would say, there is a reason assignable, not only for every word, but for the position of every word.

He seems to have made much use of verse compositions as an instrument of mental training, and to have shown, in commenting on them, a critical instinct somewhat in advance of his age. The stock imagery and periphrases of the Augustan poets were an abomination to him.

In fancy I can almost hear him now, exclaiming, 'Harp? Harp? Lyre? Pen and ink, boy, you mean! Muse, boy, Muse? Your Nurse's daughter, you mean! Pierian spring? Oh aye! the cloister-pump, I suppose!'

Certain recurrent similes, of the poisonous manchineel fruit, for example, or of Alexander and Clytus, were placed upon a special *index expurgatorius*. It is a rather refreshing sidelight upon eighteenth-century pedagogy.[1] Coleridge received some kindness from Boyer in a later time of trouble, and when he died, expressed the hope that his soul was now in heaven, 'borne by a host of cherubs, all face and wing, and without anything to excite his whipping propensities'.[2]

We do not know how Coleridge spent his earlier school holidays. Probably he had to remain at the Hospital. Apart from the expense involved, he was too young to travel alone. But the first letter of his which has been preserved, to his mother on 4 February 1785, suggests that he had paid a visit

[1] B.L. i. 4; G. 258, 398; P.W. 3; *Studies*, 69.
[2] C. 23; Robinson, *Diary*, ii. 36.

to Ottery not long before. He asks after boys with whom he had played, and sends his love to Molly, the tyrant of his youth. An escort may have been found in his brother Luke, who was in London when he wrote, presumably already walking the wards of the recently established London Hospital as a budding surgeon.[1] It may have been on his return after this visit that Boyer found him crying, and expostulated:

Boy! the school is your father! Boy! the school is your mother! Boy! the school is your brother! the school is your sister! the school is your first cousin, and your second cousin, and all the rest of your relations! Let's have no more crying![2]

His brother George also came to London about 1785 as a master at Newcome's School, and for both these brothers he learnt to feel much affection, due, he says, in part to the undomesticating influences of Christ's Hospital, and in part to his own intellectual precocity.[3] With George his relations were destined to become chequered, but for the time he played a father's part, ready to encourage the boy's early attempts at writing, or to supply a pair of Sunday breeches or a new tea-kettle, when occasion arose. To Luke Samuel writes in 1787, congratulating him on a 'success', dwelling on George's kindness, and announcing his own expectation of shortly becoming a Grecian, as in fact he did in 1788.[4] Luke married, took a practice at Thorverton near Exeter, and died there in 1790.[5] But his course at the London Hospital led to the first stage of Coleridge's very rapid mental development during his early years in the Upper Grammar School. He, too, would be a surgeon. He devoured medical books, spent his Saturdays at the hospital, thought it bliss if he was allowed to hold a plaster or watch a dressing.[6] The craze soon passed, and gave way to one for metaphysics and theology. He read *Cato's Letters* and Voltaire's *Philosophical Dictionary*.[7] The Church, to which admission to the select class of Grecians and thereafter to a

[1] C. 6.   [2] T.T. 196.   [3] G. 320.
[4] C. 7; G. 373; I.L.N.; D.H. 57.   [5] D.H. 54.   [6] Gillman, 22.
[7] B.L. i. 9; Gillman, 23. *Cato's Letters* (1755) were by John Trenchard and Thomas Gordon.

University was the natural avenue, was still regarded as his destiny. His Anglo-Indian brother John, indeed, had hoped that a General Goddard of his acquaintance would provide for the boy, and when the General died in 1783, planned to procure him an Indian cadetship. But John himself died in 1787, and the Church still held the field.[1] Clearly, however, it was not consistent with Voltaireanism. Coleridge decided that he would become, not a Grecian, but an artisan, and arranged with a shoemaker to visit Boyer and apply for him as an apprentice. ' 'Ods my life, man, what d'ye mean?' said Boyer, and thrust Crispin out of the room. Coleridge pointed out that he was an infidel. And then, he tells us, he had the one just flogging of his life-time.[2] Voltaireanism soon gave way to Platonism, and even Neoplatonism, of which he may have learnt through the recent translation by Thomas Taylor. It is of this stage that Lamb writes:

Come back into memory, like as thou wert in the day-spring of thy fancies, with hope like a fiery column before thee—the dark pillar not yet turned—Samuel Taylor Coleridge—Logician, Metaphysician, Bard! —How have I seen the casual passer through the Cloisters stand still, intranced with admiration (while he weighed the disproportion between the *speech* and the *garb* of the young Mirandula), to hear thee unfold, in thy deep and sweet intonations, the mysteries of Jamblichus, or Plotinus (for even in those years thou waxedst not pale at such philosophic draughts), or reciting Homer in his Greek, or Pindar—while the walls of the old Grey Friars re-echoed to the accents of the inspired *charity-boy*![3]

In 1789, now already well in the Grecian fairway, Coleridge paid a visit to Ottery, of which a memorial long remained in a dated inscription of his name at the entrance of a cave, known as the Pixies' Parlour, beside the bank of the Otter. It has gone now, but the recollection of Lord Coleridge and others is clear as to the date. A poem, which records his wanderings beside the river and the illness of his sister Ann, is a confirmation.[4] His attention had been diverted to poetry by the gift from his friend and protector Middleton of the recently published *Sonnets* of William Lisle Bowles, which

[1] D.H. 31, 39. [2] T.T. 83; Gillman, 23.
[3] B.L. i. 94, 170; Lamb, *Works*, ii. 21.
[4] D.H. 59 (with an old photo, which leaves the date obscure); P.W. 11.

delighted him so much that he copied them out forty times for the benefit of others.[1] It was the era, not only of poetry, but of love. Some kindness to a newly arrived Welsh junior, one John Evans, had brought about an introduction to the boy's mother, now living in London with her three daughters, Mary, Anne, and Bessy. Mary was the object of Coleridge's affections.

Oh, from sixteen to nineteen what hours of Paradise had Allen and I in escorting the Miss Evanses home on a Saturday, who were then at a milliner's whom we used to think, and who I believe really was, such a nice lady;—and we used to carry thither, of a summer morning, the pillage of the flower gardens within six miles of town, with Sonnet or Love Rhyme wrapped round the nose-gay.[2]

An added delight of those walks around London was the bathing in the New River, near Newington. Coleridge was an inveterate bather to the end of his days. A note about some early verses on the Evening Star records that they were written, 'as I was returning from the New River, and it looked newly bathed as well as I'. But Coleridge apparently swam in his clothes, and then did not change them, which led to a long period mainly spent in the sick-ward with jaundice and rheumatic fever. It was probably this which inspired *Genevieve*, although he dated it much earlier. Christ's Hospital tradition makes Genevieve the daughter of his nurse, conceivably a Mrs. Brewman, whom he helped long after. But she is 'Maid of my Love', and surely this points to Mary Evans.[3]

On the whole Coleridge may have been happier during the last years of his school life than at any other period, except possibly a brief one at Stowey. His chief friend appears to have been Robert Allen, of whose good looks Leigh Hunt tells a story.[4] With Charles Valentine Le Grice he had wit-combats, described by Lamb, in which Le Grice, who had a nimbler, if more shallow, mind, got the better of him. 'Le Grice and I', he writes to Luke in 1787, 'are

[1] *B.L.* i. 8.
[2] *A.* 27; *B.L.* i. 10; Gillman, 28; A. W. Lockhart, *Ch. H. Exhibitioners*, 36. Lamb's friend William Evans (L. 3, 180, 343) was another brother.
[3] *P.W.* 16, 19; *A.P.* 247; Lamb, *Works*, ii. 13; Gillman, 33; G. 172.
[4] Leigh Hunt, ch. iii.

very polite, very civil, and very cold.' In the same letter, as printed, is mention of one 'Alia'. Is this a slip for Allen, or is it the mysterious F. Augustus Elia, whose name Lamb borrowed?[1] Lamb himself was more than two years Coleridge's junior, and the long intimacy between them probably had its origin in 1794. A younger Samuel Le Grice and a Samuel Favell will appear later in this narrative; also a John Mathew Gutch and a Frederick William Franklin, of both of whom Coleridge had unfortunate experiences. George Dyer, the eccentric poet and scholar, whom he came to know, was of an older generation, Leigh Hunt of a younger one. Thomas Hartwell Horne was coached by Coleridge during the summer vacation of 1790. A Reverend Mr. Smith, whom I cannot identify, calls him his 'old satrap', and claims to have cleaned his shoes.[2] We may be quite sure that Coleridge did not clean them himself.

On 12 January 1791 Coleridge was granted a Christ's Hospital exhibition of £40 for the liberal period of seven years, with a reduction to £30 in the last three; and on 5 February he was elected to a sizarship at Jesus College, Cambridge.[3] His career seemed now to be marked out for him, if the gods would have had it so. He showed his gratitude long after by a newspaper defence of the policy of the Governors in using their endowments for the benefit, not of the very poor, but of children of reputable parents, threatened through death or calamity with lapse into a state of penury.[4] Verses written during the months of waiting record his budding hopes, not unmingled with regret at leaving the 'much-lov'd cloisters pale', and 'this maternal seat'. There are hints of a friend and once more a 'lovely maid'. Another set is of grief for the death of his sister Ann, which followed hard upon that of Luke.[5] From Christ's Hospital Coleridge carried away, besides a trained intelligence, and a store of wide and varied reading, two other things. One was the habit of walking bare-headed, with his hat in his hand.[6] The other, which he himself acknowledges, was the

---

[1] W. 1406; Lamb, *Works*, ii. 21; *I.L.N.*   [2] *Studies*, 61.
[3] Lockhart, *Ch. H. Exhibitioners*, 36.
[4] *O.T.* iii. 854.   [5] *P.W.* 20, 29, 30, 78; *D.H.* 19.
[6] Leslie, i. 51; H. A. Eaton, *Diary of De Quincey*, 191.

instinct of reverence to superiors in worldly rank, represented to his youth by the dignified Governors who occasionally visited the school.[1] This 'inferiority-complex' as
modern jargon has it, explains the singular deference with
which he always approached such men as Sir George Beaumont and J. H. Frere, and sometimes even extended to those
of his own standing, much to the annoyance of Southey,
who disliked being called 'dear and honoured', and of
John Rickman, who called it 'a habit of *assentation*'.[2] The
formal discharge from the Hospital is dated on 7 September. But Coleridge was able to spend the August holidays
at Ottery, where he may have found none but his mother
to greet him. Frank was now in India, where he died next
year; and of all that long tale of children, only James,
Edward, and George, besides Samuel himself, lived to
maturity. James had left the army on his marriage to a
woman of means, and was now living at Tiverton. In 1796
he bought the Chanter's House at Ottery, where he devoted
himself to the Volunteer movement, and became the pro-
genitor of a long line of Coleridges, mostly in the legal
profession. Edward, a witty but not very high-principled
man, of whom Samuel came to see and think little, was
now living at Salisbury, but later also returned to Ottery.
George was still in London until 1794, when he became
master of the Ottery Grammar School, as his father had
been before him.[3]

I do not think that there is anything very remarkable
about the poems of Coleridge's boyhood. The earliest which
can be dated is of 1787, on the joys of starting for Easter
holidays, joys in which he probably did not himself share.
Several are school exercises, thought by Boyer worthy of
being entered in a *Liber Aureus* which he kept.[4] One called
Dura Navis, which does not appear in the *Liber*, is interesting because of Boyer's criticisms upon it, which Coleridge
recorded in a note. He told him to avoid 'apostrophes' and
'O thou's' as 'the grimaces of lunacy', and to leave out as
many epithets as would reduce decasyllabic into octosyllabic
lines and then ask himself whether the exercise would not

[1] A. 27.   [2] Cf. pp. 169, 181.   [3] D.H. 24, 56, 57, 62.   [4] P.W. 1, 4, 6, 7, 12, 13.

be greatly improved.[1] It was long, however, before Coleridge's Muse could shake herself free of apostrophes. It may
be added that the manchineel, so abhorred of Boyer, and the
cognate upas tree had always a fatal attraction for Coleridge.
Thus in 1797 he writes of 'chance-started friendships' how:

> Some most false,
> False and fair-foliaged as the Manchineel,
> Have tempted me to slumber in their shade,
> E'en mid the storm; then breathing subtlest damps,
> Mix'd their own venom with the rain from Heaven,
> That I woke poison'd!

Lamb chaffs him, 'If you don't write to me, I shall get angry,
and call you hard names—Manchineel and I don't know what
else'.[2] The elegiac influence of Bowles does not, of course,
show itself until near the end of the period. It was to become
stronger afterwards. And it must have largely counteracted
Boyer's, for Bowles's tender reflections on his eventide walks
by river and ruined castle are soft with otiose epithets.

[1] *P.W.* 2.
[2] *P.W.* 174; *O.T.* i. 69; *L.* 31; *Addl. MS.* 27901, ff. 4ª, 19ª; cf. Lowes, 18.

II

CAMBRIDGE

October 1791—December 1794

COLERIDGE came up to Cambridge in October 1791. His exhibition was soon augmented by a Rustat Scholarship, tenable at Jesus by sons of clergymen, and he had the promise of some help from his family. His destiny was still regarded as the Church, and Bishop William Buller of Exeter had promised him a title to Orders.[1] At Jesus he as yet knew no one, and was rather shocked to find that Dr. William Pearce, the Master, and the tutors were still on vacation. But he was befriended by Middleton at Pembroke. Rooms were assigned to him, and he was approached by an upholsterer, who asked him how he would like them furnished. 'Just as you please, Sir,' said Coleridge, supposing the man to be employed by the College. It was, he maintained, the *fons et origo* of all his misfortunes. Three or four rush chairs and a deal table would have served his turn.[2] Unfortunately, the source lay deeper. The first year, however, seems to have been one of steady reading, more in classics than mathematics. He took to writing Greek verse, and planned to compete for all the University prizes. His nights were spent with Middleton over their books for some hours, and then became *Noctes Atticae* over size and college ale until midnight. He lived soberly, avoiding for the most part convivial suppers and wine parties, although he does describe one, at which several freshmen got drunk. His chief friend at Jesus was George Caldwell, who seems also to have been a good influence. Middleton, however, left Cambridge in the spring of 1792, having been disappointed in his hopes of obtaining a Fellowship.[3]

There are several letters to George. Coleridge has rheumatism, and here we get the first reference to opium, which he

[1] C. 9; G. 1, 365, 374; Carlyon, i. 242.
[2] C. 8; G. 316; Gillman, 41.
[3] C. 9–12; G. 1, 2, 323; Gillman, 43, 49, 51; C. W. Le Bas, *Life of Middleton*.

says never used to have any disagreeable effects on him. George also is ill, and Coleridge employs his spare moments in writing sermons for him, which he sends through Le Grice at Christ's Hospital.[1] In January, however, George has been perturbed by hearing of relations with William Frend, a Fellow of Jesus, who was a Unitarian. Frend's company is by no means invidious, says Coleridge. He is intimate with Dr. Pearce himself. Moreover, 'though I am not an *Alderman*, I have yet *prudence* enough to respect that *gluttony of faith* waggishly yclept orthodoxy'. There is some camouflage about this. We know from a later statement of Coleridge that he still considered himself an infidel, when he began a deep study of the subject, which left him a religious man, but a necessitarian. And one can hardly doubt that the development he describes was largely due to the influence of Frend.[2]

Christmas was spent in London with the Evans family, and through the tenderness of Mrs. Evans Coleridge's health improved. There are now several letters to her, to Mary, and to Anne. There is no evidence as yet of any deep affection for Mary. They are the half-chaffing letters of a 'brother Coly'. He sends compliments to the girls, encloses poems he has written, tells stories of Cambridge happenings. He keeps a cat and has acquired a swanskin waistcoat.[3] In April he tells George that he means to write for all the prizes, and he was in fact successful in winning the medal for a Greek Sapphic Ode on the Slave-Trade, which he read at the Encaenia on 3 July 1792. It was not of great merit; Richard Porson offered to show a hundred and thirty-four examples of bad Greek in it.[4] That he then paid another visit to London, and probably spoke of love to Mary, is suggested by an invocation, a year later, to Fancy:[5]

O bid the Maid arise,
Chaste Joyance dancing in her bright-blue eyes;
As erst when from the Muses' calm abode
I came, with Learning's meed not unbestowed;

[1] C. 8, 9, 15; G. 1, 2.   [2] C. 9; G. 28; A, p. 32.   [3] C. 10-14.
[4] Campbell, *Poems*, 476; C. 15; *Blackwood's Magazine* (Oct. 1817), 12.
[5] *P.W.* 51.

When as she twin'd a laurel round my brow,
And met my kiss, and half return'd my vow,
O'er all my frame shot rapid my thrill'd heart,
And every nerve confess'd the electric dart.

And so once more to a holiday in the west, with Edward at Salisbury, James at Tiverton, and at Exeter, presumably with his half-sister Mrs. Phillips, as well as at Ottery itself, where he expected George to join him.[1]

On his return to Cambridge, he was again unwell. He entered for the University Craven Scholarship in January, and met with ill fortune. He was bracketed equal with three others, but under the terms of the bequest the award had to be made to the youngest of the four, Samuel Butler, afterwards headmaster of Shrewsbury.[2] His letters to the Evans family are in the old vein, but less cheerful. He has lost his brother Frank and a friend, probably Middleton. He is learning the violin, but 'the evils of life are crowding upon me'. To George he writes of debts which have corroded his spirits, but which he hopes to meet through a volume of translations from the Greek and Latin writers, to be published by subscription. It was the first and one of the most persistent of his literary air-castles. He owes his tutor about £50 and more than £8 elsewhere. But Dr. Pearce has given him the Librarian and Chapel Clerk's place, which will be worth £33, and with strict economy he hopes to manage, if he abandons the idea of a summer holiday in Devonshire.[3] Unfortunately, this was not the whole story as it emerged in a burst of penitence more than a year later. Coleridge had in fact broken down morally, as well as financially, under the 'stupefying effect' of a large claim for the furnishing of his rooms which came in with his tutor's bill, and the 'pure terror and hauntings of mind' which it caused him. He wasted his time in 'wild schemes of impossible extrication', and 'became a proverb to the University for Idleness'. Then he 'fled to Debauchery'. His alleged severe reading for the Craven was a mere pretence; for six weeks before the examination he was almost constantly intoxicated. There

[1] G. 3, 4.　　　　[2] C. 16; G. 5, 7; Gillman, 50; 2 Gent. Mag. ii. 605.
[3] C. 16-18; G. 7.

may be some exaggeration in all this. Coleridge did indeed get an anonymous letter in 1796, which referred to him as 'the *digito-monstratus* of Cambridge'.[1] But Charles Le Grice, who came up in 1792 and was on friendly terms with him, says nothing of dissipation. He describes Coleridge as studious, but desultory and capricious in his reading. He took little exercise, and his rooms, on the right-hand ground-floor of the staircase facing the great gate, were a centre of conversation, largely on politics.

> What evenings have I spent in those rooms! What little suppers, or *sizings*, as they were called, have I enjoyed; when Aeschylus, and Plato, and Thucydides were pushed aside, with a pile of lexicons, &c., to discuss the pamphlets of the day. Ever and anon, a pamphlet issued from the pen of Burke. There was no need of having the book before us. Coleridge had read it in the morning, and in the evening he would repeat whole pages verbatim.[2]

Coleridge was an admirer of Burke's genius, and was ultimately to become, in some sense, the inheritor of his convictions. But his politics of 1793, if not strictly democratic, were certainly anti-war and anti-Pitt. This was the general tone of undergraduate Cambridge, and in Coleridge's case we may once more suspect the influence of William Frend. Early in 1793, at the very moment when the French declaration of war was forcing Pitt's hand, Frend published a pamphlet on *Peace and Union*, which caused an uproar. Its theology was attacked as derogatory to the doctrines and rites of the Church, and its politics as disturbing the harmony of society. The Fellows of Jesus excluded Frend from residence, and the Visitor upheld them. In May, Frend was brought before the Vice-Chancellor's court, on a charge of offending against a University statute by his publication. The undergraduates demonstrated in his favour. Coleridge and John Copley of Trinity, afterwards Lord Lyndhurst, were active among them. 'Frend for Ever' was chalked upon the walls of all the colleges. A train of gunpowder traced 'Liberty' and 'Equality' on the shaven lawns of Trinity and St. John's. At the trial, which dragged on throughout the month, Coleridge made himself conspicuous by

---

[1] C. 94; G. 8, 27, 316.   [2] 2 *Gent. Mag.* ii. 605.

clapping his hands at a defence of Frend. The Proctor,
Charles Farish of Queens, accused his next-door neighbour,
Edmund Charnock of Clare, who extended the stump of a
hand, unable to clap. According to Gillman, Coleridge
afterwards went to the Proctor and took the blame, when
the Proctor told him that he knew very well who it was, but
had deliberately picked out a man who could not have been
in fault. Henry Gunning, however, then Esquire Bedell,
himself a Whig, who thought the pamphlet flippant on
religion but in no way seditious, says that Coleridge had
asked Charnock to change places with him, and incurred the
censure of the undergraduates for his conduct. Frend was
expelled from the University, became an insurance official in
London, and thenceforward played no great part in Coleridge's life.[1]

After all, Coleridge did once more pay a visit to Ottery,
his last for several years. It was probably then that for the
first time he saw Bowles, now the chief inspirer of his muse,
in the market-place of Salisbury, where he again stopped
with Edward on his way. At Ottery he led a party of young
ladies to the Pixies' Parlour, and wrote an ode on the event.
James took him to Sidmouth and to Plymouth, where he
indited verses to a Miss Fanny Nesbitt, with whom he had
travelled in the coach from Exeter to Tiverton. All this
seems care-free enough.[2] But a letter to George indicates
that he was awaiting with some trepidation a discussion of
his debts. His brothers seem to have treated him generously,
but when he left Ottery he loitered away more money on
the road and in London, and on his return to Cambridge
found himself with so small a sum that he thought he could
not mock his tutor with it. He rushed up to London again
with a party of friends, lived for three days in a 'tempest of
Pleasure', and then went back to Cambridge for a week—
'such a week!'—intending a course with which he would not
shock George's religious feelings. It was, no doubt, suicide.[3]
Once more the account of a Cambridge acquaintance gives a

[1] Gillman, 49, 54; *Studies*, 92; 2 *Gent. Mag.* x. 124; H. Gunning, *Reminiscences of Cambridge*, i. 280; Estlin, 25.
[2] C. 19, 20; *P.W.* 40, 45, 46.   [3] C. 20; G. 8.

very different picture. Christopher Wordsworth, the poet's brother, then at Trinity, kept a diary, in which he recorded that on 5 November 1793 Le Grice invited him to join a literary society, of which Coleridge was to be a member. Later in the day he met Coleridge, who spouted Bowles and spoke of the esteem in which William Wordsworth's poetry was held at Exeter. On the 7th he was at breakfast with William Rough of Trinity, when Coleridge came in, and a discussion of his poems followed. Next day he saw Coleridge's lines *To Fortune* in the *Morning Chronicle*. On the 13th the first meeting of the literary society took place in Wordsworth's rooms. Coleridge was to have read a paper, but had neglected to prepare it, and recited poems instead. There the diary breaks off. But it has covered just that miserable week of Coleridge's return to Cambridge.[1] The lines *To Fortune*, written on a walk between Gray's Inn Lane and Cornhill, must have been sent to the newspaper during the hectic three days in London, and belong to an attempt to restore financial equilibrium by buying a ticket for an Irish lottery.[2]

Coleridge now went once more to London, still with grim thoughts of putting an end to it all in his bosom.[3] One thing that he did not tell his brothers afterwards, although it seems to have come to their knowledge, was that his pecuniary troubles were complicated by a 'love-fit'. Evidently his sentimental affair with Mary Evans had at last flamed into something like a passion. Probably he had seen her in London during October and had come to fear the existence of a rival. His own fortunes did not permit him to make a declaration, he wrote a year afterwards. 'I never durst even in a whisper avow my passion, though I knew she loved me.' A still later letter makes it clear that he means 'could have dared' and 'even had I known'.[4] His brothers seem to have believed that this last week in London was again one of debauchery.[5] It was in fact one of dull misery, until on 2 December he stumbled upon a recruiting officer in Chancery

[1] C. Wordsworth, *Social Life at the English Universities in the 18th Century*, 587–92.
[2] *P.W.* 54; *2 Gent. Mag.* x. 124. [3] G. 8.
[4] C. 33, 85; *Rem.* 279; De Q. ii. 167; *M.P.* xxviii. 471; Hamilton, i. 576; cf. p. 34. [5] Gillman, 64.

Lane and enlisted as a trooper in Eliot's Horse, the 15th Light Dragoons. On 4 December he was sworn in at Reading, where the regiment was quartered.[1] When asked his name, he gave it as Silas Titus Comberbacke, 'and verily', he says, 'my habits were so little equestrian, that my horse, I doubt not, was of that opinion'. His adventures at Reading seem to have won their way to the mythical; he may himself have been the chief mythologist. He had frequent tumbles from the saddle. He could not rub down his horse, or pick the hairs from its heels. He did not keep his accoutrements in order. 'Whose is this rusty carbine?' said an officer. 'Is it very rusty?' said Coleridge. 'Very rusty!' 'Then, Sir, it must be mine.' His comrades took pity on him, and helped him. In return, he wrote their love-letters for them, putting in stanzas of verse. At last, suspicion arose that he was a University man. He told the men stories from the classics, and wrote a Greek letter for one who had committed a capital offence. He corrected an officer who ascribed to Euripides a quotation which was really from Sophocles. He chalked up the sentence '*Eheu! quam infortunii miserrimum est fuisse felicem*'! A Greek book was found in his saddle-holsters.[2] However this may be, when the regiment moved to Henley in January 1794, he was removed from strictly military duties, and set as an orderly, to nurse a comrade sick with small-pox, in a little room built in the workhouse garden. The presence of a beautiful girl in the neighbourhood soothed his captivity.[3] Meanwhile he had revealed his condition to friends at Christ's Hospital, and they in turn to those at Cambridge. George Tuckett got into touch with him and communicated with his brothers. Coleridge charged Tuckett with a breach of confidence, in part on account of a reference to Mary Evans, but the disclosure of his position must have been a relief.[4] Throughout February he was in correspondence with George and James, abounding in confessions of his past, willing to return to Cambridge if his discharge could be secured, grateful for

[1] C. 24; G. 12 (note); Gillman, 57.
[2] G. 11; A., p. 101; L. 366 (note); *Rem.* 279; *2 Gent. Mag.* x. 124; De Q. ii. 167; Carlyon, i. 29; Gillman, 59.
[3] C. 21; G. 9; *Rem.* 282.   [4] C. 21; G. 7; *M.P.* xxviii. 471.

the kindness of Boyer, who presumably had concealed the affair from the Hospital authorities. His officers, in particular Captain Nathaniel Ogle, also appear to have exerted themselves on his behalf. Early in March he was moved to High Wycombe, missing a visit to Henley by Le Grice, and was billeted at the Compasses, now the Chequers, Inn. Here he employed himself in talking philosophy with a frequenter of the pot-house and writing a declamation for Robert Allen on the good and evil of novels. Shortly afterwards he was back at Reading, where one George Cornish found him at the 'White Hart' and gave him a guinea. The 'Jesuites' wrote, hoping for his return. But the negotiations for his release lingered on, because the Army authorities asked for a substitute recruit. Meanwhile the brothers arranged for the payment of his college debts, which after all did not amount to more than £132. Coleridge had lost all his civilian clothes, and needed a new outfit. He was anxious, too, about some books which he had sold at Reading and wanted for his projected volume of translations. But he was reflecting on his past attitude to religion, when he 'had too much vanity to be altogether a Christian, too much tenderness of nature to be utterly an infidel'. He doubted whether his faith was very different yet.[1]

While awaiting his discharge, Coleridge walked arm-in-arm with the handsome daughter of Charles Clagget, a musician, who set songs for him and advised him to write an opera. He also made the acquaintance of a gentleman at Bray who promised to take him to London on his way to Cambridge and introduce him to his bookseller.[2] The discharge was granted on 7 April, and by 10 April Coleridge was at Jesus again. His reception was a somewhat mixed one. His tutor, James Plampin, behaved with 'exceeding and most delicate kindness', and wrote to George that his conduct was extremely proper. Dr. Pearce, on the other hand, showed 'great asperity'. Coleridge was convened before the Fellows, gated for a month, and required to translate the works of Demetrius Phalereus, whom he found a dull writer. Caldwell and others greeted him with almost

<hr>

[1] C. 22-9; G. 9-11.   [2] C. 30; 2 Gent. Mag. x. 124.

fraternal affection. Some from outside colleges stood aloof.
Rough, he says, cut him, until he learnt that he was alone
in so doing. Samuel Butler waited until the very end of term
before paying him a call, which he acknowledged with a
grateful letter and an invitation to bread and cheese. His
more disreputable acquaintance he himself dropped. He
was full of good resolutions. 'Every enjoyment, except of
necessary comforts, I look upon as criminal.' Once more he
would write for all the prizes. He feared that he would
either have to go out at a by-term or postpone his degree
to the Christmas of 1795.[1]

Early in June Coleridge sent to the *Cambridge Intelligencer*
an advertisement of his *Imitations from the Modern Latin
Poets*, which were to include some of the lyrics of the seven-
teenth-century Polish Jesuit, Matthias Casimir Sarbiewski,
and the *Basia* of the sixteenth-century Batavian Joannes
Nicholaus Secundus. One lyric from Casimir alone represents the ambitious design.[2] On 9 June he set out with one
Joseph Hucks for a pedestrian tour to Oxford, and then on
through Wales.[3] At Oxford his primary object was to see
Robert Allen, now a sizar at University College, and receiving
the usual treatment then meted out to sizars. Of this Coleridge
had already written, "'Tis a childish University! Thank God!
I am at Cambridge.' And when he saw Oxford he did not like
it any better. The visit, however, was another turning-point
in his life, for Allen introduced him to Robert Southey
of Balliol, whom he found 'a nightingale among owls'.[4]
Southey's father, a Bristol linen-draper, had died recently,
but the boy had been mainly brought up by a half-aunt,
Elizabeth Tyler, who now lived in College Green, Bristol.
He went to Westminster, which he had to leave for writing
an attack on flogging in a school journal called *The Flagellant*.
He came to Oxford with the prospect, like Coleridge himself,
of taking Orders, but his religious principles had been shaken
by Gibbon, and he was now a republican and Stoic, after
the manner of Epictetus, with a head full of Rousseau and
Werther.[5] His morals were austere, and Coleridge claims

---

[1] C. 31, 74; G. 12–14.   [2] *P.W.* 59.   [3] G. 14.
[4] C. 15, 32.   [5] Southey (*L.*), i. 161–4; iv. 185.

to have abandoned, through his example, the sexual irregu-
larities of which he had always been ashamed.[1] It may have
been in Southey's mind, rather than in Coleridge's, that the
germ of the scheme which came to be known as Pantisocracy originated. In 1793 he had written to friends of the
attraction he found in the poet Cowley's dream of retiring
with books to a cottage in America, and there seeking the
happiness in solitude which he could not find in society.[2]

My asylum there would be sought for different reasons (and no prospect in life gives me half the pleasure this visionary one affords). I
should be pleased to reside in a country where man's abilities would
ensure respect; where society was upon a proper footing, and man was
considered as more valuable than money; and where I could till the
earth, and provide by honest industry the meat which my wife would
dress with pleasing care—*redeunt spectacula mane*—reason comes with
the end of the paper.

In similar vein he must have spoken to Coleridge, and
Coleridge, who never knew the difference between a dream
and a way of life, jumped at the hint. It could be done and
should be done. He had already read William Godwin's
Political Justice, published the year before, in which, amongst
so much that is merely negative, the idea of human perfectibility is the one constructive feature. In America, by a
small society, combining, at least in the second generation,
'the innocence of the patriarchal age with the knowledge
and genuine refinements of European culture'—here, surely,
the idea could be tried out, as in a laboratory experiment.[3]
It was, no doubt, also Coleridge's classical imagination that
invented the names Pantisocracy and Aspheterism to christen
the plan. Robert Allen and a Balliol friend of Southey,
George Burnett, would surely join in. As for funds, Coleridge's volume of translations and a poem entitled *Joan of
Arc*, upon which Southey was engaged, would supply them.[4]
    Having discussed this, Coleridge set off with Hucks for
his Welsh tour, leaving Southey to look for further recruits.
He found one in Robert Lovell, a young poet on the point
of marriage with Mary Fricker, one of the five daughters

[1] B.L. i. 49; Gillman, 64.
[2] Southey (L.), i. 191, 195, 197; cf. Cowley, Preface to *Poems* (1656).
[3] *P.W.* 86; *Fr.* ii. 29.   [4] Southey (L.), i. 210, 213, 221; (*W.*), ii. 194; *Rem.* 404.

(Mary, Edith, Sara, Martha, and Eliza) of a Gloucestershire manufacturer of sugar-pans, who had been ruined by the stoppage of trade with America. The elder girls supported themselves by their needles. Byron meant to be annoying when he described them in *Don Juan* as 'milliners' [1] Southey had known the Frickers from childhood, and was in love with Mary's sister Edith, to whom, on the strength of his new prospect, he now became engaged. The Welsh tour, described by Hucks in a printed narrative, and by Coleridge in letters to Southey and a Jesus friend, Henry Martin, took them through Herefordshire and Shropshire and most of North Wales. They climbed Penmaenmawr, Plynlimon, and Snowdon. Coleridge wrote some verses, talked Pantisocracy in inns, and feared that he would catch the itch from a Welsh democrat who grasped his hand. At Wrexham, on 15 July, he had an unexpected *rencontre*. In the church he caught sight of Elizabeth Evans, then living there with her grandmother. He retreated to his inn, and from the window saw her again, accompanied by Mary, '*quam efflictim et perdite amabam*'. They evidently saw him, but again he retired.

Had I appeared to recognise her, my fortitude would not have supported me.

> Vivit, sed mihi non vivit—nova forte marita,
> Ah dolor! alterius cara a cervice pependit.
> Vos, malefida valete accensae insomnia mentis,
> Littora amata valete! vale, ah! formosa Maria!

Hucks informed me that the two sisters walked by the window four or five times, as if anxiously. Doubtless they think themselves deceived by some face strikingly like me.

Next day he fled to Ruthin, sixteen miles away. 'Love is a local anguish,' he says. It was probably there that he wrote *The Sigh*, although he dated it in June.[2]

Southey had meant to join Coleridge in Wales, but towards the end of July was surprised by the unexpected arrival of his friend at Bristol. America was now definitely decided upon as the scene for the experiment. In the middle

---

[1] C. 32; *Rem.* 2; S.C. (*M.*) i. 9; Southey (*L.*), i. 195, 217, 223; Byron, *D.J.* III, xciii; *Letters*, vi. 112.   [2] C. 32, 33; T. 8; *P.W.* 62.

of August Southey took Coleridge to his mother's house in Bath, and from there they started on a long walk through Somersetshire, by Chilcompton, where Coleridge wrote his *Lines to a Beautiful Spring in a Village*, and then by Wells to Cheddar, where they were impressed by the high and fantastic cliffs. 'A stream of water cold and clear', writes Southey, 'flows from under the rocks where we paused to drink and pour libations to the Naiad.' At Cheddar they could only get a single bed, and Coleridge proved 'a vile bedfellow'. Thence they went to Huntspill, where George Burnett lived, and on to Nether Stowey to visit 'a friend of Coleridge'.[1] It was a turning-point in Coleridge's life even more momentous than the visit to Oxford, for this friend was Thomas Poole, whom he can only have met before for a day or so at Reading in December 1793, but with whom for several years he was now destined to be in the closest relations.[2] Thomas Poole was a well-to-do tanner, somewhat rough in his manners, but a widely read and public-spirited man, the mainstay of his neighbourhood in all local affairs, in spite of qualms which his democratic sympathies aroused, even among his own kindred. He was unmarried, and lived with his mother hard by his tannery. He was much interested in hearing of Pantisocracy, since he had himself looked upon America as 'the only asylum of peace and liberty', and had some idea of migrating thither.[3] A month after the meeting, he wrote to a friend, describing the scheme as it had been detailed to him. Twelve men and twelve ladies, already familiar with each other's dispositions, were to embark in April. They calculated that the produce of the men's labour for two or three hours a day, to be held in common, would suffice to maintain the colony. Leisure hours would be spent, with the aid of a good library, in study, discussion, and the education of children, on a system which he would not attempt to set out. The women would have the care of infants and other occupations suited to their strength. The greatest attention

---

[1] Southey (L.), i. 216; *Bodl. MS. English Letters*, C. 22, f. 124; *Rem.* 404; *P.W.* 58. The 'Kirkhampton' of a MS. must be an error.

[2] P. i. 73-84, but the writer did not know Southey's evidence, which, as contemporary, outweighs his statement in *Rem.* 404 that he and Coleridge saw Poole for the first time in August 1794.   [3] P. i. 77, 98.

was to be paid to the cultivation of their minds. It was not yet settled whether the marriage contract was to be dissoluble, if desired by one or both parties. Religious opinion was to be free, and any member of the society might withdraw at will. It was thought that a contribution of £125 by each man would enable the plan to proceed. He regarded 'Coldridge', of whom he had heard much before he saw him, as the principal in the undertaking, and was impressed by his scholarship and powers of conversation.

But he, as it generally happens to men of his class, feels the justice of Providence in the want of those inferiour abilities which are necessary to the rational discharge of the common duties of life. His aberrations from prudence, to use his own expression, have been great; but he now promises to be as sober and rational as his most sober friends could wish. In religion he is a Unitarian, if not a Deist; in politicks a Democrat, to the utmost extent of the word.

Coleridge himself would probably have qualified this last phrase. Poole thought Southey the more violent of the two in his principles. 'In Religion, shocking to say in a mere Boy as he is, I fear he wavers between Deism and Atheism.' Poole's orthodox cousin John, whom he took his guests to see, was even more shocked. *'Uterque verò rabie Democratica, quoad Politiam; et Infidelis quoad Religionem spectat, turpiter fervet. Ego maxime indignor'*, he confided to his diary.[1]

From Stowey, Coleridge and Southey went back to Bristol, passing again through Bath, where, says Southey, Coleridge engaged himself to Sara Fricker, 'not a little to my astonishment, for he had talked of being deeply in love with a certain Mary Evans'. Love, in this case, was assuredly 'a local anguish'. George Burnett, in his turn, proposed to Martha Fricker, who, more wise than her sister, rejected him, saying that he wanted not her but 'a wife in a hurry'.[2] Towards the end of September Southey thought that the American party was made up: himself, his mother, his brothers, and his cousin Margaret Hill; all the Frickers; Lovell, with a brother and two sisters; Allen and Burnett; Charles Heath of Monmouth, an apothecary. He had hoped to bring in his dearest friend, Edmund Seward of Balliol, but Seward, a strong Churchman,

---

[1] P. i. 95, 102.   [2] *Rem.* 404; Sara Coleridge, *Memoir*, i. 9.

thought that the company would split on religion, and remained critical. In the middle of October, Southey's aunt heard of the scheme, and turned him out of her house. The 'apostle of Pantisocracy' fled in a rainstorm to Bath.[1]

Coleridge had gone to London on 21 August, losing his Casimir on the way, but taking with him *The Fall of Robespierre*, of which he had written the first act and Southey the rest in two days, Lovell, who undertook the third, having failed them. In London he met Southey's friend Grosvenor Bedford, and Franklin introduced him to George Dyer, of an older Christ's Hospital generation, who was enraptured with Pantisocracy, pronounced it impregnable, and was sure that Joseph Priestley, already an exile in America, would join the enterprise. Coleridge stayed at the 'Angel' in Newgate St. but spent his evenings at a neighbouring coffee-house called the 'Salutation and Cat', where he fell in with an American land-agent, from whom it is not surprising to learn that he also received encouragement. They could do the thing on £2,000. The passage would not cost more than £400. Land could be bought more cheaply over there, and twelve men could easily clear three hundred acres in four or five months. A thousand could be cleared and houses built on them for six hundred dollars. He advised the district of the Susquehanna in Pennsylvania, which was free from hostile Indians. The bisons were quite 'backwards', and the mosquitoes not so bad as English gnats. Literary characters made money there. Evidently the land-agent knew his business. Coleridge sent fraternal love to the Lovells and Frickers and to Miss Fricker 'more'. Favell and the younger Le Grice wanted to join Pantisocracy when they left college. According to Cottle and Gillman, Coleridge was much attracted by the name Susquehanna.[2]

On 17 September he reached Cambridge, where he evidently meant to complete another term before starting for America in the spring, and sat down to write to Miss Fricker and then to Southey.

My God! how tumultuous are the movements of my heart. Since

---

[1] C. 41 (note); Southey (L.), i. 211, 214, 220, 222; *Bodl. MS. English Letters*, C. 22, f. 126.   [2] C. 35; G. 15; *Rem.* 21; Gillman, 69; Lowes, 554.

I quitted this room what and how important events have been evolved!
America! Southey! Miss Fricker! Yes Southey, you are right. Even
Love is the creature of strong motive. I certainly love her. I *think* of
her incessantly and with unspeakable tenderness,—with that inward
melting away of soul that symptomatizes it.

Perhaps this would have reassured Southey, if it was
Southey who needed reassuring. But before the letters were
dispatched, Coleridge received a rebuke from Southey for
not having written earlier to his intended bride. He was
hurt. He had promised to write the moment he arrived at
Cambridge, and had done so, 'pouring forth the heart'.
He would have written from London, but had stayed on day
by day. 'Languid, sick at heart, in the back room of an inn!
Lofty conjunction of circumstances for me to write to
Miss F.' Southey should not be so precipitate. It was unfortunate that after all the 'parcel' of Coleridge's letters had
somehow not reached Bath nearly a week later, and Southey
had to send to Favell in London for news of him. Coleridge
explained, but added, 'I am in the queerest humour in the
world, and am out of love with everybody.'[1]

Meanwhile, the fame of Pantisocracy had been brought
to Cambridge by Jesus friends who had met Coleridge in
Wales, and he was plunged in controversy. Caldwell laughed
at him. 'Up I arose, terrible in reasoning.' Dr. Pearce tried
to restrain him, but misunderstood his position. 'Sir,' he
said, 'I am neither Jacobin, nor Democrat, but a Pantiso-
crat.' He planned a 'Book of Pantisocracy', which should
'comprise all that is good in Godwin'. In preparation for
his future labours, he began to learn carpentry. This, however, left him time for other occupations. *Robespierre*, which
he had failed to dispose of in London, was published in Cambridge, under his own name only, which would carry greater
weight there than Southey's. To it was appended a further
advertisement of his *Imitations*. But these depressed his
spirits. 'When a man is unhappy, he writes damned bad
poetry, I find.' And they would take at least two quartos,
instead of the two octavos he had intended. He revised his
school *Monody on Chatterton* for Lancelot Sharpe's edition of

[1] C. 34-6.

Chatterton's *Poems*, introducing the beloved name Susquehanna; contributed a few verses, old and new, to the *Cambridge
Intelligencer* and *Morning Chronicle*; and wrote criticisms of
others by Southey and by another friend, but *'pitier* of my
principles', Francis Wrangham of Trinity Hall. He read and
trembled at Schiller. And he found time to enter into rivalry
with Caldwell for the favours of a Miss Brunton, 'the most
literary of the beautiful, and the most beautiful of the
literatae', whose father was manager of a company now acting at Cambridge. He contemplated Christmas visits to the
Bruntons and Middleton at Norwich, and Wrangham at
Cobham.[1]

These, however, were not to be. On 24 October Coleridge composed a *Monologue to a Young Jack Ass in Jesus
Piece*.[2]

> Innocent foal! thou despised and forlorn!
> I hail thee *Brother*,—spite of the fool's scorn!
> And fain I'd take thee with me, to the Dell
> Where high-soul'd Pantisocracy shall dwell!

There is no evidence that he wrote in irony. But there is
much that this term, beneath its apparent occupations, was
really one of qualms about Pantisocracy and its inevitable
consequence. Southey had expressed a desire to take with
him to America one Shadrach Weekes, a servant of his aunt.
Coleridge was at first delighted: 'Shad is my brother.' But
he was perturbed when he gathered that Southey had in
mind the introduction of a servant class into the colony.
Servitude was not consistent with the pure milk of the
gospel. He would not refuse to go, but 'this is *not our plan*,
nor can I defend it'. Later, he became uneasy at the idea
of taking mothers and children with them. He doubted
whether the women, other than Edith and Sara, were Pantisocrats at heart. Would there not be difficulties about the
education of the rising generation?

That Mrs Fricker! We shall have her teaching the infants *Christianity*,—I mean that mongrel whelp that goes under its name,—teaching
them by stealth in some ague fit of superstition.[3]

---

[1] C. 34–9; G. 16, 17, 25; T. 12; Carlyon, i. 27; *P.W.* 16, 19, 29, 57, 66, 67,
68, 69, 125.   [2] *P.W.* 74.   [3] C. 34, 37, 38.

Coleridge's family were, of course, protesting. They suggested that he was deranged. Southey feared that he would be confined, but Coleridge saw no prospect of that. He wrote to George, defending himself against the charge of democracy. He reasserted his religious principles, and promised to come and see George in London. His friend Potter of Emanuel would drive him up in a phaeton. Indolence had been his real vice, but he hoped that the kingdom of reason was now coming. He enclosed some lines written on the death of an Ottery friend, Fulwood Smerdon, full of self-criticism.[1]

> To me hath Heaven with liberal hand assign'd
> Energic Reason and a shaping mind,
> The daring soul of Truth, the Patriot's part,
> And Pity's sigh, that breathes the gentle heart—
> Sloth-jaundic'd all! and from my graspless hand
> Drop Friendship's precious pearls, like hour-glass sand.

The real trouble about Pantisocracy was, of course, that it entailed Miss Fricker, and Coleridge was by now quite clear that he did not love Miss Fricker. Early in October he had received a letter which he did not reveal to Southey until three weeks later. It was from Mary Evans, written in a purely sisterly vein, and with some hesitation lest she should be 'violating the rules of female delicacy'. But she had heard that he was to leave England on a plan so absurd and extravagant that she could not imagine it to be true, and also that he doubted of the existence of God, and disbelieved a hereafter. This, too, she did not credit. At the end of October, Coleridge wrote his lines *On a Discovery Made Too Late*, and sent them to Wrangham with a brief explanation, and to Southey with a very full one.

I loved her, Southey, even to madness. Her image was never absent from me for three years, for *more* than three years. My resolution has not faltered, but I want a comforter.

He had sought the company of Miss Brunton, in the hope that one passion would be cured by another.

The latter I could easily have dissipated in her absence, and so have restored my affections to her whom I do not love, but whom by every tie of reason and honour I ought to love. I am resolved, but wretched!

[1] C. 37, 38, 40; P.W. 76.

Southey expressed sympathy, but did not give him the obvious advice, which would have spelt the end of Pantisocracy.[1]

But Coleridge was not yet resigned to his fate. To Southey he replied:

She *was very* lovely, Southey! We formed each other's minds; our ideas were blended. Heaven bless her! I cannot forget her. Every day her memory sinks deeper into my heart.

He then meant to come down to Southey, after seeing George in London. But he did not do so. Mary had asked him not to answer her letter. One thinks that he could hardly have refrained from refuting its imputation of infidelity. This he could have done with justice, since it seems clear that his fundamental temper, whatever cloud of metaphysics his mind threw about it, was always a religious one. However this may be, he summoned up courage, while still in town, probably early in November, to avow his long passion, and to entreat Mary to let him know whether or not she is engaged to 'M^r ——'. The phrases he uses echo those of the *Discovery* sonnet. He is returning to Cambridge next day, and expects in a few months to enter the Temple. There may have been further correspondence, now lost, since it is not until 24 December that he acknowledges a final rejection:

I have this moment received your letter, Mary Evans. Its firmness does honour to your understanding, its gentleness to your humanity. You condescend to accuse yourself—most unjustly! You have been altogether blameless. In my wildest day-dream of vanity, I never supposed that you entertained for me any other than a common friendship.

To love you, habit has made unalterable. This passion, however, divested as it now is of all shadow of hope, will lose its disquieting power. Far distant from you I shall journey through the vale of men in calmness. He cannot long be wretched, who dares be actively virtuous.

I have burnt your letters—forget mine; and that I have pained you, forgive me!

May God infinitely love you!

He communicated the result to Southey.

To lose her! I can rise above that selfish pang. But to marry

---

[1] C. 37, 38; G. 17; *P.W.* 72.

another. O Southey! bear with my weakness. Love makes all things
pure and heavenly like itself,—but to marry a woman whom I do *not*
love, to degrade her whom I call my wife by making her the instrument
of low desire, and on the removal of a desultory appetite to be perhaps
not displeased with her absence! Enough! These refinements are the
wildering fires that lead me into vice. Mark you, Southey! *I will do
my duty*.

If he thought that Southey would now relent, he was mistaken.[1]

The return to Cambridge in November, if there was one,
can only have been for a short time. From 11 December
onwards Coleridge was writing from London, and by 17
December he had heard that they were 'making a row about
him at Jesus'. Nevertheless, a long-suffering College allowed
his name to remain on the books until the following June, and
even his Army freak of 1793 does not seem to have become
known to the Christ's Hospital authorities before April
1795. Evidently Boyer had been very discreet. The intention expressed to Mary Evans of entering at the Temple
suggests that the idea of Pantisocracy, if not definitely abandoned, was now dormant. Coleridge is no longer discussing
it with Southey in December, except for a defence of Robert
Allen, who had declared his defection. 'Wherein has he
offended? He did never promise to form one of our party.'[2]
Apart from Mary Evans, his letters are concerned with 'indifferent subjects'. He met Godwin, whom he thought a sophist,
and Holcroft, whom, although repelled by his atheism and
his scorn of Pantisocracy and the poems of Bowles, he at first
liked better than Godwin. Later he came to hold him in
detestation. His own metaphysics remain mechanical.

I am a complete necessitarian, and understand the subject as well
almost as Hartley himself, but I go farther than Hartley, and believe
the corporeality of *thought*, namely, that it is motion.[3]

He is still reading Bowles. He criticizes the poems which
Southey and Lovell are publishing in a joint volume. He
is in touch with the proprietors of the *Morning Chronicle*,

[1] C. 37, 38, 44-6, 52; *Bodl. MS. English Letters*, C. 22, f. 136.
[2] C. 38, note (? misdated), 42, 44, 46; Carlyon, i. 27; Brandl, 80; A. W. Lockhart,
Chr. H. Exhibitioners, 36.   [3] C. 42, 57; Godwin, i. 119; *Rem.* 329.

to which he contributes a series of sonnets on eminent contemporaries. The list is a landmark of his intellectual development at this time: Erskine, Burke, Priestley, La Fayette, Kosciusko, Pitt, Bowles, Mrs. Siddons, Godwin, Southey, Sheridan, Stanhope. All are laudatory, except that on Pitt, the 'dark Scowler', and that on Burke, which is regretful.[1] He is intimate with Lamb, 'a man of uncommon genius', and with his sister, whose illness reminds him of his own sister.

> O! I have woke at midnight, and have wept,
> Because she was not!—Cheerily, dear Charles!
> Thou thy best friend shalt cherish many a year;
> Such high presages feel I of warm Hope.
> For not uninterested the dear Maid
> I've view'd—her soul affectionate yet wise,
> Her polish'd wit as mild as lambent glories
> That play around a holy infant's head.

From reminiscences by Lamb we learn of nights spent over metaphysics and poetry, with the help of Welsh rabbits, egg-hot, and Oronooko in the little smoky room of the 'Salutation and Cat.' Lamb, too, was a Unitarian.[2] The Christmas Eve of 1794 Coleridge employed in writing his *Religious Musings*, which he sent to Lamb, still unfinished, with covering lines, in which he described it as a

rhyme
Elaborate and swelling.

It was no doubt that. Even in the extant versions, which contain later work, Coleridge has not yet shaken himself free from the obsession of apostrophes, condemned by Boyer.[3]

[1] C. 41, 42; *P.W.* 79.
[2] C. 46; *L.* 3, 4, 15, 21; A., p. 110; *P.W.* 21 (? misdated), 78.
[3] C. 41, 46; *P.W.* 78, 108.

III

THE 'WATCHMAN'

January 1795—May 1796

ABOUT Christmas 1794 Coleridge told Southey that he
meant to walk down to Bath. He did not come, but
remained in London, considering a proposal, apparently made
to him through George Dyer, of tutorship to some young
Erskines, relatives of the Earl of Buchan. They were probably
sons of the Earl's brother, Henry Erskine, the Whig lawyer,
to whom one of the *Morning Chronicle* sonnets had been addressed. Early in January, however, Southey came up to
reclaim his stray, tracked him to the 'Angel', and shepherded
him down, first to Bath, and a few days later to Bristol.
Coleridge meant to return to London.[1] But now Pantisocracy
seems to have resumed its appeal, in spite of a modification
in the scheme, suggested by Southey's Welsh friend Charles
Wynn, and supported by Lovell. Wynn's idea was that,
before attempting America, an experiment should be made by
taking a co-operative farm in Wales. Coleridge protested that
the conditions of Pantisocracy could not be realized there,
and accused Southey of wrapping himself 'in the mantle of
self-centring resolve', instead of reasoning. Finally, however, he gave way, America, of course, still remaining as
the ultimate objective for all parties.[2] It was probably now
that he added to his *Chatterton* poem these autobiographical
verses.[3]

> Poor Chatterton! *he* sorrows for thy fate,
> Who would have prais'd and lov'd thee, ere too late.
> Poor Chatterton! farewell! of darkest hues
> This chaplet cast I on thy unshaped tomb;
> But dare no longer on the sad theme muse,
> Lest kindred woes persuade a kindred doom:
> For oh! big gall-drops, shook from Folly's wing,
> Have blacken'd the fair promise of my spring;
> And the stern Fate transpierc'd with viewless dart
> The last pale Hope that shiver'd at my heart!

[1] C. 46; G. 18; *Rem.* 405.
[2] C. 43 (misdated), 52; *Rem.* 406; Southey (L.), i. 232.   [3] *P.W.* 130.

Hence, gloomy thoughts! no more my soul shall dwell
On joys that were! no more endure to weigh
The shame and anguish of the evil day,
Wisely forgetful! O'er the ocean swell
Sublime of Hope I seek the cottag'd dell
Where Virtue calm with careless step may stray;
And, dancing to the moon-light roundelay,
The wizard Passions weave an holy spell!

O Chatterton! that thou wert yet alive!
Sure thou would'st spread the canvass to the gale,
And love with us the tinkling team to drive
O'er peaceful Freedom's undivided dale;
And we, at sober eve, would round thee throng,
Hanging, enraptur'd, on thy stately song,
And greet with smiles the young-eyed Poesy
All deftly mask'd as hoar Antiquity.

Alas, vain Phantasies! the fleeting brood
Of woe self-solac'd in her dreamy mood!
Yet will I love to follow the sweet dream,
Where Susquehanna pours his untamed stream;
And on some hill, whose forest-frowning side
Waves o'er the murmurs of his calmer tide,
Will raise a solemn Cenotaph to thee,
Sweet Harper of time-shrouded Minstrelsy!
And there, sooth'd sadly by the dirgeful wind,
Muse on the sore ills I had left behind.

On his arrival at Bristol Coleridge bought a new note-book, now in the British Museum and known as the Gutch note-book. It is a curious record, extending over the years from 1795 to 1798, and containing in its first part a medley of literary notes, personal reflections, and business memoranda in chronological sequence, and in its second part similar jottings, apparently set down irregularly during the same period.[1] While it was yet virgin, Coleridge entered upon the first page the following lines:[2]

I mix in life, and labour to seem free,
    With common persons pleas'd and common things,
While every thought and action tends to thee,
    And every impulse from thy influence springs.

It was his farewell to Mary Evans. He does not appear to

[1] B.M. Addl. MS. 27901 (Archiv f. neueren Sprachen und Literaturen, xcvii. 334); cf. Lowes, 5-31, 451, and passim, and Essays and Studies (English Association), xix. 99.   [2] P.W. 292.

have ever seen her again until 1808, when he met her, a
distressed waif, in a London street.[1] Once more, Pantisocracy entailed Sara Fricker. Of her he wrote in January
to George Dyer. Over and above the attractions of her
person and 'polished understanding', he had learnt that
during his absence she had disobliged her relations by
rejecting the addresses of two men, one of them of large
fortune. This, with her usual delicacy, she had concealed
from him until his arrival at Bristol. But now, under family
pressure, she must either marry him whom she loves, or one
whom she strongly dislikes, in spite of his fortune and solici-
tous attentions. And so the decision was made, somewhat
to the disapproval of Lovell, perhaps a little more percipient
than Southey.[2]

Even Wales entailed the preliminary collection of funds.
It was thought that at least £300 would be necessary. A
beginning was made by giving public lectures. Coleridge
had already given three by the end of January, and published
one, 'it having been confidently asserted that there was
Treason in it'. Other plans were soon on foot. Southey had
some hopes from the reversion of a family estate, which,
however, came to nothing. Journalistic work on the *Tele-
graph* or the *Citizen* seemed a possibility. It might mean
living in London, but they would prefer Wales. If they
could secure a fixed £100 between them, their literary industry should supply the rest. On £150 they might marry.
The *Imitations* were still in prospect, and Southey relied on
his *Joan of Arc*. A *Provincial Magazine* was thought of, 'to be
the vehicle of all our poetry'.[3] Coleridge had taken lodgings
with Burnett at 25 College St., and here at the end of
January Southey came from Bath to join them. 'Coleridge
is writing at the same table', he told his friend Grosvenor
Bedford. 'Our names are written in the book of destiny, on
the same page.'[4] At Bristol Coleridge had the advantage of a

[1] Cf. p. 211.   [2] G. 18; *Rem.* 20.
[3] C. 51; G. 18, 19; *Rem.* 13, 406; Southey (*L.*), i. 230, 234; Wise, 9 (post-dated);
O.T. i. 6.
[4] C. 47, 139; Southey (*L.*), i. 231; (*W.*), i. 40. Coleridge writes from No. 25 in
January (G. 18) and July (C. 48), and Southey in May (*Bodl. MS. English Letters*, C. 22,
f. 148). Cottle's '48, College St.' (*Rem.* 11, 27) must be an error, unfortunately
perpetuated at Bristol by a tablet on that house (now No. 54).

public library, from which he became a frequent borrower.[1]
And he soon made many friendships, some of which long
clung to him. There was Josiah Wade, a well-to-do tradesman. There was John Prior Estlin, a Unitarian minister and
schoolmaster, with a wife for whom Coleridge made a copy
of his early verses, which still survives. There was Mrs.
Morgan, the widow of a man of fortune, with a son John.
There was Thomas Beddoes, the physician, now planning
his Pneumatic Institute at Clifton. There was Charles
Danvers, already known to Southey. There was one Michael
Castle. Above all, there was Joseph Cottle, an Evangelical
bookseller and publisher on a small scale, with a turn for
poetry, and a brother of the same persuasion, immortalized
by a line of Byron—'O Amos Cottle! Phoebus, what a name!'
To the muddled reminiscences of Joseph Cottle, based on
misdated and sometimes mutilated letters, we owe much of
our knowledge of Coleridge's life in Bristol at this and other
periods. Among these and others he talked Pantisocracy
incessantly.[2] And friendship, as was to be his frequent experience throughout life, took a financial form. After a few
weeks the young poets found themselves in debt for their
lodgings, and applied to Cottle for a loan. He asked about
Coleridge's poetry, and, on learning that the best sum he
could get for it in London had been six guineas, advanced
him thirty for the copyright, and offered Southey the same
amount for a miscellaneous volume, and fifty for his *Joan of
Arc*. He found it, however, very difficult to get any copy
out of Coleridge.[3] Meanwhile the lectures continued. Cottle
prints advertisements issued in June for six on the English
Rebellion and French Revolution, six on Revealed Religion, and one on the Slave Trade. These were to be by
Coleridge, and Cottle thought that there was one also on
the Hair Powder Tax. Southey offered a course of twelve
on History. It must, however, be doubted whether all of
Coleridge's matured. He says himself that he had given
eleven by mid-November, and wrote half of Southey's, to

[1] J. Baker, *Lit. and Bibl. Studies*, 211; P. Kaufman (*M.P.* xxi. 317).   [2] *Rem*. 6.
[3] *Rem*. 11, 35, 39. Apparently Cottle overestimates his own generosity in each case
by ten guineas, but Coleridge came to underestimate it; cf. G. 256; Murray, i. 300;
Southey (*W*.), i. 40.

which he contributed 'all the *tug* of brain'. Southey, however, claims that, in all, his earnings were as four to one
of Coleridge's.[1] A sidelight is afforded by a curious skit
on forty youths of Bristol, published about June under the
title of *The Observer*. The Slave Trade lecture is recorded,
and on Coleridge the writer adds:

> I must now remark what are the exceptionable features belonging to
> him; his speech is perfect monotonism; his person is slovenly; a clean
> appearance is as good a criterion whereby to know a scholar as the
> person of mean appearance: it is exemplified in the preceding char-
> acter [Southey]. M^r C—— would therefore do well to appear with
> cleaner stockings in public, and if his hair were combed out every time
> he appeared in public it would not depreciate him in the esteem of his
> friends.[2]

Much of the lecturing seems to have been concerned with
public affairs, and won for Coleridge some notoriety as a
democrat. In later moods of reaction, he was inclined to
regard his politics of 1795 as seditious. Herein, perhaps, he
hardly did himself justice. He was still, as at Cambridge,
strongly 'anti-polemic and anti-Pittite', disliked the 'aristocrats' in whom the ministry found their support, and resented the system of spies and informers, and the repressive
legislation against the rights of free speech. But he held
aloof from the revolutionary clubs of the day, and was at
heart no Jacobin, with a merely negative attitude to the
existing institutions of society. True patriots must be constructive in their outlook. 'Accustomed to regard all the affairs
of man as a process, they never hurry and they never pause'.
It is probable that, in the intoxication of his own eloquence,
he often spoke more violently than his calmer moments of
reflection would justify. He had, he says, some 'flame-
coloured epithets' to regret.[3]

During the lectures, the first signs appeared of a rift
between the two friends, which quickly widened into a
chasm. We have the story from both sides. Coleridge
thought that Southey was beginning to recede from the
broad principles of Pantisocracy, and to make 'Self an un-

[1] C. 52; G. 19; S. (*W*.), i. 40; *Rem.* 13, 25; Wise, 10; *O.T.* i. 1, 29–55.
[2] J. L. Lowes in *Times Lit. Suppl.* (11 Oct. 1928).
[3] *O.T.* i. 17; ii. 542; C. 80; B. i. 12; *Rem.* 109; *B.L.* i. 121; F. ii. 16.

diverging Center'. He found him cold and gloomy. There is some confirmation of this in Southey's letters to Bedford. He had not Coleridge's social instincts, and in the middle of May was shunning all company but Edith Fricker's. He was evidently much in love, and can have seen little prospect of an early marriage. A fortnight later he wrote that Coleridge was applying the medicine of argument to his misanthropical system of indifference, but a strange dreariness of mind had seized him. He was looking forward with distaste to a two days' party of pleasure into which he was to be dragged. The party was an excursion to Chepstow, Tintern Abbey, and Piercefield Walks. Cottle, who was the host, describes it. The day before, Coleridge had undertaken to give one of the lectures in Southey's historical course, but had disappointed the audience by failing to turn up. After dinner at Chepstow, Southey rebuked Coleridge for this, and an altercation took place, in which to Cottle's dismay Edith and Sara Fricker took part, each speaking up for her man. Cottle smoothed the matter over, and the party proceeded, incidentally losing the way to Tintern. Coleridge's suspicion had been renewed by the dispute, and he was 'agitated, even to many tears'. But in Piercefield Walks Southey assured him that their differences were merely speculative, and that he would certainly go to Wales. On another occasion he declared that he liked Coleridge better than ever, which provoked Sara Fricker, who was present, to affront him by exclaiming, 'What a story!' In June Southey's unhappiness was increased by the death of his friend Edmund Seward. Soon after, Coleridge learnt of a conversation between Southey and Burnett during a strawberry party at Ashton.

It scorched my throat. Your private resources were to remain your individual property, and everything to be separate except a farm of five or six acres. In short, we were to commence partners in a petty farming trade. This was the mouse of which the mountain Pantisocracy was at last safely delivered.

He became convinced that Southey was now determined upon separation, but Southey again assured him through Burnett that he would go to Wales or whatever place Coleridge

liked.[1] In August Southey's uncle, Herbert Hill, came to
England from Lisbon, where he was chaplain, and wrote to
Southey, offering him financial assistance, and urging him
to take Orders. Southey showed the letter to Coleridge, who
thought it best to put his views in writing. This he did,
temperately, and even affectionately, enough. 'Pantisocracy',
he said, 'is not the question: its realization is distant—perhaps a miraculous millennium', but he did not see how
Southey, disapproving of a religious establishment, could
possibly accept his uncle's offer. 'Domestic happiness is the
greatest of things sublunary', but in the present morbid
state of society the best things might be the most perilous
temptations. For himself, 'your desertion or adhesion will
in no wise affect my feelings, opinions, or conduct, and
in a very inconsiderable degree my fortunes!' Whatever
Southey's decision, God, wrote the convinced optimist,
would make it ultimately the best. Later, Southey accused
Coleridge of trumpeting his uncle's letter abroad. To this
his reply is not very convincing. To Cottle and to another
close friend of Southey he had spoken out of a full heart,
but to Mrs. Morgan and others he had merely said that
Southey had received a splendid offer which might take him
back to Oxford, but was quite undetermined whether to
accept it. Southey, indeed, had told him as much when he
asked what answer had gone to Mr. Hill, and he got the
impression in subsequent conversation that acceptance was
probable. It would have been better if Southey had been
more explicit with Coleridge, since it is clear from his correspondence with Bedford that he had not seriously contemplated the proposal. His own religious convictions were by
now much the same as Coleridge's, and of Orders he felt
that 'the gate is perjury'. Wynn's advice had confirmed his
own opinion. What he would do, if his uncle approved,
was to study the Law, with the hope of marrying in fifteen
months. When Coleridge at last heard of the decision, he
wrote to Cottle:

I congratulate Virtue and her Friends, that Robert Southey has

[1] C. 52; Southey (L.), i. 236; (W.), i. 40; Bodl. MS. English Letters, C. 22, f. 148;
Rem. 26.

relinquished all intentions of taking Orders—he leaves our Party however, and means, he thinks, to study the Law.

In the eyes of Coleridge the Law seemed even more inconsistent with Southey's avowed principles than the Church itself. But by now he had decided to treat his former friend as no more than a mere acquaintance. He behaved to him with cold civility, and on the receipt of a letter charging him with the withdrawal of confidence intensified his attitude. Their conversation was limited to literary topics. 'Our Muses had not quarrelled.' The situation had already become intolerable. About 20 August Southey wrote to Bedford of a plan for the publication of his poems and Coleridge's in companion volumes. They had, he says, sense enough and taste enough to be glad of mutual correction.

As for his—*meo periculo*—they will be of more various excellence than any one volume that this country has ever yet seen. I will rest all my pretensions to poetical taste on the truth of this assertion.

On 1 September he left Bristol, ostensibly for financial reasons, and retired to his mother's house at Bath.[1] His only further mention of Coleridge to Bedford, on 1 October, is again a literary one, acknowledging the melioration of his own literary taste by Bowles's poetry and Coleridge's constant company. 'He did me much good—I him more.'[2]

Southey was of course still coming and going between Bath and the Frickers' house at Bristol. Once at least he and Coleridge met and shook hands. There was also some acrimonious correspondence between them, which did not take matters any further. Charles Wynn had promised to settle an annuity of £100 a year upon Southey, when he reached his majority next year, and Burnett suspected that his defection was due to an unwillingness to share it with them. The final break does not seem to have come until the end of October, by which time, says Southey, 'I had seen that *no dependence could* be placed on Coleridge'. His uncle had been slow in responding to his suggestion of the Law, and now proposed that before he did anything else he should

---

[1] C. 50 (misdated Oct. for Aug.), 52; Southey (L.), i. 236, 240, 245; (W.), i. 40; Bodl. MS. *English Letters*, C. 22, ff. 142, 158, 160; Forster, *Landor*, i. 353 (from *Forster MS.* 113, misdated 1796).
[2] Southey (L.), i. 247; Bodl. MS. *English Letters*, C. 22, f. 163.

spend six months at Lisbon. He told Coleridge of this, and Coleridge made no remonstrance. Nor did he suspect that Coleridge meant to quarrel with him until he gathered it from Burnett's insolence, and then learnt of an outbreak at Mrs. Morgan's, in which Coleridge, 'roused', as he admits, 'to an agony of passion', inveighed against his conduct, and was supported by Burnett. Apparently Southey did not regard what had already passed as amounting to a quarrel. He went reluctantly to Lisbon, but before doing so contracted, on 14 November, a secret marriage with Edith Fricker and left her in charge of Cottle's sisters. On the day before the wedding Coleridge wrote a comprehensive indictment, covering all the incidents of the past months, and sent a draft or copy of it to Josiah Wade. Whether it ever reached Southey is not clear; possibly Wade had the sense to advise its suppression. Before it was finished, Coleridge met Southey in the street, 'and, unsaluted and unsaluting, passed by the man to whom for almost a year I had told my last thoughts when I closed my eyes, and the first when I awoke'. The allegations of the letter have already been drawn upon for this narrative. But it was also a farewell. 'You are *lost* to *me*, because you are lost to Virtue'; but, 'You have left a large void in my heart. I know no man big enough to fill it.' And of course it was a farewell, not only to Southey, but to Pantisocracy, Southey's own plan, 'the plan for which I abandoned my friends, and every prospect, and every certainty, and the woman whom I loved to an excess which you in your warmest dream of fancy could never shadow out'.[1] *Joan of Arc*, with Coleridge's contributions, appeared a few months after Southey's departure.

Coleridge's own marriage had taken place more than a month before Southey's. Propinquity had had its usual effect upon him. In the letter just described he writes:

My addresses to Sara, which I at first paid from principle, not feeling, from feeling and from principle I renewed; and I met a reward more than proportionate to the greatness of the effort. I love, and I am beloved, and I am happy!

[1] C. 50, 52, 54; *Rem.* 406; Southey (L.), i. 247, 250, 258; (*W.*) i. 40; *Bodl. MS. English Letters,* C. 22, ff. 165, 169, 171, 173.

Half a dozen poems confirm this. The first, written while a clerical friend was teaching Sara the flute, still lays stress on the 'undivided dell', where the poet will wander with 'the dear-lov'd maid'. The others are more personal. A climb on Brockley Coomb in May inspires the reflection, 'Enchanting spot! O were my Sara here!' In lines to the nightingale, its soft diversities of tone

> Are not so sweet as is the voice of her,
> My Sara—best beloved of human kind!
> When breathing the pure soul of tenderness,
> She thrills me with the Husband's promised name.

A set of Spenserian stanzas records an occasion when Coleridge, characteristically enough, failed to meet his lady at break of day. Verses written at Shurton Bars in September answer a letter written in some distress at home, and recall a 'tumultuous evil hour' of his own, 'ere Peace with Sara came'.[1] The distress was soon, for a time, to be relieved. Coleridge had taken a cottage at Clevedon, on the coast near Bristol, at a rent of £5 a year. *The Eolian Harp*, which describes the charms of that jasmine-and myrtle-covered retreat, and incidentally Sara's advice to her metaphysician to walk humbly with his God, is dated in a manuscript as written on 20 August, and possibly the cottage was taken then. But the poem was shown to Cottle just after Coleridge's marriage, and its terms suggest that it can hardly have been finished earlier.[2] A quotation in the Shurton Bars poem from Wordsworth's *Evening Walk* may have been inspired by a first meeting between the two poets, which is now known with certainty from a letter recently discovered by Professor de Selincourt to have taken place while Wordsworth was on a visit to his friend John Pinney at Bristol in this year. He was there by 2 September and on 24 October wrote to William Mathews:

Coleridge was at Bristol part of the time I was there, I saw but little of him. I wished indeed to have seen more—his talent appears to me very great. I met with Southey also, his manners pleased me exceedingly and I have every reason to think very highly of his powers of mind.

[1] C. 52; De Quincey, ii. 21; *P.W.* 92, 93, 94, 96.
[2] *P.W.* 100; *Rem.* 63.

In May 1796 Coleridge had in his hands an unpublished poem by Wordsworth, 'a very dear friend of mine', presumably *Guilt and Sorrow*, then known as *Salisbury Plain*, which he sent back to him in London through Lamb. He must have been in error when he himself dated the first acquaintance later than March 1796, and again as a year and some months earlier than May 1798.[1] At Shurton Bars Coleridge was on his way for a week's visit to Thomas Poole at Stowey. Here Poole wrote him on 12 September some extremely bad verses, in which he still calls him 'Coldridge', and Poole's orthodox cousin Charlotte recorded in her diary on 19 September the presence of 'Coldridge, a young man of brilliant understanding, great eloquence, desperate fortune, and entirely led away by the feelings of the moment'.[2] The marriage was at St. Mary Redcliffe's in Bristol on 4 October, with Martha Fricker and Josiah Wade for witnesses. The plenishing of the cottage proved inadequate and Coleridge wrote in haste to Cottle, begging him to send

A riddle slice; a candle box, two ventilators; two glasses for the washhand stand; one tin dust pan; one small tin tea kettle; one pair of candlesticks; one carpet brush; one flower dredge; three tin extinguishers; two mats; a pair of slippers; a cheese toaster; two large tin spoons; a bible; a keg of porter; coffee; raisins; currants; catsup; nutmegs; allspice; cinnamon; rice; ginger; and mace.

And, since the taste of 1795 was not ours, Cottle also, on his own initiative, sent an upholsterer to cover the whitewashed walls with 'a few pieces of sprightly paper'.[3] Apparently George Burnett took up his abode with the bridal pair. An entry in the Gutch note-book records a meticulous division of household duties among the three, which, so far as Coleridge was concerned, may not have been precisely carried out.[4] On 7 October he wrote to Poole of his happiness with 'the woman whom I love best of all created beings'. He would be at ease financially, since Cottle would give him a guinea and a half for every hundred lines of poetry he might write, and also purchase any prose works. He thought of returning to Cambridge, but not as a member

[1] C. 57, 81; W. 48, 48^b, 1584; L. 2; B.L. i. 58; S.C., *Biog. Suppl.* (T. i. 47); cf. p. 75.
[2] P. i. 123.   [3] *Rem.* 39.   [4] *Addl. MS.* 27901, f. 84.

of the University, and, once more, finishing his *Imitations*.
His former works may prove something of genius and erudition. 'This will be better; it will show great industry and
manly consistency.' Later he would publish proposals for
a school. Poole wrote affectionately in reply, but discouraged
the Cambridge project. He wanted Coleridge to set about
some work of consequence, which would give him a reputation.[1]

In November Coleridge gave another political lecture,
inspired by Pitt's measures against 'seditious meetings' and
'treasonable practices', which seemed to him to cut at the
foundations of constitutional liberty, and published it in two
forms, one of which bore the title of *The Plot Discovered*, and
the other that of *A Protest against Certain Bills*. He also
reprinted that already issued in the spring, which now became the introduction to a later one, *On the Present War*,
under the general heading of *Conciones ad Populum*. These
were followed in December by *An Answer to A Letter to
Edward Long Fox, M.D.*[2] It was probably about the same
time that he began his career as a preacher, at a Unitarian
chapel in Bath, wearing a blue coat and white waistcoat.[3]
Cottle's datings for this winter are even more than usually
muddled, but it is clear that during the earlier part of it there
was also some work on the volume of *Poems* for Cottle.
There had, of course, been further delays with this. Coleridge explained that he had very little 'finger industry',
although his mind was always on 'full stretch'.[4] But about
half seems to have been already in print before the marriage.
The rest was mainly to consist of some *Epistles*—of which
one was to Cottle himself, and another was ascribed by
Coleridge to the authorship of his wife, although she says
herself that she wrote very little of it—and of the Christmas
poem, of which a fragment had been sent to Charles Lamb
a year before. This Coleridge wrote and rewrote. It bore
the title at first of *The Nativity* and later of *Religious Musings*.[5]
An *Epistle to Tom Poole*, which Coleridge thought one of his
'most pleasing compositions', was also to have been included

[1] C. 51; P. i. 121.   [2] Wise, 9–18; O.T. i. 1–98; Gillman, 73.
[3] *Rem.* 92.   [4] *Rem.* 38.   [5] G. 20; P.W. 102, 104, 108.

in the volume, but never appeared, and is now, but for a fragment quoted in a letter, unknown.[1]

In December, however, a new enterprise caused further delay. Coleridge had the idea of starting a periodical, to be made up partly of political articles and partly of literary reviews. It was, no doubt, a revival of the scheme for a *Provincial Magazine*, which he had framed with Southey and told Poole in October he had abandoned. It received some local support at a meeting held in the 'Rummer Tavern'. Coleridge at once began to write some reviews, in the intervals of digging his Clevedon garden. The new year he unfortunately celebrated by drinking two glasses of punch at John Morgan's card-club, and had a renewal of a bilious attack originally brought on by an imprudent bathe in the sea after smoking. The periodical received the name of the *Watchman*, and its appearance was announced, in a prospectus which bore the motto 'That All may know the Truth; And that the Truth may make us Free!!', for 5 February. This date was afterwards altered to 1 March.[2] On 9 January Coleridge started on an advertising tour to the industrial towns of the midlands and the north, which extended to five weeks. It took him to Worcester, Birmingham, Derby, Nottingham, Sheffield, Manchester, and Lichfield. In the *Biographia Literaria* he gives an account of some amusing episodes, which can be supplemented from a series of letters, mostly to Josiah Wade, who was giving active personal and financial help to the project. At Worcester Coleridge was kindly received by Mr. Barr, the porcelain manufacturer, and was touched by the spectacle of his children sitting round and singing hymns after church, like the different orders of the blessed in heaven. But Worcester was so full of aristocrats, and the clerical influence so strong, that no bookseller was likely to take up the *Watchman*. At Birmingham he was more fortunate, and thought that he had secured a hundred subscribers. He describes an interview with a Calvinist tallow-chandler, 'a tall dingy man', with 'lank, black, twine-like hair, *pinguinitescent*, cut in a straight line along the black stubble of his thin gunpowder eye-brows', but yet 'one of the *thorough-*

[1] C. 70; *P.W.* 976; *Rem.* 66.   [2] C. 51; *Rem.* 74, 97; Wise, 19.

bred, a true lover of liberty', who 'had proved to the satisfaction of many, that Mr. Pitt was one of the horns of the
second beast in the Revelations, that *spoke like a dragon*'. Him
Coleridge harangued for half an hour, at the end of which
the tallow-chandler asked the price. Only fourpence, Coleridge told him, for thirty-two pages, large octavo, closely
printed.

Thirty and two pages? Bless me! why except what I does in a
family way on the Sabbath, that's more than I ever reads, Sir! all the
year round. I am as great a one, as any man in Brummagem, Sir! for
liberty and truth and all them sort of things, but as to this (no offence,
I hope, Sir!) I must beg to be excused.

Coleridge then went to dinner with one of his supporters,
and was asked to smoke a pipe afterwards. He says he had
never smoked before, except once or twice, and then herb tobacco mixed with Oronooko. Perhaps his memory had failed
him; at least two occasions are upon record, not to speak
of the 'Salutation and Cat', where indeed Lamb may have
done most of the smoking. However, he took half a pipe,
filling, for some odd reason, the lower half of the bowl with
salt. Presently he felt dizzy. A walk to a neighbouring
minister's house revived him for a time, but there he sank
into a swoon on a sofa, while a company who had been
asked to meet him arrived. As, however, 'the poison of
tobacco acts but for a short time', he presently awoke again,
whereupon, to relieve his embarrassment, a gentleman asked
him if he had seen a paper that day. 'Sir,' replied the advertising agent, rubbing his eyes, 'I am far from convinced,
that a Christian is permitted to read either newspapers or any
other works of merely political and temporary interest.'
Solvuntur risu tabulae. Coleridge varied his activities on this
journey by preaching, still 'as an hireless volunteer, in a blue
coat and white waistcoat, that not a rag of the woman of
Babylon might be seen on me'. But at Birmingham, where
he gave two sermons, 'preciously peppered with politics', he
allowed himself to be over-persuaded into wearing a gown,
which gave him an uneasy conscience. Here, too, he met
Charles Lloyd, the son of a Quaker banker, with whom he

was later to have close relations. At Derby he saw Joseph Wright the painter, and disputed on religion with the atheistical Erasmus Darwin, whose poems he had once described as a 'Russian palace of ice, glittering, cold, and transitory'. From Derby, with the help of Jedediah Strutt, the maker of spinning-frames, he expected to enrol forty or fifty names. At Nottingham he was amused by an aristocrat who read the motto on his prospectus, said that it must have been written by some 'seditious dog', and was told that the words were those of Christ, in the eighth chapter of St. John. 'This is one proof among thousands that Aristocrats do not read the Bible.' Coleridge was well received at Nottingham, but was now beginning to feel home-sick for his 'comfortable little cottage'. On his way to Sheffield he wrote some lines to a primrose, which he saw flowering in the 'dark, frieze-coated, hoarse, teeth-chattering month' of February. From Sheffield his expectations were small, since he had refrained from advertising the *Watchman*, lest he should injure the sale of the *Sheffield Iris*, the editor of which was in prison for libel.[1]

At Sheffield Coleridge heard that his wife, then with child, was ill. He dropped intended visits to Liverpool and London, and returned hastily to Bristol, apparently by way of Lichfield, where he wrote of himself as 'in a quickset hedge of embarrassments'. He arrived at Bristol on 13 February, having collected, he thought, nearly a thousand subscribers. Sara had gone to her mother's house on Redcliffe Hill, and here Coleridge joined her. The cottage at Clevedon was given up, as too far from the Bristol printers, and also from the Bristol Library. In his *Reflections on Having Left a Place of Retirement*, Clevedon has become a memory of happiness rejected for the sake of duty:[2]

> Was it right,
> While my unnumber'd brethren toil'd and bled,
> That I should dream away the entrusted hours
> On rose-leaf beds, pampering the coward heart
> With feelings all too delicate for use?

[1] C. 53; G. 22-4; *Rem.* 84; B.L. i. 114; P.W. 148.
[2] *Rem.* 64, 88; B.L. i. 119; P.W. 106.

And so:

> I therefore go, and join head, heart, and hand,
> Active and firm, to fight the bloodless fight
> Of Science, Freedom, and the Truth in Christ.

At Redcliffe Hill Coleridge was distracted between his wife's groans, the prospects of the *Watchman*, and the *Poems*, for which he had still to write a preface and notes. He found his wife's mother and her brother George, still a boy, and George Burnett largely depending on him, 'five mouths opening and shutting as I pull the string'. He was obliged to take laudanum almost every night for a fortnight. Hearing of a letter from Cottle, which he thought to be a demand for copy, but which was really an invitation to dinner, he broke out into a bitter protest. He wished God had made him a journeyman shoemaker, instead of an author.

> I have left my friends; I have left plenty; I have left that ease which would have secured a literary immortality, and have enabled me to give the public works conceived in moments of inspiration, and polished with leisurely solicitude; and alas! for what have I left them? for ——, who deserted me in the hour of distress and for a scheme of virtue impracticable and romantic.

He repeats his phrase about a 'quick-set hedge of embarrassment'.[1]

> The future is cloud, and thick darkness! Poverty, perhaps, and the thin faces of them that want bread, looking up to me! Nor is this all. My happiest moments for composition are broken in upon by the reflection that I must make haste. I am too late! I am already months behind! I have received my pay beforehand! Oh, wayward and desultory spirit of genius! Ill canst thou brook a taskmaster! The tenderest touch from the hand of obligation wounds thee like a scourge of scorpions.

Cottle sent him some money, and he was comforted. A visit with his wife to Stowey, which Cottle puts here, but of which there is no other record, can hardly have taken place. Poole came to Bristol, but Sara was too ill to see him. She was better by the end of March, and a new house was taken in Oxford Street, Kingsdown.[2]

While Coleridge was on tour, Wade had gone to London,

---

[1] C. 54, 55; G. 26, 27.   [2] C. 55; G. 26; *Rem.* 65, 69.

and ventilated the scheme of the *Watchman*, without much
success, in spite of bills in larger letters than had ever been
seen before. An agency was, however, accepted by Parsons
of Paternoster Row. In Bristol itself Cottle and another
bookseller had collected nearly four hundred orders. Cottle
provided an initial supply of paper, and obtained favourable
terms for the printing from Nathaniel Biggs. Coleridge says
that he was himself more than half convinced that prudence
dictated the abandonment of the scheme, but at that time
thought that whatever was contrary to prudence was the
dictate of duty.[1] And so the *Watchman* made its first appearance, not indeed on, but soon after, 1 March.[2] In addition
to original matter in verse and prose, it contained running
summaries of foreign and domestic events, and of parliamentary debates. These last were entrusted to George
Burnett, who did them so badly that Coleridge had to throw
his attempts into the fire, and do the work over again.[3]
There was a poets' corner, with contributions by others,
as well as Coleridge himself. But the original prose was
practically all Coleridge's. In the first number he preached
the diffusion of knowledge, and defined his programme. He
wrote essays on a public fast proclaimed by the Government,
on Pitt's budgetary loan, on Church establishment, on the
manners and religion of the ancient Germans, on modern
patriotism, on the slave trade, and on the writings of Godwin. Here he repudiated the praise of his *Morning Chronicle*
sonnet, since he now considered Godwin's 'principles as
vicious; and his book as a pandar to sensuality'. He would
print an examination of it in later numbers. He reviewed
Burke's *Letter to a Noble Lord*, with much criticism of Burke's
pensions; also Ireland's *Shakespearean Papers*, of which he
was sceptical, and the *Essays* of Count Rumford. The
chief prose contribution from outside was by Thomas
Poole, who also wrote on the slave trade.[4] The first number
raised Coleridge's hopes. '*All* admire the Poetry in the
Watchman', he wrote.[5] But the second gave him a shock.
To the essay on fasts he had prefixed a motto from Isaiah,

[1] G. 25; *B.L.* i. 119; *Rem.* 76, 82.   [2] *B.L.* i. 119.
[3] C. 55; G. 26; *Rem.* 79.   [4] *O.T.* i. 99–176.   [5] C. 55; G. 25.

'Wherefore my Bowels shall sound like an Harp.' And the essay itself was flippantly written. It lost him, he says, near five hundred subscribers at a blow. Even his Unitarian friend Estlin did not 'altogether relish it'. And he regretted it himself. 'It was conceived in the spirit, and clothed in the harsh scoffing, of an Infidel.' On the other hand, the criticism of 'patriots' in the third number displeased his democratic supporters.[1] At the end of March, indeed, he thought he saw hopes of 'a *bread-and-cheesish* profit'.[2] A fortnight later these were gone. The sales were hardly paying the expenses. The objective was too much divided. People in London and Bristol cared only for the original matter; those in the north and midlands only for the newspaper element. In the tenth number, which appeared on 13 May, Coleridge announced the termination of the enterprise. 'Henceforward I shall cease to cry the state of the political atmosphere.' And once more he resorted to Scripture for a quotation, 'O Watchman! thou hast watched in vain!'[3]

Another scheme, 'unconnected with politics', had also broken down. Something in Count Rumford's *Essays*, when he read them for the *Watchman* in April, had struck him. It is not quite clear what it was; probably a plan for garden cities, with which Rumford had already experimented in Bavaria, rather than a cure for smoking chimneys, which proved successful in London and to which Coleridge refers later. At any rate, Coleridge proposed to Cottle a pamphlet on the subject, to be adapted with variations for issue in Manchester and Birmingham, as well as in Bristol. For the copyright he asked three guineas. Cottle sent him the three guineas, but declined the publication.[4] Meanwhile, the *Poems* at last struggled into print. Once the preface and notes were finished, it was Coleridge who became impatient. On 4 March he asked whether a few copies could not be ready to send to Parsons with copies of the *Watchman* on the next day. Presentation copies should go to his brother George and to Beddoes, Wrangham, and others, and on

---

[1] *O.T.* i. 120; C. 55; G. 26, 27; T. 29; *B.L.* i. 119.   [2] C. 55.
[3] *O.T.* i. 177; C. 56; T. 29, 33.
[4] *Rem.* 70; C. 55; T. 29; *Watchman*, No. 5; cf. C. 69; G. 31.

blank leaves of these he would write sonnets. It was not, however, until 30 March that he could tell Poole of the actual completion of printing. By 15 April he was able to inscribe a copy with a grateful dedication to Cottle.[1] Apart from the long *Religious Musings*, the volume contained fifty short poems, mainly representing a judicious selection from those written during the Cambridge, London, and Bristol periods. Only two, *Genevieve* and *Absence*, are of earlier date. In some, originally addressed to Miss Nesbitt or Miss Brunton, Sara's name is substituted, but that of Mary remains in *The Sigh*. The arrangement is rather eccentric. Nine odes and elegies come first; then thirty-six sonnets and other verses, all called 'effusions'; then five epistles. In a preface Coleridge explained his use of the term 'effusions', against which Lamb was later to protest. He did not think that he had achieved the '*one*ness of thought' which would justify that of sonnets, and he did not want to challenge a comparison with Bowles, which 'would have sunk me below that mediocrity, on the surface of which I am at present enabled to float'. Only twenty-one, however, of the so-called 'effusions' are in sonnet form; the rest are lyrics and elegiacs, in a variety of metres. Among them are three examples of the easy meditative poem in blank verse, which came to be, apart from the fleeting ballad inspiration and the one great ode called *Dejection*, Coleridge's most successful form of expression in verse. He once invented for it the term Conversation Poem.

[1] C. 54, 55; G. 20, 21, 25; *Rem.* 36, 65, 69.

IV

BREAD AND CHEESE

May 1796—March 1797

ON 12 May 1796, the very day, as it happened, on which the last number of the *Watchman* appeared, Coleridge received a notification from Poole that a group of friends and admirers of his poetry would contribute annually, for a period of seven years, five guineas apiece to a sum of £35 or £40 for his benefit. John Cruikshank, Lord Egmont's agent at Stowey, would act as treasurer. Later Estlin seems to have replaced him. Coleridge replied in a letter full of gratitude. He was undetermined. He was not ashamed to receive, but hoped to rely on his own exertions. He would come over to Stowey, however, if Poole would send a horse 'of tolerable meekness' to meet the Bristol caravan at Bridgwater. He arrived on 15 May, waived, no doubt, all scruples about accepting the bounty, and returned to Bristol on 29 May, meditating by the way on the filth of the river Parret at Bridgwater in comparison with the 'dear gutter of Stowey'.[1] Poole's letter arrived at a happy moment, for the failure of the *Watchman* had wrecked Coleridge's finances. The facts are not quite clear, since in after years his own recollection and Cottle's differed. But on 6 May he had calculated that after paying for the printing and for paper to supplement the initial supply given him by Cottle, he should be £5 to the bad. In the *Biographia Literaria*, however, he says that when the time came for settlement with the booksellers, who had been his distributing agents, he could not get a shilling from Parsons, and very little from elsewhere, and should have been jailed by his printer for £80 or £90, had not a dear friend, by no means affluent, paid the sum. Cottle claims to have financed the supply of paper for the *Watchman*, and not to have been fully repaid. Prob-

[1] C. 56, 58; G. 34; P. i. 142; *Harvard MS.* 19478·5 F.

ably Coleridge had also had help from Wade, to whom, in an undated letter, he acknowledges 'a long, long bill', which he then hoped to discharge. But these were more or less affluent, and I think that the friend here referred to was George Dyer, to whom Coleridge wrote warm thanks for extricating him from his difficulties on 29 May. Charles Lamb, also, had settled for him an old debt to his London landlord of 1794, and refused to accept repayment.[1] Coleridge and Lamb appear to have lost sight of each other for the last eighteen months, part of which Lamb had spent in a mad-house at Hoxton, as the result of an unfortunate love-affair. But now a correspondence began, of which, except for one letter, only Lamb's side is known to us. He wrote much of poetry, Coleridge's and his own, and that of Bowles, Burns, and Cowper, whom both in varying degrees admired. Coleridge's phrase of 'the divine chit-chat of Cowper' delighted him. He sent Coleridge news of Charles Le Grice, now a tutor in Cornwall, and of Allen, married to a widow with some money and more children, and a confirmed atheist under the influence of Godwin. He planned a visit to Bristol, but to his annoyance could not get leave of absence from the India House. Sara Coleridge had been inspired to send him a verse letter of invitation, which he repaid with one of regret. Then, in September, came the shock of Mary Lamb's tragedy. Lamb dropped all the 'vanities' of poetry, and devoted himself to grief, and to the care of his father, with the help of Samuel Le Grice. When he told Coleridge the news, he begged for a religious letter. Coleridge's prompt reply brought consolation, although one passage in it struck his fellow Unitarian with some doubt. 'You are a temporary sharer in human misery,' Coleridge had written, 'that you may be an eternal partaker of the Divine nature.' Lamb thought this lacking in humility and theologically unsound.

What more than this do those men say, who are for exalting the man Christ Jesus into the second person of an unknown Trinity—men, whom you or I scruple not to call idolaters?[2]

[1] G. 40 (misdated); T. 33; B.L. i. 120; L. 1, 2; Rem. 82; Harvard MS. 19478·5 F.; Appendix, No. I.   [2] L. 1-12.

In his first letter Lamb had sent his compliments to Southey, should he be then in Bristol. No doubt he heard in reply of the breach between the two Pantisocrats, which he regretted. In October he wrote, 'Have you made it up with Southey yet?' To some extent Coleridge had. Southey had returned from Lisbon in May, and taken lodgings opposite Coleridge in Bristol. If we can trust Cottle, some further recriminations passed between them. In June Southey intended, when he reprinted *Joan of Arc*, to omit Coleridge's contributions. In July he was contemplating a novel, to be called *Edmund Oliver*. But in September he sent across the street a slip of paper with a translated sentence from Schiller, 'Fiesco! Fiesco! thou leavest a void in my bosom which the human race, thrice told, will never fill up.' And in an hour's time, says Coleridge's daughter, 'these two extraordinary youths were arm in arm again'. They called on Cottle after a walk in the country, and Cottle claims to have suspected a stage effect. The reconciliation was probably rather a hollow one. In December Coleridge sent Southey a letter on his recently printed poems, which begins, 'I thank you, Robert Southey', and ends with a bare signature. And about the same time he wrote to John Thelwall:

Between ourselves the *enthusiasm* of friendship is not with S. and me. We quarrelled, and the quarrel lasted for a twelvemonth. We are now reconciled; but the cause of the differences was solemn, and 'the blasted oak puts not forth its buds anew'. We are *acquaintances*, and feel *kindliness* towards each other, but I do not *esteem* or *love* Southey, as I must esteem and love the man whom I dared call by the holy name of *friend*: and vice versâ Southey of me. I say no more. It is a painful subject.[1]

During the summer of 1796 Coleridge was in active pursuit of the 'two giants leagued together, whose most imperious commands I must obey, however reluctant—their names are BREAD and CHEESE'. His domestic anxieties had been increased by the death of Robert Lovell, leaving a widow and child, and the dangerous illness of Mrs. Fricker. He had the subsidy collected by Poole, and secured

---

[1] C. 70; G. 37; Southey (L.), i. 286; (W.), i. 32; *Bodl. MS. English Letters*, C. 22, ff. 183, 191; L. 1, 2, 12; *Rem.* 106; *Biog. Suppl.* (T. i. 92).

some literary work on the *Critical Review* and the *Monthly Magazine*, started in July by Richard Phillips, who became 'obsequious' to him at Mrs. Barbauld's. These 'shilling-scavenger employments', he reckoned later, would bring in about £40 a year. Some samples of his work have been exhumed from the *Critical Review*, but they are very slight.[1] In May two alternative plans had been before him. He might waive his objections to preaching for hire, and become a dissenting minister. He might try for a commission from George Robinson, the London bookseller, to translate the whole works of Schiller, with as part remuneration the cost of maintenance for himself and his wife at Jena, whence he would bring back the writings of Kant and others, and on his return start a school for eight young men at £105 each, on a philosophical system. He was already studying German.[2] A little later, he had a fleeting idea of reviving the *Watchman*.[3] A prospect of a tutorship, held out by his friend John Fellowes of Nottingham, was slow to materialize.[4] Meanwhile came, at the beginning of July, an offer from James Perry through Dr. Beddoes of work in the editorial office of the *Morning Chronicle*. About this he was in two minds. He did not love London, and 'local and temporary politics' had now become his aversion. It would mean the abandonment of philosophy and the Muse. He thought of hiring a horse and 'galloping' down to consult Poole. But he sent a provisional acceptance and asked Lamb to find him a house. Lamb was delighted at the anticipation of his company. In Lamb's eyes London was 'the only fostering soil for Genius'. Poole thought the employment unworthy of his friend.[5] Before, however, Coleridge was finally committed, the suggestion of a tutorship matured. It would be in the household of a widowed Mrs. Evans of Darley, near Derby, the daughter of Jedediah Strutt the cotton-spinner, to whom Fellowes had already introduced Coleridge during the *Watchman* tour. A visit with Sara to Darley raised the highest hopes. The salary would be £150,

---

[1] C. 56, 67, 68; G. 29; T. 36; A., p. 194; L. 2; *Studies*, 22; Bowles, 165; Raysor (M.), 355. [2] T. 33. [3] L. 2.
[4] G. 23; T. 36; *Sotheby Catalogue* (28 April 1931), Nos. 511, 512.
[5] G. 29; T. 36; L. 3, 7; P. i. 151; Prideaux, 1.

and Coleridge's ideas of education appealed to Mrs. Evans. Her father-in-law and other relatives were opposed to the plan, but she would not sacrifice her children to 'Mammon, gloomy as Moloch'.[1] Pending a definite decision Coleridge left his wife at Darley, and went to Ottery, where he was received 'by my mother with transport, by my brother George with joy and tenderness, and by my other brothers with affectionate civility'. Both Poole and Lamb hailed Coleridge's reconciliation with his family.[2] On his return to Bristol he found a letter from Mrs. Evans, telling him that she had now learnt for the first time that her children's fortunes were largely dependent on their grandfather's will, and that if the engagement were carried out his resentment would be implacable. Coleridge sent the letter on to Poole. It had given him a pang, but he would not be an apostate from his divine philosophy.

The black clouds, which hide the Sun from my view, are they not big with fertility? And will they not drop it on me?

He now paid a second visit to Darley, to bring back his wife and release Mrs. Evans from her promise. She behaved with great kindness, kept the Coleridges there for a week, during which they had excursions to Matlock, immortalized by Bowles, to Oakover with its Raphaels and Titians, to Ilam and to Dovedale, and at their departure presented Coleridge with £95 and his wife with her valuable set of baby-clothes. The sojourn with Mrs. Evans remained in memory as 'a sunny spot' in his life. Many years later, in 1823, Mrs. Coleridge met their hostess again. She was then still Mrs. Evans, but remarried, possibly to a Walter Evans, who had been one of the recalcitrant relatives of 1796.[3]

It was now nearly the end of August. But, if one hare had slipped away, others were soon started. Dr. Crompton of Derby, another acquaintance of the *Watchman* tour, proposed to Coleridge the opening of a day-school in Derby, to which he would send his sons, guaranteeing £100 a year until the number of pupils reached a limit of twelve. Coleridge went so far as to engage a house, the landlord of which

---

[1] Prideaux, 1. [2] Estlin, 11; L. 14; P. i. 152.
[3] C. 72, 75, 124; G. 30, 31; P. i. 152; M. 23; Estlin, 11.

promised to employ a device invented by Count Rumford
for curing smoky chimneys, and planned to open the school
in November. An alternative suggestion by William Roscoe
that he should settle in Liverpool does not seem to have
been pursued.[1] On his way home he stopped with Thomas
Hawkes at Moseley, near Birmingham, and preached his
chef-d'œuvre sermon, which he thought of publishing with
two others.[2] Here, too, he once more fell in with Charles
Lloyd. This was a young man of 21, already a poet, disabled
by nervous instability for his father's banking business, and
disinclined through the reading of Rousseau and Godwin
for his father's Quakerism. He now asked Coleridge to take
him as a pupil. The father invited Coleridge to Birmingham
for a discussion of the proposal. He made a good impression
as 'a very sensible, religious man'. Consent was given and
the terms fixed at £80 a year. While at Birmingham Coleridge heard of the birth, earlier than had been expected, of
a son on 19 September, and returned to Bristol in haste,
taking, surely somewhat inconsiderately, Charles with him.
The birth was celebrated in three sonnets, and the child
named, but not baptized, David Hartley, after 'that great
master of *Christian* Philosophy'. There was a rush of affection to Sara:

> So for the mother's sake the child was dear,
> And dearer was the mother for the child.[3]

The original idea had been that Charles would reside with
Coleridge at Derby, but on 24 September Coleridge's heart
was 'heavy' respecting Derby, and he wrote to Poole proposing to come down with Lloyd and consult him. This he
did, and then decided to give up Derby, and to live, with
his family, Mrs. Fricker, Lloyd, and a servant, near his
friend at Stowey. He would cultivate a garden, and write
in the evenings. It seemed possible that John Cruikshank
could find him a house at Adscombe, hard by. Lamb gently
regretted Coleridge's 'veering' plans, but hoped that the
'dancing demon' might conduct him at last to the 'life and

---

[1] C. 60; G. 31; T. 38, 42; Estlin, 11; cf. pp. 53, 72.
[2] Estlin, 11.   [3] C. 60, 67; Lucas, *Lloyds*, 12, 15, 20; *P.W.* 152.

labors of a cottager'. He must remember, however, that
the west of England was not Arcadia. Coleridge, for the
present, thought that it was. Crompton took the change of
plan kindly, and Coleridge explained it to the elder Lloyd.
At Derby, with a school, as well as Charles, on his hands,
he would have no time for literature. Town life would
injure his health. He wanted his children 'bred up from
earliest infancy in the simplicity of peasants, their food, dress,
and habits completely rustic'. Evidently he believed that
the 'gutter of Stowey' was something like the Susquehanna.
Politics he now regarded as a study 'highly unfavourable to
all Christian graces'.

> I have accordingly snapped my squeaking baby-trumpet of sedition,
> and have hung up its fragments in the chamber of Penitences.

Mr. Lloyd replied that the scheme seemed to him 'monastic
rather than Christian', and received a programme for the
study by Charles of languages, science, metaphysics, history,
and Christianity, in preparation for his contemplated career
as a physician.[1]

Early in November Coleridge had a violent attack of
neuralgia, which was checked by the use of laudanum.
Difficulties arose about securing Adscombe, and he asked
Poole to look for some temporary abode, and also for a
servant, 'simple of heart, physiognomically handsome, and
scientific in vaccimulgence'. Charles Lloyd now fell ill in
his turn, with fits, apparently epileptic, which gave him
delirious visions, and left an 'occasional flightiness'. And
his father, perhaps now a little uneasy about the experiment
to which he had consented, notified Coleridge that it could
only last for a twelvemonth. This upset Coleridge's plans.
Moreover, Mrs. Fricker had been unable to apprentice out
her son, and was herself unwilling to leave Bristol. Coleridge decided to give her an allowance of £20, not to take
Charles, to have no servant, and to live alone with his wife
and child at Stowey, treating horticulture now not as a
mere amusement, but as a means of livelihood. An acre and
a half would provide everything but clothes and rent. What

---

[1] C. 60, 62; P. i. 160, 174; L. 10; Lucas, *Lloyds*, 20, 26.

else could he do? 'I could not love the man who advised
me to keep a school, or write for a newspaper. He must
have a hard heart.' Charles Lloyd naturally protested, and
Coleridge finally agreed to take him, not as a pupil, but as an
inmate. He would furnish his own room, and be his own
servant, and Coleridge would receive only the actual cost
of his maintenance, which he reckoned at half a guinea a
week. So it was settled in the second week of December,
when Charles had gone home to Birmingham for Christmas and persuaded his father to waive the twelvemonth
limitation.[1]

A possible habitation, no more than a poor cottage, had
been found at Stowey. But a new trouble had arisen. Poole
himself had begun to feel qualms as to Coleridge's adap-
tability to a purely country life, and these, rather indiscreetly
at this late stage, he expressed. Would not Coleridge be
more comfortable in some place nearer Bristol, such as
Acton, where he would have the company of his friends,
and be in touch with libraries and printers? Coleridge
replied that his habits and feelings had suffered a total alteration. He now systematically avoided general company, and
when in it kept silence so far as social humanity would permit him. That very day he had answered a similar question
by Mr. Lloyd:

> I shall have six companions: my Sara, my babe, my own shaping
> and disquisitive mind, my books, my beloved friend Thomas Poole,
> and lastly Nature looking at me with a thousand looks of beauty, and
> speaking to me in a thousand melodies of love.

Why had Poole sent him this 'hasty and heart-chilling letter'?
He suspected that the cause must lie in something which had
passed between Poole's mother and his sister, Mrs. King,
whom Coleridge had just visited at Acton. He brooded over
this idea, and later in the day sat down to write another long
and frenzied epistle, in the same vein. All his plans of the
last three months have been upset. His wife is watching the
workings of his face as he writes, and entreating to know
what is the matter. He dreads to show her Poole's letter.

---

[1] C. 62, 63, 65, 66, 67; G. 34; Lucas, *Lloyds*, 30–4.

'What if she should dare to think that my most beloved friend has grown cold towards me!' He cannot live at Acton and support himself by literature alone. Poole had apparently said something about a ghost.

> Ghosts indeed! I should be haunted with ghosts enough—the ghosts of Otway and Chatterton, and the phantasms of a wife broken-hearted, and a hunger-bitten baby![1]

He entreats Poole to declare the true reasons which led him to discourage a move to Stowey, and to reveal anything which may have seemed to lessen his love or esteem or confidence. If there is nothing, then 'I adhere to Stowey, and consider the time from last evening as a distempered dream'. Poole, of course, had no difficulty in reassuring him. 'An angry letter, but the breach was soon healed', runs his endorsement. Coleridge acknowledged that he had written 'with improper impetuosity'. Another attack of illness and the need to finish a job of reviewing led to some delay, but on 31 December 1796 the move to Stowey was finally accomplished.[2]

There can be little doubt that Coleridge's craving for a rural retirement was motived not only by the desire to be near Poole but also by the reaction from practical politics, of which he had written to the elder Lloyd. This is apparent also in a correspondence with John Thelwall, which began in May. 'Citizen' Thelwall had been deeply involved in anti-Government agitation, as a member of democratic societies and one of the group acquitted of sedition in the trials of 1794. In 1796 he was lecturing in the provinces, professedly on Roman history. Coleridge did not know him personally, but heard that he had taken offence at a reference to him in *The Plot Discovered*, which was meant to be complimentary, and wrote in explanation. Thelwall's reply seems to have attracted him, and several letters of rapidly growing intimacy followed.[3] They deal more with poetry than with politics, since Thelwall also had published poems, and more with religion than with either. Coleridge still regards himself as an ally of Thelwall against the aristocrats, although

---

[1] C. 66, 67, 69; G. 35; P. i. 179-95.   [2] C. 68, 69; G. 36, 37; Estlin, 25.
[3] C. 57, 59, 64, 68; G. 28, 33; C. Cestre, *Thelwall*, 140.

he thinks that they must pursue the same end by different roads.

I am not *fit* for *public* life; yet the light shall stream to a far distance from my cottage window.

And he upholds the doctrine, which had given offence in the *Watchman*, that a man of bad moral principles cannot be a true patriot. He does not think Thelwall a man of bad moral principles, but he does believe him to be an atheist, or something like it, and is concerned to defend his own version of Christianity against Thelwall's criticisms.

You say the Christian is a *mean* religion. Now the religion which Christ taught is simply, first, that there is an omnipresent Father of infinite power, wisdom, and goodness, in whom we all of us move and have our being; and secondly, that when we appear to men to die we do not utterly perish, but after this life shall continue to enjoy or suffer the consequences and natural effects of the habits we have formed here, whether good or evil. This is the Christian *religion*, and all of the Christian *religion*.

At this stage, Coleridge's special bugbear was William Godwin; not for the belief in human perfectibility, which, as we have seen, lay at the root of Pantisocracy, but for the atheism and repudiation of family and sexual morality which went with it. A scheme for a work on the evidences of religion, probably as an expansion of the lectures on Christianity given in 1795, now took the form of an *Answer to Godwin*. Coleridge was hot upon this towards the end of the year. 'I am daily more and more a religionist.' He hoped that it would appear soon after Christmas, as a six-shilling octavo. It was still in contemplation during the spring of 1797, but thereafter no more is heard of it.[1] To the fact that Coleridge had not yet met Thelwall, when the correspondence with him took place, we owe the following self-portrait:

As to me, my face, unless when animated by immediate eloquence, expresses great sloth, and great, indeed, almost idiotic good-nature. 'Tis a mere carcase of a face; fat, flabby, and expressive chiefly of inexpression. Yet I am told that my eyes, eyebrows, and forehead are physiognomically good; but of this the deponent knoweth not. As to

[1] C. 55, 57, 59, 70; G. 33, 36; L. 1, 20: *Addl. MS.* 27901, f. 21ᵃ.

my shape, 'tis a good enough shape if measured, but my gait is awk-
ward, and the walk of the whole man indicates *indolence capable of
energies*. I am, and ever have been, a great reader, and have read almost
everything—a library cormorant. I am *deep* in all out of the way books,
whether of the monkish times, or of the puritanical era. I have read
and digested most of the historical writers; but I do not *like* history.
Metaphysics and poetry and 'facts of mind', that is, accounts of all the
strange phantasms that ever possessed 'your philosophy'; dreamers,
from Thoth the Egyptian to Taylor the English pagan, are my darling
studies. In short, I seldom read except to amuse myself, and I am
almost always reading. Of useful knowledge, I am a so-so chemist,
and I love chemistry. All else is *blank*; but I *will* be (please God) an
horticulturist and a farmer. I compose very little, and I absolutely hate
composition, and such is my dislike that even a sense of duty is sometimes too weak to overpower it. I cannot breathe through my nose,
so my mouth, with sensual thick lips, is almost always open. In conversation I am impassioned, and oppose what I deem error with an
eagerness which is often mistaken for personal asperity; but I am ever
so swallowed up in the *thing* that I perfectly forget my *opponent*. Such
am I.[1]

In some early lines Coleridge had already written of his 'fat
vacuity of face'.[2] A Stowey tradition records that he was
wont to say, 'I have the brow of an angel, and the mouth
of a beast.'[3] William Hazlitt, who first met him in 1798,
gives his own impression:

His complexion was at that time clear and even bright—

'As are the children of yon azure sheen.'

His forehead was broad and high, light as if built of ivory, with large
projecting eyebrows, and his eyes rolling beneath them like a sea with
darkened lustre. 'A certain tender bloom his face o'erspread', a purple
tinge as we see it in the pale thoughtful complexions of the Spanish
portrait-painters, Murillo and Velasquez. His mouth was gross,
voluptuous, open, eloquent; his chin good-humoured and round; but
his nose, the rudder of the face, the index of the will, was small, feeble,
nothing—like what he has done. . . . Coleridge, in his person, was
rather above the common size, inclining to be corpulent, or, like Lord
Hamlet, 'somewhat fat and pursy'. His hair (now, alas! grey) was then
black and glossy as the raven's, and fell in smooth masses over his
forehead.[4]

Portraits of 1795, 1796, and 1799 confirm the hair, worn
long behind, and unpowdered, since opponents of the

---

[1] C. 64.   [2] *P.W.* 32.   [3] P. i. 224.
[4] *My First Acquaintance with Poets* (Hazlitt, xvii. 106); cf. p. 88.

Government would not pay the Hair Powder Tax, which was part of Pitt's war finance. The open mouth is conspicuous; probably Coleridge had adenoids.[1]

Entries of 1796 in the Gutch note-book record many ideas for literary work which were passing through Coleridge's mind. Some of these, even when they appear under the ambitious title of 'My Works', were mere fleeting visions, which he never seriously pursued. But here, side by side with the 'Imitations', or 'Pantisocracy', or the 'Letter to Godwin', are an epic on 'The Origin of Evil', of which he had spoken to Lamb in 1794, and a sequence of six 'Hymns to the Sun, the Moon and the Elements', to which also Lamb more than once refers. Professor Livingston Lowes has shown how greatly the reading and thinking done for these 'Hymns', as well as for an earlier notion of a romance on 'The Wandering Jew', have contributed to the store of ideas and images which welled up in *The Ancient Mariner*. But evidently Coleridge did not think that he had so exhausted the possibilities of the scheme. It was still before him in 1802, but as a 'mere dream', and even in 1821 he had not forgotten it.

Alas! for the proud time when I planned, when I had present to my mind, the materials, as well as the scheme, of the Hymns entitled Spirit, Sun, Earth, Air, Water, Fire, and Man: and the Epic Poem on —what still appears to me the one only fit subject remaining for an Epic Poem—Jerusalem besieged and destroyed by Titus.

But here Spirit and Man are additions to the original list, and the Moon has dropped out. There is nothing in the note-book about the Siege of Jerusalem.[2]

Some poetry was written during the period of Lloyd's domestication with Coleridge at Bristol. Both Coleridge and, at his request, Lamb contributed to Lloyd's memorial volume on his grandmother, Priscilla Farmer, and this led to an epistolary friendship between Lamb and Lloyd.[3] A poem on Burns, printed in a Bristol newspaper, and also separately, 'to be dispersed among friends', made an appeal

---

[1] *Rem.* f.p.; Lucas, *Life of Lamb*, i. 118 (misdated); C. i. 262.
[2] *Addl. MS.* 27901, ff. 5ᵛ, 21, 24ᵛ–25ᵛ, 45ᵛ, 47, 49; C. 127; A. 15; cf. Lowes, 74–92, 157, 169, 189, 193, 208, 376, 379, 384, 483.　　[3] L. 17, 19; *P.W.* 155.

to Lamb not to abandon versifying.[1] A joint volume by
Coleridge and Lloyd was abandoned. Some proof-sheets
for it were sent to Lamb and Thelwall, but are not now
traceable.[2] Coleridge, however, had a stock of unused
paper, presumably left over from the *Watchman*, and on this
he printed a small anthology of sonnets by himself and
others, in a form suitable for binding up with the *Sonnets*
of Bowles. One copy, so bound up, still exists.[3] And in the
last days of December, on the eve of leaving Bristol, he
wrote his *Ode to the Departing Year*, which he published in
the *Cambridge Intelligencer*, and also as a separate pamphlet,
with a dedicatory letter to Poole and some verses to Lloyd.
It is once more a chant, in the exalted vein of the *Religious
Musings*, on behalf of liberty and against war, inspired by the
sudden death of 'the Northern Conqueress', Catharine of
Russia. And with it Coleridge takes his leave of politics.

> Away, my soul, away!
> I unpartaking of the evil thing,
> With daily prayer and daily toil,
> Soliciting my scant and blameless soil,
> Have wail'd my country with a loud Lament.
> Now I recentre my immortal mind
> In the long sabbath of high self-content.
> Cleans'd from the fleshly passions that bedim
> God's Image, sister of the Seraphim.[4]

Yet another enterprise was already in hand. Coleridge's
volume of 1796 had been well received by the reviewers.
'The Monthly has *cataracted* panegyric on my poems, the
Critical has *cascaded* it; and the Analytical has *dribbled* it with
very tolerable civility', he wrote in July. Lamb thought
that the writer in the *Critical Review* was George Dyer.[5]
Cottle now wanted a second edition, and, as new pieces
would be available, offered another twenty guineas. Coleridge contemplated a complete recast, in a new order, with
considerable omissions, as well as additions. He would give
nothing but his 'choicest fish, pick'd, gutted, and clean'd'.

[1] C. 68; L. 18; Wise, 204; *P.W.* 158.
[2] C. 68; L. 17; *Athenaeum* (13 June 1891).
[3] C. 63, 68; *P.W.* 1138; Wise, 31.
[4] L. 19; *P.W.* 160, 1142; Wise, 33.   [5] G. 29; L. 7.

By December he thought that he had 'swept the book with the expurgation-besom to a fine tune'.[1] With his own poems were now to be printed a fuller collection of Lamb's. These Lamb had burnt at the time of Mary's disaster. Of some of them, however, Coleridge already had copies. And after a month or two Lamb, while still protesting that he had done with the 'idle trade of versifying' as 'unprofitable to my soul', began to take an interest in the scheme. He sent some fragments which he had salvaged, and even wrote a few new pieces. 'I do long to see our names together', he was ready to think by January. When the volume of 1796 had reached him, he had been annoyed by some substantial alterations of his own which Coleridge had made in the few sonnets there borrowed from him. 'Spare my ewe lambs', he had written, and he now insisted that his contributions shall be printed, 'all of 'em as I last made 'em'. Wisely, too, he persuaded Coleridge that sonnets should be called 'sonnets', and not 'effusions'.[2] A little later, Lloyd also gave Coleridge leave to use his poems, and so the book became a three-fold concern.[3] The actual printing does not seem to have begun until after Christmas, and a number of letters, again much disordered by Cottle, show that it was a troublesome process. Perhaps Coleridge, as he feverishly put together his parcels for Milton the carrier, realized that there was after all something to be said for Poole's suggestion that he would find Stowey inconveniently far from the printing-office. In the end he seems to have had to go to Bristol, to see the last stages through.[4] Originally the volume was to have begun with a poem called *The Progress of Liberty, or the Visions of the Maid of Orleans*. It was to be an expansion of his contribution to the second book of *Joan of Arc*, now rejected by Southey. He wrote about 150 new lines, and then deferred setting up the result until he could send it for criticism to Wordsworth and to Lamb, whose taste and judgement he thought 'more correct and philosophical than my own, which yet I place pretty high'. What Wordsworth

---

[1] C. 68; *Rem.* 115; *Harvard MS.* 19478·25 F.
[2] L. 3, 8, 13–16, 18–21, 24–6.   [3] *Rem.* 132; L. 26.
[4] *Rem.* 118, 122, 126, 132, 136; C. 72, 73; G. 38, 39, 41, 43; Campbell-White, *passim*; *Harvard MSS.* 19478·5 F., 25 F., 35 F.

said we do not know. But Lamb was critical, thinking that the new lines were discordant in matter and style with the old ones, and a disheartened Coleridge abandoned the poem. Later he regretted that his slothfulness and anxieties had prevented him from finishing it. It was printed, still a fragment, as *The Destiny of Nations*, in 1817.[1] The volume was not ready until the end of June 1797, and publication in London seems to have been deferred to October.[2] Twenty of the old poems were omitted, and twelve new ones added. There were fifteen of Lamb's, and twenty-eight of Lloyd's.[3] In a preface Coleridge admitted the justice of some criticisms which had reached him.

My poems have been rightly charged with a profusion of double-epithets and a general turgidness. I have pruned the double-epithets with no sparing hand; and used my best efforts to tame the swell and glitter both of thought and diction. This latter fault however had insinuated itself into my Religious Musings with such intricacy of union, that sometimes I have omitted to disentangle the weed from the fear of snapping the flower.

Another charge, that of obscurity, he repudiated. Every poet of warm and rapid imagination had had to face that. Milton, Gray, and Collins were not exempt. 'Intelligibilia non intellectum adfero.' A separate preface to the Sonnets contains a depreciation of Petrarch, afterwards explained away by Coleridge on the ground that he then knew that 'divine poet' only through half a dozen bald translations, and a eulogy of Bowles, in whose sonnets 'moral Sentiments, Affections or Feelings, are deduced from, and associated with, the scenery of Nature'.[4] Coleridge had at one time delighted Lamb by contemplating a dedication of the whole volume to Bowles.[5] But in the end he substituted one to his brother George, which is among his best 'Conversation' pieces.

To me the Eternal Wisdom hath dispens'd
A different fortune and more different mind—
Me from the spot where first I sprang to light
Too soon transplanted, ere my soul had fix'd

[1] C. 67, 68; L. 22, 23; *Rem.* 129; E.R. ii. 241; *P.W.* 131, cf. p. 271.
[2] Wise, 39; cf. p. 77.   [3] *P.W.* 1142.   [4] *P.W.* 1139, 1145.   [5] L. 14.

Its first domestic loves; and hence through life
Chasing chance-started friendships. A brief while
Some have preserv'd me from life's pelting ills;
But, like a tree with leaves of feeble stem,
If the clouds lasted, and a sudden breeze
Ruffled the boughs, they on my head at once
Dropped the collected shower; and some most false,
False and fair-foliag'd as the Manchineel,
Have tempted me to slumber in their shade
E'en mid the storm; then breathing subtlest damps,
Mix'd their own venom with the rain from Heaven,
That I woke poison'd! But, all praise to Him
Who gives us all things, more have yielded me
Permanent shelter; and beside one Friend,
Beneath the impervious covert of one oak,
I've rais'd a lowly shed, and know the names
Of Husband and of Father; nor unhearing
Of that divine and nightly-whispering Voice,
Which from my childhood to maturer years
Spake to me of predestinated wreaths,
Bright with no fading colours!

So Coleridge now saw his own past, justly or not, and his own future. At the end of the poem he indicates a doubt whether a clerical brother, however affectionate, would altogether appreciate some of the sentiments expressed in the book.

If aught of error or intemperate truth
Should meet thine ear, think thou that riper Age
Will calm it down, and let thy love forgive it!

And later he felt impelled to write upon a copy:

If this volume should ever be delivered according to its direction, *i.e.* to Posterity, let it be known that the Reverend George Coleridge was displeased and thought his character endangered by the Dedication.[1]

The early days at Stowey were cheerful. The house, which still exists in a much altered condition, was to be spoken of in later years as a 'little hovel', and its locality as 'odoriferous Lime Grove St.'. But for the present it was better than had been expected. There were two small sitting-rooms and an old-fashioned kitchen with an open

[1] *P.W.* 173.

hearth below, and three or four bedrooms above, although the only window in one of them was a pane of glass slid by a wire. Coleridge had again thought of Rumfordizing one of the chimneys. Mice played the devil, but he thought it unfair to set a trap. Before the door ran a clear brook of very soft water. Behind were a kitchen garden and a 'sweet' orchard, communicating across a lane with Poole's domain, where was a pleasant arbour.¹ There was after all a servant, one Nanny, who when reproved for using too much paper in lighting the fire replied, 'La, Sir! why, it is only WATCH-MEN.'² Sara quickly made friends with Poole and his mother, and the Cruikshanks, who lived hard by. Coleridge found himself a social success. 'I pun, conundrumize, *listen*, and dance.' He delighted in Hartley, who became 'a very Seraph in Clouts'. He sat with his eye rolling up to the ceiling in a lyric fury, and on his knee a diaper pinned to warm.³ He was quickly 'an expert gardener', with a callus on each hand in proof of it. Lamb wrote in some bewilderment, 'Is it a farm you have got? and what does your worship know about farming?' and of Hartley, 'I did not distinctly understand you,—you don't mean to make an actual ploughman of him?' A month later Coleridge was still working in his garden for an hour and a half every morning, and feeding pigs and poultry. He grew potatoes and all manner of vegetables, and expected to raise enough corn for his family with the spade. Milk he got from Thomas Poole. And there, one supposes, it stopped. When Thelwall visited him a year later, they disputed about education. Thelwall held with Rousseau, that a child's mind should not be influenced by inculcating opinions before it was of age to judge for itself. They then stepped into the garden, and Thelwall pointed out that it was full of weeds.

'Oh,' I replied, '*that* is only because it has not yet come to its age of discretion and choice. The weeds, you see, have taken the liberty to grow, and I thought it unfair in me to prejudice the soil towards roses and strawberries.'

¹ C. 65, 69, 71; G. 65; I.L.N.; P. i. 200, 305; *Rem.* 100, 140; *Harvard MS.* 19478·25 F.; W. Knight, *Coleridge and Wordsworth in the West Country*, 17, 53, 58, 101, 104, 111.   ² B.L. i. 121; C. 87, 97; G. 45; M. 3.   ³ C. 72; G. 39.

Dialectically, Coleridge had scored, but no doubt the weeds grew on.[1]

Charles Lloyd, after leaving Bristol about the beginning of December, had recovered his mental balance in the less stimulating atmosphere of his father's house. After Christmas he went to London and made the personal acquaintance of Lamb by a surprise visit, which Lamb recorded in verse. Early in February he reached Stowey, where he was put up at Poole's for a fortnight, while rooms in the cottage were furnished for him, and joined the Coleridge household on 22 February. Mrs. Coleridge found him a pleasant inmate, and kind to her Hartley. But early in March epilepsy seized him again. Coleridge wore himself out in attendance on his fits, and at some time between 16 March and 14 April the experiment was abandoned, and he went home once more.[2] Coleridge's plan of life was now again in fragments. His reviewing got into arrears. He dropped the biographical letters which he had begun to write for Poole, and Lamb heard nothing of him between 10 February and 7 April.[3] He came and went between Bristol and Stowey, presumably for the press-correction of his poems, stopping on one occasion at Huntspill to see George Burnett, who was ill with jaundice, and hearing incidentally from a village woman that George had been led astray by a 'vile jacobin villain' called Coleridge.[4] It was after a visit to Bristol that he wrote a melancholy letter to Cottle, which introduces a significant name.

On the Saturday, the Sunday, and the ten days after my arrival at Stowey I felt a depression too dreadful to be described.

> So much I felt my genial spirits droop!
> My hopes all flat, nature within me seem'd
> In all her functions weary of herself.

Wordsworth's conversation, &c., roused me somewhat, but even now I am not the man I have been—and I think I never shall. A sort of calm hopelessness diffuses itself over my heart. Indeed every mode of life, which has promised me bread and cheese, has been, one after another, torn away from me—but God remains.

[1] C. 71, 72; L. 20; G. 299; *T.T.* 105.
[2] G. 39; L. 21, 22, 24, 25; Bowles, 29; Lucas, *Lloyds*, 19, 37.
[3] G. 39; L. 24.   [4] *Rem.* 137, 140.

He was not in immediate pecuniary distress, since Lloyd's father had sent him £10, and was working on his answer to Godwin, and a tragedy, which Richard Sheridan through a friend of Bowles, probably Sheridan's brother-in-law William Linley, had asked him to try his hand upon, with a view to performance at Drury Lane.[1]

[1] G. 38, 39; *Rem.* 102 (with errors); *Quaritch Cat.* 500, No. 121; *Sotheby Cat.* (24 March 1936), No. 408; *Harvard MSS.* 19478·25 F.

V

THE ANNUS MIRABILIS
March 1797—September 1798

THE advent of Wordsworth was perhaps the most important turning-point in Coleridge's life. It is not likely that they had seen each other in the flesh since their first meeting during the autumn of 1795. Wordsworth was then awaiting the arrival of his sister Dorothy in order to start for Racedown, which had been put at his disposal by the Pinney family, and at Racedown, so far as we know, he mainly stayed for the next eighteen months, working on his *Salisbury Plain* and his tragedy *The Borderers*. But it is certain that, directly or indirectly, he was still in touch with Coleridge by correspondence. On 7 January 1796 he wrote to Cottle, sending his compliments to Coleridge and saying that he much wished to hear from him. The same letter promised Cottle a copy of *Salisbury Plain*. This was duly sent, and by 25 March had been read and interleaved by Coleridge, who undertook to return it with his comments to Wordsworth. If it could be printed, he would like to get his agents for the *Watchman* to ventilate it. What in fact he did was to send it to Lamb, asking him to return it to Wordsworth, who must have been on a visit to London. 'I shall be too ill to call on Wordsworth myself,' wrote Lamb, towards the end of May, 'but will take care to transmit him his poem, when I have read it.' On 13 May Coleridge had written to Thelwall of comments on his own poems by 'a very dear friend of mine, who is, in my opinion, the best poet of the age'. He would send Thelwall his friend's poem, when published. 'And this man', he adds, 'is a republican, and at least, a *semi*-atheist.' In January 1797, as we have seen, he was delaying the printing of his *Visions*, in order to get Wordsworth's criticisms upon them. In the spring of 1797 Mary Hutchinson, Wordsworth's future wife, was on a visit to Racedown, and in the course

of it, on 19 March, Wordsworth went off with his friend
Basil Montagu to spend a week or ten days in Bristol. Here
he may well have met Coleridge, coming and going about
his proofs. But, in any case, his biographers have overlooked
the evidence furnished by the letter quoted at the end of the
last chapter, that on his return to Racedown he went not far
out of his way to see Coleridge at Stowey. It is true that
Cottle, by one of his blunders, endorsed that letter as of
1796. But it is clear from its terms, and in particular from
the mention of a remittance by the elder Lloyd, that it can
only have been written shortly after Charles Lloyd, at some
time after 16 March, took his departure from Coleridge's
cottage. It must, I think, be inferred that, when Coleridge
wrote on a copy of his *Poems* of 1797 that he had no personal
acquaintance with Wordsworth as early as March 1796, and
when he told Estlin on 17 May 1798 that he had then known
Wordsworth a year and some months, he was dating the
personal acquaintance, not from the casual meeting of 1795,
but from the closer association which began about March
1797.[1]

   Coleridge's visit to Racedown in June was therefore a
return visit. He arrived on Monday, 5 June, probably in the
evening, since he had preached at Bridgwater on the Sunday
before, and breakfasted at Taunton the next morning. He
therefore just missed Mary Hutchinson, who had gone to
London on the same day. To her Dorothy Wordsworth
wrote regretting this, and giving a description of Coleridge,
whom she apparently now met for the first time.

   You had a great loss in not seeing Coleridge. He is a wonderful
man. His conversation teems with soul, mind, and spirit. Then he is
so benevolent, so good tempered and cheerful, and, like William,
interests himself so much about every little trifle. At first I thought
him very plain, that is, for about three minutes: he is pale and thin,
has a wide mouth, thick lips, and not very good teeth, longish loose-
growing half-curling rough black hair. But if you hear him speak for
five minutes you think no more of them. His eye is large and full, not
dark but grey; such an eye as would receive from a heavy soul the
dullest expression; but it speaks every emotion of his animated mind;
it has more of the 'poet's eye in a fine frenzy rolling' than I ever witnessed. He has fine dark eyebrows, and an overhanging forehead.

   [1] C. 57, 81; W. 51, 56; L. 2; *R.E.S.* viii. 12; cf. p. 46.

I am not sure that Dorothy's own eye was quite so closely
upon the object as usual, when she called Coleridge 'thin'.
Her picture may be filled out from a reminiscence late in
life of how Coleridge 'did not keep to the high road, but
leapt over a gate and bounded down the pathless field by
which he cut off an angle' at the meeting.[1]

Coleridge was much impressed by Wordsworth, whom
he now thought more inclined to Christianity than to
Theism. 'I feel myself *a little man by his side.*' Poole too,
he said, considered him the greatest man he ever knew.
Incidentally, this helps to confirm the belief that Wordsworth had visited Stowey. The poets admired each other's
tragedies, which does not indicate any great development of
critical power in either of them. Coleridge thought of walking on with his to see Bowles, but there is no evidence that
he did, or that he came back to Stowey on a Friday, as he
told Cottle he should do. It seems more likely that the stay
at Racedown was continuous to Wednesday, 28 June, when
Coleridge certainly came to Stowey, only to leave almost
at once and come again on 2 July, bringing with him
the Wordsworths, whom he drove over forty miles of
execrable roads, which made him, he claims, 'no inexpert
whip'.[2] From Stowey he wrote to Cottle, giving a portrait
of Dorothy, which forms a counterpart to hers of him. I
print the letter in full, but for its list of *errata* in the *Poems*,
since Cottle has mangled it, even beyond his wont.[3]

My dear friend
    These are the errors, & the alterations—Now, I conceive, that as the
volumes are bound, you might employ a boy for sixpence or a shilling
to go thro them & with a fine pen, and dainty ink, make the alterations
in each volume—I am confident, it would not cost more than printing
the errata.—and then the Errata may remain, as it is *now already*
printed.—*I wish, it could be so* : for really, nobody scarcely does look at
the table of Errata — — the Volume is a most beautiful one—you have
determined that the three Bards shall walk up Parnassus,—the Hill of
Fame, in their best Bib & Tucker. Give my love to your Brother
Amos—I condole with him—but it is the fortune of War—the finest
poem, I ever wrote, lost the prize—& that which gained it, was

[1] Estlin, 38; P. i. 231; W. 59, 61; *D.W.* (L.), 73.
[2] C. 73, 74; G. 42, 43; W. 63, 64; Campbell, 68.
[3] *Harvard MSS.* 19478·5 F.; cf. G. 25; *Rem.* 81, 144, 149.

contemptible—but an ode may *sometimes* be too bad for the prize; but *very often too good*.

Wordsworth & his exquisite Sister are with me—She is a woman indeed!—in mind, I mean, & heart—for her person is such, that if you expected to see a pretty woman, you would think her ordinary —if you expected to find an ordinary woman, you would think her pretty!—But her manners are simple, ardent, impressive—.

> In every motion her most innocent soul
> Outbeams so brightly, that who saw would say,
> Guilt was a thing impossible in her.—

Her information various—her eye watchful in minutest observation of nature—and her taste a perfect electrometer—it bends, protrudes, and draws in, at subtlest beauties & most recondite faults. — — She with her Brother desire their kindest respects to you. If you can pick up a Hamlet, an Othello, & a Romeo & Juliet, separately, in *numbers*, or an odd volume—Wordsworth would thank you to get it for him — — —

T. Poole will be collecting the names of the persons, who want my poems here—when I have got them, I will send the Number & you will put it to Poole's account. For my self I want one, for C. Lamb *one*, for Wordsworth in *your* name *one*, for my Brother *one*, and one I shall send with a sonnet to Dr *Parr*—

God love you
& your ever affectionate
S. T. COLERIDGE.

This was a favourite form of subscription with Coleridge. The lines on Dorothy are a variant of those recently written on Joan of Arc for the *Visions*. Amos Cottle had been competing for a prize at Cambridge. Coleridge had promised to look over his composition, but had failed to do so in time.[1]

On the second day after the Wordsworths arrived 'dear Sara' emptied a skillet of boiling milk over Coleridge's foot, which lamed him for some time. He was still unable to walk when Charles Lamb came, probably on 7 July, to pay the visit of which he had been disappointed the year before. The *Lime-Tree Bower* records a solitary evening spent by Coleridge in Poole's garden, while Charles and the Wordsworths roamed the Quantock coombs without him. Copies of the poem were sent to Southey and to Charles Lloyd. Lamb stayed for a week, and in the flurry of departure left

[1] *P.W.* 137; *Rem.* 136.

behind him a great-coat, which, incidentally, Coleridge had failed to return towards the end of September.[1] An invitation of the Southeys to Stowey was apparently not accepted.[2] But shortly after Lamb came Cottle. He too recalls the bower as a 'jasmine harbour', in which he feasted with Poole and Coleridge and, if he is right, Charles Lloyd, on bread and cheese and a brown mug of true Taunton ale. Poole had built it of sheets of bark from his tanyard.[3] Meanwhile the Wordsworths had been fascinated by the scenery of the Quantocks, which reminded them of the Lakes. Racedown had become uncomfortable, since the elder Pinney had learnt with some annoyance that they were living there rent-free, and they now heard of a vacant house, belonging to the St. Albyn family, at Alfoxton, which they called Alfoxden, in the village of Holford, some three miles from Stowey. It was a considerable mansion standing in a deerpark. But through the good offices of Poole they secured a year's sub-lease from the tenant of the home farm to which it was attached, at a rent of £23, and to Alfoxden they moved, after a fortnight spent in the cottage, about the middle of July.[4]

Alfoxden soon became almost as much Coleridge's home as Stowey itself. He was already there, for change of air, by 17 July.[5] At both houses there was much hospitality during the summer. Coleridge invited Wade, who perhaps did not accept.[6] Cottle came again, this time to Alfoxden, and gives an amusing account of his drive from Stowey, with a picnic lunch—consisting mainly of a stout piece of cheese, which was stolen on the way by a beggar, and a bottle of brandy, which was broken by Coleridge—and of the unavailing attempts of Wordsworth and Coleridge to get a collar off the horse. Ultimately the fare was reduced to a superb brown loaf and a pile of cos lettuces, the salt for which had been forgotten.[7] There was, however, another visitor, who brought much trouble with him. This was John Thelwall, Coleridge's friendly but long-unseen corre-

---

[1] C. 74; G. 44; L. 26, 28, 29, 31; P.W. 178; Poems (ed. J.D.C.) 591. The letter sending the poem to Lloyd is unprinted, and I do not know where it is.
[2] C. 74.   [3] Rem. 149, 174, 182; P. i. 202; Hazlitt, xvii, 119.
[4] W. 63, 64; P. i. 225; R.E.S. viii. 17.   [5] C. 74.   [6] G. 46.   [7] W. 65, 66; Rem. 182

spondent. He had been expected before Lamb left, and
Lamb had looked out for him in vain on his way home. He
arrived on 17 July, and found Sara, in Coleridge's absence,
engaged at the wash-tub. Next day they joined the party at
Alfoxden. Coleridge was impressed by him. They differed
on almost every point of religion, morals, politics, and
philosophy, but here, thought Coleridge, was the only active
democrat who was also an honest man. Thelwall enjoyed
the repose of the Quantocks.

'Citizen John,' I said to him, 'this is a fine place to talk treason in!'
'Nay! Citizen Samuel,' replied he, 'it is rather a place to make a man
forget that there is any necessity for treason.'

Unfortunately, it was the general belief in the neighbourhood that treason was talked, and even more than talked.
It was a time of considerable political stress. There had
been mutinies in the fleets at Portsmouth and Sheerness,
and a French invasion was confidently expected. Thomas
Poole's own democratic tendencies had long been looked at
askance. He had incurred very great odium, says Coleridge,
by bringing him, but 'my peaceable manners and known
attachment to Christianity had almost worn it away'. Then
came Wordsworth. Charlotte Poole's diary records the
shock. 'Alfoxton house is taken by one of the fraternity. To
what are we coming?' And now here was Thelwall, whose
reputation was notorious. Strange rumours flew about the
country-side. Wordsworth's movements were extremely
suspicious. He roamed over the hills like a partridge. He
was seen tramping away towards the sea. He would wander
about at night and look rather strangely at the moon. One
thought he was a smuggler. Another was confident that he
kept an illicit still. 'I could smell the spirits, as plain as an
ashen fagot at Christmas.' But the favourite idea was that he
was 'a desperate French jacobin, for he is so silent and dark,
that nobody ever heard him say one word about politics'.
The county gentlemen now took the alarm. Coleridge tells
in the *Biographia Literaria* how 'a titled Dogberry', whom he
also calls 'Sir Dogberry', brought down a spy, who tracked
Wordsworth and himself for three weeks and reported
that they seemed very good subjects. He had talked to

Coleridge on the road, professing to be himself a democrat, and had found him no friend to Jacobinism. It was
true that he heard Coleridge speak of one 'Spy Nozy', and
thought at first that the reference was to his own features,
but afterwards gathered that 'Spy Nozy' was a man who
lived long ago and wrote a book. This is probably only
Coleridge's fun. He had discovered that the man was a spy
from the innkeeper with whom he lodged, and the innkeeper, he says, also did his best to disabuse Dogberry. He
was asked whether the suspects had not been walking near
the Channel, and taking charts and maps, and replied that
he understood that Coleridge was a poet, who was going to
put Quantock and all about it in print, and that he supposed
Wordsworth to be concerned in the affair. Some years later,
Southey learnt that a connexion of his own, John Southey,
Lord Somerville of Fitzhead Court, near Taunton, had been
one of the promoters of the local agitation. But the full
story of the spy has only lately been exhumed from Home
Office papers. Lord Somerville was not the Government's
only informant. Another was Sir Philip Hale of Boymore,
near Bridgwater. Either he or Somerville might have been
Coleridge's Dogberry. A third was Dr. Daniel Lysons, a
Bath physician and uncle of the topographers. It was really
he who moved the Home Office to take action. He had
learnt through one Charles Mogg, a friend of his cook and
once a fellow servant with her at Alfoxden, of an emigrant
family who had got possession of the house. The man had
no wife with him, but only a woman who passed for his
sister. They and their visitors went about, by day and night,
with camp-stools and a portfolio, and were apparently
taking observations on a small river which ran into the sea
from near Alfoxden. Lysons thought that they might be
agents for some persons at Bristol. The Home Office
instructed an agent at Hungerford, one Walsh, to make
inquiries. He saw Mogg, whom he found 'by no means the
most intelligent man in the world', and learnt that suspicion
of the 'French people' was general. They had no servant,
but many visitors, and were often abroad at night. Thomas
Jones, who lived at the Alfoxden farm, said they were

washing and mending their clothes all Sunday, and he should not stay, as he did not like it. Christopher Trickie and his wife, of the 'Dog Pound', said that they had taken plans of his house and of many other places, had asked him whether a brook that ran in front of his house was navigable all down to the sea, and had carefully examined it. Walsh was then told to go down to the district himself and keep a careful watch. On 15 August he reported a conversation between his landlord at Stowey and a frequenter of the inn about the nest of rascals protected at Alfoxden by Poole, among whom had been and perhaps was still the famous Thelwall. They were not, however, he gathered, French, but 'a mischiefuous gang of disaffected Englishmen'. The master of the house was Wordsworth, whose name he thought was known to the Home Office. Next day he had learnt that Thelwall was no longer there. But he had been there on the Sunday after Wordsworth came, a little stout man with dark cropped hair, who wore a white hat and glasses, and, after a dinner of fourteen persons, on whom Thomas Jones was asked to wait, got up and talked so loud and in such a passion that Jones was frightened and avoided the house. Walsh had, however, bribed him to take a job of weeding in the garden, and report further. Wordsworth had been to his former home and brought back a woman servant, who was very chatty and said that her master was a philosopher. Other gentlemen were shortly expected. One was a great counsellor from London, the other from Bristol. This last was probably Cottle. I do not know who the counsellor may have been. Basil Montagu was not yet called to the bar. Poole, says Walsh, had supported, since Christmas last, 'a Mr. Coldridge and his wife'. Coldridge was reckoned a man of superior ability, had a press in the house, and was believed to print as well as publish his own productions. The press, by the way, lacks confirmation. Here the Home Office record stops. It may be that later investigation convinced the spy, as Coleridge believed, that the local wiseacres had only found a mare's nest.[1] Their suspicions, however, were

[1] C. 77; B.L. i. 126; Rem. 181; P. i. 232, 235; T.T. 105; Southey (L.), ii. 343; A. J. Eagleston, Wordsworth, Coleridge, and the Spy (Studies, 71).

not entirely laid aside. Thelwall had in fact left before the
spying began, but hoped to return. On 29 July he was at
Bridgwater, and there put into verse his desire to live next
door to Coleridge,

> With kindly interchange of mutual aid
> To delve our little garden plots, the while
> Sweet converse flowed, suspending oft the arm
> And half-driven spade.[1]

In October Coleridge was busy trying to find a house for
him, but had to give it up as hopeless. 'The aristocrats', he
wrote, 'seem to persecute even Wordsworth', and he could
not ask Poole, who had already borne so much for his
friends, to use his influence. One may perhaps read between
the lines that he was not himself altogether anxious, in his
then political mood, to have Thelwall for a neighbour. An
apologetic letter from Poole tells us that he had incurred
the disapproval of the St. Albyn family by negotiating the
lease of Alfoxden to Wordsworth.[2]

If Coleridge can be trusted, the intelligent emissary of the
Home Office had in the long run plucked out the heart of
the Quantock mystery. The poets who roamed the hills by
day and night, and looked so strangely at the moon, were
in fact engaged upon their business of versifying, and not
upon a fantastic scheme of invasion. The little water-course
which runs from Holford to the sea at Kilve had taken shape
in Coleridge's mind as the symbol of a great philosophic
poem.

> I sought for a subject, that should give equal room and freedom for
> description, incident, and impassioned reflections on men, nature, and
> society, yet supply in itself a natural connection to the parts, and unity
> to the whole. Such a subject I conceived myself to have found in a
> stream, traced from its source in the hills among the yellow-red moss
> and conical glass-shaped tufts of bent, to the first break or fall, where its
> drops become audible, and it begins to form a channel; thence to the
> peat and turf barn, itself built of the same dark squares as it sheltered;
> to the sheepfold; to the first cultivated plot of ground; to the lonely
> cottage and its bleak garden won from the heath; to the hamlet, the
> villages, the market-town, the manufactories, and the sea-port.

---

[1] *Poems Chiefly Written in Retirement* (1802).   [2] C. 75-7; G. 47; P. i. 240.

The poem, of course, was not to be. 'Many circumstances, evil and good, intervened.' *The Brook* is only represented to-day by a stray jotting in the Gutch note-book.

> The Brook runs over Sea-weeds.
> Sabbath day—from the Miller's mossy wheel
> The water-drops dripped leisurely.[1]

One other visit of August must be recorded, for the picture which it gives of happiness in the Stowey cottage. One Richard Reynell, probably of a Devonshire family, writes to his brother. Coleridge was away from home, having gone to make the acquaintance of Mrs. Barbauld at Bristol. But he found George Burnett there, and with him went to see Wordsworth at Alfoxden. Shortly Coleridge returned, having walked forty miles without much appearance of fatigue. Reynell thought Stowey idyllic. 'Here you can be happy without superfluities.' And the household was in keeping with it. 'I have seen domestic life in all its beauty and simplicity, affection founded on a much stronger basis than wealth —on esteem.' With Sara, of whom we hear so much and know so little at this period, he was much taken. He found her 'sensible, affable, and good natured, thrifty and industrious, and always neat and prettily dressed'; and withal 'indeed a pretty woman'. He notices the child Hartley, over whom Coleridge would hang, 'talking to it, and fancying what he will be in later days'. Coleridge had hoped that Reynell might replace Lloyd as an inmate of his household, but nothing came of it.[2] On the happenings of the later autumn we have little information, except that at the beginning of September Coleridge paid a visit to Bowles at Donhead in Wilts. He had thought of going on to Salisbury and to Christ Church to see Southey, but there is no evidence that he did so. He was, however, again away from home for a day or two in the middle of October.[3] In November two fragments of letters by Dorothy Wordsworth tell of walks which were now extending beyond the limits of the Quantocks. One went by Porlock to Lynmouth, whence the travellers were guided to the Valley of

[1] *B.L.* i. 128; *P.W.* 992 ('merry' for 'mossy'); *Addl. MS.* 27901, f. 30ᵛ; Lowes, 207.
[2] Estlin, 38; *I.L.N.*   [3] C. 75; W. 66; *Rem.* 21, 133.

Rocks, near Lynton. The other, which began at half-past four in the afternoon of 13 November, took them on that day eight miles, probably to Watchet. In the course of it Wordsworth and Coleridge employed themselves in laying the plan of a ballad, to be published with some pieces of Wordsworth's. To this ballad I shall return.[1]

Behind all the ardent talk among friends and all the planning of poetry, there still lay for Coleridge the unsolved problem of bread and cheese. At Racedown he was 'almost shillingless', but a second instalment from the fund raised by Poole and Estlin came to the rescue. Poole asked Charles Lloyd to join the contributors, but we do not know whether he assented. The contributions to the *Critical Review* were dropped, apparently because Dorothy laughed at instead of with a batch which Coleridge had thought 'clever and epigrammatic and devilishly severe', and he threw them into the fire. If they were not better than those which survive, they deserved their fate.[2] He worked at the tragedy suggested by Sheridan, which he called *Osorio*, but it made slow progress. In June he expected to finish it in a few days. 'I hope you are only Coleridgeizing', wrote Lamb. 'Shakespeare was a more modest man; but you best know your own power.' In September he took it to Bowles for criticism, and on 16 October sent it to him for transmission to Sheridan. 'It is done: and I would rather mend hedges and follow the plough, than write another.' By November he had become impatient for a decision. Sheridan had not used him with common justice. The proposal for the play had come from him, and he was bound to pay it the earliest attention. Probably it lay snugly in his green bag. By 2 December it had been rejected. Sheridan suggested that some revision might make it fit for the stage. But Coleridge long nursed a grievance. Sheridan had failed to return the manuscript, of which he had lost his only copy. He was, however, able to give one to a friend in 1799. Parts of it had been allowed to get abroad. A scene in a dank cave had begun with the lines:

> Drip! drip! drip!—in such a place as this
> It has nothing else to do but drip! drip! drip!

---

[1] W. 68, 69.   [2] G. 42, 374; Estlin, 38; P. i. 228.

This Sheridan had parodied before company as:

> Drip! drip! drip! there's nothing here but dripping!

and had based his refusal on a pretence of Coleridge's un-willingness to alter the passage. Coleridge claimed in 1813 that it really ran:

> Drip! drip! a ceaseless sound of water-drops.

But the evidence of manuscripts is against him.[1]

In despair, Coleridge had begun to think, about July, of taking a salaried post as a Unitarian minister. One offered itself at Norwich, but Norwich he rejected as ugly and dear, and distant from all he loved. Moreover, even if he no longer believed that it was wrong to preach for hire, he had scruples against taking part in sacramental rites. On this point, however, discussion with Estlin seems to have modi-fied his view.[2] In September he must have met for the first time Thomas Wedgwood, who was then staying with Wordsworth at Alfoxden. Thomas was an invalid son of the founder of the Etruria pottery, and a devotee of science and philosophy. The pottery was now in the hands of his brother Josiah, and a banker brother John dwelt at Cote House, near Bristol. Early in December the Wordsworths went for a time to London, and Coleridge was invited to Cote House. Here he again met Thomas and probably also Josiah Wedgwood. And here too was James Mackintosh, already, like Coleridge himself, drifting from his early demo-cratic ardour. He too was a conversationalist. But while Coleridge 'riveted' Thomas Wedgwood and bored the rest of the party with his monologue, Mackintosh was the more dexterous debater, and when urged to attack him soon reduced him to confusion. In after life relations were always strained between them, although Mackintosh says that the dislike was mainly on Coleridge's side. Mackintosh, how-ever, now introduced him to his brother-in-law, Daniel Stuart, the editor of the *Morning Post*, and Stuart gave him

---

[1] C. 75; G. 41, 42, 48; L. 26; W. 71; Estlin, 38; Bowles, 32; *Rem.* 133; *I.L.N.*; L.P. 5; Southey (*W.*), i. 66; Carlyon i. 142, 179; Greenough, 561; De Q. ii. 169; *Essays and Studies*, xix. 86 from *Harvard MSS.* 19478·5 F.; *P.W.* 812.
[2] C. 75; G. 44, 53; Estlin, 46.

a salary of a guinea a week, in return for expected contributions. These took the form of verses, of which the first
appeared on 7 December. But they came slowly, and by
January Stuart was remonstrating.[1] In Bristol Coleridge
also met Basil Montagu, and with him discussed a plan for
taking pupils which seemed unlikely to prove practicable.[2]
On his return to Stowey he heard of the possibility of
another ministry, at Shrewsbury, whence one John Rowe
was on the point of retirement, to become a colleague of
Estlin. Shrewsbury attracted him more than Norwich, but
a second intimation suggested that another candidate might
be preferred. On 26 December he received a draft from
Josiah Wedgwood for £100 as a gift from himself and
Thomas. This he gratefully accepted next day. On the same
evening came a definite invitation to offer himself for the
Shrewsbury vacancy. He consulted Estlin, and after some
sleepless nights returned the Wedgwood draft on 5 January,
with an elaborate explanation of his motives. The £100,
with his salary from the *Morning Post*, would keep him, in
his frugal way of living, for two years. But journalism,
which meant politics, and incidentally the regular dispatch
of contributions, he thought 'only not the worst occupation
for a man who would wish to preserve any delicacy of moral
feeling'. Shrewsbury was in fine country. He would have
£150 a year, a house worth £30, five days of leisure in the
week, and, if he left a family in want, the likelihood of their
maintenance by the congregation. Moreover, he would
have legal exemption from military service, which meant a
relief from the fear that, in the case of invasion, the Government would put him and their other opponents, like Uriah,
in the forefront of the battle. On the other hand, he still
thought it warping to the intellect to let livelihood depend
upon the profession of particular opinions, and that there
were further dangers of truckling to the wishes of a paying
congregation, and of falling into a sectarian mannerism
through the routine of duty. But against these things he

[1] G. 48, 55; W. 70–2; S. (T.), i. 302; T.T. 14; 2 *Gent. Mag.* ix. 485; Estlin, 46;
Litchfield, 51; Robinson (D.), iii. 486; Mackintosh, *Memoirs,* i. 326; Carlyon, i. 68;
P. i. 261; Wise, 207; *P.W.* 171.   [2] W. 72; Estlin, 46.

would be forearmed, and after all the Unitarian creed only required belief that Jesus Christ was the Messiah. 'In all other points I may play off my Intellect *ad libitum*.' On the whole, feeling that 'whatever is conducive to a man's real comforts is in the same degree conducive to his utility', he had decided to go to Shrewsbury, and to return the £100, in the hope that his vacillation would not forfeit the esteem of the donors. He then borrowed £10 of Estlin and £5 of Wade, and on 13 January 1798 arrived at Shrewsbury, where he preached his first trial sermon the next day.[1]

Of this visit we have the immortal account in William Hazlitt's *My First Acquaintance with Poets*.[2] It was written long after, but is only slightly touched by Hazlitt's later antipathy to Coleridge. William was then a young man of nineteen, living with his father, himself a Unitarian minister, at Wem, ten miles from Shrewsbury. Rowe, he says, had met the coach, in some anxiety at the preacher's late arrival, but could see no one but a round-faced man in a short black coat, like a shooting-jacket, talking at a great rate to his fellow passengers. He had scarcely got back in a state of disappointment, when the round-faced man entered, and again began to talk. 'He did not cease while he stayed; nor has he since, that I know of.' On the Sunday, Hazlitt walked over to hear the sermon. Hackneyed as his description is, I must quote from it.

When I got there, the organ was playing the 100th Psalm, and when it was done Mr Coleridge rose and gave out his text, 'And he went up into the mountain to pray, HIMSELF, ALONE.' As he gave out this text, his voice 'rose like a steam of rich distilled perfumes'; and when he came to the two last words, which he pronounced loud, deep, and distinct, it seemed to me, who was then young, as if the sounds had echoed from the bottom of the human heart, and as if that prayer might have floated in solemn silence through the universe. The idea of St John came into my mind, 'of one crying in the wilderness, who had his loins girt about, and whose food was locusts and wild honey'. The preacher then launched into his subject, like an eagle dallying with the wind. The sermon was upon peace and war; upon church and state—not their alliance but their separation; on the spirit of the world and the spirit of Christianity—not as the same, but as opposed to one another.

---

[1] G. 49–52; Estlin, 45, 46; *R.E.S.* vi. 63.　　　[2] Hazlitt, vii. 128; xvii. 106.

On the following Monday Coleridge paid Hazlitt's father the professional courtesy of a night's visit to Wem. Here he talked for two hours, saying afterwards that he was 'conversing with William Hazlitt's forehead'. Hazlitt's account of his personal appearance has already been given. There was much further discourse at supper, to the delight of both hosts. 'I remember the leg of Welsh mutton and the turnips on the table that day had the finest flavour imaginable.' Coleridge spoke of Burke and Mackintosh, Godwin and Holcroft. Neither Mackintosh nor Wedgwood, he said, thought much of Wordsworth, but he had told them, 'He strides on so far before you, that he dwindles in the distance.' Next morning Coleridge received a letter from Josiah Wedgwood, offering him, on behalf of his brother and himself, an annuity of £150 a year for life, independent of anything but the wreck of their fortune. No condition was annexed, but the abandonment of any professional ties was of course implied. Poole himself urged acceptance.[1] Coleridge, indeed, had no hesitation now. He seemed to make up his mind, says Hazlitt, 'in the act of tying on one of his shoes'. Hazlitt himself felt little gratitude, but was uplifted when Coleridge, after writing his name and address on a card, advanced to him 'with undulating step', and gave it him with an invitation to come and see him shortly at Stowey. They walked back towards Shrewsbury together, discussing philosophy. Coleridge said that, before accepting the post at Shrewsbury, he should have preached two more sermons, one on Infant Baptism, the other on the Lord's Supper, showing that he could not administer either. Hazlitt also noticed a habit, which in fact clung to Coleridge in later years, of constantly shifting from one side to the other of the footpath, as he walked. When he wrote, Hazlitt had come to think this symbolic. From Shrewsbury Coleridge wrote a grateful letter of acceptance, and attempted to mitigate Estlin's disappointment by an exposition of his motives. But Estlin did not respond. The resignation of Coleridge's candidature was received with regret. He had won golden opinions from his congregation, in spite of

[1] P. i. 257.

some resentment aroused by an unfortunate reference to one Arthur Aikin, the nephew of Mrs. Barbauld, as a 'booby', in ignorance of the fact that Aikin had at one time been connected with the church. He felt bound to take duty at Shrewsbury for two more Sundays, in order to enable Rowe to make his arrangements at Bristol. But on 30 January he left, paying a visit to Thomas Wedgwood on his way home, and by 2 February he was once more at Stowey.[1]

Perhaps the worst thing possible had happened to him. He had talked long enough; sown enough wild oats. I do not suggest that he should have become a Unitarian minister. But it was time for him, in one way or another, to take up his share of the economic burden which is, or ought to be, the common lot of humanity. Instead, here was an endowment which, in terms at least, left it possible for him to go on just as he had always done. It is true that his first impulse was to recognize in full the moral obligation which it imposed upon him. 'Now I am enabled, as I have received freely, freely to give', he wrote to Estlin, and to Josiah Wedgwood himself in more formal acknowledgement:

> Disembarrassed from all pecuniary anxieties yet unshackled by any regular profession, with powerful motives and no less powerful propensities to honourable effort, it is my duty to indulge the hope that at some future period I shall have given a proof that as your intentions were eminently virtuous, so the action itself was not unbeneficent.

The thought recurred to him from time to time for many years. But, unfortunately, the longer Coleridge looked at a moral obligation the more he became inclined in practice to shy away from it.[2]

The next two or three months at Stowey must have been of great happiness. Dorothy Wordsworth's *Alfoxden Journal*, which runs from 20 January to 17 May, records the constant wanderings out of doors, in a spring which began early, then for a time came slowly up that way, and in the second week of April moved rapidly to summer. It was the summer which Wordsworth long remembered.[3]

[1] C. 78; G. 53–6, 58; Estlin, 59; *R.E.S.* vi. 67.
[2] G. 53, 54.
[3] D. W. (*J.*), i. 6, 14, 16; *Prelude*, xiii. 395.

That summer when on Quantock's grassy Hills
Far ranging, and among her sylvan Combs,
Thou in delicious words, with happy heart,
Didst speak the Vision of that Ancient Man,
The bright-eyed Mariner, and rueful woes
Didst utter of the Lady Christabel.

In February Coleridge wrote his beautiful lines on *Frost at Midnight*, and also the ode called both *The Recantation* and *France*, inspired by the aggression of the Republic on the liberties of Switzerland.[1] Wordsworth was also busy with poetry, writing pieces which afterwards found their place in the *Prelude* and the *Excursion*. He had already conceived the idea of the *Recluse*. Coleridge claimed to have partly suggested it, and it would have been a pendant to his own design for *The Brook*. He was himself still much under the spell of Wordsworth. 'The Giant Wordsworth—God love him!' But on one subject they were habitually silent. Wordsworth's attitude to religion had not developed, as Coleridge hoped. 'He loves and venerates Christ and Christianity. I wish he did more'. Perhaps the rambles were mainly with Dorothy. The two poets had different habits. Coleridge liked to compose in walking over uneven ground, or breaking through the straggling branches of a copse-wood. Wordsworth preferred the uninterrupted continuity of a straight gravel walk.[2] Coleridge's health was not good. Wordsworth recalled the attacks of 'a frightful internal pain, which sometimes caused him, when they walked together in Somersetshire, to throw himself down and writhe like a worm upon the ground', and to this he ascribed the use of opium.[3] Early in March Coleridge had a fever caused by an inflamed tooth, and afterwards went for a week with his wife to recover at Alfoxden.[4] A letter to his brother George, written during his convalescence, gives a long account of his political and religious attitude, which is tempered no doubt as usual to the shorn clerical lamb, but confirms the revulsion from French sympathies expressed in his ode of February. He still thinks the present ministry weak and unprincipled men, but is 'no

[1] *P.W.* 240, 243.   [2] C. 79, 81; W. 73–6; *T.T.* 185; Hazlitt, xvii. 119.
[3] Batho, 368, from R. P. Graves (*Afternoon Lectures*).
[4] C. 79, 80; D. W. (*J.*), i. 12, 13.

Whig, no Reformist, no Republican'. He repeats the phrase about his 'squeaking baby-trumpet of sedition' which he had already used to the elder Lloyd eighteen months before. For the inherent depravity of mankind he now believes that the *spirit* of the Gospel is the sole cure, although, he must add, he looks for it 'neither in the mountain, nor at Jerusalem'. He has withdrawn himself to muse on fundamental and general causes.

I devote myself to such works as encroach not on the anti-social passions—in poetry, to elevate the imagination and set the affections in right tune by the beauty of the inanimate impregnated as with a living soul by the presence of life—in prose to the seeking with patience and a slow, very slow mind, 'Quid sumus, et quidnam victuri gignimus,'—what our faculties are and what they are capable of becoming. I love fields and woods and mountains with an almost visionary fondness.

So Coleridge saw himself in 1798. At the end of the letter he expressed a hope of walking down to Ottery shortly.[1] This he did, returning on 18 April, but we have no details of his reception.[2] In April he wrote *The Nightingale* and *Fears in Solitude*, in which his growing disillusion with France is the stronger for apprehensions of an invasion. The sin, on both sides, of warfare is emphasized by contrast with the peace of the Quantocks and of his own lowly cottage.

> With light
> And quickened footsteps thitherward I tend,
> Remembering thee, O green and silent dell!
> And grateful, that by nature's quietness
> And solitary musings, all my heart
> Is softened, and made worthy to indulge
> Love, and the thoughts that yearn for human kind.

The poem was sent to George, as one that might appeal even to his brother James, 'who is no admirer of the art'.[3] The shift in Coleridge's political attitude must have added to the irritation with which he found himself pilloried a few months later by the lively poets of the *Anti-Jacobin*. George

[1] C. 80.   [2] D. W. (J.), i. 17.   [3] P.W. 256, 264; G. 59.

Canning appears to have been mainly responsible for *The New Morality*, printed in July with the lines

> And ye five other wandering Bards that move
> In sweet accord of harmony and love,
> C—DGE and S—TH—Y, L—D, and L—BE and Co.,
> Tune all your mystic harps to praise LEPAUX.[1]

In August Gillray added a caricature, which shows 'Colridge' wearing an ass's head and carrying a scroll of dactylics.[2] In September the attack was renewed by *The Anarchists*.[3]

> See! faithful to their mighty dam,
> C.....DGE, S..TH.Y, L...D and L..BE,
> In splay-foot madrigals of love,
> Soft moaning like the widow'd dove,
> Pour, side by side, their sympathetic notes;
> Of equal rights and civic feasts,
> And tyrant Kings and knavish priests,
> Swift through the land the tuneful mischief floats.
> And now to softer strains they struck the lyre,
> They sung the beetle, or the mole,
> The dying kid, or ass's foal,
> By cruel man permitted to expire.

On 14 May was born a child, who was given the name Berkeley. The event found Coleridge in a state of deep distress.[4] To Estlin he wrote, 'I have had many sorrows and some that bite deep; calumny and ingratitude from men who have been fostered in the bosom of my confidence'; and to Poole on 20 May, 'So many unpleasant and shocking circumstances have happened to me in my immediate knowledge within the last fortnight, that I am in a nervous state, and the most trifling thing makes me weep.' We can only in part reconstruct the story, which concerns Lloyd, Southey, and Lamb. After Lloyd left Stowey in the spring of 1797, he once more recovered his health under Dr. Darwin at Lichfield. He was evidently on friendly terms with Coleridge during the summer, even if Cottle is wrong in thinking he saw him at Stowey. Possibly he is, since by August Lloyd had fallen in love with one Sophia Pemberton. There was

---

[1] *Anti-Jacobin* (9 July 1798).
[2] Lucas, *Life of Lamb*, i. 136, from *Anti-Jacobin Review and Magazine* (1 Aug. 1798).
[3] *A.-J. R. and M.* (Sept. 1798).   [4] C. 82–4; G. 59.

family opposition. Lloyd went to consult Lamb in London, and at his request Lamb took him down to Southey, at Burton, near Christ Church, and left him there. 'He thought of going to consult you,' wrote Lamb to Coleridge, 'but said if he *had* come to you, he could never have brought himself to leave you.' From Burton, Lloyd and Southey went together to Bath and then to Birmingham, with the idea of persuading Sophia to a Scottish marriage. De Quincey's story that Southey stole her away for Lloyd by proxy is an exaggeration. They went back to Burton and then again to Bath in September. Lamb wrote again to Coleridge:

> You use Lloyd very ill, never writing to him. I tell you again that his is not a mind with which you should play tricks. He deserves more tenderness from you.

By 11 November Lloyd had written a novel.[1] Coleridge failed to take Lamb's hint, and did play tricks with Lloyd's mind. He sent to the *Monthly Magazine* three 'mock sonnets', which he signed Nehemiah Higginbottom and thought would 'do good to our young Bards'. They were, he told Cottle, in ridicule of his own, Lloyd's, and Lamb's, and the instances almost all taken from his own and Lloyd's. The sonnets duly appeared at the end of November 1797. Coleridge was never happy with humorous verse, but the parody of Lloyd is faintly traceable in the first and second, which hit respectively at '*doleful egotism*' and at 'low, creeping language and thoughts, under the pretence of *simplicity*'. Oddly enough, Southey had just written to his friend Wynn that he was 'aware of the danger of studying simplicity of language', and it was in the first instance he, and not Lloyd, who supposed himself the mark for Coleridge's shafts. Coleridge, now regretting the publication, attempted to disabuse him. He was 'sorry to perceive a disposition in you to believe evil of me'. He had also been writing to Lloyd. Probably he convinced neither of them.[2] Apparently Lamb took no offence. Certainly none is traceable in a letter of 28 January

---

[1] L. 25, 26, 30, 31; P. i. 228; Southey (*W*.), i. 46; *Bodl. MS. English Letters*, C 23, ff. 15, 20, 28ᵛ; Lucas, *Lloyds*, 43; De Q., ii. 389; *Annus Mirabilis*, 105.

[2] C. 85, and note; *Rem*. 159; *B.L.* i. 17; *Annus Mirabilis*, 86; Southey (*L*.), i. 324; *P.W.* 209.

1798 to Coleridge, rejecting an invitation to Mary Lamb as too stimulating for her. 'I think you would almost make her dance within an inch of the precipice.' He had then himself almost quarrelled with Lloyd, now living in London with the volatile James White, in high spirits which did not consort with Lamb's gloomy mood. An outcome was Lamb's *Old Familiar Faces*, in which I do not think that there is any reference to Coleridge.[1] Chronology now becomes difficult, but at some time Lloyd wrote a letter to Dorothy Wordsworth, in which he called Coleridge 'a villain', and said that she had expressed the same opinion in conversation with him. Perhaps she had, if not at Stowey, then in London at Christmas, but obviously not with any serious intention. She brought the letter from Alfoxden to Coleridge in tears, and he laughed at it. Then, he says, followed 'a series of wicked calumnies & irritations—infamous Lies to Southey & to poor dear Lamb', which by a supernatural effort he took patiently, although it preyed upon him. Possibly the letter to Dorothy was in March 1798, when her journal shows that she walked over to see Coleridge, then ill, on the 6th, and on the 16th wrote to some one whose name is left blank.[2] Unfortunately the editor of the journal confesses omissions, and the manuscript is lost. At any rate, it was early in March that, on hearing that a third edition of Coleridge's *Poems* was in contemplation, Lloyd asked Cottle that his might be omitted. Coleridge assented. They had been included at Lloyd's own request, but times change and people change. 'By past experiences we build up our moral being.' He assured Cottle that he did not involve him in the bickering, and would write to Lloyd.[3] On 4 April Lloyd told Southey:

> Coleridge has written a very odd letter to Lamb. I don't know what may be his sentiments with regard to our conduct, but I can perceive that he is bent on dissociating himself with us—particularly Lamb I think he has used unkindly.[4]

In the course of April appeared Lloyd's novel, with the title *Edmund Oliver* and a dedication to Lamb. This it must

[1] L. 32.   [2] *R.E.S.* xi. 78; D. W. (*J.*), i. 12, 13.
[3] *Rem.* 164, 165, 167.   [4] L. 24, note (antedated, I think, by a year).

have been which threw Coleridge into such a state of agitation during the first fortnight of May. The hero was evidently modelled on himself. He had the same dark hair and large glistening eye. He left college in a love-fit, and became a recruit in a regiment of light horse, as Coleridge had done. He was given to a strange dreaminess, and if at any time thought-troubled swallowed some spirits or had recourse to his laudanum. No doubt Coleridge recognized that Lloyd's was a diseased mentality. Hearing that he was at Bristol, he set out on 16 May with Wordsworth and Dorothy, in the hope of reclaiming him. On the way they learnt that he had gone, and Coleridge returned. He was convinced that Lloyd's infirmities had been 'made the instruments of another man's darker passions'. Clearly he was thinking of Southey, who must in fact have given Lloyd the name Edmund Oliver, and may have been the intimate friend who told him of the incidents in the Army, although he cannot have been, as Lloyd says in the preface, an 'eye-witness of one of them'.[1] An epigram by Coleridge, however, suggests that he had himself told Lloyd much.[2]

*To One who Published in Print what had been
entrusted to him by my Fireside.*

Two things thou hast made known to half the nation,
My secrets and my want of penetration:
For Oh! far more than all which thou hast penn'd,
It shames me to have call'd a wretch, like thee, my friend!

Most of what must have been a voluminous correspondence has disappeared. One letter from Coleridge to Lamb can hardly be later than May 1798. Possibly it was never sent, as the manuscript was found among Coleridge's papers. It is reasonable, and good-tempered, and even affectionate.[3] Lloyd has let Coleridge know through Dorothy that Lamb will no longer correspond with him. He believes that Lamb regards himself as performing a painful duty of friendship. His own letters have been such that 'the best and kindest wish which, as a Christian, I can offer in return is that he may feel remorse'. Lamb disbelieved him when he denied

---

[1] C. 81, 82, 85, 101; G. 63; D. W. (J.), i. 18 ('22nd' for '17th' May).
[2] *P.W.* 964.   [3] C. 85.

that the sonnet on simplicity was aimed at Southey, and he will not therefore be too hasty in expressing his own disbelief of Lloyd's assertion that *Edmund Oliver* was not aimed at him. He now wants Lamb to arrange for him to meet Lloyd, alone or in the presence of 'all whose esteem I value'.

He assigned as reasons for his rupture my vices; and he is either right or wrong. If right, it is fit that others should know it and follow his example; if wrong, he has acted very wrong.

For himself, he feels that he has been unfortunate in his connexions.

Both you and Lloyd became acquainted with me when your minds were far from being in a composed or natural state, and you clothed my image with a suit of notions and feelings which could belong to nothing human. You are restored to comparative saneness, and are merely wondering what is become of the Coleridge with whom you were so passionately in love; *Charles Lloyd's* mind has only changed his disease, and he is now arraying his ci-devant Angel in a flaming San Benito—the whole ground of the garment a dark brimstone and plenty of little devils flourished out in black. Oh, me! Lamb, 'even in laughter the heart is sad!'

By June Lloyd had come to his senses. 'I love Coleridge', he told Cottle, 'and can forget all that has happened. At present I could not well go to Stowey. . . . I shall write to Coleridge to-day.'[1] But with Lamb there was an aftermath. Hearing that Coleridge was going to Germany, he sent him a number of burlesque scholastic theses, with the implication that, under the guise of an angel, he was a liar, a sneerer, a contemplator of himself in a vision beatific, and to be damned at the last, without suspecting it beforehand. Coleridge, wisely, did not reply. He showed the letter to Cottle, with the comment, 'These young visionaries will do each other no good.' On 28 July, Lamb sent a copy to Southey, explaining that Coleridge's last words had been, 'Poor Lamb, if he wants any *knowledge*, he may apply to me.' I do not suppose that Coleridge, who had not in fact yet gone, had said just that, but if we can trust a report of his young friend Thomas Allsop, many years later, Lloyd had shown Lamb a letter, in which Coleridge cited himself and

[1] Lucas, *Lloyds*, 54.

Lamb as examples respectively of genius and talent. About that time, Lamb had written to Coleridge of Lloyd, 'He is a sad tattler', and

> He almost alienated you (also) from me, or me from you, I don't know which. But that breach is closed. The dreary sea is filled up.

In 1832 he repeated:

> If you ever thought an offence, much more wrote it, against me, it must have been in the times of Noah; and the great waters swept it away.

The episode of 1798 was in fact the only breach in an enduring friendship.[1]

Meanwhile, the Wordsworths had failed to secure a renewal of their Alfoxden lease, and the idea of a joint tour to Germany had emerged. They, at any rate, needed to raise funds for the purpose. Cottle came once more to Alfoxden, and the plan of the *Lyrical Ballads* was formed. With Coleridge and Wordsworth he walked to Lynton. This was probably during the last week of May 1798.[2] On the day after Cottle left, Coleridge walked to Lynton again, making one day of it in each direction. A third walk, with a stay of two nights at Lynton, is described by Hazlitt, who now paid the visit for which Coleridge had invited him in January. With them went John Chester, a native of Stowey and a dog-like admirer of Coleridge. They talked of *Hamlet* and many other things, and saw the Valley of Rocks, where Hazlitt learnt of an abandoned intention of Coleridge and Wordsworth to use the spot as the scene of a prose tale, which was clearly *The Wanderings of Cain*. Hazlitt stayed for three weeks, and made the acquaintance of Wordsworth, about whom he has much to say.[3] When he left, in the course of June, Coleridge went to see Poole's friend Samuel Purkis at Brentford, and thence to Josiah Wedgwood's house at Stoke d'Abernon in Surrey, where he metaphysicized with Thomas Wedgwood until he was a *caput mortuum*.[4] The Wordsworths left Alfoxden at midsummer, spent a week at

---

[1] L. 33, 34, 349, 899; A., p. 141; *Rem.* 168.
[2] W. 76–81; D. W. (J.), 15; *B.L.* ii. 5; P. i. 240; *Rem.* 167, 174–9; *Harvard MS.* 19478·25 F.
[3] G. 58; *Rem.* 180; Hazlitt, xvii. 116; Raysor, i. 19; *P.W.* 285.   [4] P. i. 271.

the Stowey cottage, and then went to Bristol. Now Wordsworth wrote his *Tintern Abbey*, after an excursion with
Dorothy to the Wye. There was a second Welsh trip in
August, when a sudden fancy of Coleridge's took them to
Liswyn on Wye, where Thelwall now had a farm.[1] We
know no more of Coleridge's movements until the middle
of September, when he was in London, arranging for the
publication of some of his recent poems as a pamphlet,
neglecting to call upon Stuart, and preparing to start for
Germany.[2]

It is intelligible enough that under the stimulus of companionship with the Wordsworths, and in the joy which,
for all his financial troubles, that companionship brought
to him, Coleridge should have written good meditative
poems of the 'Conversation' type, since these were in the
natural line of development from less successful attempts
in the past. The amazing thing about the *Annus Mirabilis* is
of course that sudden emergence, at the highest levels of
imaginative power and verbal felicity, of the more objective
triumph of balladry, which, however much the materials may
have been shaping themselves in his subliminal consciousness, he had never essayed before, and was never to recover
again. What god or daimon for a few months walked with
him we do not know; it is perhaps the ultimate test of the
greatest poetry that we should not know. I have discussed
elsewhere the difficulties involved in the dating of the
greater poems.[3] The initiation both of the *Ancient Mariner*
and of *Christabel* he himself ascribed to 1797. On the whole it
seems likely that the first of the two November walks described
by Dorothy gave rise to *Cain*, and the second, which in that
case went as far as Dulverton, to the *Ancient Mariner*; and
if so the *Ancient Mariner* may be the ballad of which Coleridge wrote to Cottle in November and January, and as
'finished' in February, and brought to Alfoxden, again
'finished', in March. Echoes, alike of the *Ancient Mariner*
and of *Christabel*, in Dorothy's journal, suggest that both

[1] G. 60; W. 87, 1281; Wordsworth, *Poems* (1857), i. 190, ii. 160.
[2] P. i. 282; Wise, 52.
[3] *Annus Mirabilis*, 85. Another reminiscence by Wordsworth of the initiation of
the *Ancient Mariner* is in Robinson (D.), iii. 86.

were still in progress during the first three months of 1798. The *Ancient Mariner* went for printing with the *Lyrical Ballads* about the end of May. *Christabel* remained unfinished. Coleridge says that the trouble with Lloyd stopped his work on it.

The date of *Kubla Khan* is even more uncertain. When Coleridge first published the lines in 1816, he gave an account of their composition, with others amounting to two or three hundred, during a deep sleep due to an anodyne prescribed for a slight indisposition. On awaking, he recalled the whole, and began to write it down. A business visitor delayed him for an hour, and when he left, all beyond the fragment had gone from his mind, except some eight or ten scattered lines and images. Southey once ventured to suggest that he had dreamed that he had made a poem in a dream. However that may be, he gave in 1816 a date to the episode.[1]

In the summer of the year 1797, the Author, then in ill health, had retired to a lonely farm-house between Porlock and Linton, on the Exmoor confines of Somerset and Devonshire.

This date has been questioned on the strength of a notebook entry of 3 November 1810, which relates the ill health to the distress caused him by the quarrel with Charles Lloyd. The entry itself long remained unpublished, but through the kindness of the Rev. G. H. B. Coleridge I was enabled to recover it.[2] Part of its contents I have already summarized, but after describing Lloyd's correspondence with Dorothy Wordsworth, Southey, and Lamb, and recording his own forbearance, Coleridge adds:

Yet this supernatural effort injured me—what I did not suffer to act on my mind, preyed on my body—it prevented my finishing the Christabel—& at the retirement between Linton & Porlock was the first occasion of my having recourse to Opium.

On the strength of this more than one writer has rejected Coleridge's own dating for *Kubla Khan*, and referred it to the period of controversy with Lloyd, which began with the withdrawal by Lloyd of his poems, and culminated in the

---

[1] *P.W.* 295; S. C., *Memoir*, ii. 21.   [2] *R.E.S.* xi. 78.

fortnight of distress of which Coleridge wrote to Poole on
20 May 1798. I was myself at one time inclined to accept
that view, and to regard a day or two round about 9 May
1798 as likely enough for Coleridge's retirement.[1] But
several considerations now lead me to take a different view.
One is that I now mistrust Knight's entry for 9 May in
his edition of Dorothy Wordsworth's journal, which he
prints as 'Wrote to Coleridge'.[2] This naturally suggested
an absence from Stowey. The manuscript of the journal is
now lost, but 9 May is the date of an important letter from
Wordsworth to Cottle, which broaches the scheme of the
Lyrical Ballads, and I feel fairly sure that Knight has mis-
read 'Col' for 'Cot'.[3] Secondly, Mrs. Coleridge was confined
on 14 May. That is not very conclusive, since it was during
an absence of Coleridge that Hartley's birth had taken place.
It is of course just possible, although not very easy, to find
another conceivable date for Porlock between 6 March and
the middle of May. After that come the visits of Cottle
and Hazlitt, and, although we know of three walks to
Lynton, the first, in company with Wordsworth and Cottle,
can hardly have been broken by a retirement, and the other
two were certainly done without spending a night on the
way.[4] Dorothy's journal shows Coleridge continuously at
or near Stowey during most of March and April, and on
some days in May. On 21 March he had just returned from
'a little excursion' for the benefit of his health, but that
was, I think, only to Alfoxden, between 9 and 18 March.[5]
It is just conceivable that he left his wife there and
went to Porlock, but I think Dorothy would have noted
it. She does not name him between 9 and 18 April, if I
am right in taking Knight's 'Mr Coleridge' as an error for
'Mrs Coleridge'. She never calls him 'M^r' elsewhere in this
journal. But on 18 April he returned from a visit to his
brother George, and I do not think he would have gone
round by Porlock on his way from Stowey to Ottery.[6]
There are two other points. One is the emergence at the
National Portrait Gallery in 1934 of an autograph copy of

---

[1] *Annus Mirabilis*, 110.   [2] D. W. (*J.*), i. 18.   [3] W. 78; *Rem.* 175.   [4] Cf. p. 98.
[5] *Rem.* 165; D. W. (*J.*), i. 13.   [6] D. W. (*J.*), i. 16, 17.

Kubla Khan from the collection of Lord Crewe. A pencil note records it as sent by 'M^rs' (or possibly 'M^r') Southey. There are some variants from the text of 1816, and two of these, 'Cubla' for 'Kubla' and 'Amara' for 'Abora', seem to stand nearer to the probable sources of the poem. It has also been noted that the watermark of the paper is the same as that of a letter written by Coleridge in 1796. Experts tell me that little is known about the dating of late eighteenth-century paper. I may add that paper of 1795 was used for the *Lyrical Ballads* of 1800.[1] It is, however, quite possible that the Crewe MS. may be much earlier than 1816. And in it Coleridge gives much the same account of what happened.

This fragment with a good deal more, not recoverable, composed in a sort of Reverie brought on by two grains of Opium, taken to check a dysentery, at a Farm House between Porlock & Linton, a quarter of a mile from Culbone Church, in the fall of the year, 1797.

This repeated testimony now seems to me on the whole to outweigh the inference drawn from the note-book entry of 1810, made, as will appear later, in a condition of considerable mental disturbance.[2] And after all, although the actual quarrel with Lloyd dates from March 1798, Coleridge must have known that it largely owed its origin to the Nehemiah Higginbottom sonnets, themselves written in the fall of 1797. Finally, I am impressed by the terms of a letter written by Coleridge in 1798 to his brother George.[3] After describing the illness due to inflammation from the stump of a tooth, from which he was suffering on 6 March 1798, and which was followed by the excursion to Alfoxden, he says:

Laudanum gave me repose, not sleep; but you, I believe, know how divine that repose is, what a spot of enchantment, a green spot of fountain and flowers and trees in the very heart of a waste of sands.

Professor Lowes has already called attention to this passage as·evidence for Coleridge's knowledge, when he wrote *Kubla Khan*, of the 'blessed unviolated spot of earth' and 'enchanting spot' described in William Bartram's *Travels*.[4] But I think we can go farther. In the letter the 'spot' is already linked with laudanum, and surely that link

[1] Lowes, 358, 373; A. D. Snyder in *T.L.S.* (2. viii. 34); Wise, *Bibl. of Words-worth*, 34.   [2] Cf. p. 237.   [3] C. 80.   [4] Lowes, 364.

was first forged when *Kubla Khan* itself was written. The letter, then, is later than the poem. Unfortunately, it cannot be dated with certainty. The original bears no date, but a copy preserved among Thomas Poole's papers, in the hand of his apprentice Thomas Ward, is endorsed 'April 1798'.[1] It promises the visit from which Coleridge returned on 18 April. I strongly suspect, however, that it was written, not in April, but during the Alfoxden visit of 9 to 18 March, since in it Coleridge describes himself as 'now recovering apace', and enjoying 'that newness of sensation from the fields, the air, and the sun, which makes convalescence almost repay one for disease'. This is very close to what he wrote to Cottle from Alfoxden, 'I am much better, and my new and tender health is all over me like a voluptuous feeling'. The endorsement of the manuscript may have been influenced by the expectation in the letter of the birth of a child in 'five or six weeks' and the knowledge that the birth took place on 14 May. This, however, is not final. Mrs. Coleridge's anticipations could not be relied upon. Hartley's birth had come as a surprise. On 30 January and again between 9 and 18 March 1798, Coleridge was expecting a second child, not in May, but in April.[2]

If, then, *Kubla Khan* belongs to 1797, can we date it more closely? I think we can. On 16 October 1797 Coleridge sent his completed *Osorio* to Bowles.[3] On a Saturday, presumably 14 October, he wrote to Thelwall at Derby that it was to be sent off 'to-day'. He had just been 'absent a day or two'. In the same letter he notes that 'rocks or waterfalls, mountains or caverns, give me the sense of sublimity or majesty'.[4] That is, I believe, as near as the complicated evidence enables us to get to the date of *Kubla Khan*.

[1] *Addl. MS.* 35343, f. 177.   [2] G. 56; *Rem.* 165, 168.   [3] Bowles, 32.
[4] C. 75. A reference in this letter to an article in the *Courier*, two days before, might confirm the date, but I cannot find a copy of the number.

VI

GERMANY

September 1798—July 1799

THE idea of a German tour had floated into Coleridge's
mind during the spring of 1796, but was then impracti-
cable. At the end of 1797 he was studying the language,
and translating the *Oberon* of C. M. Wieland.[1] The Wedgwood annuity put him in funds, and in March 1798, when
the Wordsworths had learnt that they must leave Alfoxden,
a definite scheme shaped itself. Both families would go for
a period of two years, and settle near some university town.
By August it was modified. Coleridge still thought it 'of
high importance to my intellectual utility; and of course to
my moral happiness'. But it would be better and cheaper
to leave his wife and children at home in the first instance,
and to return for them, if all went well, after three or four
months. He believed that Mrs. Coleridge's wishes tended
the same way.[2] So it was settled, and on 16 September
Coleridge, with his young Stowey friend John Chester and
the Wordsworths, embarked at Yarmouth. Three days
later they reached Hamburg. Coleridge observed everything with the keenest interest, but it was 'an ugly city that
stinks in every corner', and their inn, 'Der Wildemann', was
uncomfortable. An introduction was obtained to the old
German poet F. G. Klopstock, best known by his *Messiah*,
and with him Wordsworth was able to converse, not in
German but in French, while Coleridge, who was not, for
once remained silent. Klopstock spoke much of his own
poetry, and of Lessing, Goethe, Schiller, and others; also of
the 'incomprehensible' Kant, whose influence he believed
and hoped was on the wane. He was described to Coleridge
as 'the German Milton', but when Coleridge read the *Messiah*
he thought him 'a very *German* Milton indeed'.[3]

After a few days at Hamburg, Coleridge went to Ratze-

[1] Cf. p. 59; *Annus Mirabilis*, 86. [2] G. 60; *Rem.* 176; W. 75, 77, 81.
[3] C. 87; *B.L.* ii. 132–65, 168–80; *Rem.* 254; W. 85–7; D. W. (*J.*), i. 21.

burg, some thirty-five miles to the south-east, to look for lodgings, and on his return it was decided, a little surprisingly, that after all the friends should part company. Lamb, still rather maliciously disposed towards Coleridge, wrote to Southey, when he learnt of it:

I hear that the Two Noble Englishmen have parted no sooner than they set foot on German earth, but I have not heard the reason— possibly to give novelists an handle to exclaim, 'Ah me! what things are perfect?'

Letters, however, from Poole and the Wordsworths make it clear that Lamb's suggestion was unfounded. Poole had always been doubtful about the amalgamation. Coleridge's object was to be where he could learn pure German; theirs rather to see the country. And they had to do it as economically as possible; Ratzeburg they found too expensive for them.[1] Here, on 1 October, Coleridge and Chester took up their abode in the house of a pastor, and stayed to 6 February, paying a visit to Lübeck in the course of October. Coleridge was well received by the notables of the place, since the English were then popular in Germany, and made rapid progress in his study of the language, although he never acquired a good accent. Ratzeburg was in fine wooded country, on the edge of a lake nine miles long, and Coleridge describes with enthusiasm the scenes of skating during the winter.[2] Meanwhile the Wordsworths had gone to Goslar, where they found social conditions not very comfortable for a man and his sister travelling together. They had meant to travel on foot through Upper Saxony, but inclement weather detained them. Wordsworth learnt little German, and wrote a good deal of poetry. With Coleridge they kept in touch through correspondence.[3]

In February, during the coldest nights for a century, Coleridge went to Hanover, where he obtained further influential introductions, and thence to Göttingen, which he reached, still accompanied by the faithful Chester, on 12 February. Here he had the company of other Englishmen, Charles and Frederick Parry (brothers of the Arctic

---

[1] *B.L.* ii. 165, 168; D. W. (*J.*), i. 24; W. 86; L. 43; P. i. 277.
[2] C. 88, 92, 93; *B.L.* ii. 165; D. W. (*J.*), i. 26.   [3] C. 93; W. 88–92.

explorer), Clement Carlyon, George Greenough, and
Anthony Hamilton, of St. John's, Cambridge. He matriculated at the University, and was taken to a students' club,
where he witnessed a scene of drunken revelry.

> I thought of what I had been at Cambridge, and of what I was, of
> the wild bacchanalian sympathy with which I had formerly joined
> similar parties, and of my total inability now to do aught but meditate,
> and the feeling of the deep alteration in my moral being gave the scene
> a melancholy interest to me.

He had himself been an abstainer from wine or fermented
liquor for over three months, and felt the better for it.
There seems, however, to have been some recourse to
opium.[1] Both Carlyon and Greenough have left reminiscences of him. To Carlyon, originally prepossessed against
him by his 'political frenzy' at Cambridge, he seems to have
talked freely: of Pantisocracy, which he now thought 'absurd
and visionary'; of Shakespeare, whose powers he believed
to have owed their vast expansion to 'the cheering breath
of popular applause' and the absence of 'stings of a traffick-
ing criticism'; of revealed religion, to which he was no
enemy, although Carlyon noted that, like other Göttingen
students, he did not go to church; of metaphysics, but 'an
old woman's grain of faith was worth them all'. Carlyon
noted his bad dress, which he asserted, 'with a singularly
coxcombical expression of countenance', was sure to be lost
sight of as soon as he began to talk, and his habit of fixing
his prominent eyes upon himself in a mirror, whenever
there was one in the room.[2] The months at Göttingen
appear to have been laborious ones. Coleridge came with
introductions to C. G. Heyne, the University Librarian. His
concern was still mainly with the language, including the
'Gothic and Theotuscan' origins, which he studied under
Olaus Tychsen. But he had conceived the idea of a life of
Lessing, and for this he collected copious materials, working harder than he hoped ever to have to work again.
'This endless transcription is such a body-and-soul-wearying
Purgatory.' He attended the physiological lectures of J. F.
Blumenbach, and heard of the new process of extracting

---

[1] C. 94; Lowes, 599.   [2] Carlyon, i. 16, 29, 92, 100.

sugar from beet, about which he said all Germany was mad.
With the rationalist J. G. Eichhorn he disputed on theology.
He spent £30 on buying books, chiefly on metaphysics,
'with a view to the one work to which I hope to dedicate
in silence the prime of my life'.[1] It is doubtful whether he
actually devoted much attention to metaphysics during his
stay in Germany. He seems, however, to have begun to
read Kant, who had been to him in 1796 'the most unintelligible Immanuel Kant', and Carlyon confirms a story
of the surprise of a German girl who found that he could
understand what was beyond her. In the version of this
story ascribed by Hazlitt to Coleridge himself the work of
Kant named is unfortunately one which does not exist.[2]

The Wordsworths left Goslar towards the end of February, and walked through the Harz forest to Nordhausen.
They contemplated further travels, and hoped to get to
Göttingen. Towards the end of April they came, but did
little more than pass through, and by the middle of May
were back in England. An ascent of the Brocken had been
planned, but it was thought too much for Dorothy, and
Wordsworth would not go without her.[3] The expedition,
of which we have accounts from Carlyon and Greenough,
as well as from Coleridge himself, took place in May.[4] The
two Parrys, Chester, and a son of Professor Blumenbach
went with the party. Coleridge was in high spirits and
loquacious. The start was on 11 May, and on the second
day they reached the Brocken. Climbing over boggy ground,
Coleridge discussed the sublime and beautiful, but there was
more of Coleridge in it than of Burke. They were too late
in the day for the spectre, but they saw the ring of stones
in which fairies danced on May-day. In the *Stammbuch* of
the Brocken inn Coleridge inscribed some verses of an exile,
which he had sent to Poole not long before, and in that of
Elbingerode, where they spent the third night, others descriptive of the Brocken itself and of thoughts of England

---

[1] C. 92, 94, 98; *B.L.* i. 137; *F.* i. 207, 209; Carlyon, i. 186, 191; Litchfield, 70.
[2] C. 68; *B.L.* i. 99, ii. 179; Carlyon, i. 162; Hazlitt, xii. 37; Wellek, 69.
[3] C. 97, 98; W. 90–4, 97; Carlyon, i. 196; Greenough, 555.
[4] G. 61; *New Monthly Mag.* (Oct. 1835); *Archiv* cxviii. 38; Gillman, 125; Carlyon,
i.32; Greenough, 559.

there.[1] He has much to say about the beauty of the spring scenery, with snow still lying over the higher slopes. On the fourth day they watched a Whit-Tuesday dance of peasants round a May-pole at Rubilland, and reached Blankenburg. The fifth, similarly diversified by a shooting-match at a stuffed bird on a Wernigerode May-pole, took them to Goslar, 'an ugly silent old desert of a city', and the sixth to Clausthal, where Coleridge thought writing a long letter to Sara preferable to going down a mine. They were then 'a hospital of bruised toes, swelled ancles, blistered soles, and excoriated heels', and were no doubt glad to see Göttingen again on 18 May. There were further expeditions a little later to the Hübichen-Stein, and by Hardenburg, where the King and Queen of Prussia were on a visit, to Hesse-Cassel, which was the most southern point in Germany reached by Coleridge. Here he lost his temper at some inhospitality in the ale-house, and said that the Hessians could not be Christians, with the result that the party was turned out and had to bivouac in a wood.[2]

When at Hamburg Coleridge expressed an intention of writing home twice a week, to his wife and Poole alternately. He did not, we may be sure, quite live up to this ideal, but more letters are upon record than have been preserved. He also meant to keep a journal and send it regularly.[3] The beginnings of this, rather than the letters, are probably the basis of the *Satyrane's Letters*, which he printed first in *The Friend* and afterwards in the *Biographia Literaria*.[4] They do not take him beyond Hamburg. Later the long descriptive letters on the Brocken tour suggest that the idea of a separate journal had been dropped. Towards the end of his life Coleridge gave two of these to S. C. Hall, who published extracts from them in the *Amulet* for 1829. Coleridge sent to Poole for a third, and all three appeared in full, after his death, in the *New Monthly Magazine* for 1835.[5] We have also some of Poole's letters to Coleridge.[6] They are full of good advice. He warns Coleridge against a disease

[1] *P.W.* 314, 315. [2] *Fr.* i. 39; Carlyon, i. 35, 151; Greenough, 556.
[3] C. 86, 87, 89, 92; P. i. 278. [4] *Fr.* (ed. 1), Nos. 14, 16, 18; *B.L.* ii. 132.
[5] C. 249 (misdated 1830 for 1821); *Addl. MS.* 35343, f. 382; P. ii. 258, 279; G. 72.
[6] P. i. 277.

of his mind, in the activity of imagination, which makes it death to him to chain his thoughts long to any particular object. 'This many of your friends falsely call irresolution.' Coleridge admits the disease, but hopes, if he cannot cure it, to suspend its operation for the next three months, while he works on Lessing. 'The journey to Germany has certainly *done me good*. My habits are less irregular, and my *mind* more in my own power.' He wrote also, as in duty bound, to Josiah Wedgwood. For him he had compiled 'six huge letters', apparently on social conditions in Germany. One of these, dealing with the system of land-tenure, has survived.[1] But he did not write to Daniel Stuart, who had asked him to send communications on German literature to the *Morning Post*;[2] and he failed to keep a promise of writing to the Wordsworths after they left him at Göttingen.[3]

Coleridge's letters to his wife are very affectionate. 'Over what place does the moon hang to your eye, my dearest Sara?' begins the first, and ends with a note of the sky and colours of the clouds which he sees at night, 'quite English, just as if I were coming out of T. Poole's homeward with you in my arm'. The subscription is elaborate. 'In the full and noblest sense of the word, and after the antique principles of *Religion*, unsophisticated by Philosophy', he will be, he trusts, 'your husband faithful unto death'; and the 'faithful' is iterated in several other letters. He sees 'a very beautiful little woman—less, I think, than you'. Carlyon noted that he spoke affectionately of his wife at Göttingen.[4] To his children, also, the letters have many tender references. It is clear that, although he enjoyed his new experiences and could be animated in company, Coleridge was constantly homesick. He felt uprooted, and if he remained long among aliens would wholly lose his powers of intellect.

Love is the vital air of my genius, and I have not seen one human being in Germany whom I can conceive it *possible* for me to *love*, no, not *one*; in my mind they are an unlovely race, these Germans.

To be abroad, he thought, must make every man a patriot and a loyalist, 'almost a Pittite'. It is not inconsistent with

[1] C. 92; G. 62; Litchfield, 68.   [2] P. i. 279, 282.   [3] W. 97.   [4] C. 87, 88, 96, 97.

this that in old age he looked back to his sojourn in Germany as 'a spot of sunshine in my past life'.[1] The sense of isolation was aggravated by the lack of regular news from England. The mails were often delayed, especially in winter, when ice blocked the mouth of the Elbe; and on every post-day Coleridge was in an agony of expectation. When a letter came he trembled to open it. When it did not, he fancied that Sara wished to shorten his absence by making it insupportable. He had misgivings about his babies. 'Absence makes it painful to be a father.'[2]

The misgivings were only too well justified. In November Berkeley was inoculated with small-pox, and appeared to have taken it well, although Coleridge cried himself blind over the news. Afterwards the child developed a cough, and change of air was advised. On 31 December Mrs. Coleridge took him to her mother's at Bristol. Here the cough proved to be consumptive, and on 10 February Berkeley died in convulsions. By Poole's advice, nothing was said for a time to Coleridge. But a month later it was thought better to let him know, probably because there was an obvious chance of the tidings coming to him indirectly. His reaction was a characteristic one, less of grief than of intellectual perplexity. 'For the death of the baby I have *not* wept', he wrote; and again, 'The few, the slow, the quiet tears which I shed, are the accompaniments of high and solemn thought, not the workings of pain or sorrow.' He turned into the fields, and mused on the riddles of life. 'Oh this strange, strange, strange scene-shifter Death!—that giddies one with insecurity and so unsubstantiates the living things that one has grasped and handled!' What is life? Can vital force perish? Is not the death of a child in itself a sign of immortality? 'I find it wise and human to believe, even on slight evidence, opinions, the contrary of which cannot be proved, and which promote our happiness without hampering our intellect.' To his wife he wrote hoping that a shared sorrow would always be a restraining thought, 'when in moments of fretfulness and imbecility I am disposed to anger or reproach'. He now, of course, became full of fears for Hartley, linked

[1] C. 94; *Archiv* cxviii, 58; Watson, 53.   [2] C. 89, 90, 92–4.

up with the songs of nightingales in the spring woods and
his own poem *The Nightingale*. Would Hartley, too, be
dead before he got home? He had a strange sensation as
if none whom he entirely loved could die while he was
present.[1]

It was, indeed, time for Coleridge to return. The three
or four months which he had originally contemplated had
already doubled their number. In January he had hoped to
be at Stowey by 1 May. By February the provision he had
made for his wife's maintenance was exhausted, and she had
more than once to borrow from Poole. In April Coleridge
wrote of coming in another ten or eleven weeks, and when
she protested explained that, with reading and transcribing
from eight to ten hours a day, it would still take him into
June to finish collecting material for a work, no doubt that
on Lessing, which alone could save them from embarrassment and debt, and would also establish his character for
industry and erudition, and he hoped also for reflection and
genius.[2] He had, of course, spent more in Germany than he
had expected. Ratzeburg had been costly, but at Göttingen
he took cheap lodgings 'in a damned dirty hole in the Burg
Strasse', and bought his own food at a cook-shop. At the
end of May he told Josiah Wedgwood, with whose German
agents, the Von Axens, he had a credit, that he had drawn
£103, and asked leave to anticipate his next year's annuity
by £40 or £50. By Christmas he felt sure that he should
have got straight. No doubt he was relying upon the proceeds of the Lessing book. A debt to Carlyon was repaid
after his return.[3] The letters to Poole are much concerned
with the question of his future residence. He did not want
to leave the neighbourhood of Stowey. But the Lime Street
cottage would not do any longer. He could not be either
comfortable or useful there; and certainly its conditions
were not well adapted to literary work. Woodlands, not
far away, had taken his fancy, but Poole found that no suitable house there could be had. There was one in Stowey

---

[1] C. 90, 92–8; P. i. 281, 284, 288; M. 1.
[2] C. 93, 96–8; M. 1–3; Litchfield, 68.
[3] C. 92, 93, 96; Litchfield, 68; Greenough, 565.

itself, but Coleridge disliked the idea of living opposite to a man who had been rude to his wife. The problem was further complicated by his personal relations, on the one hand to Poole, and on the other to Wordsworth. He was at this period like a piece of metal between two equally powerful magnets. To Poole he had written, when he left England:

> Of many friends whom I love and esteem, my head and heart have ever chosen you as the friend—as the one being in whom is involved the full and whole meaning of that sacred title.

But he did not want to part with Wordsworth, and Wordsworth did not want to part with him. The best solution would be that Wordsworth too should return to Stowey. Wordsworth's own mind, however, was divided. Evidently he hankered after the Lakes. He gave the want of books as his chief objection to Stowey. At the Lakes he would have free access to the great libraries of Sir Wilfrid Lawson and Sir Frederick Vane. Would not Coleridge come too? Coleridge thought that a country gentleman's fashionable library would be of little use to him.

> I think it better once in a year to walk to Cambridge, in the summer vacation—perhaps I may be able to get rooms for nothing, and there for a couple of months read like a Turk on a given plan, and return home with a mass of materials which, with dear, *independent* Poetry, will fully employ the remaining year.

At last, when Wordsworth passed through Göttingen, Coleridge came, for the time, to a resolution, which he reported to Poole.

> I told him plainly that *you* had been the man in whom *first* and in whom alone I had felt an *anchor*! With all my other connections I felt a dim sense of insecurity and uncertainty, terribly incompatible. W. was affected *to tears*, very much affected; but he deemed the vicinity of a library absolutely *necessary* to his health, nay to his existence. It is painful to me, too, to think of not living near him; for he is a *good* and *kind* man, and the only one whom in *all* things I feel my superior —and you will believe me when I say that I have few feelings more pleasurable than to find myself, in intellectual faculties, an inferior. But my resolve is fixed, *not to leave you till you leave me*!

So for the present the matter rested. In June Wordsworth was still not quite determined against Stowey; and when he

finally settled at Grasmere, one cannot think that the neighbourhood of libraries had much to do with it.[1] At last, on
24 June, Coleridge made up his mind to return. Rather
amazingly, he had contemplated an extension of his tour
through Denmark, Sweden, and Norway, but company
failed him until too late, and he put it off until next spring,
the Greek Kalends. Carlyon and Greenough went with
him and Chester as far as Brunswick, and there left them.
On their way they once more climbed the Brocken, and
once more failed to see the spectre. They stopped also at
Wolfenbüttel, where Coleridge wanted to make further
researches on Lessing, 'which it would be criminal to
neglect', but found the librarian discourteous. By 18 July
he was at Cuxhaven, having lost his chests of books, which,
however, followed him to England; and by 29 July he was
at Stowey.[2]

The *Lyrical Ballads* had been published in September 1798,
during the absence of the authors, and without their names.
But it was not long before these became known.[3] Coleridge's
contributions, besides the *Ancient Mariner*, were *The Nightingale* and two fragments from *Osorio*, under the titles of *The
Foster-mother's Tale* and *The Dungeon*.[4] But *The Nightingale*
had replaced *Lewti*, which had actually been set up in proof,
and then cancelled, presumably to secure anonymity, since
it had already appeared in the *Morning Post*. Manuscript
copies of *Lewti* show that the name had replaced an original
Mary, and an intermediate Cora. According to a note by
Southey, Coleridge had here 'corrected' a poem written by
Wordsworth as a boy, and if so 'Mary' may point to Mary
Hutchinson, rather than Mary Evans.[5] A notice of the
Ballads in the *Critical Review* for October 1798 gave them
very qualified praise.[6] The writer admired *The Foster-
mother's Tale* and *The Dungeon*. But of the *Ancient Mariner* he
writes:

The piece appears to be perfectly original in style as well as in story.

---

[1] C. 86, 92, 98; W. 89, 97; P. i. 286.
[2] C. 99; Carlyon, i. 161, 170, 186; Greenough, 562.
[3] W. 82, 84; *Monthly Mag.* vi. 297; De Q. ii. 139.　　[4] *P.W.* 182, 185, 264.
[5] *P.W.* 253, 1049; Wise, *Bibl. of Wordsworth*, 14; Lowes, 513.
[6] 2 *Critical Review*, xxiv. 197; cf. S. (T.), i. 221.

Many of the stanzas are laboriously beautiful, but in connection they are absurd or unintelligible.

After a quotation of the passage on the 'roaring wind' he adds:

It is a Dutch attempt at German sublimity. Genius has here been employed in producing a poem of little merit.

Wordsworth comes off no better. *Tintern Abbey* was admired, but the reviewer was altogether displeased with *The Thorn*, and did not think that *The Idiot Boy* deserved the labour bestowed on it. Nevertheless 'every piece discovers genius; and ill as the author has frequently employed his talents, they certainly rank him with the best of living poets'. There is no indication here of any knowledge of a dual authorship, but the writer was generally taken to be Southey, and to him Lamb protested:

If you wrote that review in 'Crit. Rev.' I am sorry you are so sparing of praise to the 'Ancient Marinere';—so far from calling it, as you do, with some wit, but more severity, 'A Dutch attempt', &c., I call it a right English attempt, and a successful one, to dethrone German sublimity. You have selected a passage fertile in unmeaning miracles, but have passed by fifty passages as miraculous as the miracles they celebrate. I never so deeply felt the pathetic as in that part,

> A spring of love gush'd from my heart,
> And I bless'd them unaware—

It stung me into high pleasure through sufferings. Lloyd does not like it; his head is too metaphysical, and your taste too correct; at least I must allege something against you both, to excuse my own dotage—

> So lonely 'twas, that God himself
> Scarce seemèd there to be!—&c., &c.

But you allow some elaborate beauties—you should have extracted 'em. 'The Ancient Marinere' plays more tricks with the mind than that last poem, which is yet one of the finest written.

It is hard to see a contemporary poem in its true perspective, but I do not know that the *Ancient Mariner* has been better criticized than by Lamb.[1] Wordsworth was also much annoyed, but he takes rather an odd line.[2]

Southey's review I have seen. He knew that I published those poems for money and money alone. He knew that money was of

[1] L. 40; *M.L.R.* xxxiii. 409. The 'last poem' was *Tintern Abbey.*   [2] W. 99.

importance to me. If he could not conscientiously have spoken differently of the volume, he ought to have declined the task of reviewing it.

A later notice in the *Monthly Review* is attributed by a note in the Hope copy at the Bodleian to 'D^r B . . . y'—Charles Burney.[1] Here the *Ancient Mariner* is 'the strangest story of a cock and a bull that we ever saw on paper', and 'a rhapsody of unintelligible wildness and incoherence', although with 'poetical touches of an exquisite kind'. On the other hand, 'The Nightingale sings a strain of true and beautiful poetry; Miltonic, yet original; reflective, and interesting in an uncommon degree'. Burney, too, does not seem to have discerned more than one hand in the volume. The *Lyrical Ballads* did not sell well. Sara Coleridge wrote placidly to Poole in March 1799, 'The Lyrical Ballads are laughed at and disliked by all with very few excepted'; and again in April, 'The Lyrical Ballads are not liked at all by any.'[2] Coleridge himself says in jest that the purchasers were mostly seafaring men, who misapprehended the title of the *Ancient Mariner*.[3] Cottle had given up bookselling. He had sold most of the issue of five hundred copies to John and Arthur Arch of Paternoster Row, whose imprint is on some that survive, and the copyright to Longman, whose is on others. But Longman valued it at nothing, and Cottle then begged it back from him, and gave it to Wordsworth.[4] Wordsworth's own view was that the *Ancient Mariner*, with its old words and its 'strangeness', had on the whole been an injury to the book and, if it should ever come to a second edition, thought of substituting 'some little things which would be more likely to suit the common taste'.[5]

[1] W. 98; *Monthly Review* (June 1799), xxix. 204.
[2] M. 2, 3.   [3] A., p. 128.
[4] W. 93–5; *Rem.* 185, 257, 259; *M.L.R.* xxxiii. 406; Wise, *Bibl. of Wordsworth*, 28.
[5] W. 96.

VII

THE JOURNALIST

August 1799—July 1800

COLERIDGE did not, after all, sit down to restore his finances, and establish his character for industry, erudition, and genius, with the help of Lessing, by the Christmas of 1799. One of his first acts at Stowey was to make overtures for a reconciliation with Southey. Domestic affection, he wrote, was hard upon him, and his health was declining. He did not expect 'participation in each other's moral being'. But he could not forget their common past, and begged that Southey would be tolerant of him, and that, if they met, they might not 'withhold from each other the outward expressions of daily kindliness'. Southey at first hung back, on the ground that Coleridge had slandered him, but on being assured that 'I never charged you with aught but your deep and implacable enmity towards me', and on receiving a confirmation from Poole that Coleridge had always spoken of him with affection, he gave way, and in August spent some time at Stowey, where he was once more writing 'at the same table with Coleridge'.[1] They composed joint verses entitled *The Devil's Thoughts*, which attracted some attention in the *Morning Post*, although their humour has perhaps rather evaporated to-day. They also planned a poem on Mohammed of which only a fragment remains. Southey expected that he would have nearly the whole work to do, as Coleridge's ardour was not lasting.[2] A joint tour followed in September, which took them to Ottery, and on to Exeter and South Devon, which Coleridge thought 'tame to Quantock, Porlock, Culbone, and Linton'. Both men have recorded impressions of the Ottery kinsfolk. Southey respected George's character, but 'he told me that from the age of eighteen he had never leisure to read a book through'.

[1] C. 99 and note; G. 63; Southey (*W.*), i. 78. I suspect that Coleridge wrote 'domestic affliction'.

[2] C. 101, 103; G. 64; Southey (*L.*), ii. 47; (*T.*), i. 293; *P.W.* 319.

Edward, he thought, 'seldom talks much to the purpose'. He was amused by the old mother, who broke in upon an argument between Samuel and his brothers with, 'Ah, if your poor father had been alive, he'd soon have convinced you.' Coleridge believed that he himself practised reservation.

I have three brothers, that is to say, relations by gore. Two are parsons, and one is a colonel. George and the colonel, good men as times go—very good men—but alas! we have neither tastes nor feelings in common. This I wisely learnt from their conversation, and did not suffer them to learn it from mine.

He enjoyed the clouted cream, however, and drank 'Church and King', keeping his comments to himself. The neighbourhood of Hucks and of some local free-thinkers afforded relaxation.[1]

Coleridge left Southey at Exeter, but many letters passed between them during the next few months. The return to Stowey was hastened by the fact that Hartley had caught the itch, and Coleridge was now tortured by the mercurial girdle which the medical science of the day thought prophylactic. He had also a rheumatic attack, the worst since his school-days, but nevertheless remained 'sunk in Spinoza, as undisturbed as a Toad in a Rock'. Spinoza, not Lessing! Meanwhile, 'poor Sara', who had lost her domestic, was 'tired off her legs with servantry' in their 'little Hovel'. Coleridge also planned a school-book, and thought he would get a couple of pupils. He spent a few days with Josiah Wedgwood, then at Upcott in Devonshire.[2] Like Southey, who reviewed the book, he was interested in Landor's *Gebir*, but could not learn the name of the author.[3] In October he was at Bristol, contemplating a visit to London, and there made a new friend in Humphry Davy, whom Beddoes had brought to take charge of the laboratory at his Pneumatic Institute. Davy was studying nitrous oxide, then regarded not as an anaesthetic, but as an exhilarant, which at twopence a dose would supersede alcohol. Both Coleridge

[1] C. 100; G. 64; Southey (*W.*), i. 81; (*T.*), i. 293; *App.* no. ii.
[2] C. 101; G. 64, 65.   [3] C. 101, 107.

and Southey seem to have experimented with it.¹ While at
Bristol Coleridge, who had been urging Wordsworth, since
his return, to finish *The Recluse*, and if possible to re-take
Alfoxden, which he would not do, now received alarming
news, in fact unfounded, of his friend's health, and hurried
up to the North, with Joseph Cottle, who already had an
invitation, to see him. The Wordsworths, when they came
from Germany, had gone to Durham.² Here, in a grazing
farm on the banks of the Tees, lived Thomas Hutchinson,
with his brother George, and three sisters, Mary, Sara, and
Joanna. Another brother, John, was a ham-factor and
banker at Stockton on Tees. Mary had been a close friend of
Dorothy in her youth at Penrith, and is believed to have been
an early flame of William's. Coleridge arrived at Sockburn
towards the end of October, and recorded in his notebook:

Few moments in life are so interesting as those of our affectionate
reception from a stranger who is the dear friend of your dear friend!
How often you have been the subject of conversation, and how
affectionately!³

The reference is no doubt to Mary Hutchinson, who, as we
have seen, had just missed meeting him at Racedown, in
1797. It was not, however, Mary, but Sara, who was
destined to bring a tragic element into his life. After a few
days together at Sockburn, Coleridge and Wordsworth
started for a walking-tour in the Lakes, which took them
to Grasmere, where Wordsworth saw Dove Cottage, soon
afterwards to become his home. On the way they dropped
Cottle, and were joined by Wordsworth's sailor brother
John.⁴ On 10 and 15 November Coleridge was at Keswick,
meaning to go to London. But instead he seems to have
left Wordsworth to finish his tour alone, and to have returned himself to Sockburn. An incident of this second
visit is the subject of another note-book entry:⁵

Nov. 24ᵗʰ—the Sunday—Conundrums & Puns & Stories & Laughter

¹ C. 101, 103, 105, 106; G. 66, 70, 71; *Rem.* 259; T. E. Thorpe, *Davy*, 40.
² C. 101, 102; *Rem.* 258; W. 101, 102; W. *Memoirs*, i. 159; *Addl. MS.* 35343, f. 213.
³ *A.P.* 8. Harper, 302, gives the precise date of 26 October for Coleridge's
arrival, but for that I can find no evidence. A note-book shows him on the road
during 22–4 October.   ⁴ W. 103.
⁵ *Asra*, 307. I owe the precise facts to Miss K. H. Coburn, who kindly examined
the note-books for me.

—with Jack Hutchinson — — Stood up round the Fire, et Sarae
manum a tergo longum in tempus prensatam / and tunc temporis, tunc
primum, amor me levi spiculo, venenato, eheu! & insanabili, &c.

This, however, as its terms suggest, is not a contemporary
record; it was added when copying entries of 1799 into a
note-book of 1803. But it is certain that in 1799 or later
Coleridge fell in love with Sara Hutchinson, and that for
many years this hopeless passion continued to dominate
him. Its beginnings inspired the poem *Love*, which appeared
on 21 December in the *Morning Post*, as an *Introduction
to the Tale of the Dark Ladie*. The *Dark Ladie* itself is a
ballad fragment from the *Annus Mirabilis*, and only a 'sister
tale' to that sketched in *Love*. But 'the statue of an armed
knight', against which Genevieve leans in *Love*, is at Sockburn, and there too is a 'grey stone', which is merged with
the statue in the first draft of the poem. To Sockburn may
also belong an undated fragment.[1]

> All look and likeness caught from earth,
> All accident of kin and birth,
> Had pass'd away. There was no trace
> Of aught on that illumined face,
> Uprais'd beneath the rifted stone
> But of one spirit all her own;—
> She, she herself, and only she,
> Shone through her body visibly.

At Keswick Coleridge had 'by accident' an offer 'of a
pleasant kind', which would take him to London for four
or five months. This offer, which he may have himself
invited, was no doubt from Stuart, who, in spite of Coleridge's cavalier attitude in the past, was now prepared to give
him regular employment on the staff of the *Morning Post*.
His poetical contributions had already been resumed in
August, and in September had come *The Devil's Thoughts*.
He reached London about 27 November, recording in
his note-book the contrast of the immovable city, 'a huge
place of sepulchres through which hosts of spirits were
gliding', with 'the universal motion, the harmonious system
of motions in the country, and everywhere in Nature'; took

[1] *P.W.* 293, 330, 393, 1052.

lodgings at 21 Buckingham Street, Strand; and wrote for
his wife at Stowey to join him.¹ His first prose contribution
to the *Morning Post* may have been on 7 December. Between
that and 21 April 1800, forty have been identified, some
with certainty, others by plausible conjecture.² He writes
of himself as engaged to 'undertake the literary and political
department'. But that is putting it rather high. Daniel
Stuart, the proprietor of the paper, himself acted as editor,
and Coleridge's position was clearly that of what would now
be called a leader-writer. His salary paid all his London expenses; his grandson found some evidence that it was four
guineas a week; he says, himself, of this or a later period,
five guineas or five pounds. The duties occupied only his
afternoons and evenings, leaving the mornings free for
other literary work, by which he hoped to make £150, as he
had already anticipated the whole of his annuity for 1800.
'I work from I-rise to I-set', he says.³ He claims to have
stipulated with Stuart that the paper should 'thenceforwards
be conducted on certain fixed and announced principles', by
which it became *anti-ministerial* indeed, yet with a very
qualified approbation of the opposition, and with far greater
earnestness and zeal both anti-jacobin and anti-gallican'.
This Stuart repudiates. The politics of the *Morning Post*, he
says, were already such as Coleridge indicates.⁴ His own
political development had in fact been much like Coleridge's
own. As an official, with his brother-in-law Mackintosh, of
the Friends of the People, he had been even more deeply
involved in democratic agitation. But the Friends had ceased
to exist, and the *Morning Post* was an independent paper of
liberal and moderate views, opposed to Jacobinism, but also
opposed to Pitt, and to the continuance of war with France.
It was again unfortunate for Coleridge that just at this
juncture *The New Morality* should reappear in *The Beauties
of the Anti-Jacobin*, with a note upon him which asserts that:

He has left his native country, commenced citizen of the world, left

---

¹ C. 102, 103; *Rem.* 149 (misdated); *B.L.* i. 141; *L.* 53; 2 *Gent. Mag.* ix. 485;
A.P. 8.
² *O.T.* 179-408; Wise, 213-19, 257-64.
³ C. 104; G. 305, 375; Litchfield, 74; *B.L.* i. 141; *P.* i. 1.
⁴ *B.L.* i. 141; 2 *Gent. Mag.* ix. 485, 577; *Studies*, 43.

his poor children fatherless and his wife destitute. *Ex his disce* his
friends Lamb and Southey!

It was premature. Coleridge was advised that an action for
libel would lie, but did not bring one.[1]

He was well satisfied with his first attempts for Stuart.
'Anything not bad in the paper, that is not yours, is mine',
he wrote to Southey.[2] Stuart, in retrospection, is critical.
He found Coleridge's conversation brilliant. But even when
not disabled by illness, he could not write daily on the
occurrences of the day. 'The thought of compulsion dis-
armed him.'[3] The actual record, so far as we can trace it,
does not, at any rate at first, quite bear this out. Contributions, some certainly Coleridge's, others reasonably ascribed
to him on internal grounds, appeared with regularity every
day or two from the last week of December to the end of
January, with the exception of one week, during which he
may have been ill. They are almost all upon foreign politics,
and amount to an effective and well-sustained attack upon
the refusal of Pitt's government to accept Bonaparte's offer
of peace negotiations, when he became First Consul under
the new French constitution established by the *coup d'état* of
9 November 1799. There is a good deal of sound political
thinking in them. The actual constitution Coleridge regarded
as a makeshift, not destined to endure. He condemned
the methods by which Bonaparte had arrived at power,
and in private called him a 'reptile'.[4] But he argued that
the power was being used to a good end. The government of the republic had returned to stability on the basis,
not of personal rights, but of the rights of property. Jacobinism, at any rate, was dead, and with Jacobinism the alleged
justification for war. Rightly or wrongly, he thought at this
stage that Bonaparte was sincere in his desire for peace.
The articles are effectively written in a less involved style
than became habitual with Coleridge later. They are fully
on a level with the best of modern political leaders; rather
more literary in tone, since the range of readers was less
wide and better cultivated. There is much pungency of

expression; William Windham, in particular, the Secretary
for War, must have writhed under some of the hits directed at
him. Coleridge's mind, one may judge, more capable of
bursts of energy than of prolonged occupation with a single
theme, was well adapted to the swallow-flights of journalism. Towards the end of January he was frequenting the
theatres, with the idea of writing dramatic essays in the
paper. If he wrote any, they have not been identified.[1]
Greenough was told that he went to Drury Lane pit four
times a week, in order to make himself known, and was
introduced to Sheridan, 'whom he detests'. About the same
time he began to attend the debates in Parliament.[2] Upon
his report of a speech by Pitt in favour of a subsidy to
Austria he liked to look back. It was written out from
'heads and torsos of sentences' scrawled in a note-book, and
comparison with other reports shows that, although Coleridge succeeded in preserving Pitt's logic, the eloquent expression was all his own. He claims that Canning, calling
on business at the *Morning Post* office, said of the report, 'It
does more credit to the author's head than to his memory.'
Stuart, however, denies that Canning was ever at the *Morning Post* in those days. He thinks that Coleridge's most
effective contributions were a leader on a speech by Lord
Grenville, and an elaborate *Character of Pitt*, which is certainly a vigorous piece of writing. A *Character of Bonaparte*
was announced to follow, and was promised to Stuart at
intervals during a period of ten or twelve years, but never
written. According to Coleridge, an agent of Bonaparte in
London had hopes that it would be a favourable one.[3]
But by February Coleridge was already tired of his job. The
attendances at debates, in particular, he found an unpleasant
activity and 'too, too fatiguing'. He had sat in the House,
which was 'hideously crowded' for nineteen hours, and then
written for another five. More than once he sent Stuart
apologies for failing him, and on 18 February he declared,
'I shall do no more for Stuart.' He did not at once retire,
but the identified contributions become more and more

---

[1] Litchfield, 74.   [2] C. 106; Litchfield, 79; Greenough, 564.
[3] C. 107; G. 127; Gillman, 193, 207; 2 *Gent. Mag.* ix. 485; cf. pp. 136, 230, 267, 283.

sparse, and on 27 March they end. Thereafter, Coleridge
told Stuart, he would do what he could, but not for a regular
stipend. 'That harasses me'.[1]

Stuart was unwilling to lose Coleridge, and offered him
shares both in the *Morning Post* and in the evening *Courier*,
of which he was part proprietor. Wordsworth thought
that it would be a good opening for his friend. To Poole
Coleridge wrote that, if he accepted the proposal, he could
make almost sure of £2,000 a year.[2]

But I told him I would not give up the country and the lazy reading
of old folios for two thousand times two thousand pounds; in short,
that beyond £250 a year I consider money as a real evil—at which he
stared.

It must have been mainly on the strength of this winter's
work, although also no doubt on some attacks upon Bonaparte in the *Morning Post* of 1802 and some sporadic contributions to the *Courier*, that Coleridge stressed in later
years his services to journalism, and regretted the withdrawal from more valuable activities which they involved.
To Stuart himself he wrote of them modestly enough. But
the claim in the *Biographia Literaria* to have made it a condition
of his employment that the political tone of the paper should
be modified to his approval not unnaturally met with resentment from Stuart, although no breach of friendship was the
result.[3] After Coleridge's death, however, his nephew was
indiscreet enough to publish in the first edition of the *Table
Talk* two passages, in one of which Coleridge referred to
Stuart as 'a very knowing person' and in the other asserted
that his own participation had raised the sale of the *Morning
Post* from an inconsiderable number to 7,000 a day in the
course of one year. Correspondence between Stuart and the
editor followed, and the offending statements were modified
or withdrawn.[4] In the *Gentleman's Magazine* for 1838 Stuart
gave a full account of his relations with Coleridge, and while
doing full justice to Coleridge's abilities, if he would only

[1] C. 106, 107; Litchfield, 79; L.P. 1–3.
[2] O.T. xc; *Addl. MS.* 35343, f. 225; Greenough, 564.
[3] C. 209; G. 205; A. 15; *L.P.* 24; *B.L.* i. 141, 144.
[4] *T.T.* (1835), i. 172; ii. 49; cf. 3rd ed., 174.

have taken the pains to apply them in a practical way, made
it very clear that his actual contribution to the fortunes
of the *Post* and the *Courier* was comparatively slight. A
further discussion of the subject by Sara Coleridge in the
Biographical Supplement gives no ground for modifying this
conclusion.[1]

It was an over-estimate of his powers which led Coleridge
to suppose that he could effectively combine journalism in
the afternoons with other remunerative literary work in the
mornings. The nature of that work is not at first quite clear.
He writes of compilations for booksellers.[2] One of these,
if there were more than one, was certainly Richard Phillips,
who published school-books and popular treatises. It is
doubtful whether Coleridge ever finished anything for
Phillips, who was pressing him in August 1800, and to
whom he was still in debt for an advance of £25 in January
1801. He could get another £25 by a fortnight's labour, 'but
the fellow's name is become so infamous, that it would be
worse than any thing I have yet done to appear in public as
his Hack'.[3] A start had also been made in London with an
essay on the progressiveness of man and the principles of
population. Coleridge apologizes to Tom Wedgwood for
turning from his personal interests to so abstract a subject.
But that was always his disease, and now he could not get
rid of it, even if he wished to.

Life was so flat a thing without enthusiasm, that if for a moment
it leaves me, I have a sort of a stomach-sensation attached to all my
Thoughts, like those which succeed to the pleasurable operation of a
dose of opium.

The work on Lessing, too, was still looming in the background.[4] Probably all other schemes were diverted by a
proposal from Longman for a translation of Schiller's plays
on *Wallenstein*. At this Coleridge was 'fagging' by 1 March.
It had to be done in a hurry, so that the publication in
England might synchronize with that of the German originals
abroad; and no doubt it accounts in part for the fall-off in
journalistic output. 'These cursed Plays play the devil with

---

[1] 2 *Gent. Mag.* ix. 485, 577; x. 22, 124; *Biog. Suppl.* (T. ii. 76).
[2] C. 103–4; Litchfield, 74.
[3] C. 106, 107, 114; G. 81, 83; P. ii. 11.   [4] C. 104, 105; Litchfield, 74.

me', he says in one of his apologies to Stuart. Later he notes 'the deep unutterable Disgust, which I had suffered in the translation of that accursed Wallenstein'. However, *The Piccolomini* duly appeared in the summer, and was shortly followed by *The Death of Wallenstein*. But *Wallenstein's Camp* and an essay on the genius of Schiller, which were also advertised, passed into oblivion. Coleridge treated his text with freedom, and here and there pruned or amplified it to his own taste. In the following passage, perhaps the best in the volumes, twelve lines of Schiller have become twenty of Coleridge.

> For fable is Love's world, his home, his birth-place;
> Delightedly dwells he 'mong fays and talismans,
> And spirits; and delightedly believes
> Divinities, being himself divine.
> The intelligible forms of ancient poets,
> The fair humanities of old religion,
> The Power, the Beauty, and the Majesty,
> That had their haunts in dale, or piny mountain,
> Or forest by slow stream, or pebbly spring,
> Or chasms and wat'ry depths; all these have vanished.
> They live no longer in the faith of reason!
> But still the heart doth need a language, still
> Doth the old instinct bring back the old names,
> And to yon starry world they now are gone,
> Spirits or gods, that used to share this earth
> With man as with their friend; and to the lover
> Yonder they move, from yonder visible sky
> Shoot influence down: and even at this day
> 'Tis Jupiter who brings whate'er is great,
> And Venus who brings everything that's fair.

The translations were not a financial success. The copies became 'winding-sheets for pilchards' or 'extant only by the kind partiality of the trunk-makers'. Coleridge claims to have warned Longman that this would be so. Longman lost £250, of which Coleridge had £50, 'poor pay, Heaven knows'. But in after life he spoke of *Wallenstein* as 'a specimen of my happiest attempt, during the prime manhood of my intellect, before I had been buffeted by adversity or crossed by fatality'.[1]

[1] C. 109, 130, 194; G. 68, 69, 75, 76, 78, 195, 282; T. 101; Litchfield, 104, 105; L.P. 3; L. 62, 65, 75; Fr. iii. 79; A, p. 51; Grattan, ii. 112; P.W. 598, 648; Schiller, *Piccolomini*, iii. 4.

There are several letters from London to Southey and replies by Southey. For his friend's literary work Coleridge is full of suggestions, and ready with offers of collaboration. They might even 'toss up' a novel together, since Godwin had made £400 by *St. Leon*. He introduced Southey's *Thalaba* to Longman, who published it a year later. They discussed the second volume of the *Annual Anthology*, which Southey was editing, and for which he tried to persuade Coleridge to finish *Christabel*. Coleridge wanted him to come to London. But Southey's health was failing. Could not Coleridge go abroad with him, to Italy or the East? Coleridge could not, at present. Lessing stood in the way. But he dreamed of a pleasant little colony for a few years in Italy or the south of France later. 'Peace will soon come.'[1] The *Annual Anthology* duly appeared, without *Christabel*, but with twenty-seven other contributions by Coleridge, mostly reprints or trifling epigrams, with the exception of the *Lime-Tree Bower*, here for the first time published.[2] A third volume, left for Coleridge to supervise, if he should be in Bristol, got no farther. Southey himself went to Lisbon in April. There was an exchange of farewell letters. 'Be my executor', wrote Southey, 'in case I am summoned upon the grand tour of the universe.' He was taking Coleridge's poems, and begged him to write often. Coleridge, on his side, was affectionate.

The time returns upon me, Southey! when we dreamt our dream, and that a glorious one—when we ate together, and thought each other greater and better than all the world beside. Those days can never be forgotten, and till they are forgotten, we cannot, if we would, cease to love each other.

But he did not write to Southey in Portugal, nor did Southey much expect it.[3]

After a couple of months in London Coleridge's wife went to friends in the country. He seems to have paid a visit to Purkis at Brentford, and then taken up his abode with Charles Lamb at Pentonville.[4] With Lamb, as well as with Southey, there must have been a reconciliation on the

---

[1] C. 101–9; Southey (L.), ii. 24, 36, 39. [2] Wise, 58.
[3] *I.L.N.*; Southey (L.), ii. 53; (*W.*), i. 101, 104, 117; (*T.*), i. 358.
[4] C. 106, 107; L. 62.

return from Germany. A correspondence in the autumn had left Coleridge faintly annoyed.[1]

I have a great affection for Lamb, but I have likewise a perfect Lloyd and Lambophobia! Independent of the irritation attending an epistolary controversy with them, their *prose* comes so damn'd dear. Lloyd especially writes with a woman's fluency in a large rambling hand, most dull though profuse of feeling. I received from them in last quarter letters so many, that with the postage I might have bought Birch's Milton.

Clearly the reconciliation did not, except perhaps on paper, extend to Lloyd. Coleridge still thought that he had not a good heart and was a perilous acquaintance.[2] Even the tolerant Lamb may have been rather disillusioned with him. Lloyd had been flirting with one Mary Hayes, an authoress and friend of Godwin, and laughing over the letters he received from her. He had maligned Coleridge to Lamb, who took it lightly.

I cannot but smile at Lloyd's beginning to find out, that Coleridge can tell lyes. He brings a serious charge against him—that he told Caldwell he had no engagement with the Newspapers! As long as Lloyd or I have known Col., so long have we known him in the daily & hourly habit of quizzing the world by lyes, most unaccountable & most disinterested fictions.

Afterwards he learnt that Caldwell had declared Lloyd's story to be itself untrue. In December he knew that Coleridge was in London, although he had not yet seen him, and by February he had been drunk two nights running at Coleridge's lodgings.[3] The association at Pentonville seems to have been a pleasant one. On 17 March Lamb writes:

I am living in a continuous feast. Coleridge has been with me now for nigh three weeks, and the more I see of him in the quotidian undress and relaxation of his mind, the more cause I see to love him, and believe him a *very good man*, and all those foolish impressions to the contrary fly off like morning slumbers. He is engaged in translations, which I hope will keep him this month to come. He is uncommonly kind and friendly to me. He ferrets me day and night to *do something*. He tends me, amidst all his own worrying and heart-oppressing occupations, as a gardener tends his young *tulip*. Marry come up! what a pretty similitude, and how like your humble servant! He has lugged me to the brink of engaging to a newspaper.

[1] C. 101.   [2] C. 101.   [3] C. 105; L. 58, 59 and *n*.

Later he recalls how Coleridge would sit in a dressing-gown and look like a conjuror, while he was translating *Wallenstein*.[1] Coleridge himself, when he had left Lamb, is in his turn enthusiastic.[2]

He has an affectionate heart, a mind *sui generis*; his taste acts so as to appear like the unmechanic simplicity of an instinct—in brief he is worth an hundred men of *mere* talents. Conversation with the latter tribe is like the use of leaden balls—one warms by exercise—Lamb every now and then *irradiates*, and the beam, though single and fine as a hair, is yet rich with colours, and I both see and feel it.

This friendship, at least, was never again to be broken.

Coleridge's avocations, strenuous as they were, were not inconsistent with a good deal of social intercourse. He became acquainted with Lamb's Cambridge friend, Thomas Manning, by whom he was much impressed.[3] Basil Montagu he found very cool to him.[4] He saw much of Mrs. Barbauld, a woman of 'wonderful *Propriety* of Mind'.[5] He greatly admired Mrs. Robinson, the rejected Perdita of the Prince, and her poems, some of which he secured for the *Annual Anthology*. 'She is a woman of undoubted genius.' A year later she died, after writing an 'affecting, heart-rending' death-bed letter to Coleridge, who quoted his own early verses:

> O'er her pil'd grave the gale of evening sighs;
> And flowers will grow upon it's grassy slope.
> I wipe the dimming water from mine eyes—
> E'en in the cold Grave dwells the Cherub Hope.[6]

She was only one of a tribe of literary ladies, Miss Hayes 'ugly and petticoated', Miss Benger, Miss Sarah Wesley 'that mopsey', who hung about him, and afterwards pestered Lamb for news of him.[7] Coleridge was catholic in his choice of company, and Poole became uneasy on hearing that Purkis had met at his house 'those I would not have given a button to meet'. He gathered that they talked boldly of atheism.[8] Coleridge had in fact dined with Horne Tooke,

[1] L. 62, 75.   [2] G. 69.   [3] L. 57, 58.   [4] Litchfield, 77.
[5] G. 68.   [6] C. 105, 109; G. 69, 83; *M.L.N.* xlv. 90; *P.W.* 996.
[7] C. 105; L. 65.   [8] P. ii. 4.

and became familiar with Godwin, whom he found a great admirer of Davy. Godwin himself he thought 'no great things in intellect', but the better in heart and manner for having been the husband of Mary Wollstonecraft. The 'cadaverous silence' of Godwin's children, however, oppressed him.[1] So far as religion was concerned, the conversation was no doubt philosophically open-minded. Coleridge's tongue sometimes ran away with him. There is a curious letter to Godwin, in which he retracts things which he had said the night before, in a state of tipsiness.[2]

An idea starts up in my head,—away I follow through thick and thin, wood and marsh, brake and briar, with all the apparent interest of a man who was defending one of his old and long-established principles. Exactly of this kind was the conversation with which I quitted you. I do not believe it possible for a human being to have a greater horror of the feelings that usually accompany such principles as I then supported, or a deeper conviction of their irrationality, than myself; but the whole thinking of my life will not bear me up against the accidental crowd and press of my mind, when it is elevated beyond its natural pitch.

And after all it was Coleridge who modified Godwin's convictions, not Godwin Coleridge's. Godwin wrote in 1813 :[3]

My theism, if such I may be permitted to call it, consists in a reverent and soothing contemplation of all that is beautiful, grand, or mysterious in the system of the universe, and in a certain conscious intercourse and correspondence with the principles of these attributes, without attempting the idle task of developing and defining it—into this train of thinking I was first led by the conversations of S. T. Coleridge.

It may have been at this period that Godwin took Coleridge to meet Sir Francis Burdett. It was 'an Attic feast'. But on a subsequent visit to Burdett, Coleridge found him with boon companions, and the talk was so lewd that he got into a hackney-coach, which happened to be at the door, and fled.[4]

At the back of his mind was still the problem of a residence. His wife must be settled by August. The family at Ottery wanted him to live there.

But *that* I must decline in the names of public liberty and individual

[1] C. 103, 104; G. 66, 69; Litchfield, 76.
[2] Godwin, ii. 2 ('supposed' for 'supported'?).   [3] Godwin, i. 357.   [4] A. p. 164

free-agency. Elder brothers, not senior in intellect, and not sympathis-
ing in main opinions, are subjects of occasional visits, not temptations
to a co-township.

Poole was still hunting for him in Somerset. There was a
house at Aisholt, in a delicious situation, but too solitary.
He must have a house with a garden and a study out of the
noise of women and children. Part of a farm-house would
not do. It entailed the use of a joint kitchen, and squabbles
between his servant and the farmer's wife would be worse
than 'the old hovel' fifty times over. To Bristol his objections were insurmountable.

God knows where we can go; for that situation which suits my wife
does not suit me, and what suits me does not suit my wife. However,
that which is, is—a truth which always remains equally clear, but not
always equally pleasant.

Poole, of course, still wanted to have him near Stowey.
Although he thought well of the journalism and wished
Coleridge to fulfil his obligations to Stuart, he longed for
the time when the debts would be clear, and the days of devo-
tion to the permanent could begin. But the admirable Poole,
a solitary man and sensitive in spite of his ruggedness, was
apt to brood over what lay in his heart, and not always
tactful in the expression of it. Coleridge had treated him
with 'unmerited silence' during the autumn, and when he
did write at Christmas, the letter, in spite of its iteration that
he was 'the Friend', seemed to him sent as a duty, rather than
as a pleasure. Coleridge repudiated the suggestion. 'My
affections are what they are, and, in all human probability,
ever will be.' Later he expressed a doubt whether Poole
fully appreciated Wordsworth, a man 'of whom I do not
hesitate in saying that, since Milton, no one has *manifested*
himself equal to him'. He still wished he could get Wordsworth to retake Alfoxden with him. He protested when Poole,
in reply, charged him with 'prostration in regard to Wordsworth'. But, although Poole would have done better not to
let it appear, he had probably realized by this time that the
pull of the north upon Coleridge had become stronger than
the pull of Stowey.[1] Lamb, too, had become conscious
where his friend's affections lay. 'Coleridge has left us', he

[1] C. 106; P. ii. 1–10.

wrote on 5 April, 'on a visit to his god Wordsworth.' Lamb was to finish his proof-sheets of *Wallenstein* for him. It was only a short visit. Coleridge was still 'in excessive perplexity of mind', although he contemplated writing a novel and rewriting his tragedy, and had material, perhaps derived from Bonaparte's 'intercepted letters', for an essay on Literary Forgery.[1] On 4 May he left Grasmere for Bristol, where a renewed acquaintance, which ripened into a friendship, with Davy probably gave him the idea of translating Blumenbach's *Manual of Natural History*. By 21 May he was at Stowey, and by 12 June at Bristol again.[2] The search for a house continued, and was extended to Porlock. But it was fruitless. Moreover, Coleridge believed that it was Poole's intention, if peace came and his mother died, to go to the Continent for a year or two. Meanwhile he had heard of a house at Keswick with such a prospect that 'if impressions and ideas *constitute* our being, I shall have a tendency to become a god, so sublime and beautiful will be the series of my visual existence'. Dorothy Wordsworth, whose *Grasmere Journal* begins in May, was already in treaty for him with the owner, Mr. Jackson. The house was called Greta Hall.[3]

And so, parting from Poole with 'pain and dejection', Coleridge set out once more, with his family, for the Lakes. They moved slowly, stopping for a week with Dr. Crompton at Liverpool, and Dorothy had been in expectation of them for some days before at last, on 29 June 1800, they came. She had thought of taking lodgings for them in Ambleside, but evidently they went to Dove Cottage. Here Coleridge was ominously ill for a fortnight, with a touch of rheumatic fever, from a cold caught at Liverpool. Writing to Davy, with an invitation to come to Keswick in the autumn, he wishes he could wrap up the view from his house in a pill of opium, and send it. He was, however, well enough to take up his abode at Keswick on 24 July 1800, and recorded for Poole's benefit a final picnic at his departure.[4]

We drank tea the night before I left Grasmere, on the Island in that

[1] *I.L.N.*; W. 107; L. 63, 65; Rickman, 27; *O.T.* 275.
[2] G. 69, 70; Litchfield, 93.   [3] G. 69; Litchfield, 93, 102; D.W. (*J.*), i. 36.
[4] G. 71–3; *L.P.* 5; W. 109, 110; D.W. (*J.*), i. 36, 38, 43.

lovely lake, our kettle swung over the fire hanging from the branch
of a Fir-tree, and I lay and saw the woods, and mountains, and lake
all trembling, and as it were *idealized* thro' the subtle smoke which rose
up from the clear red embers of the fir-apples, which we had collected;
afterwards, we made a glorious Bonfire on the margin, by some elder
bushes, whose twigs heaved and sobbed in the uprushing column of
smoke—and the Image of the Bonfire, and of us that danced round it—
ruddy laughing faces in the twilight—the Image of this in a Lake
smooth as that sea, to whose waves the Son of God had said, *Peace!*
May God and all his Sons love you as I do.

VIII

DISASTER

July 1800—April 1802

IT must have become apparent during the course of this chronicle that Coleridge's failure to make good was primarily due to a fundamental instability of character. He had dreamed of the permanent, but had lived wholly in the present, talking brilliantly and incessantly, and snatching at every will-o'-the-wisp interest which a vivid imagination suggested to him. He could not integrate his life, and when troubles, for which he was not wholly responsible, came upon him, he had no reserve of endurance to make head against them. His gift of introspection sometimes gave him a whisper of this. 'Sloth-jaundic'd all', he had once said of himself, and had bewailed his 'chance-started friendships'. It was not exactly sloth.[1] His mind was always actively at work upon something, only it was generally the wrong thing. And 'chance-started friendships' were to serve him well throughout life. So Coleridge drifted to disaster.

There was happiness in the early months at Keswick. The spell of 'the glory of the place' was strong upon him.

I question if there be a room in England which commands a view of mountains, and lakes, and woods and vales superior to that in which I am now sitting.

Cloud-effects and moon-effects fill his letters, with invitations to his friends, Poole, Godwin, Purkis, Wrangham, as well as Davy, to come and see. Jackson, his landlord and Wordsworth's 'Waggoner', who lived next door, was an admirable man, with a good library of his own.[2] He delighted, too, in his boy Hartley, 'a spirit dancing on an aspen leaf' and 'the darling of the sun and of the breeze'.[3] A second son born on 14 September was called Derwent from

---

[1] *P.W.* 77, 174; cf. pp. 16, 33.
[2] C. 110, 111; G. 73–5, 78, 80; T. 106; Litchfield, 102.
[3] G. 73, 74, 76, 78; Prideaux, 3.

the local river. He was not expected to live, and was baptized, rather against the father's views, to please 'the good
people'. But before long he was a 'stout boy'.[1] The close
association of Stowey with the Wordsworths was renewed.
These intrepid walkers thought nothing of the thirteen
miles over Dunmail Raise, which lay between Keswick and
Grasmere. Coleridge would come over for two or three
nights, and in August the Wordsworths spent a week at
Keswick, during which Coleridge went to church. It is one
of the few occasions on which this is recorded of him. John
Wordsworth was of the company until the end of September,
when the chance of becoming captain of a ship took him to
the south.[2] Coleridge renamed Dorothy Rotha, again from
a river, that which flows through Grasmere.[3] It was rather
annoying that in the course of the autumn Charles Lloyd
settled at Ambleside. The Wordsworths could not altogether avoid him, because Wordsworth's brother Christopher
was engaged to his sister Priscilla, but they thought him 'a
dangerous acquaintance'. Coleridge professed indifference.
'I have no wish to see him, and likewise no wish not to see
him'.[4]

The talk at Grasmere was largely of poetry. The first
edition of the *Lyrical Ballads* was exhausted, and Longman
was prepared to undertake another. It was to be in two
volumes, and for the second Coleridge's *Christabel* was to
be finished. He brought the second Book to Grasmere
on 4 October, probably much as we have it, except for the
'Conclusion', which seems to have been originally a distinct
poem on Hartley. The Wordsworths were 'exceedingly
delighted' with it. But two days later it was decided not to
put it in the *Lyrical Ballads*, and the sheets already printed
of the first Book were cancelled. Coleridge wrote to Davy,
who was superintending the printing at Bristol.

The 'Christabel' was running up to 1,300 lines, and was so much
admired by Wordsworth, that he thought it indelicate to print two
volumes with his name, in which so much of another man's was

---

[1] C. 110, 111; G. 78; *L.P.* 6.
[2] D.W. (*J.*), i. 45, 50, and *passim*.   [3] T. 109.
[4] C. 114; L. 72; Godwin, ii. 13; W. 110; D.W. (*J.*), i. 49, 50, 55, 58–60; Lucas,
Lloyds, 121; *R.E.S.* xi. 78.

included; and, which was of more consequence, the poem was in direct opposition to the very purpose for which the lyrical ballads were published, viz., an experiment to see how far those passions which alone give any value to extraordinary incidents were capable of interesting, in and for themselves, in the incidents of common life.

It was then intended to publish *Christabel* and Wordsworth's *Pedlar* together, but apart from the *Ballads*. But this plan was in turn altered. The *Pedlar*, which must be the *Ruined Cottage*, became part of the *Excursion*, and by March 1801 *Christabel* was to be published separately by Longman, in five books, with vignettes and two annexed essays on the 'Preternatural' and on 'metre'. It never so appeared. Coleridge was no longer inspired. Even the second book had been written with difficulty. His own explanation was that he had been 'stricken with barrenness', by his disgust with *Wallenstein*.[1]

I tried and tried, and nothing would come of it. I desisted with a deeper dejection than I am willing to remember. The wind from the Skiddaw and Borrowdale was often as loud as wind need be—and many a walk in the clouds on the mountains did I take; but all would not do—till one day I dined out at the house of a clergyman, and somehow or other drank so much wine, that I found some effort and dexterity requisite to balance myself on the hither edge of sobriety. The next day, my verse making faculties returned to me, and I proceeded successfully—till my poem grew so long and in Wordsworth's opinion so impressive, that he rejected it from his volume as disproportionate both in size and merit, and as discordant in it's character.

The puzzle is that, although Coleridge wrote to Davy of nearly 1,300 lines as done, and to Poole about the same date of 1,400 lines, we have only 655, or at most 677, nor does any more appear to have got abroad, either through Coleridge's own recitation, or through a copy which he gave to John Stoddart, who visited him at Keswick in October 1800, and which Stoddart later read to Walter Scott.[2] Perhaps the solution is to be found in the reminiscences of one Richard Warner, who both in 1801 and in 1802 heard Coleridge recite a poem which was 'not printed nor a word of it committed to paper'. This he believed to have been

---

[1] C. iii, 113, 116, 118; G. 77, 78, 81; T. 97; W. iii, 112, 114, 119; D.W. (J.), 47, 51, 52, 54, 55.
[2] G. 77, 78, 111, 222 n.; D.W. (J.), i. 55, 56; Godwin, ii. 79; Lockhart, ii. 23; cf. pp. 198, 246, 273, 308, 350.

published two years later as *Christabel*.[1] Of course *Christabel* was not published in 1804, and certainly part of it had been written down before 1801. But conceivably part remained only in Coleridge's head. This was the case, according to his own statement, with another poem in 1811.[2]

The second edition of the *Lyrical Ballads* was published in January 1801 with Wordsworth's name on the title-page, but he acknowledged the contribution of five pieces as by 'a Friend'. These were Coleridge's. Four were carried on from the first edition, but much of the original archaic diction was now removed from the *Ancient Mariner*, and it was given the sub-title of 'A Poet's Reverie', which incurred the criticism of Lamb. The fifth was *Love*, much altered from the version printed in the *Morning Post*.[3] Wordsworth sent a copy of the *Lyrical Ballads* to Charles Fox among others, and Fox expressed the opinion that *Love*, the authorship of which he did not know, was 'the most beautiful poem in the language'. The edition also contained a critical preface on poetry, which had certainly arisen out of discussions on the subject between Coleridge and Wordsworth. It was 'half a child of my own brain', Coleridge told Southey, and to Stuart he described it as containing 'our joint opinions on Poetry'. In 1838 Wordsworth said that he had been prevailed upon by Coleridge to write it, and in 1845 that he wrote it wholly to gratify Coleridge. When Coleridge, however, came to discuss the diction of poetry in the *Biographia Literaria*, he criticized the views expressed, as if the responsibility for them was solely Wordsworth's.[4]

The struggle to finish *Christabel* had thrown Coleridge behindhand with his 'bread and beef occupations'.[5] His obligations to Stuart had been met by a few more contributions to the *Morning Post*, but the most important of these, upon 'Monopolists and Farmers', were in fact mainly written for him by Thomas Poole. *Bonaparte*, however, he declared, should not 'loiter'.[6] Sheridan had urged him to make another

---

[1] Warner, *Literary Recollections*, ii. 155.   [2] C. 183.
[3] L. 96; W. 112, 114, 116; A, p. 129; Wise, *Bibl. of Wordsworth*, 34; *P.W.* 293, 330.
[4] C. 127; L.P. 7; P. ii. 27; D.W. (*J*.) 50; W. 1244, 1565; B.L. i. 50; ii. 6.
[5] T. 97.
[6] C. 111; G. 77; L.P. 5–8; P. ii. 11; D.W. (*J*.), i. 54; O.T. 409–56.

attempt at fitting *Osorio* for the stage. This he would not do.
He was still under the grievance of the old controversy, and
called Sheridan 'a damned impudent Dog'. But for some
time he played with the idea of rewriting *Osorio*, and publishing it as a poem.[1] He was under an agreement with
Longman for the *Life of Lessing*, to which he thought of
appending an *Essay on Poetry*, which would be 'in reality a
disguised system of morals and politics'. But he persuaded
Longman to let him substitute a volume of *Letters from
Germany*. This he regarded as 'a decent lounge book, and not
an atom more'. But it came from him 'with mortal pangs',
and in a few months to go on with it would be 'suicide of
my very soul'. He would propose to Longman, instead of
it a book on Locke, Hobbes, and Hume, as '*pioneer* to my
greater work'.[2] There were other and vaguer notions. He
would start a fresh periodical of his own. He had a half-
finished dramatic romance, and a sort of farce, 'written
purposely vile'. He might even try a school-book on
geography.[3]

> To one resolution I am wholly made up, to wit, that as soon as I
> am a freeman in the world of money I will never write a line for the
> express purpose of money (but only as believing it good and useful,
> in some way or other).[4]

All these schemes, even the long-contemplated Lessing,
now pass into oblivion. Before the end of 1800 Coleridge's
health had broken down. The climate of the Lakes, with
its excess of rainfall, is the worst possible for a rheumatic
subject, and Greta Hall, however attractive its outlook, was
a badly built house. The illness at Grasmere in June had
left Coleridge's eyes weak and inflamed. He did not improve
matters by long mountain walks in wind and hail. In the
middle of November news that he was very ill with dysentery
made Wordsworth hurry over to Keswick to see him. There
were ups and downs, but part of December was spent in bed,
with boils. At the end of the month he was better, and
started, by way of Grasmere, to pay a promised Christmas

[1] C. 119; G. 72, 81; *L.P.* 5.
[2] C. 111, 113, 115, 116; G. 78, 79; *I.L.N.*; Litchfield, 104; Prideaux, 3.
[3] C. 114; G. 77, 78, 81; Godwin, ii. 13.   [4] C. 114.

visit to Poole. It was not paid, for he got wet through in walking to Grasmere, and a bout of rheumatic fever held him there. Others followed on his return to Keswick, and during much of the early part of 1801 he was bed-ridden. By May he had swollen knees and knotty fingers, and his doctor was diagnosing the disease as gout. The examination taken after his death suggests that the root-trouble lay in rheumatic tendencies due to his illness at Christ's Hospital, which had caused adhesions of the membranes around his heart. During the summer he recovered in warm weeks, but fell back again whenever it was cold and wet. In July he describes himself as 'a poor fellow with a sick stomach, a giddy head, and swoln and limping limbs' and as 'a man on whom the dews of heaven cannot fall without diseasing him', and again as 'climbing up that rock of convalescence from which I have been so often washed off and hurried back'. He had then had nine months of it.[1] But of course this was not all. It is clear from many after admissions by Coleridge himself, that it was during his illness of 1801 that opium took hold of him. He had read, he says, in a medical journal of the effects of the drug, in a form known as the Kendal Black Drop, as a cure for swollen knees, if used as a liniment, and at the same time taken internally. He resolved to try the experiment. 'It acted like a charm, like a miracle!' Unfortunately the operation of a given dose of opium tends to decrease, and Coleridge doubtless went on increasing the doses, until he was taking some 80 or 100 drops a day. He is very clear that he never took it as a stimulus or for any craving after pleasurable sensation. 'My sole sensuality was *not* to be in pain.' His account of what he found in a medical journal may be true enough, but of course we have had abundant evidence that he had been familiar with the curative use of opium, and even with its 'pleasurable operation' and the 'divine repose' it gave from very early years. I do not suppose that there was much secret about the growing habit at Keswick among those who knew him best. Poole had heard of it by February 1802, and Professor de Selin-

[1] C. 113–16, 118–20; G. 77, 79, 81–5, 101, 111; T. 100, 105, 107; P. ii. 26, 43, 48; W. 117, 119, 121, 122; D.W. (J.), 57–60; Godwin, ii. 79.

court may be right in thinking that Dorothy Wordsworth first learnt of it in the March of that year.[1]

There was another anodyne. During his illness Coleridge's mind turned to metaphysics, a term from which he does not at this stage clearly distinguish psychology. The impulse came from his own pain, and the desire to understand the psychological nature of pain. In December 1800 he thought himself 'a kind of a metaphysician' and by February 'a purus putus metaphysician'. Thinking with 'the most intense energy', he had become dissatisfied with the traditional philosophies based upon Locke, which had served him in the past, and believed that he had 'extricated the notions of time and space' and overthrown the 'association' and 'necessity' of his former master Hartley. He reverted, with Giordano Bruno, to his earlier studies in Neoplatonism. And now, for the first time, he seems to have become familiar with the writings of Kant. He is concerned with 'the relations of thoughts to things'. He is conscious of the conflict within himself between the call to speculation and the call to poetry. 'I hope, Philosophy and Poetry will not neutralize each other, and leave me an inert mass', he writes in February, and in March he is 'chasing down metaphysical game' and 'the Poet is dead in me'. In July he is reading Scotus Erigena, and 'burning Locke, Hume, and Hobbes under his nose'. But in August he regards the composition of a set of verses as a symptom of convalescence. 'It is a long time since I have cropt a flowering weed on the sweet Hill of Poesy.'[2] At one time he seems to have thought that the study of chemistry would assist his researches, and consulted Davy as to the possibility of fitting up a small laboratory at Keswick.[3]

Whether for poetry or for philosophy, however, a recovery of health was now the first requisite. Moreover, Coleridge had become dissatisfied with the social conditions at home, in particular for writers with high ideals. 'Such is the depravity of the public mind, that no literary man can

[1] C. 132, 254; G. 266, 390; A. 9; *Rem.* 366; Gillman, 246; P. ii. 77; D.W. (*J.*), i, 103, (*L.*), 130; cf. p. 150.
[2] C. 113–17, 119; G. 80, 83, 84, 87; T. 100, 105; *A.P.* 16; P. ii. 43; Wellek, 71.
[3] C. 115; T. 107.

find bread in England except by misemploying and debasing
his talents.' He had no doubt that he could make £500 a
year if he liked, but then he must 'forego all desire of truth
and excellence'. He felt that he might be holding his annuity
by a very precarious tenure, but, if he retained it, he would
like to settle near Priestley in America, and would try to get
Wordsworth to go with him.[1] This was little more than an
aftermath of Pantisocracy. But the need for a more genial
climate also pointed to a residence, temporary or permanent,
abroad. He thought of St. Michael's in the Azores, where
John Wordsworth had assured him that living was cheap,
and medical baths were available. If it answered, he would
send for his wife and children. The Wordsworths had
generously promised to come too, and he hoped for Southey.
But finance stood in the way. He owed Wordsworth £30
and Poole £37. He was now square with the Wedgwoods
and had enough to go on with at home to the end of 1801.
But he could not travel without funds, and would not make
any further application either to the Wedgwoods or to
Poole. Possibly he could raise enough from booksellers, if
he could give them security.[2] In July he put his difficulties
before Poole, who was not very sympathetic, being himself
financially embarrassed, and feeling some doubt whether
Coleridge's disease was 'really bodily, and not the consequence of an irritated mind', and whether a warmer climate
would be of any avail. Coleridge in reply gave the full
details of his illness.[3] Then Wordsworth committed a bad
blunder. Without telling Coleridge what he was going to
say, he wrote himself to Poole, confirming the medical facts,
giving his own opinion that a change of climate was desirable, and deprecating any further engagement with booksellers, which it was ten to one Coleridge would not be able
to fulfil. Poole must do what he thought proper on this
statement of the case, but if he could risk £50, that would
probably be sufficient. If not, he thought that Wade or
some other friend might be willing to help.[4] Poole's answer
was not to Wordsworth, but direct to Coleridge. He had

[1] C. 117.   [2] C. 118; G. 85; T. 107, 109; P. ii. 48; Godwin, ii. 79.
[3] P. ii. 44.   [4] W. 123; P. ii. 51, 58.

many claims upon him, but he could manage £20, if Coleridge could raise the rest in other ways. He had suggested
to Josiah Wedgwood that his brother Thomas, who was
going to Sicily, might take Coleridge as a companion. This
had, indeed, been an idea of Coleridge's own, before his
illness became serious.[1] Coleridge now kept silence for a
month, and then wrote in rather a bitter mood. He wished
he had followed his own instinct and restrained Wordsworth, who did not know Poole as he did.

> It is impossible that you should feel, as to pecuniary affairs, as
> Wordsworth or as I feel—or even as men greatly inferior to you in
> all other things that make man a noble being.

He regretted the application to the Wedgwoods; the last
thing he could submit to would be to go as a companion to
another invalid, and one so unlike himself in opinions,
habits, requirements, and feelings.

> But enough of this. Let us, for the future, abstain from all pecuniary
> matters. If I live, I shall soon pay all I at present owe—and if I die,
> the thought of being in your debt will never disquiet me on my sick-
> bed. I love you too well to have one injurious thought respecting you.
> You deem me, too often perhaps, an enthusiast. Enthusiast as I may
> be, Poole! I have not passed through life without knowing that it is
> a heart-sickening degradation to borrow of the rich, and a heart-
> withering affliction to owe to the poor.

He had given up the idea of the Azores, and now thought of
wintering at Nevis in the West Indies, where he believed he
could get a house belonging to John Pinney.[2] An 'outrageous' letter, Poole called it, and Coleridge could not see
why. But it was followed a fortnight later by an affectionate
one on the death of Poole's mother. Will not Poole come
to Keswick? 'You have none that love you so well as I.'
Yet another regrets the pain given to Poole, although Coleridge still thinks that his own attitude towards property is
one which his friend could not possibly share. He could not
himself have refused the £50, had it been his last. And by
the end of October he was willing to borrow £25 for four
months. He hoped soon to visit Poole.[3] But in 1809 he wrote

---

[1] P. ii. 61; Litchfield, 104.
[2] P. ii. 63; *Addl. MS.* 35343, f. 286.   [3] C. 122; G. 89; P. ii. 65–72.

of a 'healed indeed but yet scarred wound' which the episode had left for years.[1]

Meanwhile, for the moment in better health, Coleridge had taken a holiday towards the end of July, professedly for the purpose of reading Duns Scotus in the cathedral library at Durham. Here he was within reach of the Hutchinsons, who had left Sockburn in the spring of 1800. George had taken a farm at Bishop's Middleham, near Durham, and Thomas another at Gallow Hill, near Scarborough in Yorkshire. The sisters seem to have divided their time between them. Coleridge stayed at Bishop's Middleham, occasionally spending a night or two in Durham. He describes the Hutchinsons.

A quiet good family that love me dearly—a young farmer and his sister, and he makes very droll verses in the northern dialects and in the metre of Burns, and is a great humourist, and the woman is so very good a woman that I have seldom indeed seen the like of her.

It is not quite clear whether this was Sara or Mary. In any case Sara came to Bishop's Middleham. Walking back one day from Durham Coleridge had a relapse of gout, and his knee swelled up. A physician recommended baths in warm sea-water, and for this purpose he took the opportunity of riding back with Sara to Gallow Hill. Contrary to the physician's advice he preferred using the open sea, of which he was always fond, benefited by it, and wrote verses upon it.[2]

> O ye hopes, that stir within me,
>   Health comes with you from above!
> God is with me, God is in me!
>   I cannot die, if Life be Love.

In spite of the memorandum on the Sockburn visit of 1799, I suspect that it was now that Coleridge for the first time realized that he was in love with Sara Hutchinson. Some other verses to Asra, which was his poetical name for her, may be of the same date.[3] He had, of course, seen a good deal of her at Grasmere. She had come there, by way of Greta Hall, early in December 1800, was there during his

[1] L.P. 48.
[2] C. 119–21; G. 86, 87; L.P. 10; W. 117; P.W. 359.   [3] P.W. 361, 362.

illness at Christmas, and if the original plan for her visit
was carried out, remained there for three or four months.
Dorothy's journal here fails us, but she was gone by the end
of April. During part of this period, however, Coleridge
was confined to his bed.[1]

After ten days at Gallow Hill, Coleridge returned to
Bishop's Middleham. He was looking for a visit from
Southey at Keswick, but there was a delay, and he planned
to take sulphur baths for a week at Dimsdale in Stafford-
shire. Southey had returned from Lisbon in July and at
Bristol found letters from Coleridge who had expected him
earlier. An active correspondence followed, very warm-
hearted on both sides. Southey wrote:

> Time and absence make strange work upon our affections; but mine
> are ever returning to rest upon you. I have other and dear friends, but
> none with whom the whole of my being is intimate—with whom every
> thought and feeling can amalgamate.

And Coleridge replied:

> Oh, how I have dreamt about you! Times that *have been*, and never
> can return, have been with me on my bed of pain.

He had hoped that Southey would winter with him at Greta
Hall, where there was plenty of room for both families.
Southey had a prospect of a secretaryship in the south of
Italy or at Constantinople. This did not attract Coleridge,
but the idea of a general exodus to the West Indies was still
with him. Southey paid his visit and then went off to Dublin
as secretary to Isaac Corry, the Chancellor of the Irish
Exchequer.[2] Here he had a letter which made clear to him,
if he had not already realized it, a deplorable state of things
at Greta Hall. Coleridge was going to London.[3]

> Sara—alas! we are not suited to each other. But the months of my
> absence I devote to *self*-discipline, and to the attempt to draw her
> nearer to me by a regular development of all the sources of our
> unhappiness—then for another trial *fair* as I hold the love of good men
> dear to me—*patient* as I myself love my own dear children. I will go
> believing that it will end happily—if not, if our mutual unsuitableness
> continues, and (as it assuredly will do, if it continue) increases and
> strengthens—why then, it is better for her and my children that I

---

[1] W. 110, 121, 205; D.W. (*J.*), i. 58–60; cf. p. 237 ('ten years').
[2] C. 118–21; G. 86–8; Southey (*L.*), ii. 131, 136, 149, 151, 154, 157, 167, 171;
(*W.*), i. 153; (*T.*), i. 369.   [3] G. 88, 90.

should live apart, than that she should be a widow and they orphans. Carefully have I *thought thro'* the subject of marriage, and deeply am I convinced of its indissolubleness. If I separate, I do it in the earnest desire to provide for her and them, that while I live she may enjoy the comforts of life and that when I die, something may have been accumulated that may secure her from degrading dependence. When I least love her, then most do I feel anxiety for her peace, comfort and welfare. Is she not the mother of my children? And am I the man not to know and feel this? Enough of this.

We cannot tell precisely what causes, other than Sara Hutchinson, had led up to this disaster. The marriage, of course, had been more of Southey's making than of Coleridge's own. To that he does not refer here, although later letters show that he had not forgotten it.[1] There had, however, been much affection at Bristol and Clevedon, which lasted, if not without occasional ruffles, up to the end of the visit to Germany. As to the ruffles, we know little. Reynell found an idyllic household at Stowey.[2] John Payne Collier, who came to know Coleridge in 1811, recorded in his old age a singular story, as given to him by Hugh James Rose. According to this Coleridge came to Rose one day in tears. He wanted to consult Rose about the conduct of his wife. He could never live with her again, if she was not brought to her senses. Was she insane? asked Rose.

No, but a sane woman could hardly have required of her husband what she had expected from him; viz., that on the coldest mornings, even when the snow was on the ground, and icicles hanging from the eaves of their cottage, she compelled him to get out of bed in his night-shirt and light the fire before she began to dress herself and the baby.

This, as it stands, is absurd. Hugh James Rose became a correspondent of Coleridge. But he was born in 1795, and could not possibly have known Coleridge when he lived in a cottage, or even before he left his wife. Collier has, of course, the worst of reputations for literary dishonesty, but this narrative reads to me more like an old man's muddle than a deliberate fabrication.[3] Unless it is a mere myth, it points to the servantless period at Stowey in the autumn of 1799, although that seems rather early for snow.[4] More important, perhaps, is De Quincey's account of a young lady, with 'no

[1] Cf. pp. 157, 205.   [2] Cf. pp. 84, 110.
[3] Collier, *Old Man's Diary*, iii. 80.   [4] Cf. p. 117.

personal charms', but 'intellectually very much superior to
Mrs Coleridge', who with her brother became the daily companion of Coleridge's walks, and sometimes, when she
returned drenched with rain, 'would run up to Mrs Coleridge's wardrobe, array herself, without leave asked, in M^rs
Coleridge's dresses, and make herself merry with her own
unceremoniousness and Mrs Coleridge's gravity'. Coleridge, he says, treated his wife's resentment as narrow-
mindedness. But her servant and others gossiped about
the situation.[1] Dykes Campbell rejects all that De Quincey
says about Coleridge on the ground that his own opium-
eating had deprived him of the power of distinguishing
between facts and fancies.[2] This is, I think, an exaggeration.
Opium disordered De Quincey's life, but did not much
affect his literary powers. His misstatements about Coleridge and Wordsworth are mostly gossip on matters about
which he had no direct evidence. He did not, of course,
know the Coleridges before 1807, but this particular story
he claims to have heard from two of those concerned, with
some confirmation from a third; and this he may well have
done when he and Coleridge were housemates with the
Wordsworths at Allan Bank in 1808. Probably the beginnings of the definite rift between Coleridge and his wife
may be safely put in 1800. We have seen that they did not
then agree about the situation for a house.[3] In January 1801
John Chester told Greenough that Mrs. Coleridge was not
so partial to Greta Hall as her husband.[4] It was natural
enough. All her own friends were at Bristol or Stowey.
The Lakes had no attractions for her. She was no walker;
did not mount Skiddaw until she had been nine years at
Keswick, and then stuck in a bog.[5] It is uncertain how far
she ever knew of her husband's feelings for Sara Hutchinson, which, indeed, his views on the indissolubility of
marriage may have kept on a plane of sentiment and imagination that would have been incomprehensible to her.
Some petulance at a visit to Penrith in 1802 is the only suggestion of it.[6] But it is clear that her relations with the

[1] De Q., ii. 159.   [2] Campbell, 125.   [3] Cf. p. 130.
[4] Greenough, 565.   [5] Southey (W.), ii. 159.   [6] Cf. pp. 161, 162, 164.

Wordsworths, although they often stayed at each other's houses, were never cordial. In April 1801 Dorothy wrote to Mary Hutchinson, after a visit to Keswick, that 'we are never comfortable there after the first two or three days'. She had by then learnt something of what was afterwards revealed to Southey.

Mrs C is in excellent health. She is indeed a bad nurse for C., but she has several great merits. She is much, very much to be pitied, for when one party is ill-matched the other necessarily must be so too. She would have made a very good wife to many another man, but for Coleridge!! Her radical fault is want of sensibility and what can such a woman be to Coleridge?

Even with her children, although an excellent nurse to them, she wasted her time. 'She is to be sure a sad fiddle faddler.'[1] All Dorothy's references to Mrs. Coleridge have just this touch of pungency, coupled with an evident desire to be fair. The marriage, indeed, even if Coleridge first realized it at Sockburn, was a typical case of incompatibility. Again, one may quote De Quincey.[2]

Wanting all cordial admiration, or indeed comprehension, of her husband's intellectual powers, Mrs Coleridge wanted the original basis for affectionate patience and candour. Hearing from everybody that Coleridge was a man of most extraordinary endowments, and attaching little weight, perhaps, to the distinction between popular talents and such as by their very nature are doomed to a slower progress in the public esteem, she naturally looked to see, at least, an extraordinary measure of worldly consequence attend upon their exercise. Now, had Coleridge been as persevering and punctual as the great mass of professional men, and had he given no reason to throw the *onus* of the different result upon his own different habits, in that case this result might, possibly and eventually, have been set down to the peculiar constitution of his powers, and their essential maladaptation to the English market. But, this trial having never fairly been made, it was natural to impute his non-success exclusively to his own irregular application, and to his carelessness in forming judicious connections. In circumstances such as these, however, no matter how caused or how palliated, was laid a sure ground of discontent and fretfulness in any woman's mind, not unusually indulgent or unusually magnanimous.

This analysis, although perhaps coloured by Coleridge's

[1] W. 121.   [2] De Q. ii. 158.

own representations to De Quincey, is consistent with what
we know of Mrs. Coleridge from other sources. She was
an ordinary woman. Her married life had been a disappointment; she may have remembered the better offers she had
rejected beforehand. Her reluctance to break it seems to
have been determined less by any lingering affection for
Coleridge, than by fears of neighbourly comment. She
thought him a clown in appearance.[1] With his intellectual
life she can have had little sympathy. Her easy acceptance of
the fate of the *Lyrical Ballads* has been noted. She regretted
the publication of *Christabel* and *Kubla Khan*. She found it
unpleasant to be asked whether he had changed his political
sentiments, for she did not know properly how to reply, and
had to consult Poole.[2] We may be sure that his metaphysics
meant nothing to her. And she was not a patient woman.
A sister recorded the violence of her temper as a girl, which
made the whole household uncomfortable.[3] Certainly she
had her merits. Her daughter, whose memories would not
go back to the crisis, wrote of her with the warmest affection:

> Dear mother! what an honest, simple, lively-minded, affectionate
> woman she was, how free from disguise and artifice, how much less
> she played tricks with herself, and tried to be and seem more and better
> than she was, than the generality of the world.

She, too, however, admits the hasty temper at the moment
of provocation.[4] We have many letters from Mrs. Coleridge
to Poole during later years, when the stress was over, and
Coleridge could be referred to, not unkindly, as 'poor
Coleridge'. They are certainly lively, but deal mainly with
personalities. She tells of the doings of her children and
what she hears of her husband, and of the little social events
in life at Keswick. To Poole himself she was much attached,
and asks constantly of his family, and of other old friends at
Stowey. Nor are they unintelligent. Living with Southey,
she was still in the world of books, or at least of the writers
of books. 'We get on with Mrs Sam and let her run on
about all the literary World,' wrote James Coleridge, when

---

[1] W. 262.   [2] Cf. pp. 115, 276.
[3] Allston, 354.   [4] S. C. *Memoir,* i. 344; ii. 25, 233.

she paid a visit to Ottery.[1] 'At home', to quote her daughter
again, 'she made herself felt, dear creature, every hour in the
day.' We may gather as much from Southey's letters, which
tell of a bustling woman, who quizzed him incessantly, in
a grotesque vocabulary of her own invention.[2] Such a habit
would certainly have driven Coleridge to distraction, but
the more tolerant Southey endured it, and even parodied it
to his friends. There must have been plenty of combustible
material in the early days at Keswick, and one cannot doubt
that Mrs. Coleridge was as unfit a wife for Coleridge as
Coleridge was a husband for her, or perhaps for any wife.

On 10 October 1801 Coleridge and the Wordsworths
built a 'Sara's seat', as he was leaving Grasmere for Keswick.
It was no doubt at the spot on Dunmail Raise later referred
to by Dorothy as 'Sara's rock', and sometimes called 'the
Rock of Names'. The names seem to have been added by
Coleridge on 4 May 1802.[3] At Keswick Coleridge had a
visit from Mackintosh, whom he found entertaining but
without emotions, and his conversation 'well-worded: but
not a thought in it worthy of having been worded at all'.[4]
On 10 November he set out for London, whence he meant to
pay his promised visit to Poole. Professor de Selincourt says
that he visited Sara Hutchinson on his way, but I do not
know on what evidence.[5] He was still far from well, and
had complicated matters by getting over a fence, and running a thorn into his leg, which could not be extracted.
Once more he had found consolation in metaphysics.[6] The
Wordsworths were affected at his going. 'O! how many,
many reasons I have to be anxious for him' Dorothy recorded.[7] He too felt the parting. 'Though we were three
persons, there was but one God,' he wrote to Godwin, who
would not have been shocked.[8] On his way he stopped
at Eusemere, a house on the edge of Ullswater, just built
by Thomas Clarkson, the anti-slavery agitator, and his wife
Catherine, who soon became an intimate friend both of

[1] D.H. 282.   [2] Southey (L.), iii. 101; v. 167; (W.), i. 398; iii. 270, 417.
[3] D.W. (J.), i. 63, 117, 122, 123, 141; H. D. Rawnsley, *Literary Associations of
the English Lakes*, ii. 219; cf. p. 156.   [4] G. 89.
[5] D.W. (J.), i. 63; T. 110; *Essays and Studies*, xxii. 12.
[6] G. 90; T. 110; P. ii. 73.   [7] D.W. (J.), i. 64.   [8] Godwin, ii. 83.

Dorothy and of Coleridge himself.[1] At London, which he reached on 15 November, Stuart found him lodgings with his tailor, one Howell of King St., Covent Garden. He spent his time 'reading in the old Libraries for my curious metaphysical work', among other things, the *Parmenides* and *Timaeus* of Plato. But he also did a little for the *Morning Post*, to which he had been contributing minor poems since September, and introduced to the paper Charles Lamb, whose paragraphs, however, were not very successful.[2] But he was a sick man, physically and mentally. The Wordsworths received many letters both from him and from Sara Hutchinson. Dorothy more than once describes his letters as melancholy. She was 'uneasy', and Sara too was 'in bad spirits' about him.[3] At Christmas he made excuses to Stuart and to Southey, who was now in London, but had seen little of him, and went off with Thomas Wedgwood to Stowey. There was a fresh lament to Southey. 'What is life, gangrened, as it is with me, in its very vitals, domestic tranquillity.' He refused an invitation to Ottery, being in 'no very brotherly mood of mind', and after a month at Stowey returned with Poole to London.[4] There were further 'heart-rending' letters to the Wordsworths, and William thought of going to London to see him.[5] But by the end of February he was better, both in health and spirits. He had had 'no occasion for opiates of any kind', he told Poole.[6] He even wrote to his wife. 'It is my frequent prayer, and my almost perpetual aspiration that we may meet to part no more, and live together as affectionate husband and wife ought to do.' He had a notion of a two years' residence at Montpellier, and Joseph Mawman the bookseller would defray the expenses of a tour in France and Switzerland, in return for letters to be published. He was now quite a man of fashion, he told her, and on the best of terms with Lady Charlotte Somebody and the Honourable Mrs. Damer, but none the less still her faithful husband. He hoped to be with her early in March. If it was

[1] C. 121; G. 90; W. 110.
[2] C. 123, 124; G. 91, 93; *L.P.* 4 (misdated), 10–12; L. 116, 118, 124; Godwin, ii. 83; *O.T.* 456, 464; Wise, 222–5.　　　　　[3] D.W. (*J.*), i. 68, 71, 74.
[4] C. 123; G. 91, 101; *L.P.* 12; P. ii. 77; Southey (*W.*), i. 181, 183; D.W. (*J.*), i. 82.　　　　　[5] D.W. (*J.*), i. 83, 86.　　　　　[6] P. ii. 77.

decided that Sara Hutchinson was to come to Grasmere, he should return by York and bring her with him.[1] From Dorothy's journal we learn that the Wordsworths were 'perplexed about Sara's coming', and in fact she did not come. Apparently, however, Coleridge went to Gallow Hill, and stayed there a fortnight.[2] It was on 19 March 1802 that he arrived at Dove Cottage from Keswick. Dorothy records her reaction and William's.[3]

His eyes were a little swollen with the wind. I was much affected by the sight of him, he seemed half-stupefied. William came in soon after. Coleridge went to bed late, and William and I sate up till four o'clock. My spirits were agitated very much.

There may have been some fleeting reconciliation at Greta Hall; another child was soon in prospect. Coleridge regretted it. 'I have too much reason to suspect that she is breeding again, an event which was to have been deprecated.' Certainly only a few days can have passed, before scenes of discord recurred.[4]

Ill-tempered Speeches sent after me when I went out of the House, ill-tempered Speeches on my return, my friends received with freezing looks, the least opposition or contradiction occasioning screams of passion, and the sentiments which I held most base, ostentatiously avowed—all this added to the utter negation of all, which a Husband expects from a Wife—especially, living in retirement—and the consciousness that I was myself growing a worse man.

On 27 March Wordsworth wrote the first four stanzas of his *Ode on Intimations of Immortality*. On the next day he went with his sister for a week to Keswick, and while they were there Coleridge was writing on 4 April an ode, which he called *Dejection*. Possibly some verse fragments which Dorothy Wordsworth received from him at Eusemere on 13 April may have been part of it. On 21 April he repeated at Grasmere 'the verses he wrote to Sara'. Dorothy was 'affected with them, and in miserable spirits'. She notes on 4 May the crescent moon with the 'auld moon in her arms', from the lines in the ballad of *Sir Patrick Spence*,

---

[1] C. 124; G. 93, 94; D.W. (*J.*), i. 86, 88; G. A. Anderson, *Letters of Manning to Lamb*, 82.   [2] C. 126, *note*; D.W. (*J.*), i. 95.   [3] D.W. (*J.*), i. 103.
[4] G. 94, 95, 101; *Addl. MS.* 35343, f. 313.

which Coleridge used as a motto to his ode. The verses to
Sara came to Grasmere on 6 May.[1] In July Coleridge sent
long extracts from the ode to William Sotheby, who had
recently been with him, describing the poem as one written
to Wordsworth and in the greater part of a private nature.
A short extract he also sent to Southey, omitting some lines
which would give Southey no pleasure.[2] On 4 October, the
day of Wordsworth's wedding, the ode appeared in the
Morning Post, much as given to Sotheby, but with the name
'Edmund' as a substitute for 'Wordsworth'. The date of
writing is given as 4 April. When Coleridge reprinted it,
with slight alterations, in the *Sibylline Leaves* of 1817 the
addressee became a nameless 'Lady'.[3] On 7 May Coleridge
told Poole that on 4 April he had written him a letter in
verse, but thought it dull and doleful and did not send it.[4]
The coincidence of date suggests that this must have been
the ode. That it should be addressed to Wordsworth rather
than to Poole was natural enough. It must have owed
much of its original inspiration to Wordsworth's stanzas of
27 March, which were doubtless shown to Coleridge at
Keswick. The openings of the two poems are variations
upon a common theme, the loss of delight arising from the
apprehension of beauty in natural things. Wordsworth's
treatment of it, so far as the opening stanzas go, is merely
a statement of the fact.

> The things which I have seen I now can see no more.

He recovers the sense of bliss, and loses it again.

> Whither is fled the visionary gleam?
> Where is it now, the glory and the dream?

Later he found his own mystical interpretation of the experience. Coleridge's is different. The apprehension of
beauty is a subjective one, dependent on the presence of joy
in the heart of the beholder.

> O Sara! we receive but what we give,
> And in *our* life alone does Nature live;
> Our's is her Wedding Garment, our's her Shroud!

[1] W. 128, 129; D.W. (*J*.), i. 104, 105, 110, 118.
[2] C. 126, 127.   [3] *P.W.* 362, 1076.   [4] G. 94.

And when joy is gone out of a life, as it has out of his, the
power of delight in beauty goes with it. There are parallels
of phrase, which make clear the link between the two
poems. The search for these has been pressed rather far,
and some of those suggested are rather remote and may not
be echoes at all. Moreover, echoes may have gone either
way. We do not know the precise form in which Wordsworth's stanzas were when Coleridge first saw them. He
was still working at them on 17 June, but laid them aside, and
did not finish them until 1804.[1] And the setting, as we have it,
seems to be of May, rather than of March. But one passage
is clear enough. When Coleridge wrote 'I too will crown
me with a Coronal', he must have had before him Wordsworth's 'my head hath its coronal'. Coleridge's line is not
in the published version of *Dejection*. But whatever his first
intention with regard to the poem, it had taken, if not
already by 4 April, at latest by 21 April, a form in which it
was addressed, not to Wordsworth, and not to Poole, but
to Sara Hutchinson. This form survives in a manuscript at
Grasmere, recently revealed to us by Professor de Selincourt.[2] This, too, has the date 4 April. It is more than
twice as long as the published version, and although it does
not make so good a poem, is full of biographical interest.
The causes of Coleridge's loss of joy, and with it his 'shaping
spirit of imagination' are elaborated in passages which dwell
on his 'own peculiar lot' of domestic 'indifference or strife',
in a life which has 'no hopes of its own vintage', but is worn
out by the 'habitual ills' that arise

> When two unequal Minds
> Meet in one House and two discordant Wills.

He loves his children, but even that bliss still calls up a woe.

> I have half-wished they never had been born!

His only comfort is in Sara and in his and her friends, but
it weighs down his heart to visit them.

> Wherefore, O wherefore! should I wish to be
> A wither'd branch upon a blossoming Tree.

[1] D.W. (*J.*), i. 132.   [2] *Essays and Studies*, xxii. 7.

He has reminiscences of happy days at Gallow Hill, one
of which, incidentally, he made the subject of his *A Day-
Dream*, and regrets for a 'complaining scroll', which had
bruised Sara to bodily sickness, and made her blame her
blameless self.[1] For her he has hopes of happiness, apart
from him, in an abiding home, with those whom she loves
best. Then he too 'will crown him with a Coronal', will
give himself to 'no inglorious toils'.

> And only now and then, and not too oft,
> Some dear and memorable Eve will bless
> Dreaming of all your Loves and Quietness.

Early in May 1802 Wordsworth wrote his *Stanzas in
Thomson's Castle of Indolence*, which Dorothy says were 'about
Coleridge and himself'.

> Within our happy Castle there dwelt One
> Whom without blame I may not overlook;
> For never sun on living creature shone
> Who more devout enjoyment with us took:
> Here on his hours he hung as on a book,
> On his own time here would he float away,
> As doth a fly upon a summer brook;
> But go to-morrow, or belike to-day,
> Seek for him,—he is fled; and whither none can say.
>
> Thus often would he leave our peaceful home,
> And find elsewhere his business or delight;
> Out of our Valley's limits did he roam:
> Full many a time, upon a stormy night,
> His voice came to us from the neighbouring height:
> Oft could we see him driving full in view
> At mid-day when the sun was shining bright;
> What ill was on him, what he had to do,
> A mighty wonder bred among our quiet crew.
>
> Ah! piteous sight it was to see this Man
> When he came back to us, a withered flower,—
> Or like a sinful creature, pale and wan.
> Down would he sit; and without strength or power
> Look at the common grass from hour to hour;
> And oftentimes, how long I fear to say,
> Where apple-trees in blossom made a bower,
> Retired in that sunshiny shade he lay;
> And, like a naked Indian, slept himself away.

[1] *P.W.* 385.

Great wonder to our gentle tribe it was
Whenever from our Valley he withdrew;
For happier soul no living creature has
Than he had, being here the long day through.
Some thought he was a lover, and did woo:
Some thought far worse of him, and judged him wrong;
But verse was what he had been wedded to;
And his own mind did like a tempest strong
Come to him thus, and drove the weary Wight along.

With him there often walked in friendly guise,
Or lay upon the moss by brook or tree,
A noticeable Man with large grey eyes,
And a pale face that seemed undoubtedly
As if a blooming face it ought to be;
Heavy his low-hung lip did oft appear,
Deprest by weight of musing Phantasy;
Profound his forehead was, though not severe;
Yet some did think that he had little business here:

Sweet heaven forefend! his was a lawful right;
Noisy he was, and gamesome as a boy;
His limbs would toss about him with delight,
Like branches when strong winds the trees annoy.
Nor lacked his calmer hours device or toy
To banish listlessness and irksome care;
He would have taught you how you might employ
Yourself; and many did to him repair,—
And certes not in vain; he had inventions rare.

Expedients, too, of simplest sort he tried:
Long blades of grass, plucked round him as he lay,
Made, to his ear attentively applied,
A pipe on which the wind would deftly play;
Glasses he had, that little things display,
The beetle panoplied in gems and gold,
A mailèd angel on a battle-day;
The mysteries that cups of flowers enfold,
And all the gorgeous sights which fairies do behold.

He would entice that other Man to hear
His music, and to view his imagery;
And, sooth, these two were each to the other dear:
No livelier love in such a place could be;
There did they dwell—from earthly labour free,
As happy spirits as were ever seen;
If but a bird, to keep them company,
Or butterfly sate down, they were, I ween,
As pleased as if the same had been a Maiden-queen.

De Quincey says that the third stanza refers to Coleridge, after his return from Malta, and has been followed by some modern critics. It is, of course, impossible, as the poem stands, and could only be made possible on the assumption that the stanza was a later addition, and was inserted in the wrong place when the lines were published in 1815. Probably the reference is really to the ill health which had overtaken Wordsworth by 1802, and made the task of poetic composition both arduous and painful to him. The 'glasses that little things display' figure in a letter from Wordsworth to his London publishers in 1801, which acknowledges a joint debt by himself and Coleridge for two copies of Withering's Botany and two botanical microscopes.[1]

[1] De Q. ii. 162; D.W. (J.), i. 119, 120; W. 118.

IX

ON THE WING

May 1802—December 1803

DURING the summer of 1802 Wordsworth was making
preparations for his marriage to Mary Hutchinson.
Dove Cottage was likely to prove too small for an enlarged
household, and there was some thought of a move to
Keswick, where the Wordsworths might either share Greta
Hall or take a neighbouring Brow Top. On 20 May, however, they had a letter from Coleridge, asking them not to
go to Keswick, and two days later they met him at 'Sara's
rock', and had 'some interesting, melancholy talk, about
his private affairs'. Dorothy wrote to Mrs. Coleridge, probably abandoning the plan, and had an unsatisfactory answer.[1]

Mrs Coleridge is a most extraordinary character—she is the lightest
weakest silliest woman! She sent some clean clothes on Thursday to
meet C. (the first time she ever did such a thing in her life) from which
I guess that she is determined to be attentive to him—she wrote a
note, saying not a word about my letter, and all in her very lightest
style. . . . Is it not a hopeless case? So insensible and so irritable she
can never come to good and poor C!

A month later the Wordsworths left Grasmere, on their
way to France, where William had to close his relations with
Annette Vallon, and did not return until 6 October, after
the marriage. Perhaps their absence contributed to the
establishment of better terms between Coleridge and his
wife. After a violent quarrel, which threw him into spasms,
he made up his mind to the 'awful step' of threatening a
separation. It wounded her pride, he says, and made her
serious.

She promised to set about an alteration in her external manners and
looks and language, and to fight against her inveterate habits of puny
thwarting and unintermitting dyspathy, this immediately, and to do
her best endeavours to cherish other feelings. I, on my part, promised
to be more attentive to all her feelings of pride, etc., etc., and to try
to correct my habits of impetuous censure.

[1] W. 131, 132; D.W. (*J.*), i. 122, 123, 127.

He reported the affair to Southey, with much analysis of his own character and hers, and for the next year and a half domestic life at Greta Hall seems to have been, in the main, one at least of mutual toleration. 'We go on', he told Poole in December, 'with less of those habitual Ills that wear out life when two unequal minds meet in one house, and two discordant Wills—we have been at peace.'[1] Coleridge apparently thought that it would still further improve matters if he could persuade Southey, who had now abandoned his job with Corry and was expecting the birth of a child at Bristol, to take up his abode at Greta Hall. The house was being in part rebuilt, and Coleridge sent detailed accounts of the accommodation expected, and of the way in which it could be divided between the two families. Southey was uncertain, fearing the climate. Moreover, he wanted to bring with him his brother Tom and his wife's sister Mary Lovell, which, as Coleridge elaborately explained, would not be possible without such close packing that he would no longer have a room available for the visits of the Wordsworths or other friends. The plan was now dropped for a time, and when it was picked up again a few months later, it become apparent that the difficulties were largely personal. Mrs. Coleridge could not stand her sister as a housemate, and Tom had left an unpleasant impression on Coleridge, through an 'unbrotherly spirit of thwarting and contradicting', not himself, but Southey, who seems in fact to have been on the best of terms with his brother. Coleridge's wife, however, based her objections mainly on the overcrowding, and this, he said, must be final.[2]

Assuredly, I have no right to do anything that will in the least degree diminish Mrs Coleridge's comforts and tranquillity. In an evil hour for me did I first pay attention to Mrs Coleridge, in an evil hour for me did I marry her, but it shall be my care and my passion that it shall not be an evil day for her, and that whatever I may be, or may be represented, as a Husband, I may yet be unexceptionable as her Protector and Friend.

In the meantime, he had also offered part of the house, unsuccessfully, to a new friend, William Sotheby.[3]

---

[1] C. 127; G. 101, 107; Estlin, 82; Southey (L.), ii. 189; cf. *Dejection*, 243.
[2] C. 127, 128; G. 97, 114, 116; Southey (L.), ii. 189.   [3] G. 98.

To July and August 1802 belong two letters addressed to Sara Hutchinson. They are affectionate in tone, but mainly descriptive of Lake scenery and of the doings of the children at Greta Hall.[1] The second was written on Coleridge's return from a week's walking tour, during which he climbed Scafell, and on the top 'poured forth a hymn in the manner of the Psalms, though afterwards I thought the ideas, etc., disproportionate to our humble mountains'. And when the poem appeared in the *Morning Post* on 11 September, it bore the title of *Chamouny The Hour before Sunrise*. Nor can it have been quite so much of an improvisation as Coleridge suggests, since it owes something to the much shorter *Chamouny beym Sonnenaufgange* of Friederike Brun. Coleridge, in fact, had never been at Chamounix.[2] The last night of the tour was spent with Charles Lloyd, now settled at Old Brathay near Ambleside, and once more on some sort of terms with Coleridge.[3] At the end of August came a surprise visit from Charles and Mary Lamb, who stayed three weeks, and succeeded in getting to the top of Skiddaw. Lamb was much impressed by the view from Greta Hall, 'quite enveloped on all sides by a net of mountains: great floundering bears and monsters they seemed, all couchant and asleep'. On his return he felt that he now understood the romantic, although he still thought the Strand and Fleet Street the better places to live in.[4]

When Coleridge first came back to Keswick in March 1802, he found no comfort 'except in the driest speculations'. It is part of the theme of *Dejection*.[5]

> For not to think of what I needs must feel,
> But to be still and patient all I can;
> And haply by abstruse Research to steal
> From my own Nature, all the Natural man—
> This was my sole Resource, my wisest plan!
> And that, which suits a part, infects the whole,
> And now is almost grown the Temper of my Soul.

[1] *App.* nos. iii, iv.
[2] C. 128–30; G. 309; T.T. (1835) pref.; L. 130; De Q. ii. 143; Wordsworth, *Prose Works*, iii. 442; Campbell, 140, and *Poems*, 629; P.W. 376, 1131.
[3] C. 128; L. 129; Lucas, *Lloyds*, 121; R.E.S. xi. 79.
[4] C. 129; L. 128, 129.   [5] G. 101; *Dejection*, 265–71.

The very writing of *Dejection* may have helped to release the mood which it represents. Already in May Coleridge was hoping by the end of the year to have disburdened himself of metaphysics, and to be able to attempt a long poem. He was about to publish a second volume of his shorter pieces.[1] He did neither of these things. But during the period of domestic calm which followed, he was certainly occupied with literary plans. William Sotheby, whom he met in Keswick during the summer, seems to have put into his hands Salomon Gessner's poem *Der erste Schiffer*, with a suggestion that he should do a translation, to be published with illustrations by the engraver P. W. Tomkins. At first he thought the piece too silly, but was tempted to try his hand, and later wrote to Sotheby that it was finished and only wanted transcription. He did not, however, think it worth the fee of £10 which Tomkins offered, and would sooner make him a present of it. Some years after he said that he never got beyond the first half, and gave it up out of 'a double disgust, moral and poetical'.[2] Nothing is known of it now, although another poem by Gessner is used in *The Picture*, which appeared in the *Morning Post* on 6 September.[3] He told Sotheby that his object in making the attempt was to force himself out of metaphysical trains of thought, into which sickness and other worse afflictions had driven him. 'For I believe that by nature I have more of the poet in me.' But to Southey he expressed a doubt whether he ever really possessed any poetic genius, as distinct from 'a mere general *aptitude* of talent and quickness in imitation'. If he did, it was now gone, and he was a fool to regret that metaphysics had robbed him of it.[4] Both to Southey and to Estlin he foreshadowed a volume to be made up of letters to the *British Critic* on the use of the definitive article in New Testament Greek and its bearing on the Arian controversy. It was no mere dream, he said, like his *Hymns to the Elements*, for he had written more than half the work. A review in the *British Critic* of Christopher Wordsworth's *Six Letters* on the subject is probably his, but I can trace nothing else.[5] He had

---

[1] G. 94. [2] C. 125, 126, 129–30; G. 100; Godwin, ii. 222. [3] Lowes, 548; *P.W.* 369.
[4] C. 126, 127.   [5] C. 127; G. 97; Estlin, 82; *British Critic*, xx. 15.

other schemes to put before Southey. One was a treatise on tithes and church establishment, as to which he had already told his brother George of some departure from his earlier views. Another was a volume of essays on contemporary poets, to be accompanied by selections from their works. 'You spawn plans like a herring,' replied Southey. He should be afraid of the imprudence of the book on contemporaries, if he had any expectation that it would ever be written. That once projected on old poets would be better, and in fact Coleridge picked up this idea again later, and Southey himself gave effect to it in 1807.[1] With Basil Montagu Coleridge discussed a work on the history of English prose, which in its turn was left for Montagu to accomplish in 1805.[2] The only remunerative work of 1802 was once more for the *Morning Post*. Here, besides a number of poems and trifling epigrams, appeared in instalments, never completed, a long essay on the probable instability of the existing despotism in France, and the possible restoration of the Bourbon dynasty. It was an effective piece of writing, even if not, for the time being, a very successful prophecy. The attitude of the *Morning Post* towards Bonaparte was now more definitely hostile than in 1800, and was said by Fox to have helped to bring about the renewal of war in May 1803. Coleridge came to believe that his own contributions provoked the resentment of Bonaparte, to whom he constantly referred as a 'Corsican', and exposed him to personal danger when he was in Italy. Then followed a series of vigorous *Letters to Fox*, whom Coleridge much admired, in protest against his exchange of civilities with Bonaparte in Paris. These Stuart delayed and ultimately toned down, and Coleridge thought of reprinting them, with additions, as a pamphlet. His tale of journalism for this autumn was completed by an essay on Jacobinism and two reports of the misdoings of an adventurer, Hatfield by name, who had lured a local celebrity, one Mary of Buttermere, into a mock marriage.[3] The poems in the *Morning Post* were

---

[1] C. 127; G. 95, 96; Southey (L.), ii. 189.   [2] G. 99, 101.
[3] C. 133, 137; G. 100, 101, 111, 127; Byron, iv. 486; Gillman, 180; *B.L.* i. 145; O.T. 478–592; Wise, 226–34; cf. p. 173.

signed Ἔστησε. This he explained to Sotheby as meaning 'He hath stood'. Elsewhere he calls it 'Punic Greek'. It should have been Ἔστηκε.[1]

The summer of 1802 had been one of tolerable, although not unbroken, health, but in September came an attack of low fever, and once more the mirage of travel rose before Coleridge.[2] He had probably heard from Thomas Wedgwood's friend John Leslie, who had been at Keswick, that Wedgwood too was restless, and to Wedgwood, forgetful of his own wiser opinion in 1801 that two pernickety valetudinarians would not be helpful to each other, he sent a tentative offer of companionship. Wedgwood replied with an invitation to come at once, in the first instance for visits to Wales, where he meant to do some shooting, and to Stowey, but no doubt with a prospect of travel abroad later. Coleridge, with his wife's concurrence, and with regret at leaving his children, at once took wing. He stopped a night at Penrith, where was Sara Hutchinson, passed through London, and joined Wedgwood at Cote House by the second week in November.[3] Letters to his wife record the tour through the vale of Usk, which he found beautiful, but not comparable to any part of the Lake country, and onwards to Crescelly in Pembrokeshire, the home of one John Allen, two of whose many daughters were married to John and Josiah Wedgwood and a third to James Mackintosh. Coleridge was delighted with the company of Thomas Wedgwood. 'He possesses the *finest*, the *subtlest* mind and taste I have ever yet met with.' At Crescelly they stayed for the best part of a month, and while Wedgwood pursued woodcock, Coleridge talked to a housefull of ladies.[4] Wedgwood says that he was 'in prodigious favour', but Miss Fanny Allen remembered that he was irreverent about the Ten Commandments, and was rude to her when she laughed at a passage of Wordsworth's *Leechgatherer*, not preserved in the existing text, which described the old man's skin as so dry that the leeches would not stick to it. And the ladies

---

[1] C. 130; *P.W.* 453.　　[2] C. 127; G. 95, 99, 100; W. 132; D.W. (*J.*), i. 122.
[3] C. 133, 134; G. 101, 102, 107; Litchfield, 118, 120; D.W. (*J.*), i. 133, 156.
[4] C. 132; G. 102–6.

must have been rather surprised when, in speaking of his
early days at Bath or Bristol, he said, 'There I had the misfortune to meet with my wife'.[1] Of his host, too, one may
think that he writes with scant courtesy.[2]

> O Christ! Old Nightmair! An ancient Incubus! Every face was
> saddened, every mouth pursed up! Most solemnly civil, like the Lord
> of a stately castle 500 years ago! Doleful and plaintive eke for I believe
> that the Devil *is* twitching him home.

Crescelly, however, was a comfortable harbourage. Coleridge got more cream, he tells Poole, than Poole's dairymaid
would ever give him. But he lived soberly, taking much
ginger, no brandy, beer or tea, and only half a grain of
opium a day, less than an eighth of what he took at Keswick.[3]
The letters to his wife are friendly, even affectionate and
hopeful, although she had been a little fretful about his
delay at Penrith. He is anxious about her confinement,
wishing that she could get Sara Hutchinson or one of the
other women at Grasmere to be with her.[4]

> How much there lies at my heart with respect of the Wordsworths
> and Sara and how much of our common love and happiness depends on
> your loving those whom I love—why should I repeat? I am confident,
> my dear Love! that I have no occasion to repeat it.

Her letters sometimes upset him, and even at this moment,
he cannot, after all, refrain from sermonizing her. For a
professed psychologist, some of his letters, here and elsewhere, are singularly impercipient. Absorbed in the analysis
of his own feelings, he never stops to consider the probable
reaction upon the mind of his correspondent.[5]

> Permit me, my dear Sara, without offence to you, as Heaven knows!
> it is without any feeling of pride in myself, to say, that in sex, acquire-
> ments, and in the quantity and quality of natural endowments whether
> of feeling, or of intellect, you are the inferior. Therefore it would be
> preposterous to expect that I should see with your eyes, and dismiss
> my friends from *my* heart; but it is not preposterous in me, on the
> contrary I have a *right* to expect and demand that you should to a certain
> degree love and act kindly to those whom I deem worthy of my Love.

---

[1] Litchfield, 124, 126.   [2] G. 102.   [3] C. 132; G. 102, 107.
[4] G. 92 (misplaced), 103–6.
[5] G. 102. Here 'six' is a misreading.

Meanwhile, the hopes of further travel with
and of course at Wedgwood's expense, were
grow dim. An internal complaint, which he
think incurable, and which in fact soon led t
prevented Wedgwood from forming any fixed pl
November anything seemed possible, Cornwall, Ireland,
Cumberland, Naples, Madeira, Teneriffe—anything, wrote
Coleridge, short of the moon, the planets, or the fixed stars.
In December Coleridge thought he would have to travel
alone. Wedgwood had decided to give England a fair trial.
He took a shooting cottage near Crescelly, and thought of
securing a sporting companion in óne Captain Charles Luff,
a young friend of the Wordsworths and Clarksons, who
lived at Glenridding in Patterdale. This entailed a visit to
Keswick for consultation with Luff.[1] Coleridge wrote to
his wife with elaborate instructions for his friend's comfort
in Jackson's lodgings next door to Greta Hall, and on
Christmas Eve the travellers arrived, having passed through
Grasmere and learnt there of the birth of a daughter to the
Coleridges the day before.[2] After a week at Keswick, Coleridge went on with Wedgwood to Glenridding, and spent
several days walking to and from Grasmere over the Kirk-
stone pass. On one of these trips he was caught in a violent
storm, and a consequent attack of dysentery was relieved,
not by opium, but by ether.[3] From Glenridding on 5 January
1803 he wrote another hortatory letter to his wife on the conditions necessary for future peace and love, and in particular
as to the need for good relations with the Wordsworths.

Of course I speak *chiefly* of Dorothy and William—because Mrs
Wordsworth and her sister are far less remote from you than they—
and unless I am grievously deceived will in some things become less
so still.

He expected to go south again very shortly, but in the meantime had a plan to discuss with her. This may have been
an intention to assure his life in the event of travel.[4]

I shall *strive* to be at Keswick tomorrow night, and *possibly* may
come in on a double horse, with Sara Hutchinson, whom I have *some*

[1] C. 132, 134; G. 102–7; 109; Litchfield, 126.
[2] C. 134; G. 106; D.W. (*J.*), i. 156.
[3] C. 135; G. 110, 111; Litchfield, 130, 132; D.W. (*J.*), i. 157.   [4] G. 110.

few reasons for wishing to be with you immediately—which I will inform you of—but one of the least, and yet the most ostensible is the necessity of one or more of her teeth being drawn without delay—for I never saw a human being's health so much affected *generally* by the tooth-ache as hers appears to be—yet this tooth-ache I suspect to be in part nerves—and the cause which I more than suspect has caused this nervousness will return—I will tell you when I am alone with you. In one thing, my dear Love! I do prefer you to any woman I ever knew. I have the most unbounded confidence in your discretion, and know it to be well-grounded.

These references to Sara Hutchinson are rather cryptic. What was Coleridge going to tell his wife, perhaps in order to ward off a revelation of his own sentiment, which her fretfulness about his delay at Penrith in November may have led him to fear? One can only conjecture, and my conjecture is, that he believed Sara Hutchinson likely to become the wife of John Wordsworth. This in fact he stated to Daniel Stuart in 1808.[1] It might, at that date, have been a disordered fancy. But I think that there is some confirmation for it. Writing just after his brother's death by shipwreck on 6 February 1805, Wordsworth says that he had come to Grasmere a little over five years before and stayed for eight months, during which 'he found in his sister and me and Coleridge and in my wife and a sister of hers whom at that time he had an opportunity of seeing much of, all that was wanting to make him completely happy'. Other letters of the same period speak of John as having 'every hope about him that could render life dear', and as 'made for the best sort of happiness which is to be found in the world'.[2] Such phrases, from the pen of a man himself happily married, seem to me to point to an expectation of marriage. John Wordsworth hoped to make a fortune which would enable him to settle at Grasmere and help his brother and sister, but that he did not intend to live with them we know, since they could point to a field which he had fixed upon as the place where he would build his house.[3] The eight months' visit referred to can be shown from Dorothy's journal to have ended on 29 September 1800, the day after news came of the arrival of the *Earl of Abergavenny*, of which

[1] L.P. 25.   [2] W. 110, 199, 204, 205, 206, 207.   [3] W. 428.

ship John was to become captain. During part of the eight
months Mary Hutchinson was at Grasmere, but apparently
not Sara. On 14 May, however, John and William went
into Yorkshire, and spent three weeks at Gallow Hill. When
John left on 29 September he was only going to Penrith,
where Sara Hutchinson seems often to have been with her
relations, the Monkhouses, and might perhaps return. He
had not done so, up to the point where the unfortunate gap
in Dorothy's journal from 23 December 1800 to 9 October
1801 begins. Meanwhile Sara Hutchinson came from Penrith on 22 November for a visit which had been meant to
extend over three or four months. She had gone before
29 April 1801, when the Wordsworths sat and thought of
her and Mary in 'John's firgrove' on the road between Dove
Cottage and Rydal, opposite the wishing-gate, which they
now called 'Sara's gate'. No visit by John other than the
long one of eight months is recorded, but the *Earl of Abergavenny* does not appear to have sailed until May or June,
and it is not unlikely that he did return to bid farewell after
Christmas, while Sara was still at Grasmere.[1] He might
also, of course, have gone to Gallow Hill. At any rate, we
know from Wordsworth's reminiscence that in one way or
another he saw much of Sara before he sailed. The *Earl
of Abergavenny* reached England again in September 1802
and a second voyage began about 1 May 1803. William
and Dorothy saw John for the last time in London on
his arrival. He was not at the wedding on 4 October,
but might have found time to go to Gallow Hill before
7 November, when Coleridge saw Sara at Penrith.[2] She went
from there to Grasmere, whence Coleridge was coming
with the secret about her which he wanted to reveal to his
wife on 5 January 1803. The second voyage of the *Earl of
Abergavenny* ended in October 1804, and the third, which
proved fatal to John Wordsworth, began on 24 January
1805.[3] As he did not go to Grasmere during this short
interval, it is possible that he did not see Sara, who was then

---

[1] W. 105, 107, 108, 110, 117, 121 (misdated), 122, 145 (misdated); D.W. (*J.*),
i. 31, 38, 49, 50, 58.
[2] W. 134, 135, 137–9, 141, 205.   [3] W. 184, 192.

settled with her brother Thomas at Park House near Penrith. But she may have gone to London, and it was through a letter to her, which she brought over, not from Penrith but from Kendal, that the first news of the disaster reached Grasmere.[1] I must leave my speculation at that.

Sara did come to Keswick on 7 January 1803 for a few days and walked with Coleridge to the falls of Lodore, at the other end of Derwentwater. He was not well, but under the influence of that gentle spirit able to think it impossible 'that any bodily pains could eat out the love and joy, that is so substantially part of me, towards hills, and rocks, and steep waters'.[2] He again contemplated a second volume of his poems, and a comic poem as long as Hudibras, with less wit, but on a plan which would not exclude the utmost beauty of imagery and poetic diction. And he had written a tragedy and a farce, probably the same which he had written a year before.[3] Meanwhile Thomas Wedgwood's plan of a shooting partnership with Luff in Wales seems to have been dropped, and foreign travel again thought of, possibly with both Luff for sport and Coleridge for conversation.[4] At the end of January Coleridge went off, by way of the Wedgwood works at Etruria, to join his friend once more at Bristol. He writes from Southey's lodgings there, feeling like 'a Comet tied to a Comet's Tail', and from Southey we have the first of many letters which reflect upon what Coleridge might have been, rather than upon what he was to be. It is to William Taylor.[5]

I am grieved that you never met Coleridge; all other men whom I have ever known are mere children to him, and yet all is palsied by a total want of moral strength. He will leave nothing behind him to justify the opinion of his friends to the world; yet many of his scattered poems are such, that a man of feeling will see that the author was capable of executing the greatest works.

A little later he wrote to the same friend.[6]

Coleridge only talks, and, poor fellow!, he will not do that long, I fear . . . It provokes me when I hear a set of puppies yelping at him,

[1] W. 195.   [2] G. 111; Litchfield, 133; D.W. (J.), i. 157, 158.
[3] G. 112.   [4] C. 135; Litchfield, 131, 132.
[5] G. 112; *Addl. MS.* 35343, f. 322; Southey (L.), ii. 199; (T.), i. 452.
[6] Southey (T.), i. 459.

upon whom he, a great, good-natured mastiff, if he came up to them, would just lift up his leg and pass on. It vexes and grieves me to the heart, that when he is gone, as go he will, nobody will believe what a mind goes with him,—how infinitely and ten thousand-thousand-fold the mightiest of his generation.

Coleridge was not staying with Southey, but at Cote House. We have a curious sidelight upon him in a letter from Miss Kitty Wedgwood, one of the few people, it seems, who proved impervious to his fascination. Her brother has asked her to arrange for his accommodation. She will do her best, although he will have to be put in the tower. But she does not share her brother's sentiments about him.

I have never seen enough of him to overcome the first disagreeable impression of his accent and exterior. I confess, too, that in what I have seen and heard of Mr Coleridge there is in my opinion too great a parade of superior feeling; and an excessive goodness and sensibility is put too forward, which gives an appearance, at least, of conceit, and excites suspicion that it is acting; as real sensibility never endeavours to excite notice.

She feels that he must be an uncomfortable husband and negligent of the worldly interest of his children. At Crescelly, where she had been of the party, she had had no scruples of conscience in joining in an attack upon him. No doubt he was generally civil and obliging there, as he was bound to be in the circumstances, but she does not think that Emma Allen will celebrate his politeness.[1] The storm in a teacup at Crescelly, whatever it was, does not figure in Coleridge's own letters. He parted from Wedgwood at Cote, under an engagement to meet him again later at Tarrant Gunville in Dorsetshire, where Josiah Wedgwood had a house, and went to see Poole, whose company he much enjoyed.

Poole is a very, very good man, I like even his incorrigibility in little faults and deficiencies; it looks like a wise determination of Nature to let well alone.

Wedgwood, he believes, has now come to think that his own health would make him an unsuitable companion, and he is not altogether sorry. He does not like the idea of

[1] Litchfield, 139.

leaving Wedgwood to a hireling. But, for himself, he would prefer to go alone, to Teneriffe or the Grand Canaries or Italy and Switzerland.[1] His complaint he believes to be irregular gout, and his letters begin to abound with details of intestinal misfortunes, which need form no part of this record. He professes to have abstained for the last four months 'from all narcotics and exhilarants, whether from the vintner's Shop or the Apothecary'.[2] Nevertheless he is trying to get through Purkis or John Wordsworth a parcel of bang for Wedgwood, and when it arrives he writes to Wedgwood in anticipation of an orgy:

Do bring down some of the Hyoscyamine Pills, and I will give a fair Trial of Opium, Hensbane, and Nepenthe. By the bye, I always considered Homer's account of the *Nepenthe* as a *Banging* Lie.

For Wedgwood there was some excuse. He was suffering from an incurable thickening of the gut, and temporary alleviation of pain was the most for which he could now hope.[3] To Southey Coleridge reports an unsuccessful attempt to dispose of Mrs. Lovell by getting her a post as governess at Cote House. She had, indeed, no accomplishments and he feared that her having been on the stage would be an objection. But the real difficulty was that what John Wedgwood laid particular stress upon was sweetness of disposition and temper, and this he could not bring himself to claim for her. He wishes that Southey could pension her off.[4] After a fortnight at Stowey he went on with Poole to Tarrant Gunville, quarrelling on the way because Poole would take a one-horse chaise, which broke down and delayed them, and also about a certain John Leslie, a physicist friend of Wedgwood's, Poole's dislike of whom he thought that Coleridge had revealed to Wedgwood.[5] At Tarrant Gunville they were up to the chin in comforts, but when Wedgwood himself arrived after some delay he was 'hopeless, heartless, planless', and although he finally went abroad, in spite of the near expectation of war, Coleridge did not go with him.[6]

[1] G. 112–14, 116; Litchfield, 135, 137.   [2] G. 112, 114, 116, 117.
[3] G. 112, 113, 115.   [4] G. 114, 116–18.   [5] G. 115, 117, 129; Litchfield, 137.
[6] G. 117, 118; Litchfield, 140; P. ii. 114; Southey (L.), ii. 201.

The next move was to London in mid-March, and here Coleridge's chief business was to effect the contemplated assurance on his life for a sum of £1,000 at a premium of £27 and to make a will, leaving Poole or, in the event of Poole's death, Wordsworth, as trustee for his family.[1] He had also to arrange with Longman for a third edition of his poems, and this Charles Lamb undertook to see through the press. The attempt to add a second volume had been abandoned.[2] Mary Lamb became ill while Coleridge was in the house and it fell to him to put her into a hackney-coach and take her to the madhouse at Hoxton. During her absence he went to lodge with Charles at 16 Mitre Court Buildings.[3] Now for the first time he saw John Rickman, a friend both of Lamb and of Southey, who was secretary to the Speaker. Rickman was a man of keen and hard intellect, well versed in public affairs and particularly in statistics. He was interested in Coleridge, but likely enough to be critical of him. After a second meeting Rickman wrote to Southey :[4]

I am a little annoyed by a habit of *assentation*, which I fancy I perceive in him; and cannot but think he likes to talk well, rather than to give or receive much information. I understand he is terribly pestered with invitations to go to parties, as a singer does, to amuse the guests by his talent; a hateful task I should think: I would rather not talk finely, than talk to such a purpose.

Another impression was communicated by Humphry Davy to Poole.[5]

I saw him seldomer than usual; when I did see him, it was generally in the midst of large companies, where he is the image of power and activity. His eloquence is unimpaired; perhaps it is softer and stronger. His will is probably less than ever commensurate with his ability. Brilliant images of greatness float upon his mind: like the images of the morning clouds upon the waters, their forms are changed by the motion of the waves, they are agitated by every breeze and modified by every sunbeam. He talked in the course of one hour of beginning three works, and he recited the poem of Christabel unfinished, and as I had before heard it. What talent does he not waste in forming visions, sublime, but unconnected with the real world. I have looked to his efforts, as to the efforts of a creating being; but as yet, he has not even laid the foundations for the new world of intellectual form.

'[1] G. 114, 119.　[2] L. 140, 141; T. 120; Wise, 63.　[3] C. 136; L. 139; Rickman, 87.　[4] Rickman, 86, 88; P. ii. 107.　[5] Thorpe, *Davy*, 85; T. i. 251.

Coleridge, however, had recently expressed the opinion that Davy's own genius was likely to deteriorate under the influences of social life in London.[1] More than one of these parties was at Sotheby's, and among the guests was Sir George Beaumont of Coleorton, an amateur painter of some accomplishment, who took a great dislike to Coleridge.[2] Another group of Sotheby's friends offered to publish *Christabel* for him, and promised that in paper, printing, and decorations it should be the most magnificent thing that had yet appeared. But Coleridge declined.

The lovely lady shan't come to that pass! Many times rather would I have it printed at Soulby's on the true ballad paper.[3]

Early April saw Coleridge back at Keswick, and here he had had another bout of rheumatic fever, which kept him for some time bedridden. Throughout the summer his health seems to have been worse than in the year before.[4] For five months his mind was 'strangely shut up'. He was once more under the spell of metaphysics, which had probably been the main subject of the reading which he estimated in October as having occupied on the average eight hours a day for three years.[5] The renewed impulse to poetry which had come to him in the summer of 1802 had not endured. In December of that year he had written:

I have almost wholly weaned myself from the habit of making Verses, and for the last three years uninterruptedly devoted myself to studies only not *quite* incompatible with poetic composition.—Poetic composition has become laborious and painful to me.[6]

The 'curious metaphysical work' of December 1801 had a defined objective before it in February 1803. It was to be 'the death-blow of Hobbes, Locke and Hume'. The last of these was Coleridge's especial bugbear.[7]

I confine myself to facts in every part of the work, excepting that which treats of Mr Hume: *him* I have assuredly besprinkled copiously from the fountains of Bitterness and Contempt.

[1] Thorpe, *Davy*, 88; Paris, *Davy*, i. 176.
[2] C. 150; Farington, ii. 207.   [3] C. 136.
[4] C. 137; G. 119, 122; T. 119; W. 141.   [5] G. 126, 127.
[6] G. 108.   [7] Paris, *Davy*, i. 173; Southey (*T.*), i. 452.

In June the book had taken the form of a system of logic, preceded by a history of the subject, with the title of *Organum Verè Organum, or an Instrument of Practical Reasoning in the Business of Real Life*. It would be followed by a treatise on the *omne scibile* of human nature. 'But between me and this work there may be death.' This was true, even of the *Logic*, but Coleridge did not anticipate the thirty-one years of fruitless labour which were to intervene. He was already in search of a publisher, perhaps Phillips, whom he thought a pushing man.[1] Even Mrs. Coleridge spoke to a neighbour in high terms of her husband's coming metaphysical work.[2] Coleridge was fortifying himself for his enterprise by a further study of scholastic philosophy in the writings of Scotus Erigena. He would also prefix an essay on Hartley to an abridgement of Tucker's *Light of Nature*, which young William Hazlitt had in hand. In July and August he was still condemning the doctrines of materialism and mechanical necessity, and attempting to explain association as dependent rather on the recurrence of resembling states of feeling than on trains of ideas.[3] He had dropped the notion of publishing a second volume of poems, and had failed to respond to a request of Wordsworth to write to him at large upon a poetic subject.

It seemed a dream that I had ever *thought* on poetry, or had ever written it, so remote were my trains of ideas from composition or criticism on composition.

At moments he hoped that his 'old mind' would recur to him, and that he would be able to produce a series of letters on Chaucer and Godwin's *Life of Chaucer*, either as a volume or in the *Morning Post*.[4] And once, he says, he did tear himself away from his 'abstruse researches' to do some 'Essays and alarum trumpets' on politics in the *Morning Post*. They have not, however, been identified.[5] With Southey he discussed a scheme for a *Bibliotheca Britannica*, which should amount to a history not merely of literature, but of every branch of British learning. Southey thought it 'too gigantic',

---

[1] T. 119, 120. 　　[2] H. A. Eaton, *Diary of De Q.*, 191.
[3] C. 137, 139; T. 119, 120. 　　[4] T. 120. 　　[5] C. 137; G. 127.

and 'to rely upon you for whole quartos!' In a modified form Longman agreed to take it up, but had to drop it during a period of business depression.[1]

In July Coleridge stood godfather to Wordsworth's son John.[2] Among the tourists to Keswick in the autumn was Sir George Beaumont, who lodged at Jackson's, and was somewhat dismayed to find himself next door to Coleridge. He tried to shun him, but was caught by his conversation, and rapidly became one of his warmest and most generous admirers. 'Sir G. and Lady B. are half-mad to see you', Coleridge told Wordsworth, and after they met, Beaumont gave Wordsworth a piece of land at Applethwaite, in order that he might build himself a house near his friend. Wordsworth accepted the gift, but did not build the house, believing that Coleridge was likely to leave the country. Coleridge began a volume of 'translations' from Beaumont's drawings, but nothing survives of them.[3] At Keswick was also William Hazlitt, who painted portraits both of Coleridge and of Wordsworth in the style of Titian. That of Wordsworth was afterwards destroyed as unlike him, and that of Coleridge is unknown. Hazlitt was no longer the ingenuous youth of Wem and Stowey, but a disputatious and rather aggressive young man. He had hoped for Beaumont's patronage, but lost it by angry contradiction of Coleridge in his presence. He left Keswick rather abruptly, and turned up at Grasmere. De Quincey says that he made Dorothy Wordsworth an offer of marriage, but of that there is no confirmation.[4] At Grasmere Coleridge saw the poet Samuel Rogers. He records the 'unpleasant effect on my spirits' of the 'passions, that have made their Pandemonium in the crazy hovel of that poor man's heart'. He should feel 'tarred and feathered', if liked by him.[5]

On 15 August Coleridge started on a tour into Scotland with Wordsworth and his sister, which had been for some time planned. They went in an Irish car, which they bought for £15. Coleridge thought that they would have done better

---

[1] C. 137–9; G. 120; Southey (L.), ii. 220, 233; (T.), i. 465.   [2] W. 147.
[3] G. 121; B. i. 1, 10, 24, 50; W. 151, 156, 159; Farington, ii. 172, 207.
[4] G. 120, 121; W. 218, 220; Howe, *Hazlitt*, 71, 74; De Q. ii. 293.
[5] B. i. 1; Rogers, *Life*, i. 9.

to walk, 'with one pony and side-saddle for our Sister Gift-of-God'.[1] A journal by Dorothy minutely describes their adventures.[2] Apparently Wordsworth borrowed money from Stuart through Coleridge for his expenses, which gave rise to some confusion later.[3] They went by Carlisle, where the miscreant Hatfield was being tried, and Gretna Green, paid their respects to the grave of Burns at Dumfries, and made their way through Lanarkshire and Dumbartonshire, by the Falls of Clyde and Glasgow, to Loch Lomond. Coleridge had started with some hesitation. He now believed that his disease was gout, and meant to experiment with a new remedy introduced by Beddoes.[4] He disliked sitting in a noisy open carriage in the rain, and thought that Wordsworth's 'hypochondriacal feelings' kept him 'silent and self-centred'. Evidently solitary walking would suit him better. When they reached the head of Loch Lomond, Wordsworth suggested that they should part company. This they did at Arrochar. Coleridge sent on his clothes to Edinburgh, and was to follow them by foot. In fact, as the Wordsworths learnt by coming on his tracks later, he did nothing of the kind.[5] Ill health never prevented him from walking, and having found himself 'so happy alone (such blessing is there in perfect liberty)', he turned northwards, and went by Glencoe and Ballachulish to Fort William, and so along the line of the forts to Fort Augustus, where he arrived with a bad toe and a pair of shoes which he had burnt through in an attempt to dry them. At Fort Augustus he had the misfortune to be arrested, on suspicion of being a spy. When released, he went on by Inverness to Cullen, and then turned southwards to Perth, where he arrived after a walk which had covered 263 miles in eight days.[6] At Perth bad news awaited him. Southey had lost his daughter Margaret, and finding Bristol now intolerable, had fled with his wife and the unwelcome Mrs. Lovell to Greta Hall. Coleridge took coach to Edinburgh, where he was delayed for two or three

[1] C. 138; G. 120-2; W. 147-9.
[2] D.W. (J.), i. 159-255; ii. 3-150.   [3] G. 166; L.P. 23.
[4] G. 116, 118, 122, 125-8.
[5] C. 140; W. 150, 151; D.W. (J.), ii. 14, 17, 57, 69, 73, 103, 107.
[6] C. 140, 141; G. 123, 124, 126-8; B. i. 6; R. (D.), i. 369.

nights at the Black Bull waiting for another coach, but was
not well enough to visit Walter Scott at Lasswade. He
suffered from night horrors and sent Southey the lines on
Pains of Sleep. But he claims to have used no opiates, 'except
ether be one'. On 15 September he reached Keswick.[1]

Greta Hall, although he did not know it, was to be
Southey's home for the rest of his life. He had at first no
'fixture-feeling' or 'symptoms of root-striking'. But the
renewed association with Coleridge, in spite of the 'panto-
mimic complaints' for which he was 'quacking himself',
proved a pleasant one. 'Coleridge and I are the best of companions possible, in almost all moods of mind, for all kinds
of wisdom, and all kinds of nonsense, to the very heights and
depths thereof.' They threw stones upon Derwentwater together, like two boys.[2] Coleridge in return was impressed
by his friend's progress in vigour of mind and robustness
of understanding during the last two or three years.[3] Not
wishing to leave him, he abandoned proposed visits to
Ottery and to Beaumont at Dunmow, writing to Beaumont,
who was a strong Tory, a long and interesting letter in
which he surveyed his own earlier political development.[4]
Probably the advent of the Southeys had helped to ease the
situation at Greta Hall. He sent Poole a letter full of details
about his children and praise of Southey, although Mrs.
Southey and Mrs. Lovell he found 'a very large Bolus'. His
dislike of his wife extended to most of her sisters. Martha
was 'the only one of the Brood' for whom he had any
regard. Much later he was visiting her during an illness in
London, where 'the fine ladies at Keswick' had left her as a
laborious mantua-maker, after tantalizing her with a year's
intercourse with Sirs, Lords, and Dukes at Greta Hall. As
to his wife herself:

We go on, as usual—except that tho' I do not love her a bit better,
I quarrel with her less.[5]

[1] C. 141, 142; G. 124–6; W. 152; Southey (*W.*), i. 229; (*T.*), i. 468; *P.W.* 389.
[2] Southey (*L.*), ii. 237; (*W.*), i. 231, 234, 239, 244, 253, 256.
[3] G. 129, 131; Rickman, 104.
[4] G. 127; B. i. 12; Southey (*T.*), i. 474.
[5] G. 129, 251, 274; A. 32; M. 7; S. C. *Memoir*, i. 9; Collier, *Old Man's Diary*,
iii. 80.

A note-book entry, possibly of this period, points to an active correspondence with Sara Hutchinson.

If I have not heard from you very recently, and if the last letter had not happened to be full of explicit love and feeling, then I conjure up shadows into substances—and am miserable.[1]

His religious attitude seems to have been shifting with his metaphysics. In November all his children were publicly baptized. And the book on logic had given way in his mind to one of which he gave the title as 'Consolations and Comforts from the exercise and right application of the Reason, the Imagination, the Moral Feelings, Addressed especially to those in sickness, adversity, or distress of mind, *from speculative gloom*, etc.' This, too, however, was to be 'the very essential oil of metaphysics', and 'the absolute Impersonality of the Deity' was still the article of his faith nearest to his heart.[2] Of Wordsworth he was not at this time seeing so much as usual, still thinking him 'benetted in hypochondriachal fancies', and feeling a little hurt at a supposed lack of attention from him in illness. He records in his note-book an 'unpleasant dispute' with Wordsworth and Hazlitt on the Divine Wisdom, in which they spoke irreverently and malignantly, and he in his turn too contemptuously. Apparently Wordsworth had criticized the views of Paley and others on design in nature.

Hazlitt, how easily raised to rage and hatred self-projected! but who shall find the force that can drag him up out of the depth into one expression of kindness, into the showing of one gleam of the light of love on his countenance. Peace be with him.

Before long, however, he was priding himself on having converted Wordsworth from necessitarianism.[3]

All praise to the Great Being who has graciously enabled me to find my way out of that labyrinth-den of sophistry, and, I would fain believe, to bring with me a better clue than has hitherto been known, to enable others to do the same.

With Hazlitt he was evidently much disillusioned. In September Wedgwood had sounded him on the possibilities

---

[1] *Asra*, 310. [2] C. 143, 145; W. 154; B. i. 43; S. (*W.*), i. 244; Raysor (*M.*), 454.
[3] C. 144, 145; G. 129; *A.P.* 35; W. 150, 151, 152.

of the young man as a travelling companion. For this Coleridge thought him 'utterly unfit'. He had a high opinion of his mental powers and his gifts, in his more genial moments, of expression. 'He sends well-headed and well-feathered Thoughts straight forwards to the mark with a Twang of the Bow-string.' But 'his manners are singularly repulsive—: brow-hanging, shoe-contemplative, *strange*'. And he is 'jealous, gloomy, and of an irritable Pride—and addicted to women, as objects of sexual Indulgence'. The whole analysis is interesting.[1] Coleridge's uneasiness about Hazlitt's sexual proclivities was soon to receive confirmation. Hazlitt had returned to Keswick in October, but soon disappeared, very much under a cloud. The facts were known to Coleridge and Wordsworth, but not revealed by them until many years later. Mrs. Coleridge was apparently only told some 'ridiculous story' of behaviour to a peasant girl. But it is clear that in fact this behaviour took the form of an indecent assault, as a result of which Hazlitt had a narrow escape of being ducked by the girl's neighbours, and even of prison and transportation. Coleridge says that he gave him all the money he had in the world and even the very shoes off his feet to enable him to escape from his pursuers over the mountains to Grasmere, where he got further help from Wordsworth. The ends of justice were hardly served, but no doubt everybody was glad to be rid of him.[2]

Health was now again urgent, in spite of the new medicine, and of Coleridge's own conviction of the metaphysical secrets to be wrested from suffering.[3]

I bear Pain with a woman's Fortitude; it is constitutional with me to look quietly and steadily in it's face, as it were, and to ask it—What and Whence it is?

He had written gloomily of his state to Poole, and Poole, always a little sceptical of his friend's infirmities, had begged that, if the worst happened, some one should be under orders to let him know immediately, 'that I may be certain while I do not hear from you that you have not been dead

[1] G. 126.
[2] G. 273, 276, 279; L. 262; M. 16; W. 505; Southey (L.), ii. 237; Howe, 79, 262; Batho, 66; cf. pp. 295–7.   [3] G. 131.

long'.[1] The idea of a sojourn abroad had now become a fixed resolve. Much of the continent had been closed by war, but Madeira and Sicily remained available. Malta, too, was still in English hands, and Stoddart, who had just been appointed King's Advocate in the island, had given Coleridge an invitation to make that his starting-point.[2] One of his preparations was ominous. He wrote to his friend Thelwall, who was shortly to visit him from Kendal, asking him to bring with him an ounce of crude opium and nine ounces of laudanum, 'the latter put in a stout bottle and so packed up as that it may travel a few hundred miles with safety.'[3] On 20 December he felt better and made a start, intending to bid farewell at Grasmere on his way, and to leave his boy Derwent for the coming Christmas. But here he was taken ill again, and remained for a month, mainly bed-ridden, under the tender care of Mary and Dorothy Wordsworth.[4]

[1] G. 128; P. ii. 117. [2] C. 143, 144; G. 131; B. i. 1; Litchfield, 166.
[3] G. 130, 131. [4] C. 144; Litchfield, 166; W. 155, 158.

X

MALTA

January 1804—August 1806

ON 14 January 1804 a sudden recovery to 'a state of elastic health' enabled Coleridge to walk nineteen miles in four and a half hours through bad weather from Grasmere to Kendal. Here he stopped to write to Richard Sharp an analysis of the characters of Thomas Wedgwood and Wordsworth as the two 'genuine philosophers' among their common friends. Wedgwood's faults, he said, in view of his circumstances, impressed him 'with veneration for his moral and intellectual character more than almost any other man's virtues' For Wordsworth he did not feel 'that almost painfully profound moral admiration which the sense of the exceeding difficulty of a given virtue can alone call forth'. He thought him a happy man, in spite of the 'hypochondriacal graft in his nature', and believed that he would hereafter be admitted, on the strength of his *Recluse*, as the first and greatest philosophical poet. And here he states that distinction between Fancy and Imagination, as the 'modifying' or 'aggregating' power, 'in that sense in which it is a dim analogue of creation', which was to play so great a part, rightly or wrongly, in his later critical theory.[1]

From Kendal he went on to Liverpool, where he spent a week with Dr. Crompton, and thence on 23 January to London. Here he found Thomas Poole, who had come on John Rickman's invitation to undertake the analysis of some statistical returns upon the condition of the poor. 'God bless him! He looks so worshipful in his office, among his Clerks, that it would give you a few minutes' good spirits at least to look in upon him.' For a time Coleridge used Poole's lodgings at 16 Abingdon St., sleeping at Waghorn's coffee-house hard by.[2] Poole, however, had to return to Stowey for a time, and Coleridge invited himself for two days to Sir

---

[1] C. 144; W. 158; Litchfield, 166.
[2] C. 145; G. 132, 133; Litchfield, 166; P. ii. 121, 137-9.

George Beaumont's house at Dunmow in Essex, in order
to see Beaumont's drawings. Here he was received with
great kindness, and remained in fact for ten days, during
which he had a fall from his horse while riding, which must
have reminded him of old times.[1] On his return to London
in the middle of February he borrowed the rooms of an
absent acquaintance, James Tobin, at 17 Barnard's Inn,
Holborn, and gives as his address during the daytime the
Courier office in the Strand. The *Courier* was an evening
paper, of which Daniel Stuart, who had recently sold the
Morning Post, was joint proprietor and editor with one T. J.
Street. Whether Coleridge was now writing for it is not
clear. Nothing from his pen was traced there by his editors,
but in February he contemplated publishing some *Vindiciae
Addingtonianae*, and some essays for 'the Volunteer'.[2] At
Tobin's he was not comfortable, and it was a relief to him
when Sir George Beaumont came to town in the middle of
March, and asked him to his house in Grosvenor Square.
Here he stayed for the rest of his time in London.[3] An idea
of going to Ottery, 'to see my aged mother once more
before she dies', was abandoned.[4] He had brought with
him from Kendal his *Consolations and Comforts*, for which
he thought that one fortnight's steady reading would enable
him to complete the materials, 'and then I neither stir to the
right nor to the left, so help me God! till the work is finished'.[5]
We may be sure that the fortnight's steady reading did not
get itself done during this period. Coleridge was much
occupied with definite preparations for his sojourn abroad.
A last faint hope of Wedgwood's company had failed.
Wedgwood, now hopeless of recovery, had thought of
shutting himself up in a noise-proof room at Tarrant Gunville and waiting for death there. Coleridge suggested that
he might perhaps bring out gout by drinking freely, or
might try 'large doses of opium in a hot climate, with a diet
of grapes, and the fruits of the climate'. But 'another heart-

---

[1] C. 147; G. 135-7, 144; B. i. 50; ii. 164 (misdated); W. 162; Farington, ii. 207;
App. no. v.
[2] C. 148, 151; G. 134, 141; L. 151; Litchfield, 170; Rickman, 105; Lowes, 570;
E. O. Benger, *John Tobin*, 62, 164.   [3] G. 143, 144; W. 166-8; *App.* no. v.
[4] C. 148; W. 158; Litchfield, 168.   [5] C. 145.

withering letter of absolute despair' was the only reply.[1]
Mackintosh, who was now going to India as Recorder
of Bombay, offered to find Coleridge a place there, but this
he rejected without hesitation, having no confidence in
Mackintosh's promises.[2] His mind was still set on Madeira
or Catania in Sicily, where he hoped to get hospitality at the
Benedictine convent through the good offices of Lord Nelson
and Lady Hamilton. Possibly, he thought, he might ultimately get a vice-consulship in Sicily, if it became British,
and live there with the Wordsworths. But his starting-
point must be Malta, and here too it might prove that some
official post would be available.[3] From Sotheby he secured
letters of introduction to Sir Alexander Ball, the High Com-
missioner, and General Valette, who was in military command. Stoddart would house him on his arrival.[4] As to
finance, Wordsworth lent him £105, or more strictly, since
he could not at once find the money, stood security for a
loan of that amount from Sotheby. Another £100 Coleridge
thought that he could borrow from his brothers and from
Stuart. Perhaps this was rendered unnecessary by a gift of
£100 from Beaumont, which Coleridge at first refused, but
which Beaumont pressed into his hand when he went from
Dunmow. At any rate he was able to leave his wife free of
debt, and with the Wedgwood annuity to draw upon during
his absence. Stuart appears to have agreed to act as his
banker.[5]

The delay in London was largely due to the difficulty of
securing transport. Coleridge had hoped to obtain a passage
in a King's ship, and in February Rickman was trying to
find him one, but without success. In March, therefore, he
took a berth, which would cost him over £40, in a merchant
vessel, the *Speedwell*, which was likely to touch at Malta.
But it was still necessary to wait for a convoy, and it was
not until the end of the month that the *Leviathan* became
available for the purpose.[6] Meanwhile Coleridge was able,
not indeed to write *Consolations and Comforts*, but to enjoy

[1] Litchfield, 161, 168, 169; G. 135.   [2] C. 146.
[3] C. 147; G. 136, 139; B. i. 38, 43; Rickman, 103.   [4] G. 139, 144; L. 153.
[5] C. 147, 148, 155; G. 135, 137, 139, 143, 144; B. i. 38, 43; W. 155, 164; Litchfield,
167.   [6] C. 150; G. 138, 142; Rickman, 103, 105.

a good deal of social intercourse. He saw much of Lamb,
who had left off drinking and was unwell and low-spirited.[1]
But there was drink going in his house, and under the
influence of 'a glass of punch of most deceitful strength'
Coleridge had a violent quarrel with Godwin, whose unpleasant second wife had instigated him to speak contemptuously not only of Coleridge himself, but of Southey
and their literary ideas. Coleridge was so disgusted with
'the grossness and vulgar insanocecity of this dim-headed
prig of a philosophocide' that he 'thundered and lightened'
at him for an hour and a half. A reconciliation followed,
but Southey, to whom Coleridge reported the affair, wished
that he would not be so lavish of the outward and visible
signs of friendship to a set of fellows whom he did not care
for and ought not to care for. At any rate, Coleridge might
keep for them the open expressions of love and honour,
which, though he does not doubt them, seem to him 'out-
landish', when applied to himself.[2] Perhaps Southey is here
affected by the criticism of John Rickman, a far more reputable companion than Godwin, from Southey's point of
view. Coleridge was in fact on good terms with Rickman,
whom he thought 'a sterling man'. There was, however, some
friction when a bulky transcript of Wordsworth's poems, for
which Coleridge had sent to Grasmere, came directed under
cover to the Speaker. Coleridge apologized for this abuse of
Rickman's privilege, but when he explained that it was contrary to his own instructions, he must, one hopes, have
forgotten what he had in fact, twice over, indicated to
Wordsworth. Rickman wrote of him to Southey with more
kindly tolerance than might have been expected from a man
of so different a temper. He thought that Coleridge suffered
from the absence of steady work and laboured under a
disease, 'which is *not* the *Nostalgia*', from that cause only.
He was ill, but if he died, it would be 'from a sulky imagination, produced from the general cause of such things; i.e.
want of regular work or application: which is great pity'.[3]

[1] C. 149; G. 133, 138; L. 151; Rickman, 104.
[2] C. 147, 149; G. 133, 137; S. (*L.*), ii. 266; B. i. 49.
[3] C. 148; G. 136, 138, 140, 141, 144, 145; Rickman, 102–7.

But to Wordsworth Coleridge had just written that 'mortal life seems destined for no continuous happiness, save that which results from the exact performance of duty'.[1] Rickman and Coleridge had a common interest in the fate of the unfortunate George Burnett, the waif of Pantisocracy. Rickman had given Burnett some statistical work, but found him indolent and useless. He had tried journalism and tutoring and surgery, with consistent ill success. He went about abusing Coleridge and Southey as the causes of his misfortunes, and Lamb thought that they probably had done harm to his 'flimsy skull'. He was now going to Poland, as secretary to a Polish count, but without any knowledge of languages. And he had taken to drugs. Coleridge met him in the street, and noted his eyes, stupid with opium. 'Oh, it made the place one calls the heart feel as it was going to ache.'[2] Davy, too, was in London, and Coleridge thought him 'more and more determined to mould himself upon the Age, in order to make the Age mould itself upon him'.[3] There was an unexpected introduction to Sheridan, who promised to make Coleridge known to Addington. 'I could take that man in, but I'll be damned if he could take me in.'[4] Others with whom he dined or breakfasted or conversed were the poet Campbell, Sotheby, Richard Sharp, Southey's friend Grosvenor Bedford, and his own old Göttingen acquaintance, Greenough.[5] But he seems to have failed in a promise to Southey that he would negotiate with Longman about a book, which may have been the *Bibliotheca Britannica*.[6] Beddoes and one Welles gave him medical advice.[7] He visited the collection of antiquities formed by Richard Payne Knight, and began to take an interest in pictures.[8] His own portrait was painted by James Northcote. Both at Northcote's and at Beaumont's he met the diarist Joseph Farington, who has left some interesting impressions, of his own and others. Conversation, he says,

---

[1] C. 147.   [2] C. 149; Rickman, 8, 45, 48, 69, 71, 84, 94, 104.
[3] C. 146, 148; B. i. 55; T. i. 297–300.   [4] G. 144.
[5] C. 147, 148; G. 133, 139, 142; W. 169; B. i. 49, 55.
[6] C. 149; G. 133, 137; S. (L.), ii. 266; cf. p. 171.
[7] C. 148; W. 162; Rickman, 104.
[8] G. 144 ('Browrind' for 'Bronzino'?); B. i. 52, 55.

took the form of 'listening to a succession of opinions, and explanations delivered by Coleridge'. These were 'frequently perplexed, and certainly at times without understanding his subject'. On coming away Farington felt 'much fatigued by that sort of confinement we had been under'. He notes Coleridge's 'broad Devonshire' accent, and his good-natured and civil manner. 'He went on like one who was accustomed to take the lead in the company he goes into.' Northcote had heard him read a long poem of his own, with 'the drone of a presbyterian parson'. But Beaumont was enthusiastic.[1]

He mentioned his good fortune in having met with such a genius as Coleridge, a man of such a disposition that he would go to the end of the world to serve another; That Wordsworth, not himself, was his Theme, His friendship being above all self-love.

On 24 March Coleridge heard that the *Speedwell* was about to sail, and hurried off to meet her at Portsmouth, where he stayed at the Crown, and received much kindness from one J. C. Mottley, a local bookseller and agent for Sir Alexander Ball, the Governor of Malta. Stuart himself, with Tobin and the faithful Lamb, saw him off by the coach. He had been far from well during the last month.[2] There was a flight of farewell letters, among others to the Wordsworths, to Poole, to Davy, to the unfortunate Wedgwood, and a 'commission-abounding' one to Lamb.[3] That to his wife dealt wholly with business, but throughout the stay in London he had been writing to her in the half-affectionate, half-hopeless, terms which had become habitual during the foregoing year.

What we have been to each other, our understandings will not permit our hearts to forget! God knows, I weep tears of blood, but so it is.

He bids her write as gladsomely as she can, and is full of tenderness for his children, to whom he sends the new German game of spillekins, the intricacies of which had pleased him. He has been concerning himself to get a job for her brother, George Fricker.[4] What he said to Sara

[1] Farington, ii. 209–11, 217.
[2] C. 150; G. 142–5; S. (T.), i. 487; *App.* no. v.
[3] L. 154; T. 129; W. 168; Litchfield, 170; P. ii. 138, 174.
[4] C. 148, 150; G. 132, 135, 137, 143, 145.

Hutchinson we do not know. A fortnight before, he had addressed to her that letter on Sir Thomas Browne, with its quotation from the ode on *Dejection*, which is one of his finest bits of literary criticism.[1] The farewell letter to the Wordsworths, written when the ship was sailing, is not preserved, but an affectionate one which he sent a few days earlier has recently come to light.[2] He had written also to his brother George, but unfortunately he neglected to see the letter posted, and still had it in his desk on his return.[3] From Southey he parted with a sudden flash of retrospect.

O Southey, from Oxford to Greta Hall—a spiritual map with our tracks as if two ships had left Port in company. It is not for either of us to do it; but a Poet might make a divine allegory of it.

Southey in his turn was affected. '*Quanto minus est cum reliquis versari quam tui meminisse!*' The pair were now on the best of terms. Southey and Lamb, Coleridge had just told Rickman, were 'the two men, whom next to Wordsworth, I love the best in the world'. Tom Poole was now clearly passing into the background. And Southey's 'Trinity of living greatness' were Coleridge, Rickman, and William Taylor. 'All else whom I have seen are children to these.' But Coleridge was likely to prove an inheritor of unfulfilled renown.

The disjecta membra will be found if he does not die early: but having so much to do, so many errors to weed out of the world which he is capable of eradicating, if he does die without doing his work, it would half break my heart, for no human being has had more talents allotted.

So, in 1804, Southey still abounded in letters to his friends.[4]

The *Speedwell* sailed on 9 April, and had a prosperous run of eleven days to Gibraltar, where the *Maidstone* took up the convoy. Coleridge suffered little, except from the rolling of eighty-four guns from Trieste with which the ship was freighted. He studied the Italian grammar, and had no need of the old wine and brandy with which Beaumont had provided him. 'So very little does anything grow into a habit with me!' He spent five days at Gibraltar, enjoying the sun-

---

[1] T. 127; Raysor (M.), 269.   [2] W. 168; *App.* no. v.   [3] G. 161.
[4] G. 144; Rickman, 105; S. (L.), ii. 271, 273, 276; (W.), i. 250, 269, 297.

shine and the marvellous views, and climbing the rocks
among the monkeys. But thereafter the fair wind failed,
and during twenty-four days of storm and dead calms
between Gibraltar and La Valetta he at one time expected to
die.[1] On 18 May he appeared at Stoddart's house in Malta,
where he had not been looked for. Stoddart, he says, received
him with an explosion of surprise and welcome, 'more *fun*
than *affection* in the manner, but just as I wished it'. According
to the reminiscences, very inaccurate in detail, of one Underwood, who held a minor official post, Stoddart was at a ball
at the Governor's, when he was told that a gentleman from
England was asking for him. 'My God!', said Stoddart,
'what has brought you here?' 'To see you.' 'Well, as you
are here, one must be glad to see you. Come and have some
supper.' Mary Lamb had, however, written in advance to
Stoddart's sister Sarah, begging her and Mrs. Stoddart to
be kind, affectionate nurses to Coleridge, although it is
likely enough the message had not arrived. Later she asked
whether perhaps the absence of references to Coleridge in
Stoddart's letters meant that there had been long arguments,
'till between the two great arguers there grew a little coolness'. It is probable that the two men were not altogether
congenial to each other.[2] But in fact Coleridge's conversa-
tional gifts had excited the admiration of Sir Alexander Ball,
who gave him comfortable quarters, now in the palace at
La Valetta, and now in that of St. Antonio, in the country four
miles away, and employed him on secretarial work. Southey
heard that Sheridan had recommended him. Before long the
under-secretary to the government, one E. T. Chapman,
went on a mission, and Ball gave Coleridge the temporary
post, at a salary of £25 a month. He now wrote many official
'Sibylline Leaves' and regarded himself as a 'diplomatic under-
strapper'.[3] Malta itself he found an impressive but arid
place, and the Maltese ugly and noisy. But the hot climate
suited him, and for some time he enjoyed good health.[4] In

[1] C. 151–3; G. 144, 146; L.P. 16; I.L.N.; B. i. 58; W. 173, 179 ('April' for 'May').
[2] C. 152–4; G. 146, 150; I.L.N.; L. 153, 158, 171; A.P. 74, 107, 167; Gillman,
167; W. 179; C. W. Dilke, *Papers of a Critic*, i. 32.
[3] C. 153; G. 146, 147, 161; L.P. 16; B. i. 69; I.L.N.; S. (*W*.), ii. 178.
[4] C. 153; G. 146, 147, 150, 152; I.L.N.; W. 179; Gillman, 167.

August he was able to take a three months' holiday in Sicily. Here he spent most of his time in or near Syracuse, and twice succeeded in ascending Mount Etna. He had contemplated a further tour, but as he was on his way to Messina, he was abruptly recalled to Malta, with the result that he just missed seeing an eruption of Vesuvius.[1] There was now some idea of sending him on a commission to buy corn for the island, which would have taken him through Greece and the Balkans, and possibly into the heart of Russia. But this came to nothing.[2] In January 1805 the Public Secretary to the government died, and Coleridge was appointed as Acting Secretary, until Chapman could return to take up the permanent post. He was now entitled to half the official salary, amounting to £50 a month. He claims, indeed, that he had been promised the whole salary, and was disappointed, but that is very unlikely. The destruction of Maltese archives has left us with little record of his official activities. He describes himself as appending innumerable signatures to routine documents, but also as writing memorials on Egypt, Sicily, and the coast of Africa. Two detailed reports to Ball from Syracuse on a dispute with the Sicilian authorities about the *bona fides* of an alleged French privateer are fairly business-like. Underwood, who perhaps can hardly be trusted, seems to have thought him 'totally inefficient', and a complete 'humbug'. He tells an amusing story of how he was transcribing for Coleridge on one morning, when an official visitor arrived. Coleridge took up a little book, and made a speech about a sonnet he had translated from it, which he repeated *verbatim* to five other visitors on the same morning. It was characteristic, no doubt, but there are lucid intervals, even in government employment.[3]

But of course steady work, even if well paid, did not suit Coleridge. By the turn of the year he was becoming very unhappy, and longing to return home, although it is not clear what he meant to do when he got there.[4]

God! O God! if that, Sara, which we both know too well, were not

---

[1] C. 153, 154; G. 148-50; B. i. 69; T.T. 133.   [2] G. 150.
[3] C. 155-7; G. 148-51, 161; S. (L.), ii. 313; (T.), ii. 101; Dilke, i. 32.
[4] G. 150.

unalterably my lot, how gladly would I prefer the mere necessaries of life in England and those obtain by dint of effort.

Communications in war-time, whether by convoy or through the Continent, were very uncertain, and many letters failed to reach their destination. He describes himself as finding no gratification for a whole year except in writing to the Wordsworths, Sara Hutchinson, Southey, Stuart, Wedgwood, and Beaumont. But only thirteen letters from Malta are preserved. In some cases he knew what had happened. To Stuart he sent copies of a set of 'Sibylline Leaves' which he had written for Ball on the affairs of Egypt and Sicily, which Stuart, if he saw fit, might make use of journalistically, 'only not in the same words'. Incidentally, that is rather shocking to the official mind. The papers were entrusted to a Major Adye. But Adye died of the plague at Gibraltar, and the papers were burnt with his own. Other letters were thrown overboard from the *Arrow*, the *Acheron*, and a merchant vessel, when these were chased by hostile craft. Others again were taken by an Algerian privateer. Letters to him were equally unfortunate.[1] And when news did come, it was not reassuring. He was perturbed to learn that Jackson was obliged by financial difficulties to sell his beloved Greta Hall, although this he had rather anticipated, and in fact it came to nothing.[2] In March he had a shock through hearing suddenly from Lady Ball at a party of the death of John Wordsworth. He staggered and fell, bruising his head, and kept his bed for a fortnight.[3] Hearing of this, his wife refrained from telling him of the death of Thomas Wedgwood. His absence at this moment inspired Mary Lamb's beautiful lines, which begin:

> Why is he wandering on the sea?
> Coleridge should now with Wordsworth be.[4]

Coleridge's health had now suffered a considerable setback.[5] He told his friends that he should start home at the end of February, and then put it off to the end of May.[6] But

---

[1] C. 153–7; G. 146, 147, 150–2; *L.P.* 16; *I.L.N.*; B. i. 69; *A.P.* 134; Meteyard, 303; W. 182, 183, 186; L. 160.   [2] C. 148, 155; W. 189, 191.
[3] C. 156, 157; *H.L.* 107; *A.P.* 132.
[4] Litchfield, 178; Meteyard, 303, 324; L. 168.   [5] C. 155–7; G. 151, 152.
[6] C. 155, 156; G. 151; S. (*L.*), ii. 322, 328; L. 168; W. 211, 212, 214, 218, 223.

Chapman did not return to take up his appointment for some months yet. Ball urged Coleridge to stay on, and although he refused all offers of a permanent post, and also a good opening in America, he was persuaded, as he says, by the importunities of 'one good and great man' to consent. Rickman had heard, years later, that Coleridge and Ball 'parted on the worst terms, on a mutual notorious hatred of each other'. But of this there is no confirmation. Ball may have suffered from Coleridge's business methods. But Coleridge, although he was no doubt irritated by the delay, is insistent to the end on Ball's 'personal fondness' and 'fatherly attention' to him, and the same note recurs in the elaborate account of Ball, which he began, but never finished, for the *Friend* in 1810. He had the highest opinion of him as an administrator. Malta, he thought, was an Augean stable of moral corruption, and Ball had every inclination to be its Hercules.[1] The American prospect may have been suggested to Coleridge by Stephen Decatur, a captain in the naval service of the States, whose acquaintance he made at Malta. Others whom he met there were Captain Pasley, a writer on military subjects, and Richard Reynell, who had visited Stowey in 1797.[2]

Coleridge does not appear to have done any continuous literary writing, apart from disquisitions on Mediterranean politics, during his stay in the island. But he had much recourse to his note-books. About a third of the miscellaneous jottings collected by his grandson in *Anima Poetae* belong to this period. There are many notes of things seen, and many thoughts of home, together with much self-analysis, and reflection on points of psychology and religion, as to which his mind was still undergoing a rapid development. He seems to have been collecting material for a work to be called 'The Soother in Absence', to be related in some way to Sara Hutchinson. There are some scraps of verse, in one of which Sara appears as Asra. There are other more definite references to her, as a kind of guardian spirit. The

---

[1] C. 157, 159; G. 151, 152, 161; *Fr.* i. 227; ii. 95; iii. 226–301; *T.T.* 315; Rickman, 151; S. C. (M.), ii. 300; cf. p. 233.
[2] C. 157; *Fr.* ii. 74, 141; *T.T.* 178; cf. p. 84.

recollection of her saved him from the allurements of one
Cecilia Bartolozzi, apparently an opera-singer, at Syracuse.
All is in an exalted strain of idealism. He still writes to
his wife as 'faithful to you and to my own honour in all
things'.[1] Meanwhile his mundane position was improving.
He lived free of expense, and was able to make some savings
out of his official earnings. He reckoned that he should be
able to meet the expenses of an overland journey to England,
and to repay his debts to Sotheby and others on his return.
He sent his wife £110, largely to cover a year's renewal of
his life-assurance.[2] At the end of August he got his promise
of release, and Ball undertook to send him with dispatches
to Hugh Eliot, the British minister at Naples, in the hope
that Eliot would frank him home as their bearer. There
was constant expectation of his return at Grasmere and
Keswick during the summer and autumn of 1805, which
was prolonged through the winter by a fresh announcement
that he should leave Malta on 1 September. Thereafter no
further letter was received from him.[3] His movements now
become exceedingly obscure. He was at Syracuse on 26
September, but seems to have lingered in Sicily, and when
he finally made his way to Naples he found Eliot 'to be
everything that Sir A. Ball was not and nothing that he was'.
Through the 'villainous treatment' he received, which
probably means no more than that Eliot did not think him
a suitable King's messenger, he was obliged to retain as
journey money another £100 which he had meant for his
wife.[4] The Wordsworths, by December, believed him to have
reached Trieste, on his way to Vienna, and this was indeed
his original intention.[5] But, if he got to Trieste, he could
get no farther, since the advance of the French towards
Vienna, after the capitulation of the Austrian army at Ulm
on 19 October, had closed the continental route. He was
certainly at Naples on 15 December, and remained there

[1] G. 150; A.P. 70–167; Asra, 311, 317.   [2] C. 155–7, 159, 161; G. 150–2.
[3] C. 151, note, 157; G. 152; L.P. p. 389; W. 211–18, 220, 223–5, 229, 230, 235–46;
L. 177, 180, 181; S. (L.), iii. 18, 20, 25; (W.), i. 335, 355; (T.), ii. 113; Meteyard, 303.
In W. 235 'not' is probably a slip for 'now' or 'yet'.
[4] C. 159, 161; G. 161; A.P. 162; Gillman, 178.
[5] G. 161; W. 236, 241–6, 260; L.P. p. 389; S. (L.), iii. 18; L. 180. Probably
'Trieste' in W. 236 was an error for 'Syracuse, on the way to Trieste' (cf. W. 260).

until the end of January 1806, when an acquaintance offered
to take him to Rome. Ten days later, he says, the French
torrent rolled down upon Naples. He had left his letters of
credit and other papers there, meaning to return, although
some of these seem to have been taken by a friend to
Messina. At Rome he stayed for some months, still hoping
to get to Germany through Milan.[1] He was not sensitive to
historical associations. 'I am not certain whether I should
have seen with any emotion the mulberry-tree of Shake-
spere', he says, and 'I believe I should walk over the
plain of Marathon without taking any more interest in it
than in any other plain of similar features'. Nor did he
care about architecture.[2] But he pursued his studies in
pictorial art, and made a close friend of Washington
Allston, a young American painter, then resident in Rome,
who did a portrait of him. Coleridge used to call Rome 'the
silent city', Allston remembered, but he had not found it so
when they walked together in the gardens of the Villa
Borghese.[3] Others whom Coleridge met with interest were
Ludwig Tieck and Wilhelm von Humboldt, then Prussian
Minister at Rome.[4] But Rome itself was now under French
control, and Coleridge came to believe that Bonaparte, who
harboured resentment against him for his articles in the
Morning Post, had ordered his arrest. He claims to have
escaped through the good offices of the Pope and a noble
Benedictine. A story, which represents him as hustled from
his bed at break of dawn, and taken to Genoa in the
Cardinal Fesch's carriage under the guise of his attaché, is
probably in part apocryphal.[5] He says himself that he got
to Florence by the friendship of a young William Russell,
then apparently studying art at Rome.[6] From there he went
to Leghorn, where he fell in with one Captain Derkheim,
an American, who was so taken by his conversation, having
heard nothing like it since he left Niagara, that he offered

---

[1] C. 159; G. 161; Gillman, 179; L.P. 21; L. 182, 184, 185, 190, 191; W. 245, 246,
260; S. (L.), iii. 25; (W.), i. 355, 361.

[2] *Rem.* 313; *A.P.* 71; *T.T.* 269.

[3] Allston, 61, 64; Gillman, 179; *B.L.* ii. 237; W. 1504.

[4] *Fr.* iii. 198; *T.T.* 286; Gillman, 179.

[5] C. 158, *note*; *B.L.* i. 145; *Rem.* 310; Gillman, 179; C. Fox, *Memories of O
Friends*, i. 124.   [6] G. 161.

him a passage in his ship, the *Gosport*. According to Coleridge, Derkheim got him a passport by swearing that he was
an American and his steward, and that he knew his father
and mother, who lived in a red-brick house, about half a
mile out of New York, on the road to Boston. Had he
known what Derkheim was going to swear, Coleridge adds,
whatever the consequences might have been, he would have
prevented him.[1] There was some further delay. A quatrain,
written at Leghorn on 7 June, describes his state of mind:

> Come, come thou bleak December wind,
>   And blow the dead leaves from the tree!
> Flash, like a love-thought, thro' me, Death!
>   And take a life that wearies me.[2]

He now returned to Florence, where he was dangerously
ill for a fortnight, and thought that he had a stroke of palsy.
Finally he reached Leghorn again by way of Pisa, and set
sail with Russell on 23 June.[3] Meanwhile, no letter from
him had reached England since those written before he left
Malta in the previous autumn. At the end of February news
came from Stoddart and through another friend of the
Lambs that he had been in Rome, much noticed, and planning a visit in the country. Southey was extremely angry.

I have no doubt that the reason why we receive no letters is, that
he writes none; when he comes he will probably tell a different story,
and it will be proper to admit his excuse without believing it.

At the end of June a second letter from Stoddart gave the
whole story, so far as known to him. The Wordsworths
had long been in a quandary. The growth of their family
had made it necessary for them to leave Dove Cottage,
but they did not feel able to make any permanent settlement until they knew what Coleridge's plans would be.
On 1 August they heard of him again, as at Leghorn.[4]
At last on 11 August he reached quarantine at Portsmouth,
and finally on 17 August landed at Stangate Creek in Kent,
after a 'heart-wasting' experience since April, shirtless and

---

[1] *Rem.* 310; C. Fox, *Memories*, i. 124.
[2] *P.W.* 1001.   [3] C. 158; G. 153, 161.
[4] S. (*W.*), i. 374; Campbell, 151; W. 183, 184, 189, 191, 212, 245-7, 260, 266, 268;
L. 182, 184, 185, 190.

penniless. He now reckoned that his employments in Malta had cost him £200. The voyage had been a bad one of fifty-five days, including the quarantine, and once more he believed that his life had been thought in jeopardy. But Russell and Captain Derkheim had nursed him with the greatest tenderness. A Spanish privateer had chased the ship, and although he had preserved two large pocket-books, most of his political papers had been thrown overboard to escape capture. Probably, said the cynical Rickman, these were papers he had intended to write. During quarantine, being still ill, he sent no letters, although he dictated one to be given to Wordsworth, if the worst should happen. News of his arrival, however, came to Keswick and Grasmere from Russell, through friends of his own at Exeter and the family at Ottery. Coleridge thought that the account given of his condition was much too favourable.[1]

There is no reference to opium throughout the year and a half of absence from England. Perhaps this is in itself ominous. At any rate the deterioration apparent in Coleridge's physical and mental condition after his return suggests that it was during this period that the habit first became inveterate.

[1] C. 159; G. 153, 155, 156, 161; W. 269, 270, 272; Gillman, 181; Rickman, 143.

XI

SEPARATION

August 1806—June 1808

AT Stangate Creek Coleridge hurried to 'a curious little chapel' which he found deserted, and offered up 'as deep a prayer as ever without words or thoughts was sent up by a human Being'. He now felt health flowing in upon him 'like the mountain waters upon the dry stones of a vale-stream after rains'. He could not at first bring himself to ask for any one or of any one. But he made his way to the Bell Inn in London, called upon Lamb, and announced his arrival to Wordsworth and to Stuart, who was at Margate, but offered him lodging at his house in Brompton. Two days later he wrote to Southey, whom he felt he could address with more tranquillity than his wife.[1] To her his first letter was on 16 September 1806. He then expected to reach Keswick in a fortnight. During the interval he had been seeking ways and means for the future. He had visited Stuart, and came back with the idea of writing a character of Fox, who was just dead, in his paper, the *Courier*, but none has been identified. He also spent some time with the Clarksons, who were staying with one William Smith at Parndon in Essex. From here he seems to have visited Newmarket, where he was shocked by the gambling, and pleased by his own success in an exchange of verbal amenities with the aristocratic frequenters of the race-course. Smith, who was in Parliament, gave him an introduction to Lord Howick, the Foreign Secretary, from whom he evidently hoped to secure some official post on the strength of his familiarity with Mediterranean affairs. This, however, came to nothing. He says that he called at Howick's house and was repelled by the hall-porter with gross insults.[2] A more likely prospect was opened out by an invitation, no doubt through Davy, to deliver a course of lectures at

[1] C. 159, 160, 161; G. 153; L.P. 21; W. 272.
[2] C. 160, 161; G. 154; A.P. 168; L. 192; P. ii. 177; Meteyard, 324; Gillman, 257.

the Royal Institution. This he hoped might lead to permanent work, there or at the London Institution, and an income of £400 a year.[1] Further letters to Mrs. Coleridge apologized for an unavoidable delay in coming north. He was 'fretted almost out of all patience'. The helpful Captain Derkheim had now become a villain. Coleridge had with him in the ship a number of books and a trunk which contained, among other things, a set of engravings from Raphael, which he needed for his lectures, a quantity of Roman pearls, and five bottles of the rare attar of white roses, given him as a reward for pleading on behalf of the Dey of Tunis in the Admiralty Court at Malta, and intended for his wife and Lady Beaumont. These he wanted to take ashore with him at Stangate Creek, and had in fact bribed the custom-house officers for the purpose. But this Derkheim would not allow. He promised, however, to clear the goods at the custom-house for Coleridge, and dispatch them to him. In London, however, he became engaged to be married and, in spite of four letters of passionate entreaty, sailed without fulfilling his undertaking. Coleridge had given him the pearls in return for his kindness, and strongly suspected that he had stolen the attar of roses for his bride. Why Coleridge could not do the clearing himself is not obvious. But he seems to have walked to Tower Hill and got his feet wet in vain, and then to have put George Fricker on to the job, which was finally accomplished through Russell and Clarkson about the middle of October.[2]

Meanwhile Coleridge sat in Clarkson's house at Bury St. Edmunds writing long letters in exposition of the Trinitarian doctrines, which had now definitely replaced his earlier Unitarianism.[3] As to whether he had come home a better theologian, I offer no opinion. But I fear that he was not the wiser or the better man. The letters to his wife are still in the semi-affectionate strain of recent years. But in this there is a good deal of *camouflage*. The first letter was written under direct pressure from Mary Lamb, who insisted that it should be accomplished in her presence. And

[1] C. 161; G. 155, 157, 158; W. 276; S. (T.), i. 506; P. ii. 177; Raysor, ii. 4.
[2] G. 154–60.   [3] G. 158–60; T. 134.

both the Lambs and the Wordsworths were already well aware that the delay was really due to Coleridge's unwillingness to live with his wife, and that the probable result would be a separation. Wordsworth broke the situation to Sir George Beaumont. He thought Coleridge was in any case destined to be unhappy.

He dare not go home, he recoils so much from the thought of domesticating with Mrs. Coleridge, with whom, though on many accounts he much respects her, he is so miserable that he dare not encounter it. What a deplorable thing!

He offered to go and see Coleridge in London, but Coleridge put him off.[1] Dorothy wrote more fully to Lady Beaumont.[2]

We have long known how unfit Coleridge and his wife were for each other; but we had hoped that his ill-health, and the present need his children have of his care and fatherly instructions, and the reflections of his own mind during this long absence would have so wrought upon him that he might have returned home with comfort, ready to partake of the blessings of friendship, which he surely has in an abundant degree, and to devote himself to his studies and his children. I now trust he has brought himself into this state of mind, but as we have had no letters from him since that miserable one which we received a short time before my brother mentioned the subject to Sir George, I do not know what his views are. Poor soul! he had a struggle of many years, striving to bring Mrs Coleridge to a change of temper, and something like communion with him in his enjoyments. He is now, I trust, effectually convinced that he has no power of this sort, and he has had so long a time to know and feel this that I would gladly hope things will not be so bad as he imagines when he finds himself once again with his children under his own roof. If he *can* make use of the knowledge which he has of the utter impossibility of producing powers and qualities of mind which are not in her, or of much changing what is unsuitable to his disposition, I do not think he will be unhappy; I am sure I think he ought not to be *miserable*. While he imagined he had anything to hope for, no wonder that his perpetual disappointments made him so! But suppose him once reconciled to that one great want, an utter want of sympathy, I believe he may live in peace and quiet. Mrs C. has many excellent properties, as you observe: she is unremitting in her attentions as a nurse to her children, and, indeed, I believe she would have made an excellent wife to many persons. Coleridge is as little fitted for her as she for him, and I am truly sorry for her.

[1] W. 273–5; L. 192, 193.   [2] W. 276.

Coleridge was still at Bury on 15 October, but hoped to start for the north next day, 'God permitting', which meant, I suppose, if God offered no further excuses for delay. He had actually left by 23 October.[1]

The Wordsworths disliked his plan of lecturing, which would prevent him from settling down to some work of permanent value. But as it would take him back to London, they decided to spend the winter themselves in a farm-house lent them by Sir George Beaumont at Coleorton in Leicestershire. Sara Hutchinson was to accompany them, but when they met her at Kendal on 26 October she had with her a letter from Coleridge, who had just missed her at Penrith, and was in an 'excess of anguish' from some information there given to him. Whether this was merely the fact of her departure, or some intimation that his wife would not consent to a separation, is not clear. He followed the party to Kendal, and spent three days with them there. Dorothy was shocked at his condition. She was sure that he was ill. 'His fatness has quite changed him—it is more like the flesh of a person in a dropsy than one in health; his eyes are lost in it.' And 'the divine expression of his countenance' was gone. 'I never saw it, as it used to be—a shadow, a gleam there was at times, but how faint and transitory.' The Wordsworths offered to abandon their journey and return to Grasmere. This, however, Coleridge refused. He would go to Keswick, effect the separation, and join them at Coleorton in a month. They seem to have been convinced that it was now the wisest course. But he had been 'so dismally irresolute in all things since his return to England', that they were not sure that he would have the strength to follow it.[2] Nothing more was heard from him until the middle of November, 'a certain proof that he continues to be very unhappy'. Then came a string of agitated letters. Coleridge was maintaining his purpose. The boys were to be with him for their education, and to spend their holidays with their mother. But though at times she seemed to consent, at others she broke out into outrageous passions, urging continually 'that one argument (in fact the only one

---

[1] G. 160; L. 194.   [2] W. 276–8, 280, 284.

which has the least effect upon her mind) that this person, and that person, and everybody will talk'. Her own dislike of her husband, 'as far as her nature is capable of a *positive* feeling', was manifest, and she delighted in satirizing him with her 'self-encouraged admiration of Southey'. To the Wordsworths she wrote herself 'just as if all things were going on as usual, and we knew nothing of the intentions of Coleridge'. She said he was ill, and he himself thought he had the dropsy. Finally she seems to have given way, but to have stipulated for a joint visit to Ottery in the following spring, 'that our separation may appear free from all shadow of suspicion of any other cause than that of unfitness and unconquerable difference of temper'.[1]

Coleridge arrived with Hartley at Coleorton on 21 December, and wrote to his wife as 'your sincere friend'. Dorothy reported favourably of him.

His looks were much more like his own self, and though we only talked of common things, and of our friends, we perceived that he was contented in his mind, and had settled things at home to his satisfaction. He has been tolerably well and chearful ever since, and has begun with his books.

There were pleasant walks, too, in the woodlands, with William and Dorothy and Sara Hutchinson.[2] It must, however, now have become apparent that much of the change in Coleridge's appearance was due to the persistent use of opium, and of the brandy taken to relieve the depression due to its after effects. This was to some extent controlled at Coleorton. But Coleridge was soon taken with seizures, which led to the postponement of the scheme for lectures and the substitution of a book of travels, which never matured.[3] On 7 January 1807 Wordsworth read to Coleridge his *Prelude*, of which the greater part, including the account of their year together on the Quantocks, had been written during the absence at Malta; and Coleridge, in his turn, was moved to write his last poem of any substantial importance, the lines *To William Wordsworth*.[4]

Ah! as I listened with a heart forlorn,
The pulses of my being beat anew:

[1] W. 281–4, 286; G. 164.   [2] C. 162; W. 286, 288, 294; S. (*W*.), i. 398.
[3] C. 162; G. 157 *note*, 162, 168; W. 286, 290, 292.   [4] B. i. 213; *P.W*. 403, 1081.

And even as Life returns upon the drowned,
Life's joy rekindling roused a throng of pains—
Keen pangs of Love, awakening as a babe
Turbulent, with an outcry in the heart;
And fears, self-willed, that shunned the eye of Hope;
And Hope that scarce would know itself from Fear;
Sense of past Youth, and Manhood come in vain;
And Genius given, and Knowledge won in vain;
And all which I had culled in wood-walks wild,
And all which patient toil had reared, and all
Commune with thee had opened out—but flowers
Strewed on my corse, and borne upon my bier,
In the same coffin, for the self-same grave!

The comparison between his friend's achievement and his own failure was a bitter one. For a moment he thought that he would turn to poetry again.

Amid the howl of more than wintry storms,
The Halcyon hears the voice of vernal hours
Already on the wing.

To Southey he wrote that he 'felt that sort of stirring warmth about the Heart, which is with me the robe of incarnation of my genius, such as it is'. He had done between four and five hundred verses, of which the lines to Wordsworth only account for a quarter.[1] What else there was, we do not know. Possibly he made another attempt upon *Christabel*, to which his attention had been called by the belief of Wordsworth, Lamb, and others that it had been echoed, consciously or unconsciously, in Scott's *Lay of the Last Minstrel*. Scott certainly knew *Christabel* before he published the *Lay* in 1805. But Coleridge did not expect to find any improper resemblance, and in fact found none when he came to read the *Lay* later in 1807.[2] He had been unable to accept a recent invitation from Scott to visit him in Edinburgh, and a hope that they would meet at Coleorton seems also to have been disappointed.[3]

After all, the healing influences of poetry and country rambles in friendly converse did not prove enduring. 'We had long experience at Coleorton', wrote Dorothy later,

[1] G. 162.   [2] C. 166; G. 158, 222, 260; W. 230; cf. p. 135.
[3] W. 270ª, 280, 290, 296.

'that it was not in our power to make him happy'.[1] The separation still had to be made definite, in the face of yet another 'frantic' letter from Mrs. Coleridge.[2] There was a little friction also with Southey over Greta Hall, the tenancy of which he now in effect took over. Southey told Rickman, in explanation of the separation, that Coleridge's habits were 'murderous of all domestic comfort', and Rickman replied that stories of calls for brandy in the mornings 'without respect of persons' had reached him.[3] Coleridge began to exercise some parental responsibility towards his boys, writing to Derwent about morals and the study of Greek, and giving Hartley instructions for the sobriety of behaviour which the coming visit to Ottery would impose upon him.[4] He disliked the idea of taking his wife there, to which he was only 'impelled by a sense of Duty and of awakening affection for my Brother'.[5] But inwardly he was racked by 'far crueller calamities, and more envenomed sting', and it is clear from entries in his note-books that the companionship with Sara Hutchinson at Coleorton was ruined for him by a morbid jealousy which he took it into his head to conceive of her evident admiration and friendship for Wordsworth. Morally and intellectually, as well as physically, he was now a very sick man.[6] From Coleorton he wrote at the beginning of April to his brother George, setting out the state of affairs with his wife, and her desire to have the shadow of respectability thrown over the separation, and apparently offering, in spite of his unwillingness to be so far from Wordsworth, to 'strike root in my native place' and succeed Edward Coleridge, who had thrown up his post of assistant at the Ottery Grammar School. He was now starting to join his wife at Bristol, where a letter would find him at Wade's.[7]

The journey to Bristol was, however, deferred, and during parts of April and May Coleridge, with Hartley, the Wordsworths, and Sara Hutchinson, was at Montagu's house in London. Once more, apparently when in com-

1 W. 315.   2 W. 291, 295.
3 G. 162; S. (W.), i. 404, 408, 412, 414; ii. 1; W. 291; Rickman, 144.
4 C. 163; G. 163.   5 G. 169, 170.
6 G. 169, 170; Asra, 313.   7 G. 164, 169, 170.

pany with Wordsworth, his 'inmost feelings were lacerated'.
He was not well and during a call at Lamb's inscribed in his
friend's Beaumont and Fletcher the note 'God bless you,
dear Charles Lamb, I am dying; I feel I have not many
weeks left'. On a later occasion, however, a dose of brandy
and water and a basin of strong broth administered by Mary
relieved him. In London, at last, he met Scott. His chief
business seems to have been to settle some outstanding
debts, as to the amount of which his memory had failed
him, from Wordsworth and himself to Stuart, and for this
purpose he borrowed £50 from Sotheby. But he also saw
Longman, who agreed to give 100 guineas for two volumes of
poems, some of which, including *Christabel*, he had unfortunately still to finish. And the accidental discovery among
Godwin's books of the only copy known to him of *Osorio*,
which he had formerly given to Mrs. Robinson, led him to
think of recasting that for Covent Garden. The old grudge
against Sheridan was still rankling.[1] When he finally reached
Bristol, Mrs. Coleridge had been awaiting him for two
months at her sister Martha's. There, too, at Wade's, was
George's reply to his letter. Being ill, Coleridge, following
a course which became habitual with him, did not open it
until after the arrival of the party on 6 June at Stowey, for
a visit which was intended as a step to Ottery.[2] And when
he did read it, it was extremely disconcerting. George was
much agitated at the notion of a separation, which he
thought no argument would justify. To come to Ottery for
such a purpose would only cause his brother fresh expense
and load his own feelings with what he could not bear
without endangering his life. Moreover, he had a houseful
of invalids, and was giving up his school. He was willing
to furnish financial help, but peace of mind he must have.
Coleridge made no reply at the time, although he complained bitterly to his friends of the unkindness which had
left him with £100 to pay for bringing his family to the
south, after an implied promise that it should cost him

---

[1] G. 165–8; *L.P.* 23; L. 382; W. 299, 300; H. Coleridge, *Poems*, xxxiii, cxcix.
[2] G. 164, 167, 170, 184; P. ii. 181; *Rem.* 305; M. 4; W. 313; S. (*L.*), iii. 101;
(*W.*), i. 414; ii. 1; Meteyard, 324.

nothing. Meanwhile, Mrs. Coleridge had merely a cool formal letter from George's wife, regretting her inability to receive them, and George's own letter Coleridge would never show her. At the end of July she returned to Bristol with the children, but Coleridge remained at Stowey to the middle of September.[1] The visit was a peaceful interlude in his life. He took horse exercise, dropped spirituous liquors, and enjoyed the companionship of Poole, and the renewal of wanderings in 'my dear old walks, of Quantock and Alfoxden', although incidentally he once more had an accident, through entangling his leg in a root and spraining his ankle while leaping a high hedge.[2] He was still brooding over his suspicion of Sara Hutchinson's preference for Wordsworth, but to this period belongs, in part at least, the calmer mood of his poem on *Recollections of Love*.[3]

> How warm this woodland wild Recess!
> Love surely hath been breathing here;
> And this sweet bed of heath, my dear!
> Swells up, then sinks with faint caress,
> As if to have you yet more near.
>
> Eight springs have flown, since last I lay
> On sea-ward Quantock's heathy hills,
> Where quiet sounds from hidden rills
> Float here and there, like things astray,
> And high o'er head the sky-lark shrills.
>
> No voice as yet had made the air
> Be music with your name; yet why
> That asking look? that yearning sigh?
> That sense of promise every where?
> Belovéd! flew your spirit by?

The reminiscence is of 1799, just before the fatal visit to Sockburn. Coleridge had, indeed, been twice at Stowey during the interval, but perhaps not on the top of Quantock.

There were excursions to see neighbours, Lord Egmont at Enmore, the Brices at Aisholt, the Chubbs at Bridgwater.[4] And at Bridgwater young Thomas De Quincey, who had for some time been in correspondence with Wordsworth,

[1] G. 164, and *note*, 169, 170, 184, and *note*, 206, 209; M. 5; D.H. 167; S.C.(M.), i. 8.
[2] C. 164; G. 169, 170; P. ii. 196.
[3] *Asra*, 314; P.W. 409.   [4] S.C. (M.), i. 8; De Q. ii. 149.

but had not yet seen either of the poets, at last succeeded in running Coleridge to earth.[1] Cottle gave him at Bristol an introduction to Poole, and his *Lake Reminiscences* describe at length his visit to Stowey, only to learn that Coleridge was at Bridgwater, the meeting with him there in a reverie under Chubb's archway, the courtesy of his manner and the deference shown to him in the streets of the town, the three hours' dissertation on the Hartleian philosophy and the abandonment of Unitarianism which followed, and was broken only by the entry of Mrs. Coleridge and the most frigid of introductions to her, and the grave warning against the bondage of opium delivered in a sunset walk. De Quincey gives a portrait which may be compared with those of earlier years.

> In height he might seem to be about five feet eight (he was, in reality, about an inch and a half taller, but his figure was of an order which drowns the height); his person was broad and full, and tended even to corpulence; his complexion was fair, though not what painters technically style fair, because it was associated with black hair; his eyes were large, and soft in their expression; and it was from the peculiar appearance of haze or dreaminess which mixed with their light that I recognized my object.

Coleridge was now at last stirred up by Poole to write a long-delayed letter to Josiah Wedgwood. Josiah thought that there had been a 'total neglect' of himself and his brother during the long absence at Malta, although in fact Coleridge had written at least once to Thomas, and only learnt of his death a month after his own return. But now Josiah wanted to arrange for the publication of his brother's metaphysical work by Sir James Mackintosh, and to this he hoped that Coleridge would not be deterred by his dislike of Mackintosh from furnishing materials for a biographical introduction. Ever since he had heard that Coleridge was in quarantine, he had been making vain attempts to get in touch with him through Poole, Wordsworth, and Southey, and he had now become extremely angry. It was 'the only matter on which I wish in future to hold communication with him', he told Poole in January, 'and on that I expect

---

[1] De Q. ii. 140, 150; P. ii. 190.

nothing from him.' Subsequently he was mollified by the kindness of George Coleridge to his boy at the Ottery school, and was prepared to attribute the delay to Coleridge's 'hypochondriacal state'. But it lasted for another two months, and Wedgwood again appealed to Poole. 'I cannot write to him as a friend, and I would rather have no communication with him than as a mere stranger.' Coleridge was at last moved to an apology. 'Cowardice of pain' had often led him to keep letters from persons dear to him for weeks together unopened. But he had, among papers not yet recovered from Malta, one which he had written about Thomas and his psychology, and with this intimation Josiah was satisfied. 'I was truly glad to hear from him. His letter removed all those feelings of anger which occasionally, but not permanently, existed in my mind towards him. I am very sorry for him.' The proposed book, however, was never written, since Mackintosh also failed to do his part, and Coleridge's paper probably became material for an anonymous account of Thomas which he put in *The Friend*. The affair with Josiah seems to have left him very uneasy. He began to fear the possible loss of his annuity. Thomas's share of this had, however, been settled on him by will. Later he was much annoyed by a statement of John Wedgwood that he had neglected Thomas during his illness.[1]

The period at Stowey seems to have been one of mental inactivity. Coleridge did not feel able to carry out his engagement with Longman, and Poole's encouragements to exertion were only met by an epigram.

> Let Eagle bid the Tortoise skyward soar,
> As vainly Strength speaks to a broken mind!

If anything was attempted, it was the beginning of a Greek grammar and lexicon for the use of his boys.[2] At last a letter from Davy revived the idea of lecturing at the Royal Institution, and Coleridge began to plan a course for the following winter. He abandoned the wide theme of Taste in the Fine Arts, which originally attracted him, on the

[1] C. 156; G. 169; Meteyard, 324; T. 142; P. ii. 175, 185; Litchfield, 207, 260; *Fr.* i. 195; *App.* no. vi.   [2] G. 169, 170, 176; P. ii. 195; *P.W.* 1001; Meteyard, 324.

ground that he had not sufficient material, and decided to
confine himself to the Principles of Poetry, as illustrated
by Shakespeare, Spenser, Milton, Dryden, Pope, and modern
Poetry. This would give him scope for 'the whole result
of many years' continued reflection on the subjects of Taste,
Imagination, Fancy, Passion, the source of our pleasures in
the fine arts, in the *antithetical* balance-loving nature of man,
and the connection of such pleasures with moral excellence'.
And on one thing he came to a 'solemn Determination—not
to give a single Lecture till I have in fair writing at least
one half of the whole course, for as to trusting anything
to immediate effort, I shrink from it as from guilt, and guilt
in me it would be'. He would now start on his travel book,
and give Davy a final answer by the end of September.[1]
During that month he rejoined his wife at College Street in
Bristol, much improved in health and looks.[2] Of this visit
there is a long but rather confused account in the reminiscences of Joseph Cottle. With him Coleridge seems to have
had much converse, detailing his adventures abroad, and
expounding his new Trinitarian philosophy and his contempt for the errors alike of Atheism and of Unitarianism or,
as he now preferred to call it, Socinianism. With this change
of mind the evangelical Cottle was more pleased than another
old friend, the Unitarian minister Estlin, who moaned over
his backsliding,

His intellect is all gone, Sir! all his genius is lost, quite lost. He is
a mere superstitious Calvinist, Sir!

Between Estlin and Coleridge there does not appear to have
been at this time any open breach. Of opium Cottle learnt
nothing. But he heard of a plan for a new Review, which
presumably matured into *The Friend*.[3] And he became the
intermediary for a transaction which, for a time at least,
must have put Coleridge on his financial legs again. De
Quincey, who was still in Bristol, had just come into his
patrimony. He approached Cottle and made the generous
offer to put £500 at Coleridge's disposal. Cottle demurred

---

[1] G. 170.   [2] M. 5.
[3] G. 174; *Rem.* 305, 308, 325, 332; Estlin, 101; S. (*T.*), ii. 215.

to the amount, and it was reduced to £300, which was handed over in November. De Quincey had stipulated that the gift should be anonymous, as from a gentleman who admired Coleridge's genius, but Cottle told him that he was sure that Coleridge entertained no doubt as to its source. Probably he paid some debts; he told Cottle some years later that very little of the money had gone to himself. He was certainly borrowing again by the following April.[1]

Nothing seems to have been said at Bristol about a separation. At the end of October Coleridge announced that he must go to London to see about his lectures. The gallant De Quincey offered to act as an escort for his wife and family to the north. Mrs. Coleridge packed up her husband's clothes and departed, only to learn three weeks later that he had fallen ill in Bristol, and had passed three weeks in the house of 'a Mr. Morgan', nursed in the kindest manner by his wife and her sister.[2] She must, however, have known all about the Morgans, with whom both Coleridge and Southey had been acquainted from early Bristol days. John Morgan had married a Mary Brent, and with them dwelt her sister Charlotte. He was a lawyer, but gave up his practice. The family were now to become most helpful friends and supporters of Coleridge. A poem *To Two Sisters*, which with some lack of taste he contributed, over the signature 'Siesti', to the *Courier* of December 10, draws a parallel between Mary and Charlotte and two other sisters dear to him, who were clearly Mary Wordsworth and Sara Hutchinson. It was not unnaturally resented by Mrs. Coleridge and Southey. And a letter written to Morgan a little later even suggests that in happier circumstances he might have married Charlotte.

> But I played the fool and cut the throat of my own happiness, of my genius, of my utility, in compliment to the merest phantom of over-strained honor—O Southey, Southey, what an unthinking man were you, and an unjust![3]

Coleridge claimed to have rewritten his tragedy at Bristol, and written almost as much of *Christabel* as the Wordsworths

[1] *Rem.* 341, 386; G. 180, 255, 321; A. H. Japp, *De Quincey Memorials*, i. 127; H. A. Eaton, *De Q.*, 134.   [2] *Rem.* 347; M. 5; De Q. ii. 232; W. 312, 313.
[3] C. 167; G. 174, 177; M. 5; S. (L.), i. 86; iv. 361; v. 31; *P.W.* 410; cf. pp. 40, 43, 45.

had already seen.[1] On 23 November he came to London, but a dangerous illness of Davy led to a postponement of the lectures, and he returned twice to Bristol before he finally settled down on 13 January 1808 in rooms lent him by Stuart at the *Courier* office. Here he was extremely uncomfortable, in a noisy building, tended only by an 'unlovable old woman'. De Quincey, who followed him to town, describes him as 'picturesquely enveloped in nightcaps, surmounted by hand-kerchiefs indorsed upon handkerchiefs', and calling in vain, 'with the most lugubrious of faces' for the elusive Mistress Brainbridge.[2] No work of this period for the *Courier* has been disinterred, but there or elsewhere he wrote a defence of the bombardment of Copenhagen by the English fleet, which he later incorporated in *The Friend*.[3] He was full of interest in his friend Clarkson's *History of the Abolition of the Slave Trade*, the tale of an achievement, 'compared with which how mean all the conquests of Napoleon and Alexander!'[4]

The lectures began on 15 January, but began disastrously. Coleridge was ill and could hardly leave his bed. By the end of February only two had been given. 'Two more were attended', wrote Lamb, 'but he did not come. It is thought he has gone sick upon them.' De Quincey, who had fol-lowed Coleridge to London, and promised to take notes, records the annoyance of the fashionable ladies who drove twice a week to the doors of the Royal Institution in Albemarle Street, only to be put off with an apology for the absence of the lecturer. Many ceased attendance altogether. And when Coleridge did appear, he was ob-viously unfit.

His appearance was generally that of a person struggling with pain and overmastering illness. His lips were baked with feverish heat, and often black in colour; and, in spite of the water which he continued drinking through the whole course of his lecture, he often seemed to labour under an almost paralytic inability to raise the upper jaw from the lower.

De Quincey put down his condition to opium, and Dorothy

[1] W. 313.
[2] C. 165–7; G. 173, 177; M. 5; *A.P.* 193; De Q. ii. 188, 193; S. (*W*.), ii. 48.
[3] B. ii. 44; *Fr.* ii. 143, 161; S. (*L*.), iii. 139.
[4] G. 174; cf. p. 214.

Wordsworth suspected the same.[1] They had not heard
from him during the summer and autumn of 1807, and had
themselves given up writing, believing their letters unopened. He had failed to repay an advance made by William
for his insurance premium. They were beginning to be very
doubtful as to the desirability of his taking up his abode
with them. This they had contemplated when they left
Coleorton in June, and had in fact secured a larger house at
Grasmere, known as Allan Bank, which would hold him
and his boys. An intermittent correspondence was resumed
when he reached London. He was again full of admiration
for Wordsworth and of gratitude both to him and to
Dorothy.

That there is such a man in the World, as Wordsworth, and that
such a man enjoys such a Family, makes both Death and my inefficient
Life a less grievous Thought to me.

He concerned himself with the interests of Sara Hutchinson's sailor brother Henry, who had been seized by a press-
gang.[2] In February reports came to the Wordsworths
through Mrs. Coleridge and Southey that he did not believe
he could live three months. Wordsworth went up to
London. He found no evidence of any disease which could
not be cured or prevented by Coleridge himself, and was
annoyed by having to wait until four o'clock each day
before he could get admittance to him. The lectures were
resumed at the end of March, and Wordsworth heard two
of them before he left, after entrusting Coleridge to
negotiate with Longman on his behalf for the publication
of *The White Doe of Rylstone*.[3] The course now seems to
have gone on with some regularity until the end of April,
by which time Coleridge had finished with Shakespeare and
was ready to begin upon Milton. Little of the material used
for it has survived, but it is pretty clear that his intention
of writing out at least half the lectures in fair before he
began them was not fulfilled. De Quincey's summary report

[1] C. 167; G. 173–6; B. ii. 44; L. 207; W. 314, 319, 320; De Q. ii. 188; Morley,
102; Raysor, ii. 6.
[2] G. 175, 178, 182, 202; B. ii. 44; W. 298, 303, 305, 310, 312–16, 334; W. H.
Arnold, *Ventures in Book-Collecting*, 44.
[3] W. 317–20, 325, 327, 435; G. 185; L. 207, 209.

betrays great disappointment. Coleridge 'relied upon his extempore ability to carry him through', but he was too depressed to recover 'that free and eloquent movement of thought which he could command at any time in a private company'. The passages he read in illustration were chosen at haphazard and injudiciously, and among his accomplishments 'good reading was not one'.

However, this defect chiefly concerned the immediate impression; the most afflicting to a friend of Coleridge's was the entire absence of his own peculiar and majestic intellect; no heart, no soul, was in anything he said; no strength of feeling in recalling universal truths; no power of originality or compass of moral relations in his novelties: all was a poor faint reflection from the jewels once scattered in the highway by himself in the prodigality of his early opulence—a mendicant dependence on the alms dropped from his own overflowing treasury of happier times.

De Quincey, of course, was writing at a distance of time, and in any case had not himself had by 1808 much experience of Coleridge's early opulence.[1] Rather more favourable were the impressions of Henry Crabb Robinson, communicated to Mrs. Clarkson, from whom he had an introduction to Coleridge, although he does not seem to have made his personal acquaintance before 1810, from which date they were in intimate relations. He, too, notes that there was 'no order in his speaking', but thought that 'the digressions are not the worst parts of his lectures, or rather he is always digressing'. The lecture on Milton was the least interesting. 'The word poetry was not used till the lecture was two-thirds over, nor Milton's name till 10 minutes before the close.'[2] A third reporter was a certain Edward Jerningham, who generally conversed with Coleridge at the end of the lecture.[3]

His voice has something in it particularly plaintive and interesting. His person is short, Thick, his Countenance not inspirited with any Animation. He spoke without any Assistance from a manuscript, and therefore said several Things suddenly, struck off from the Anvil, some of which were entitled to high Applause, and others Incurred mental disapprobation. He too often Interwove Himself into the Texture of his Lecture.

[1] G. 182; De Q. ii. 189; Raysor, ii. 9.   [2] G. 183; Morley, 28, 104.
[3] E. Castle, *Jerningham Letters*, i. 314; Raysor, ii. 20.

Apart from his state of health, Coleridge had not yet, one gathers, mastered the arts of a lecturer in the disposition of his material, or the tact necessary in handling an audience. Towards the end of April Dorothy was able to write,

Poor Coleridge! he has indeed fought a good Fight, and I hope he will not yield; but come to us having accomplished a perfect victory.[1]

But trouble arose early in May, when the sequence of the course was broken for the introduction of a gratuitous double lecture on the subject of Education. It seems to have been suggested by Milton's *Tractate*. Incidentally the old story of Thelwall and the garden of weeds at Stowey appeared in it. Robinson found it excellent. But it kept the hearers 'on the rack of pleasure and offence' for over two hours, and at the end Coleridge was indiscreet enough to launch into a defence of the pedagogic system of his friend Andrew Bell, who seems to have been present, and an attack on that of Bell's rival, the Quaker Joseph Lancaster. This was an issue of burning controversy at the time, and some of the proprietors of the Institution took great offence. They expressed it to Coleridge before the next lecture, at which he appeared much dejected. 'He cou'd hardly at Times refrain from Tears: long pauses sometimes Intervened—and he seemed as if He did not well know how to proceed.'[2]

Coleridge suspended the course for a week, thinking that in self-defence he must publish the lecture, but this he did not in fact do. On the next occasion a crowded audience was faced with an apology, on the ground that the lecturer had fallen in getting out of a boat and had bruised his head. It was the case; Coleridge describes the accident in a contemporary letter. He told the Secretary that it had brought on a pain originally caused by the fall at Malta, when he heard of the death of John Wordsworth.[3] Jerningham reports:

He appeared among us again in about three weeks after. He looked sullen and told us that He previously had prepared and written down Quotations from different Authors to illustrate the present Lecture. These Quotations he had put among the leaves of his Pocket Book

[1] W. 331.　　　[2] G. 183; Morley, 104, 150; Castle, i. 315; Raysor, ii. 10, 21.
[3] Raysor, ii. 18; Castle, i. 316; *H.L.* 107; *App.* no. vi.

which was stol'n as He was coming to the Institution. This narrative was not indulgently received, and He went thro' his Lecture heavily and without advancing any Thing that was spirited and animated.—The next Day He received an Intimation from the Managers that his Lectures were no longer Expected.

Jerningham is not quite accurate. It was Coleridge himself who brought the course to an abrupt termination. On 23 May he was expecting to finish it in a fortnight. A little later he wrote to Wordsworth of his 'disgusting' lectures. He had one on modern Poetry and one on Wordsworth himself still to give. But these were never given, and on 13 June the managers of the Royal Institution had before them a letter in which he explained that he must break off on account of an illness which threatened his death.[1] There had been eighteen lectures in all, and for those he was entitled, at the rate agreed upon, to £100. Of this £40 had been advanced in February to meet his travelling-expenses of the year before. In April he wanted a further advance and was much offended at receiving by the hand of a servant a smaller sum than he had asked for. This, he said, was treating him as a hireling, and he borrowed £100 from Stuart, with the intention of repaying the original advance. He thought the lectures 'a very losing bargain'.[2]

Coleridge's health, which prevented him from increasing the amount of his insurance, probably also diminished his usual social entanglements during this period. He was gratified by a visit from his old Cambridge friend Middleton. He made the acquaintance of Matilda Betham, to whom as a stranger he had written verses some years before, and who now wanted to paint his portrait. Of the Lambs he saw comparatively little. Mary Lamb was rather hurt. 'Coleridge in a manner gave us up when he was in town.' But she would not complain.[3]

Perhaps we are both in fault, we expect *too much*, and he gives *too little*. We ought many years ago to have understood each other better. Nor is it quite all over with us yet, for he will some day or other come in with the same old face, and receive (after a few spiteful words from me) the same warm welcome as ever. But we could not submit to sit

[1] G. 185; Castle, i. 317; Raysor, ii. 19, 22; *App*. no vi.
[2] G. 180, 182, 183; Raysor, ii. 4, 6, 19.
[3] G. 174, 181; L. 213; Raysor (*M.*), 235; *H.L.* 106; *P.W.* 374; *App*. no. vi.

as hearers at his lectures and not be permitted to see our old friend when *school-hours* were over.

There was one curious and pathetic *rencontre*. In the street Coleridge met Mary Evans, now a Mrs. Todd, like himself married and like himself unhappy. He wrote to her afterwards on the 'awful' feeling, and told Stuart that he had seen 'a counterpart of the very worst parts of my own Fate, in an aggravated Form, in the Fate of the Being, who was my first attachment, and who with her family gave me the first Idea of an *Home*, and inspired my best and most permanent Feelings'. Many letters from Coleridge, according to her grandson, were destroyed by Mary Evans, when she married.[1] Needing for some reason a copy of his baptismal certificate, Coleridge now at last answered the letter in which his brother George had refused the proposed visit to Ottery. He is full of grievances, besides that of the refusal itself. A nephew, apparently the Colonel's son James, had spread the report in Bristol that the family had resolved not to receive him. George had prejudiced Josiah Wedgwood against him. Mrs. George, on an earlier visit, had told his wife, 'that I had been a very bad young man, that my Brother had done wonders for me, but she hoped now that I was reformed, I should be able to repay the money.' If George would send in an account of his alimony, he would do his best, 'even though I shorten my own and my children's simple means,' to liquidate it. His only regret was that he could not now cultivate the friendship of his nephew John, also a son of the Colonel, of whom he had high hopes. George later repudiated the charges against him, declared that the letter contained little else but declamation, and reasserted his objection to the parting with Mrs. Coleridge, which he should still hold 'while I think the Gospel to be the word of God delivered by Jesus Christ'.[2]

Meanwhile trouble had arisen about *The White Doe of Rylstone*. Coleridge had negotiated with Longman, as requested by Wordsworth, and arranged for publication. But Wordsworth could not make up his mind whether to publish or not, and when he finally decided, early in June, to with-

[1] G. 180; *Athenaeum* (18 May 1895).　　　[2] G. 184, *notes*; cf. p. 225.

hold the poem, appears to have told Longman that Coleridge
had exceeded his authority. Coleridge was not unnaturally
annoyed.[1] He wrote Wordsworth a long and temperate
protest, in which he recounted the history of the transaction,
and justified his own part in it. Incidentally the letter re-
sumes his own causes of suffering during the summer.
It also contains much interesting criticism, his own and
Lamb's, on the *Doe* itself and its chances of success with
the public. And in it occurs another reference to a journalistic scheme, which was soon to take shape in *The Friend*.[2]
But it must soon have been followed, probably early in
June, by another in a very different vein, which made some
unbalanced charges against Wordsworth, the nature of
which we only know from a reply recently published by
Professor de Selincourt.[3] There were four of them. One,
that Wordsworth had never commented on a suggestion
for a poem made to him by Coleridge while in town, was
obviously trifling. Wordsworth was then interested in
nothing but Coleridge's health and the chances of saving
him. Another concerned Coleridge's old friend and enemy
Lloyd. Coleridge had been 'convulsed' to hear that Sara
Hutchinson had spent a night at Lloyd's house, but he had
done the same himself a few years before. Wordsworth
rarely saw Lloyd, and believed him to be insane. The
women of his household were sorry for Mrs. Lloyd, and
sometimes visited her. It was untrue that Wordsworth
never blamed Lloyd until Lloyd expressed the opinion that
Coleridge was a better poet than his friend. Thirdly,
Wordsworth had taken Stoddart's side in a dispute with
Coleridge about their respective claims to originality in a
criticism of Shakespeare's sonnets. This was absurd. He
thought the criticism a worthless one and anything he said
about it was only said scoffingly. It may be added that, if
it was the opinion later expressed by Coleridge in his table-
talk that the sonnets were written to a woman, the claim to
priority was certainly not worth fighting for.[4] Coleridge
and Stoddart were, however, by now on the worst of terms.

---

[1] G. 185; W. 319, 324, 327–9, 333–5, 339.
[2] *App.* no. vi.   [3] W. 337.   [4] T.T. 245.

Stoddart had undertaken to recover for Coleridge the papers which he had left at Naples, and Coleridge had long been complaining, firstly that he delayed to do so for a twelvemonth, thereby preventing the compilation of the book of travels, and secondly that, when they arrived, he would not release them until Coleridge had paid £50 for the customs 'and some old affair before I went to Malta'.[1] Finally, and this no doubt was what was really rankling in Coleridge's mind, he had formed the suspicion that Wordsworth and his wife were attempting to persuade Sara Hutchinson that his attachment to her had been the curse of all his happiness, and had even overlooked the letters which passed between them. This Wordsworth entirely repudiates. He had himself meddled little with the affair. Mary and Dorothy had always advised Sara not to take Coleridge's passion too seriously. His mind must have had such a determination to some object or other, and if it had fixed on one of a different kind his sufferings might have been worse. But she was old enough to judge for herself, and the idea of any supervision of her correspondence was absurd. One sentence, and one only, had been seen by accident, and Dorothy had asked her to explain it. Coleridge's letter, as a whole, seemed to Wordsworth full of 'lawless thoughts' and 'wildest fancies', and its accusations could only have come 'from a man in a lamentably insane state of mind'. He had long realized the inutility of standing advocate for his friend, as Coleridge thought he ought to have done against Stoddart. 'It would be an unpardonable waste of time to notice a hundredth part of the charges against you, a man's life might be spent in that and nothing else.' Wordsworth is doing his best to write dispassionately, and in evidence of the same prefixes a long account of happenings at Grasmere. But it is doubtful whether the letter would have had the desired effect upon a man who was clearly both morally and physically sick. It only exists in two unfinished drafts and I strongly suspect that Wordsworth, on further reflection, suppressed it. Certainly no reaction to it is traceable from Coleridge's side.

[1] C. 161, 166; G. 170; Meteyard, 324.

XII

THE FRIEND

June 1808—April 1810

WHEN the lectures were over in June 1808 Coleridge took refuge with the Clarksons at Bury St. Edmunds. Mrs. Clarkson had the gift of sympathy, and in companionship with her he recovered to some extent his physical and mental balance. 'Catherine', he said, 'I shall soon be a poet again; you will make me a poet.' Later she regretted that he had not stayed longer, when 'the Truth, the awful Truth' would have been revealed to her. This is rather cryptic. Certainly Mrs. Clarkson knew all about the separation and the opium. Probably what she had not realized was the opening rift between Coleridge and Wordsworth, for she adds, 'He must have acknowledged that the cause of failure was in himself. He went to Grasmere & it was put upon the *change* he found there.'[1] Coleridge's review of the *History of the Abolition of the Slave Trade* by Thomas Clarkson, whom for his absorption in the subject he called 'the moral Steam-Engine or the Giant with one idea', appeared in the *Edinburgh Review* for July, much bedevilled, according to the usual fashion of Francis Jeffrey, by the insertion of paragraphs exalting the share of Wilberforce in the agitation above Clarkson's, and qualifying some praise which Coleridge had bestowed upon Pitt. It brought Coleridge, however, twenty guineas. Probably he would have liked nothing better than to become a regular contributor to the *Edinburgh*. In writing to Jeffrey he expressed his personal indifference to the alterations. But to others he described them as shameful mutilations, and when Jeffrey also made an attack upon Davy broke out, 'It is high Time, that the spear of Ithuriel should touch this Toad at the ear of the public.'[2]

---

[1] G. 216; R. 32; W. 277, 284, 291, 319, 341, 391; L. 211.
[2] C. 168, 169, 171; G. 192, 195, 202 (misdated); A, p. 184.

Early in August Coleridge was expected at Grasmere, where the Wordsworths and Sara Hutchinson had now moved to Allan Bank, an uncomfortable abode, in which they were pestered by smoky chimneys. On 5 September he came over to Greta Hall with Wordsworth to spend a few days, while Mary Wordsworth was confined. Southey describes him as looking 'half as big as the house'. On his return he took with him his daughter Sara, who was now old enough to have reminiscences in after life of her visits to Allan Bank, and in particular of her father's admiration and affection for Sara Hutchinson, of whom she gives the best description preserved to us.

She had fine, long, light brown hair, I think her only beauty, except a fair skin, for her features were plain and contracted, her figure dumpy, and devoid of grace and dignity. She was a plump woman, of little more than five feet.

Crabb Robinson, who was naturally curious, does not add much, on a first meeting in 1815 :[1]

She is a plain woman—rather repulsive at first—but she improves on acquaintance greatly. She is a lively and sensible little woman.

There are broodings over Sara Hutchinson of this date in Coleridge's note-books.[2] He was now, however, on friendly terms with his wife, who herself spent a week at Allan Bank during the autumn, and came again with her daughter in the following year.[3] The separation was now tacitly accepted, although it was not for some years that Coleridge paid his last visit to Keswick. Allan Bank, however, now became his head-quarters, with one considerable gap, until the spring of 1810. His boys, whom he put to school with Mr. Dawes at Ambleside, spent their holiday hours there. For some months, during the winter of 1808, De Quincey was a fellow-inmate.[4] Coleridge renewed his relations with Charles Lloyd at Old Brathay.[5] And before long he made a new acquaintance in John Wilson, a young man of fortune who had built himself a house at Elleray on Lake

[1] C. 169; G. 187; W. 343, 347, 348, 353, 371; S. (W.), ii. 15; S.C. (M.), i. 19; R. (D.), i. 253.   [2] Asra, 316.   [3] G. 187; W. 352, 393.
[4] De Q. ii. 190, 358; L.P. 36, 46; W. 353, 354, 357.
[5] Lucas, Lloyds, 240; W. 357.

Windermere. Wilson was much impressed by a reading of
Christabel and a recitation of the *Chamouny* hymn 'by sun-
rise among the caves of Helvellyn', and acknowledged his
debt to an unpublished, and still unknown, poem by
Coleridge for a fine image in some lines of his own called
The Magic Mirror.[1]

> Oft, all I heard was but a gentle swell,
> Like the wild music of the summer leaves;
> Till, like an army mustering in the dell,
> The blasts came rushing from their pine-clad caves,
> And swept the silence of the scene away,
> Even like a city storm'd upon the Sabbath-day.

At the beginning of October Coleridge was in tolerable
health and better spirits than Wordsworth had known him
in for some time. He was still cheerful in December,
although sometimes poorly in the mornings and inclined
to lie in bed for half the day.[2] He had in fact, perhaps at
the instigation of Mrs. Clarkson, at last made a definite
attempt to rid himself from the domination of opium. To
Street he had written in September:

> I am hard at work, and feel a pleasure and eagerness in it, which
> I have not known for years—a consequence and reward of my courage
> in at length overcoming the fear of dying suddenly in my Sleep, which
> Heaven knows! alone seduced me into the fatal habit of taking enor-
> mous quantities of Laudanum, and latterly, of spirits too—the latter
> merely to keep the former on my revolting Stomach.

He has forgotten the earlier explanation that laudanum was
to be a cure for rheumatism. 'I left it off *all at once*', he adds,
and, 'If I entirely recover, I shall deem it a sacred duty to
publish my cure, tho' without my name, for the practice
of taking opium is dreadfully spread.' He thinks it a matter
for legislative interference. Letters of December, to Estlin,
to Poole, to Davy, are more qualified. 'A very painful effort
of moral Courage has been remunerated by Tranquillity.'
For years he has been 'almost a paralytic in mind from
self-dissatisfaction', brooding over what he believed to be
inevitable, but had never authorized his conscience to pro-

---

[1] W. 371, 392, 393, 395, 400; A. L. Strout, *S.T.C. and J.W.* (*P.M.L.A.* xlviii.
100).   [2] W. 348, 353.

nounce inevitable, by submitting his case, 'carefully and
faithfully', to a physician. This he has now done, and the
result has been what he anticipated. Complete abandonment of the narcotic is impossible, without loss of life, but
he has reduced his allowance to one-sixth of what he used
to take. It is not clear who the physician was. In March he
had thought of consulting Thomas Beddoes, with whom
he was certainly in correspondence, when Beddoes died on
24 December. But if so, the advice can only have been
given by letter, since Beddoes was at Clifton; and it may
be doubted whether a drug-addict ever puts his case, quite
'carefully and faithfully', in a letter. Moreover, he describes
himself as being 'under the care and inspection' of his
physician. On the other hand, he says that the death of
Beddoes left him with 'no confidence in any medical man
breathing'. Probably even the modified doses were sufficient
to account for Coleridge's condition on December mornings.[1]

The confessions to his friends are accompanied by confident hopes for the future. They are to count his life from
the first of January, 1809. It is indeed, he knows, high
time.

Hitherto I have layed my Eggs with Ostrich carelessness and Ostrich
Oblivion—Most of them indeed have been crushed underfoot—yet not
a few have crawled forth into Light to furnish Feathers for the Caps of
others, and some too to plume the shafts in the Quivers of my Enemies.

This very formula he had been using as far back as 1803.[2]
His present optimism was based upon the plan for a
periodical to be known as *The Friend*, of which he had
written to Wordsworth in May or June 1808, as likely to
bring in from £12 to £20 a week. He was ripening it, he
then said, under very warm and zealous patronage, and had
already a prospectus going to the press as soon as Sotheby
and Beaumont had read it. The idea had no doubt emerged
during the lectures at the Royal Institution, since its
organizers, Davy and Thomas Bernard, had given encouragement. One William Savage, printer to the Institu-

[1] C. 170, 173; G. 177, 191, 192, 202 (misdated); *L.P.* 28; Estlin, 101; T. 142;
App. no. vii.   [2] G. 129, 190, 191; B. ii. 63; *L.P.* 28.

tion, was prepared to act as publisher.[1] A prospectus was
not in fact issued before Coleridge came to the north, but
in November he obtained a small supply of one from
William Pennington, a Kendal printer, and in December
both he and the Wordsworths were busy in sending out
copies to all whom they thought likely to be able to obtain
subscribers. The issue was of course premature. Coleridge
took it, complains Southey, 'wet from the pen to the printer,
without consulting anybody, or giving himself time for
consideration'. The impossible date of the first Saturday in
January was fixed for the opening number, although all the
technical details of publication had still to be settled. Nor,
even on the literary side, was Coleridge prepared. He had
'no one essay written', says Dorothy, 'no beginning made'.[2]
The Kendal prospectus has not, I believe, been reprinted,
but, as an exposition of Coleridge's editorial programme,
it probably did not differ much, apart from some changes
of wording introduced in deference to criticisms by Jeffrey
and others, from a later version sent to Stuart, or from the
final text in the first number of *The Friend* itself.[3] Coleridge
adopted the form of a letter to an imaginary correspondent.
Here is the central passage:

The object of the Friend, briefly and generally expressed, is—to up-
hold those truths and those merits, which are founded in the nobler and
more permanent parts of our nature, against the caprices of fashion
and such pleasures as either depend on transitory and accidental causes,
or are pursued from less worthy impulses. The chief objects of my
own essays will be:
The true and sole ground of morality or virtue, as distinguished from
prudence:
The origin and growth of moral impulses, as distinguished from
external and immediate motives:
The necessary dependence of taste on moral impulses and habits,
and the nature of taste (relatively to judgment in general and to genius)
defined, illustrated, and applied. Under this head I comprize the substance of the Lectures given, and intended to have been given, at the
Royal Institution on the distinguished English poets, in illustration of
the general principles of poetry; together with suggestions concerning

[1] *App.* no. vii; G. 192, 193; T. 141, 142.
[2] C. 170-2; G. 190-3; W. 350-4; Estlin, 101; S. (*W.*), ii. 114, 119; Wise, 70.
[3] *L.P.* 32 and p. 85; *Fr.* iii. 303.

the affinity of the fine arts to each other, and the principles common to them all;—architecture; gardening; dress; music; painting; poetry.

The opening out of new objects of just admiration in our own language, and information as to the present state and past history of Swedish, Danish, German, and Italian literature,—to which, but as supplied by a friend, I may add the Spanish, Portuguese, and French—as far as the same has not been already given to English readers, or is not to be found in common French authors.

Characters met with in real life;—anecdotes and results of my own life and travels, as far as they are illustrative of general moral laws, and have no direct bearing on personal or immediate politics:

Education in its widest sense, private and national:

Sources of consolation to the afflicted in misfortune, or disease, or dejection of mind, from the exertion and right application of the reason, the imagination, and the moral sense; and new sources of enjoyment opened out, or an attempt (as an illustrious friend once expressed the thought to me) to add sunshine to daylight, by making the happy more happy. In the words 'Dejection of mind' I refer particularly to doubt or disbelief of the moral government of the world, and the grounds and arguments for the religious hopes of human nature.

In a later number of *The Friend* Coleridge further defined his purpose to discuss in succession the Principles of Political Justice, of Morality, and of Taste, and finally to examine, in the light of Principles, the work of ancient and modern English Poets.[1]

Having delivered himself of the prospectus, he wrote to Savage, asking him, if he was still minded to act as publisher, to print another thousand copies, with his name to them, in London. The reply was disconcerting. The arrangement, as Coleridge understood it, was that Savage should print at trade prices and take a five per cent. commission for his services. Savage, however, now asked for a perpetual right of printing and publishing all editions, and half profits on each after the payment of all expenses. Coleridge suspected an attempt to take advantage of his 'apparent contempt of money'.[2]

But the whole of the Iniquity I did not perceive till it was unveiled to me by a man of the most consummate knowledge of the world, managed by a thorough strong and sound judgement, and rendered innocuous by a good heart—indeed the wisest, most disinterested and constant Friend I was ever blest with.

[1] *Fr.* no. vi.   [2] C. 170, 171; G. 192, 193; T. 141, 142; *App.* no. vii.

This was Daniel Stuart, who now found himself in the position of having to act as Coleridge's mentor through all the intricacies of his enterprise. He must obtain the fresh supply of prospectuses, and put up with Coleridge's complaints, when they did not come as quickly as he hoped. He must find a London agent, which he did in one H. J. Clement. Coleridge, however, was more or less committed by an earlier negotiation with Longman, and somewhat reluctantly added his name. Stuart had also to consult the Stamp Office, and to learn that, if the numbers of the periodical were sent by post, the stamp duty of threepence-halfpenny a sheet would be payable upon them as pamphlets. It took Coleridge a long time to satisfy himself that, as his subscribers were likely to be widely scattered, this would be a cheaper method of distribution than dispatch in parcels to booksellers by coach. And when, at the end of January 1809, he had come to a decision on this, and fixed the size of *The Friend* as a single sheet, and the price as a shilling, which would, he thought, leave him a profit of threepence-halfpenny on each copy, and rejected Stuart's suggestion of monthly instead of weekly issue, he had still to find a printer.[1] It would be cheaper, he believed, to get the work done locally, instead of in London. He tried Pennington, who declined on the ground that he was giving up business. He had vague ideas of setting up a press in Grasmere itself.[2] Then he heard of a young John Brown of Penrith, who would undertake the job, and act as nominal publisher. And so, on 12 February 1809, he left Allan Bank, and made his way over Grisedale to Penrith, spraining his knee and leg on the way, according to his usual fashion, in leaping a brook. He came to terms with Brown, and now fixed 1 April for his first issue, which seems not altogether an inappropriate date. Brown agreed to print 500 copies for £1 3s. and up to 1,000 for £1 7s. But he was not a man of capital, and Coleridge had to buy a hand-press at £22 and a set of pica type at £38 13s., which was £10 more than he

[1] C. 170, 172, 173, 175; G. 191, 193-5, 200; 207; L.P. 28, 30-5; *Addl. MS.* 34046, f. 52; W. 350; *App.* no. vii.
[2] C. 173; L.P. 35, 36 (misdated); W. 355; Lucas, *Lloyds*, 243.

had been told it would cost.[1] Meanwhile he had written
some essays and found the task 'quite delightful, by comparison with the troubles of *setting up shop*'.[2] These troubles,
however, were not yet over. Bonds had to be given as
security for the payment of stamp duty, and the local
distributor wanted Coleridge—'Me, unused to business !'—
to get instructions as to this from the Stamp Office. Stuart
must get him out of 'this embarrassment', and also see to
the advertising of The Friend in London. Still worse,
stamped paper had to be obtained from Fourdrinier, the
London stationer, who usually supplied it. Would Stuart
determine the size and quality to be used, and get a stock
sent off? And could he, as a 'newspaperist', get it on credit?
If not, he must borrow from his friends. A sum of £60 was
due to him from the Royal Institution, and this he had
ordered to be paid to Stuart, towards the discharge of the
£100 he had borrowed the year before. It is evident that
Stuart allowed this £60 to be diverted to the purchase of
paper, and early in April he sent Coleridge an instalment of
1,250 sheets. Unfortunately it was dispatched by the wrong
route, and it was not until 5 May that it reached Penrith.
It was not, therefore, until 1 June that, after much agony,
the first number of The Friend at last made its appearance.[3]

Coleridge returned to Allan Bank on 14 June, after an
absence of four months, during which he had moved
between Penrith, Keswick, Appleby, where the District
Stamp Office was, and Workington Hall, the seat of
J. C. Curwen, the member for Carlisle, who used his remarkable privilege as a legislator to frank the whole postage
of The Friend.[4] The Wordsworths had heard little from him,
and what they heard of him was not encouraging. They had
not been easy when he left, fearing that 'the journey and one
thing or other (to use one of his own favourite phrases) will
knock him up'. And it is clear that in the course of the four
months the good resolutions of the previous autumn had
broken down. He was not 'managing himself well' at the

[1] C. 174; G. 195, 196; L.P. 38; Forster MS. 112, 1.
[2] L.P. 38.   [3] C. 175; G. 196; L.P. 35-47.
[4] G. 197; L.P. 32, p. 450; W. 357, 359, 364, 366, 367, 375, 378, 382, 384; Forster
MS. 112, 6.

end of March. Early in May Wordsworth sent him a warning against 'Doctors' stuff'. There was unpleasant gossip about his habits at Penrith, where he stayed with one Anthony Harrison, an attorney.[1] Later he moved for a week to the cottage of Wordsworth's Quaker friend, Thomas Wilkinson of Yanwath, and 'was happy in Thomas's quiet and simple way of life, drank no spirits, and was comfortable all the time'.[2] Of *The Friend*, shortly before its appearance, they had little hope. It would never be carried on, Wordsworth wrote to Poole, and therefore it would be better that it should never commence. He was alarmed for the prospects of Coleridge's children.[3]

> I give it to you as my deliberate opinion, formed upon proofs which have been strengthening for years, that he neither will nor can execute any thing of important benefit either to himself his family or mankind. Neither his talents nor his genius, mighty as they are, nor his vast information will avail him anything; they are all frustrated by a derangement in his intellectual and moral constitution. In fact he has no voluntary power of mind whatsoever, nor is he capable of acting under any *constraint* of duty or moral obligation. Do not suppose I mean to say from this that The Friend may not appear—it may—but it cannot go on for any length of time, I am *sure* it cannot.

Wordsworth's wish that *The Friend* might never appear was shared by Southey. Both of them, indeed, must have given Coleridge some encouragement at the outset of his enterprise, if we can trust his later statement that their 'sad and anxious looks' had reinforced 'the sense of Duty unperformed' which was his ruling motive. And Southey, at least, was still hopeful early in December, and resolved that, if a fair start was made, he would lend a hand in any accidental delay or illness of its promoter. But already by January he had become sceptical, and was advising an issue at irregular intervals, as material became available, under the conviction that in any other shape, the thing would soon drop. The ideal of course would be to start with a stock in advance of sufficient articles for ten or twelve weeks, which he could then help to keep up, but of that he saw no chance.[4]

---

[1] G. 195; W. 357, 363, 375, 433, 441.
[2] W. 384.   [3] W. 367, 381, 382.
[4] G. 201; S. (*W.*), ii. 114, 119; (*T.*), ii. 229, 261; *L.P.* p. 402.

However, the opening number, which Lamb was one of the first to hail, although he declined at this stage to criticize, was duly followed by a second on 8 June, and Wordsworth, while disliking the intrusion into it of an allusion to the *Beauties of the Anti-Jacobin* and other personal matters, was sufficiently impressed to tell Stuart that he now felt more hopeful of steady exertion by Coleridge than at any other period of the business. Coleridge himself says that he was getting up at 5 a.m. and doing three hours of work before breakfast. He hoped that the forthcoming numbers would be 'in a very superior style of polish and easy intelligibility.[1] But now another financial hitch had arisen. The stock of stamped paper was running low; only enough was now in hand for two more issues. So far this item of cost had been met by Stuart. Some one now made an 'unauthorized and unknown application' to him, which reminded Coleridge of Wordsworth's unfortunate application to Poole in 1801. It does not appear, on this occasion, to have been Wordsworth, although he also sent Stuart a hint of his friend's difficulty. No response was made for some time, and Coleridge felt aggrieved. 'The Whale of Self-offered services, which I had mistaken for an Island, plunged away from under me.' He thought that perhaps he had by now acquired enough of 'a tradesman's character' to get his paper on credit, but learnt through Clarkson and Montagu that this was not so. Then towards the end of June came a letter from Stuart, which was read to Coleridge while he was ill in bed, and which he misunderstood. Apparently Stuart had said no more than that the first instalment of 1,250 sheets might be regarded as a present from him, and that he would advance a supply for two more numbers. Coleridge, however, got the impression that Stuart was prepared to go on financing the paper up to the twentieth number, after which he had announced that subscribers would be expected to make their initial payments. Publication had been stopped after the second number, and Southey had written to Beaumont in July,

Heaven knows when you will see another number of *The Friend.*

[1] C. 175; W. 384-6; L. 220.

To me and Wordsworth it is a sore grief and earnestly did we wish that you might never see the first.[1]

It was presumably on the strength of Stuart's supposed promise that a third number appeared on 10 August, and that from 7 September the regular weekly issues were resumed. In the meantime the writing of essays had gone on steadily, and Coleridge was soon 'months beyond the printer'. His methods were irregular, of course, but he was capable of writing a whole *Friend* in two days.[2] No more paper came from London, however, and the possibility of another suspension soon began to loom on the horizon. Coleridge felt 'like a bird whose plumage is beclammed and wings glued to its body with bird-lime'. He had waited in vain for a letter from Stuart.

For God's sake do not abandon me now! Need I say that one of my great objects in carrying out this Work is to enable me to repay by degrees what I owe you?

Then he turned up Stuart's letter of June, and discovered his blunder over it. Stuart now confirmed his promise of paper for two numbers, and as Coleridge thought that he could raise a loan from his brother or Poole, he asked Stuart to send enough for four, and printing continued. But by the middle of October no supply had come, and Coleridge believed that Stuart, who was on a holiday, had failed to order it. He was much shocked and now curiously once more believed that there had been an undertaking, to him or to Wordsworth, to see *The Friend* through to its twentieth number. Stuart, he considered, had shown great ingratitude and forgetfulness of those services on the *Morning Post*, out of which he had made a very large fortune, 'not indeed *exclusively* by my efforts, but so far that without them he could have done nothing.' Later he wrote of Stuart as 'a *Maecenas* worth £50,000', who had not treated him with common humanity, in spite of the knowledge that he had not received back 'what he lent me on the prospect of my receiving in money what I sent out in paper and stamps'.

[1] C. 175; G. 201 ('Whole' for 'Whale'), 204, 205 ('April' for 'a preliminary'?); *L.P.* 48, 49, 52; *Addl. MS.* 34046; B. ii. 77, 96; W. 384, 385.   [2] *L.P.* 50; W. 400.

Actually Stuart had spent £104 on paper for Coleridge, in addition to old advances which brought up his total indebtedness in 1809 to £300.[1]

Coleridge now turned elsewhere, and asked Thomas Hutchinson, Richard Sharp, Poole, and his brother George to divide among them a sufficient advance to cover the numbers up to the twentieth and also the cost of some unstamped paper, which would enable him to prepare some reprints for sale in book-form. He had been doubtful about Poole, in whom he thought from past experience was 'a speck' when it came to lending money. But Poole, 'my Brother by gift of God', assented, and both Hutchinson and Sharp offered to furnish the whole supply. The only recalcitrant was George, 'my Brother by accident of Midwifery', who reverted to the letter he had in 1808, and charged Coleridge with only having sent him the prospectus of *The Friend* as a step to getting money out of him. This Coleridge repudiated, regretting their long estrangement, and asserting what may very well have been true, that he had forgotten the terms of his letter of 1808, although he felt no doubt that it was an unwise and improper one. George's refusal, he told Samuel Purkis, was 'so couched that it would require an Oedipus to determine whether the baseness, the inhumanity, or the insolence of the answer was the greater'. Meanwhile the stamped paper came, after some confusion owing to conflicting instructions to Fourdrinier, and some rather obscure friction with Poole, which led to a long silence between the friends. One number of *The Friend* failed to appear on 2 November, but with this exception it ran continuously from 7 September to the end of 1809.[2]

During the incubation of *The Friend* other literary schemes, although not entirely absent from Coleridge's mind, had passed into the background. He brought with him to Allan Bank a translation or expansion of the work called *Deutschland in seiner tiefen Erniedrigung*, for the publication of which a bookseller was shot by order of Bonaparte. But

---

[1] G. 184, *notes*; 204, 205, 209, 220; *L.P.* 50, 51, 52, 54, 55; [2] *Gent. Mag.* ix. 491, cf. pp. 200, 211   [2] C. 176; G. 204-8, 210-12, 320.

the German bookseller, with whom he was in negotiation,
let him through by accepting another version, and Coleridge's,
which may not have been quite complete, has passed into
oblivion.[1] During the following winter and spring he lent
a hand to the *Courier* essays and subsequent pamphlet in
which Wordsworth expressed his disapproval of the Con-
vention of Cintra. He thought of adapting a treatise by
Bacon on ecclesiastical affairs.[2] And he intended that, as
soon as *The Friend* was '*pushed off* and in plain sailing',
Brown should print for him his Greek Grammar and Greek
and English Lexicon, for which he would buy a fount of
Greek type, and also the long contemplated two volumes
of poems, with their accompanying essays. He went so far
as to offer Longman the copyright of these for £120, and
then dropped the project, to the relief of Wordsworth, who
thought that Longman was 'an arrant Jew, like most of his
Brethren'. Both the Poems and the Grammar, however,
were still in prospect when Coleridge wrote his begging
letter to his brother George in October, together with a
volume of political memoirs, and an Introduction to Logic
with a History of Logic, all of which were ready for the press
as soon as he could procure the paper. It would be unjust
to Mrs. Coleridge and his children to sell the copyright of
these to booksellers, but he could finance them himself, if
only he could get *The Friend* to a point where it would yield
some profits. Of course he could help himself on by writing
for a party newspaper, now that he was so far beforehand
with *The Friend* essays, but he could hardly reconcile it to
his conscience, 'in this precious and ripe time of my intellectual manhood to waste the powers which the Almighty
entrusted to me and the knowledge which he has permitted
me to acquire by a life of study and meditation, with all the
advantages of Travel and various situations in the events
and passions of the day'.[3] George, as we have seen, was
not to be drawn, and in December and January Coleridge
did in fact contribute to the *Courier* a series of papers on the

---

[1] G. 191, 194; *App.* no. vi.
[2] C. 170, 173, 175; G. 191, 192, 194; *L.P.* 29–32; W. 362, 363, 372, 375; *Bodl. Montagu MS.*, d. 4, f. 107; *App.* no. vii.
[3] G. 196, 200, 205, 209, 210; W. 385; *Forster MS.* 112, 6–7.

political situation in Spain and its analogy to that in the
Netherlands under Philip II during the sixteenth century.
There was nothing in them which Coleridge's conscience
need particularly have boggled at, and, according to Stuart,
they were all the recompense which he ever received for his
services to *The Friend*.[1] In November Coleridge's mother
died. George invited him to come down to Ottery, both
before and after the event, but got no answer.

> It is strange, passing strange, but such men there are. My brother
> Sam will be admirable, in my opinion, but neither respectable, nor
> venerable.

Coleridge, however, had written to Southey, that his mother
wished to see him before her death.

> But tho' my Brother knows that I am penniless, not an offer of a
> banknote to enable me to set off. In truth, I know not what to do—for
> there is not a shilling in the whole house.

And so apparently he did, and wrote, nothing.[2]

There is no modern reprint of the original *Friend*. The
current text represents a recast of 1818, in which the matter
was entirely rearranged, and much of later date added. As
issued in periodical form, it was from the beginning a hopeless enterprise. Both Coleridge and his printer lacked experience of their business, and between them lay thirty miles
and a mountain range. Southey, who lived nearer to Penrith, undertook to correct the proof-sheets, but Coleridge
complains that either he was 'strangely oscitant', or he did
not understand the sentences, and thought that they might
have a meaning for the writer. Certainly there were many
misprints, some of which were removed when the earlier
numbers were reprinted on unstamped paper. And it was
some time before Coleridge learnt the art of so arranging his
matter as to prevent a number from ending in the middle
of a paragraph or even a sentence. A touch of humour
was provided when an issue had to be delayed because a
long passage from Hooker, which he had written out as
a motto, was eaten by rats in the printing-house before it

---

[1] C. 173; G. 204, 207; L.P. 51, 52, 54; B. ii. 96; W. 395; 2 *Gent. Mag.* ix. 491;
O.T. 593.   [2] G. 209; D.H. 177.

could be set up in type. The paper used was of poor quality.[1] Technical faults might have disappeared in the course of time. But the greater difficulty lay in Coleridge's complete failure to recognize the conditions imposed upon him by the method of publication he had adopted. He had before him the success of Cobbett's *Political Register*, but with far greater intellectual gifts than Cobbett's, he was far less able to see into the minds of his readers, and establish the relations necessary to secure and retain their sympathy. A weekly essay should be a unit in itself, written with a directness and lucidity, which quickly rivets the attention and holds it to the end. For Coleridge it was no more than the arbitrary section of a continuous treatise, which required continuous reading to effect its purpose. He could not be direct; his discussions needed the amplitude, not of a sheet, but a folio. There was much political wisdom in *The Friend*, but it hardly got beyond the vestibule to a temple which was some day to be entered. And he could not be lucid. His style was that of the seventeenth century without its architecture, encumbered by all the afterthoughts of amplification and qualification, which go to the making of doctrine, but only bewilder the reader in its exposition. Even among those of Coleridge's own circle, who were not inclined to undervalue his powers, the first impression of *The Friend* was one of its obscurity. 'There are beautiful passages', wrote Dorothy at the outset, 'and everywhere the power of thought and the originality of a great mind are visible, but there is wanting a happiness of manner; and the first number is certainly very obscure.'[2] Charles Lloyd was, perhaps naturally, even more critical.[3]

I certainly think the first number of the Friend abstruse and laboured in the style—it is evidently written with great difficulty. I cannot say that I am more pleased with the second. Coleridge has such a lamentable want of voluntary power. If he is excited by a remark in company, he will pour forth, in an evening, without the least apparent effort, what would furnish matter for a hundred essays—but the moment that he is to write—not from present impulse but from preordained

---

[1] C. 175, 176; G. 207; L.P. 52, 55, p. 415; B. ii. 89; *Forster MS.* 112, 11; *Fr.* nos. 3–5, 7, 10. [2] W. 384. [3] Lucas, *Lloyds*, 244.

deliberation—his powers fail him; and I believe that there are times
when he could not pen the commonest notes. He is one of those minds
who, except in inspired moods, can do nothing—and his inspirations
are all *oral*, and not *scriptural*. And when he is inspired he surpasses, in
my opinion, all that could be thought or imagined of a human being. . . .
But I have more *fears* than *hopes* about this publication.

Things did not improve as the numbers went on. By
the middle of September Southey was much disheartened.[1]

Never was anything so ill-adapted to its mode of publication. THIS,
I did not expect. For all other disappointments I was prepared.

A month later the charge of obscurity had reached Coleridge
himself in letters from Stuart, Poole, and Josiah Wedgwood.
He had as yet had no other outside comment except 'raptures' from Lady Beaumont. He admitted the *entortillage*
of his style to Poole, Purkis, and his brother George, but
some sort of public defence he believed he could make.[2]
And with a view to this he approached Southey. He felt
that *The Friend* was too massive, and would do his best to
lighten it by the introduction of tales and whole numbers
of amusement. He was not very hopeful, because he
realized that the real obstacle lay in the aversion of his
readers to the effort of thought which he was bound to
demand of them in order to effect any good purpose. But
would Southey write a letter in a lively style to *The Friend*
criticizing his 'Don Quixotism in expecting that the public
will ever pretend to understand my lucubrations', and there-
in comment upon his style, in a way which would enable
him to reply with a statement of his own convictions on
the nature of obscurity? Southey made the attempt.
Coleridge, he said, might understand the diseases of the
age, but he had mistaken its temper. It was a light age, and
his essays were too long for it. Moreover, he had fallen
into the same error as Burke, who, for all his talents and
reputation, produced but little effect upon the minds of the
people.

Was it not because he neither was nor could be generally understood? Because, instead of endeavouring to make difficult things easy
of comprehension, he made things, which were easy in themselves,

[1] L.P., p. 409.   [2] C. 176; G. 205, 207, 208; L.P. 55.

difficult to be comprehended by the manner in which he presented them, evolving their causes and involving their consequences, till the reader, whose mind was not habituated to metaphysical discussions, neither knew in what his arguments began nor in what they ended? You have told me that the straightest line must be the shortest; but do not you yourself sometimes nose out your way, hound-like, in pursuit of truth, turning and winding, and doubling and running, when the same object might be reached in a tenth part of the time by darting straightforward like a greyhound to the mark?

In a covering letter Southey told Coleridge that he did not think he had been very successful. A re-reading of the eight numbers had left him with no heart for jesting or irony. 'In time they will do their work; it is the form of publication only that is unlucky, and that cannot now be remedied.' He advised Coleridge to give some amusing numbers, and more poems, only not *Christabel*, which was too good for the purpose, and if possible the 'character' of Bonaparte, so long promised for 'to-morrow, and to-morrow, and to-morrow'. Coleridge did not publish Southey's criticism, but instead gave a long letter of his own to one R. L., who may be Robert Lloyd, in which he repeated much of what he wrote to Southey, and justified his own preference for 'the stately march and difficult evolutions, which characterize the eloquence of Hooker, Bacon, Milton, and Jeremy Taylor' over the 'epigrammatic unconnected periods of the fashionable *Anglo-Gallican* taste', which lacked 'all the cement of thought as well as of style, all the connections, and (if you will forgive so trivial a metaphor) all the *hooks-and-eyes* of the memory'. He admitted, however, that Hooker, Bacon, Milton, and Jeremy Taylor were not good models for a periodical essay, and hoped to correct the fault into which his own preference had led him.[1] This he hardly succeeded in doing. His broken-backed periods remained dear to him, and his formal writing yields but few examples of that swift felicity of phrase which often illumines his private correspondence. An interesting account of Luther in the eighth number made Southey hopeful that *The Friend* might yet win readers. But in a few months he was again deploring its 'rambling' and 'roundaboutness', and other

[1] T. 144, 145; G. 209; S. (L.), iii. 261.

comments from Wedgwood, from Crabb Robinson, even
from the admiring Lamb, remained critical, in particular of
the constant apologies and promises of something which
never came. The most favourable, oddly enough, was that
of Rickman, who was never inclined to over-value Coleridge,
but was now inclined to 'think the better of him for his
friendly productions', in which, for all their defects, he
found 'writing of a high order thickly interspersed'.[1] The
later numbers, moreover, were more diversified, as Coleridge
had undertaken that they should be, by the introduction of
lighter matter. Here appeared, for the first time, Coleridge's
contribution to the *Three Graves*, the earlier part of which
had been written by Wordsworth.[2] The *Chamouny* hymn
was reprinted from the *Morning Post*.[3] Coleridge's letters
home from Germany were utilized as *Satyrane's Letters*, and
a semi-autobiographical account, in prose and verse, of the
imaginary Satyrane prefixed.[4] Corners were filled with
Specimens of Rabbinical Wisdom.[5] A rather gruesome tale,
from a German source, of *Maria Eleonora Schöning* shocked
the sensibility of Dorothy Wordsworth, although Southey
found some merit in it.[6] Other hands contributed. From
Wordsworth came several sonnets, a bit of the *Prelude*,
translations from the epitaphs of Chiabrera, and the beginnings
of an essay on *Epitaphs*.[7] Some lines by F. W. may have
been Wrangham's.[8] John Wilson, with the help of his friend
Alexander Blair, and possibly of De Quincey, wrote a long
letter on the moral and intellectual weakness of the age,
over the signature of Mathetes, and to this Wordsworth
wrote an answer.[9]

On 4 January 1810 appeared the fateful twentieth number, after which Coleridge had notified his subscribers that
their initial payments would be expected. About this there
had been a further hitch. Poole had suggested that George
Ward, a London bookseller and brother of his partner
Thomas Ward, should be appointed receiver, to repay out

---

[1] *L.P.*, p. 415; S. (*L.*), iii. 273; (*W.*), ii. 188, 194; P. ii. 240; L. 228, 229; Rickman,
151; Morley, 113; Gillman, 182.   [2] No. 6; *P.W.* 267.   [3] No. 11.
[4] Nos. 14, 16, 18, 19.   [5] Nos. 11, 12, 22.   [6] No. 13; W. 393; B. ii. 86.
[7] Nos. 11, 13, 18, 19, 20, 25; W. 399, 400.   [8] No. 18.
[9] Nos. 17, 20; W. 395; *P.M.L.A.* xlviii. 101.

of the receipts the advances made for the stamped paper. Coleridge assented, but neither of them had communicated with George Ward, who naturally repudiated responsibility, and ·referred subscribers to Longman, who in his turn rebuffed them. Coleridge managed to placate Ward, who then found that subscribers were expecting him to call in all parts of London to collect their money. This, of course, he could not do, and Coleridge, in a 'supernumerary' number of instructions and explanations and projects for the future, substituted a request to make payment through local post-masters.[1] The results, however, proved extremely disconcerting. It soon became apparent that the lists of subscribers were very misleading. Many who had been approached by Coleridge's agents, if they gave their names at all, did so light-heartedly to save themselves trouble, took no real interest in *The Friend*, and if they ever read it, had certainly no intention of paying for it. The Quakers, Coleridge complained, proved particularly mean, and as for the Earl of Cork, who might as well have been the Earl of Bottle, he wrote after receiving eighteen numbers, 'reproving me in language far more lordly than courteous for my impudence in directing my pamphlets to him, who knew nothing of me or my work'. Such payments as were made arrived slowly, and in the end Coleridge came to believe that, instead of making a comfortable profit out of *The Friend*, he had incurred a loss of £200 or even £300.[2] He struggled on during the early months of 1810 and produced half a dozen more numbers. But before the end of January his hopes were 'at dead low water'. And soon came a final blow. Sara Hutchinson, who, in spite of bad health, had acted as his amanuensis throughout, taking down most of *The Friend* from his dictation, now decided to leave Allan Bank and join a brother in Wales. Coleridge's spirits failed him. Wordsworth had to supply the place of a promised essay, with which he was not ready, having been 'put out of his regular course', says Dorothy, 'by waiting for books

---

[1] G. 208, 211, 212; no. for 11 Jan. 1810.
[2] C. 178; G. 212, 233, 256, 279, 332, 377; *B.L.* i. 110; B. ii. 96; *L.P.*, p. 449; W. 399, 400, 426.

to consult respecting Duty'. I do not think that she intends
an irony.[1] The last issue of *The Friend* was on 15 March,
and ended, in the middle of an account of Sir Alexander
Ball, with the characteristic words, 'To be concluded in the
next number'. A month later Dorothy sent to Mrs. Clarkson a long report of the position at Allan Bank.[2]

I need not tell you how sadly we miss Sara, but I must add the truth
that we are all glad she is gone. True it is she was the cause of the
continuance of The Friend so long; but I am far from believing that
it would have gone on if she had stayed. He was tired, and she had
at last no power to drive him on; and now I really believe that *he* also
is glad that she is not here, because he has nobody to teize him. His
spirits have certainly been more equable, and much better. *Our* glad-
ness proceeds from a different cause. He harassed and agitated her
mind continually, and we saw that he was doing her health perpetual
injury. I tell you this, that you may no longer lament her departure.
As to Coleridge, if I thought I should distress you, I would say nothing
about him; but I hope that you are sufficiently prepared for the worst.
We have no hope of him. None that he will ever do anything more
than he has already done. If he were not under our roof, he would be
just as much the slave of stimulants as ever; and his whole time and
thoughts (except when he is reading and he reads a great deal) are
employed in deceiving himself, and seeking to deceive others. He will
tell me that he has been writing, that he *has* written, half a Friend; when
I *know* that he has not written a single line. This Habit pervades all his
words and actions, and you feel perpetually new hollowness and emptiness. Burn this letter, I entreat you. I am loath to say it, but it is the
truth. He lies in bed, always till after 12 o'clock, sometimes much
later; and never walks out. Even the finest spring day does not tempt
him to seek the fresh air; and this beautiful valley seems a blank to him.
He never leaves his own parlour except at dinner and tea, and sometimes supper, and then he always seems impatient to get back to his
solitude. He goes the moment his food is swallowed. Sometimes he
does not speak a word, and when he does talk it is always very much
upon subjects as far aloof from himself, or his friends, as possible. The
boys come every week, and he talks to them, especially to Hartley, but
he never examines them in their books. He speaks of *The Friend* always
as if it were going on, and would go on; therefore, of course, you will
drop no hint of my opinion. I heartily wish I may be mistaken.

Before the letter was closed, Coleridge came down, and
said he was going to set to work. Dorothy smiled, replied

---

[1] B. ii. 96; W. 400.   [2] W. 403.

that she supposed it would hardly be possible to get out a number that week, and added a postscript.

With respect to Coleridge, do not think that it is his love for Sara which has stopped him in his work. Do not believe it: his love for her is no more than a fanciful dream. Otherwise he would prove it by a desire to make her happy. No! He likes to have her about him as his own, as one devoted to him, but when she stood in the way of other gratifications it was all over. I speak this very unwillingly, and again I beg, *burn* this letter. I need not add, keep its contents to yourself alone.

XIII

BROKEN TIES

May 1810—April 1813

COLERIDGE had shot his bolt in *The Friend*, and it had missed its mark. Early in May 1810 he felt the need for a change of scene, and went to Keswick, while Mary Wordsworth was again confined. He had intended to return after ten days, but in fact stayed for six months, and was never thereafter a housemate of the Wordsworths. Dreams of his love for Sara Hutchinson, recorded in a temper of exalted idealism, still haunted his walks. Mrs. Coleridge describes him as on the whole in good spirits and kindly disposition, but writing nothing, although he said he was.

The last No. of the 'Friend' lies on his Desk, the sight of which fills my heart with grief and my Eyes with tears; but I am obliged to conceal my trouble as much as possible, as the slightest expression of regret never fails to excite resentment.—Poor Man!—I have not the least doubt but he is the most unhappy of the two.

He began to read Italian with her and his daughter, but the only traces of literary activity during these months are in a critical letter to Wordsworth on *The Lady of the Lake* and a few contributions to the miscellany of *Omniana* which Southey had in preparation. Hartley was now 14 and Derwent 10, and their mother did not know what would become of them unless her husband arose from his lethargy and exerted himself. Moreover, Josiah Wedgwood had written that she must henceforward pay the property tax of 10 per cent. on the annuity. Francis Jeffrey was at Keswick during the autumn, and met both Coleridge and Southey.[1]

Coleridge now had little prospect away from London, and for London he started at the end of October. He passed through Grasmere, where Mary Wordsworth thought him bloated and swollen up with fat and to her mind looking

---

[1] C. 179; G. 214; M. 6; *H.L.* 122, 125; W. 407, 410, 419, 426; *Asra.* 318: *B.L.* (ed. Shawcross), i. 217; Cockburn, *Jeffrey*, i. 199.

very ill. Basil Montagu, who had married for the third time
in 1808, and was visiting the Wordsworths, offered to take
him in his carriage, and to give him house-room at 55 Frith
Street, Soho. Coleridge says that he accepted reluctantly to
please his wife, and would really rather have gone to Edinburgh, and put himself under a doctor. He did not intend
his domestication with Montagu to be permanent, for he
had never respected or liked him. He must have forgotten
the very affectionate language of a letter he wrote to Montagu from Allan Bank. Wordsworth thought the arrangement unwise, and told Montagu something of Coleridge's
habits. What exactly he said became matter of dispute afterwards. But Montagu's experience while on the road with
Coleridge soon confirmed the warning. On 28 October, soon
after their arrival in London, there was a quarrel. According
to De Quincey, Captain Pasley, known to Coleridge from
Maltese days, was coming to dinner, and as Montagu had
written a pamphlet against the use of wine and had none at
his table, and military men cannot dine without it, Coleridge
committed the indiscretion of ordering some in himself. De
Quincey may not be quite accurate, as Montagu's pamphlet
did not appear until 1814. But whatever the origin of the dispute, Montagu was unwise enough, in the course of it, to tell
Coleridge of the warning he had received from Wordsworth.[1]
It is likely enough that he perverted its tone and intention.
But the impression of his own words upon Coleridge, so far
as we can gather from broken quotations, took some such
form as the following:[2]

Wordsworth has commissioned me to tell you that he has no hope
of you, that you have been a rotten drunkard and rotted out your
entrails by intemperance, and have been an absolute nuisance in his
family.

Coleridge left the house and betook himself to Hudson's
Hotel in Covent Garden, where he confided to his note-book
a long statement of the disillusion which had now overtaken
not only his 'consummate friendship' and 'reverential admiration' during fourteen years for Wordsworth, but also,

[1] C. 187, 188; H.L. 133; W. 425, 430, 433; R. 21; De Q. ii. 206; App. no. vii.
[2] C. 188; G. 228; Morley, 148, 149.

on account of something which had passed during the last
month, but remains hidden from us, his ten years of a love,
such as 'to an angel alone would be intelligible', for Sara
Hutchinson. To this he appended an 'Elucidation', which
in fact elucidates nothing recent, but harks back to his relations with Charles Lloyd in earlier days, and charges
Dorothy Wordsworth with disloyalty to him in her anxiety
for her brother's fame.[1] From Hudson's Hotel Coleridge was
rescued by John Morgan, who had heard of the quarrel from
a friend of the Montagus. Morgan was now living at 7 Port-
land Place, Hammersmith, and with him Coleridge was mainly
domiciled for the next year and a quarter, although on three
occasions he went off to lodgings, only to return after short
intervals. Towards the end of December 1810 he was at
Brown's Coffee House, Mitre Court, Fleet Street, from February to May 1811 at 32 or 34 Southampton Buildings, Strand,
and in October 1811 at 6 Southampton Buildings. He did
not, however, at any time break his association with the
Morgans, visiting them, even when lodged elsewhere, for a
night or two at a time.[2] The trouble at Hammersmith was,
of course, once more opium. Lamb describes him, soon after
his arrival in London.

> Coleridge has powdered his head, and looks like Bacchus, Bacchus
> ever sleek and young. He is going to turn sober, but his Clock has not
> struck yet, meantime he pours down goblet after goblet.

He put himself under Anthony Carlisle, but soon refused
to follow his prescriptions, quarrelled with him, and thought
of consulting John Abernethy. It is certain that the Morgans
did their best to restrain the habit, at a time when, according
to Southey, it had amounted to a pint a day. But the ladies
of the family were probably not quite so tactful about it as
Mrs. Clarkson. The departure from Hammersmith in October 1811 was without leave-taking, and Coleridge afterwards
explained to Morgan that on his return from a party he had
found, not for the first time, a letter making clear the 'contempt' which, Heaven knows how! I have excited for the last

---

[1] *Asra*, 321; *R.E.S.* xi. 79, from note-book.
[2] C. 180, 182, 183, 187, 188; G. 215-20; L. 239, 240, 243, 244, 247; *H.L.* 129,
132; *L.P.* 60; W. 426, 436; Morley, 46.

8 months or more in your wife and sister'. But there was obviously no permanent breach.[1]

Opium probably explains why there is little trace of Coleridge during the winter of 1810. In November he had some idea of writing for the *Courier*.[2] Crabb Robinson met him for the first time during that month at Lamb's, and thereafter at Godwin's, Rickman's, and John Collier's, where Robinson himself lived, and became a constant recorder of his conversation. It was not exactly conversation, he wrote to Dorothy Wordsworth.

> Coleridge cannot *con*verse, he *ad*dresses himself *to* his hearers. At the same time he is a much better listener than I expected.

But Coleridge had not sunk below his expectations, high as they were. To his brother Robinson wrote more fully of the first meeting, which kept him 'on the stretch of attention and admiration from ½ past 3 till 12 o'clock'. Coleridge spoke of politics, metaphysics, poetry, the Regency, Kant, and Shakespeare. Yet Robinson was not uncritical.[3]

> Tho' he practises all sorts of delightful tricks and shews admirable skill in riding his hobbies, yet he may be easily unsaddled.

Concessions leading to 'gross inconsistencies' might, without difficulty, be got out of him.

> An incomparable declaimer and speech-maker, he has neither the readiness nor the acuteness required by a colloquial disputant.

At Southampton Buildings, in the spring of 1811, Coleridge found himself almost next door neighbour to Hazlitt. It was a little uncomfortable for both of them, after what had happened at Keswick, since they could not avoid meeting at Lamb's. Hazlitt spoke of Coleridge to Robinson 'with the feelings of an injured man'.[4] Coleridge's own lack of balance at this time seems to have struck more than one observer. Early in March he had a shock from the death of George Burnett. This unfortunate man had returned from Poland in 1805, much in love with a Polish princess. He

---

[1] C. 180, 184, 188; G. 215, 217, 220; L. 238; W. 422, 426, 433, 435; *H.L.* 134; *Rem.* 373.   [2] G. 215; L. 240; W. 425.
[3] G. 216; R. 22; R. (L.) 64; Morley, 30 sqq.
[4] T. 148; Morley, 38–40; Howe, 74, 129–33.

wrote some books, not without merit, but later fell into
poverty, pestered Rickman with begging letters, and finally
met his end in a workhouse hospital. There may have been
some suspicion of suicide, but according to Rickman the
cause was a rapid decline.

I knew not why the thing was represented worse than this; and I can
tell you, that the over-acted sorrow of Coleridge has been very mis-
chievous. Would to God he had not come to London.

Both Coleridge and Hazlitt were at Lamb's when the news
arrived, and both, says Robinson, were sensibly affected.
Coleridge describes his own agitation, and that, as a result,
of Mary Lamb. She 'dropped certain ominous words at the
time', then wrote to Wordsworth, telling him to come to
town at once, because she believed Coleridge's mind to be
'seriously unhinged', and then herself collapsed, and had to
be taken to confinement. Hazlitt, however, declared that
both Mary and Charles Lamb were injured by Coleridge's
presence in town, and the frequent visits and constant company which kept their minds in perpetual fever.[1] A day after
he heard of Mary's state, Coleridge had a mournful talk with
Lamb, and then went off to dine with a Lady Jerningham,
to whom Miss Betham had introduced him. His head, he
says, was 'throbbing with long weeping and the unnecessary
haste I made in fear of being too late, and the having to act
before the curtain as it were afterwards'. Lady Jerningham
herself describes his 'superabundance of words' on this
occasion, and the fatigue caused by his evident sense of an
obligation to 'play first Violin'. He was kept until 11 o'clock
listening to music by Lady Jerningham's daughter-in-law,
and when at last he got to bed, had to remain there for the best
part of three days, thereby missing another engagement with
Miss Betham herself. Much of this he details in an elaborate
letter of apology, which when shown to Lady Jerningham,
evoked the comment, 'I am afraid he will go out of his head
also.'[2] Coleridge was now gratified by a call from the Irish
orator Henry Grattan, and met both him and the singer
Signora Catalani at dinner parties.[3] In April broken family

[1] G. 216; Rickman, 111, 152, 155; H.L. 129; R. (D.), i. 364.
[2] H.L. 128, 129; L.P. 60; Castle, ii. 7; L. 244.
[3] C. 181; Godwin, ii. 222; L. 243.

relations were renewed by a visit to Southey's friend, John
May, at Richmond, where Coleridge found his nephews
John Taylor and Henry Nelson, the sons of Colonel James.
John Taylor recorded his impressions in a letter home.

> So delightful and astonishing a man I have never met with. Every
> subject he was master of, and discussed in the most splendid eloquence,
> without pausing for a word. Whether poetry, religion, language,
> politics, or metaphysics were on the 'tapis', he was equally at home and
> equally clear.

A lady sang Italian songs to him.

> His very frame shook with pleasure, a settled smile and a sort of
> tittering noise indicated his feelings. He prayed that she might finish
> those strains in Heaven, and, sitting down by Mrs May, recited some
> extempore verses on the singer.

With his nephews he went to church, saying, as he passed
through the church-yard, that by God's favour man seemed
to have fifty-two springs every year; and, although vehement against the sermon, professed religious principles of
a most orthodox and zealous nature. 'Yet I saw and heard
some things which I did not quite like,' and although his
uncle promised to write to him by the next penny post, 'I
need hardly say that I have not heard one word from him!'
Another account of the meeting was contributed by John
Taylor to his brother's volumes of Coleridge's *Table-Talk*.[1]
In May Coleridge again recorded his expectation of early
death in one of Lamb's books, this time a copy of Donne's
Poems.[2] His mind, however, was reverting to thoughts of
literary composition, although Southey had tried in vain to
get some more *Omniana* out of him. With Godwin, who had
set up a publishing business in his wife's name, he discussed
a volume of historical lives on the model of Plutarch, and a
poem based on Gessner's *Der erste Schiffer*, which had already engaged him in 1802. There was more in Godwin, he
said, than he was at one time willing to admit, although not
so much as his admirers fancied. Once more he approached
Longman with proposals for his *Poems* and a revival of *The
Friend*. Longman offered 'a Jew bargain' for the former,

---

[1] *D.H.* 190; *T.T.* 334.　　　　　　　　　　　　[2] *L.* 382.

which Coleridge accepted in the spirit of Shakespeare's
apothecary, but did not pursue. But for *The Friend* he could
make no profitable terms, and thought of proposing a
monthly issue to another publisher, Henry Baldwin.

> Great as my affection may be for the Angels of Paternoster Row,
> that sit in the appropriate shape of Cormorants on the Tree of Know-
> ledge, I am selfish enough to have a still greater for S.T.C. and his
> three little ones.

Southey, however, had come to the conclusion that only an
improbable intellectual or moral conversion would make
Coleridge capable of any exertion for his children.[1]

Journalism again suggested itself as a resource. Coleridge approached Stuart, and offered his services as a daily
assistant and paragraph-writer to Street, who was now the
acting editor of the *Courier*, although Stuart still retained a
financial interest. The proposal was accepted. A first contribution appeared on April 19, and was followed by many
others, mostly short paragraphs on current domestic and
foreign affairs, which ran from 7 May to 27 September, with
a considerable break in the course of June.[2]

The Wordsworths had, of course, heard nothing from
Coleridge since his departure from Keswick. Dorothy was
then hopeless of him, and dismissed him from her thoughts
as far as possible. Such tidings as they got came through the
Montagus and Lambs. Montagu told Wordsworth that he
had realized Coleridge's habits on the road, had repeated to
him what Wordsworth had said, and thereby made him very
angry. Wordsworth replied that he had acted unwisely, and
heard no more of the matter at the time. 'It would pity anybody's heart', wrote Dorothy in February, 'to look at
Hartley when he inquires as if hopelessly if there has been
any news of his Father'.[3] In London, however, gossip about
the strained relations between the friends had by this time
somehow got abroad. Coleridge declares that it did not
originate with him. When he heard of it he was on his way

---

[1] C. 181; G. 216, 218, 256; Godwin, ii. 222, 224; Morley, 39; W. 433; S. (*W.*), ii.
211, 299, 301; B. ii. 126; *Bodl. Montagu MS.* d. 4, f. 102.
[2] C. 182; G. 217, 218; *L.P.* 59 (misdated); *B.L.* i. 38, 145; W. 435, 436; R. 23;
B. ii. 141; 2 *Gent. Mag.* ix. 491, 580; T. ii. 81, 82; *O.T.* 733–938.
[3] W. 422, 425, 426, 428, 430, 433.

to the Lambs, and became so agitated that he poured out
the whole story to Mary in an agony of weeping. 'Wordsworth, Wordsworth has given me up.' Afterwards he confided it to the Morgans, who certainly told no one. To
others, such as Mrs. Clarkson, whom he believed already
cognizant of the suspension of intercourse with Wordsworth, he had alluded to the fact, without going into details.
Robinson confirms this in his own case. The only thing
Coleridge could blame himself for was that he had said too
much to the Beaumonts, whom he wrongly supposed to be
aware of the position, and had even allowed himself the
comment, 'And this is cruel! this is *base*!' He may have
forgotten that he had also unbosomed himself to Stuart, to
whom he wrote in April,

> So deep and rankling is the wound, which Wordsworth has wantonly
> and without the slightest provocation inflicted in return for 15 years'
> most enthusiastic self-despising and alas! self-injuring Friendship (for
> as to his wretched agents, the Montagus, Carlisles, Knapps, etc., I
> despise them too much to be seriously hurt by any thing, they for
> themselves can say or do) that I cannot return to Grasmere or its
> vicinity.

There were, no doubt, many possibilities of leakage, but
both Coleridge and the Wordsworths seem to have come to
the conclusion later that most of the talking was done by
Mrs. Montagu. In June or July, when the Southeys were
at Richmond, Coleridge stated the whole affair to them, as a
means of transmitting it to Wordsworth.[1] It is doubtful
whether Southey, who was not as yet very intimate with
Wordsworth, would have relished the function of ambassador. But in fact the state of Coleridge's mind had already
become known at Grasmere, firstly through a letter from
Mary Lamb, written just before her illness, in which she
spoke of a 'coolness' between Coleridge and Wordsworth,
and secondly through a report by Mrs. Coleridge of a letter
from her husband to her.

> He writes as one who has been cruelly injured—He says 'If you knew
> in detail of my most unprovoked sufferings for the first month after
> I left Keswick and with what a thunder-clap that *part* came upon me

[1] C. 188; G. 216; R. 23–5; W. 433, 445; Morley, 122, 146.

which gave the whole power of anguish to all the rest—you would pity, you would less wonder at my conduct, or rather my suspension of all conduct—in short that a frenzy of the heart should produce some of the effects of a derangement of the brain, etc. etc.'

Dorothy was in arms. 'A pretty story to be told', she wrote to Mrs. Clarkson, 'Coleridge has been driven to madness by Wordsworth's cruel or unjust conduct towards him.' But on Wordsworth's side, as on Coleridge's six months before, there was no recourse to the obvious remedy of a direct communication between the old friends.

If he seek an explanation William will be ready to give it, but I think it is more likely that his fancies will die away of themselves—Poor creature! unhappy as he makes others how much more unhappy is he himself!

All that Wordsworth did was to ask Mrs. Coleridge to transmit a copy of a letter to her, which she declined, fearing that it would only prevent Coleridge from opening letters in future. Dorothy remained uneasy, not so much from resentment on behalf of her brother, as from the lack of hope for Coleridge himself.[1]

I only grieve at the waste and prostitution of his fine genius, at the sullying and perverting of what is lovely and tender in human sympathies, and noble and generous; and I do grieve whenever I think of him.

By the autumn of 1811 Coleridge had grown tired of the *Courier*. Street was not so much impressed by his abilities as Stuart, and, according to the latter, his services had only been accepted as a favour, when everything else had failed him. He became annoyed when the printing of some of his contributions was deferred, and in July there was friction because an article he had written in criticism of the appointment of the Duke of York as Commander-in-Chief was suppressed at the instigation of the Treasury, after it had been printed off. Coleridge was in general agreement with the *Courier* in its support of the Tory ministry of Perceval, but he now came to suspect that it had lost its independence; and this, according to Stuart, was to some extent the case after Street took control. Coleridge would have liked an

[1] W. 433, 435, 441.

engagement on *The Times*, but there was no room for him.
In December he told Beaumont that he should not again
attempt political journalism, unless under the compulsion of
blank necessity. 'I will write for the PERMANENT, or not at all.'
His letters to Stuart show no sign of the grudge which he
was still harbouring for the supposed betrayal of *The Friend*.[1]
A little later, when pressed by Robinson as to Stuart's connexion with a doubtful financial transaction, he burst out,
'Why, if I'm pressed as to Dan's strict honesty, which I
don't wish to be, I should say: Dan's a Scotchman who is
content to get rid of the itch when he can afford to wear
clean linen.'[2] He was, of course, still considerably in debt
to Stuart.

Coleridge's last *Courier* article appeared on 27 September
1811, and in a month he was once more essaying to take the
town as a lecturer. His locality was now Scot's Corporation
Hall, which lay between Crane Court and Flower de Luce
Court, just off Fetter Lane. The district, he said, was 're-
nowned exclusively for pork and sausages', but he hoped to
attract an audience of young men of the city.[3] Others, however, came, including Byron and Samuel Rogers. Byron
was wrapped up, but Robinson recognized him by his club
foot. He came because Coleridge was 'a kind of rage at
present', but was evidently prepossessed against this 'Mani-
chean of poesy' and 'reformed schismatic'. He had not
expected much. '"Many an old fool," said Hannibal to
some such lecturer, "but such as this, never." '[4] Of these
lectures, which ran from 18 November 1811 to 27 January
1812, we have more information than of any others given
by Coleridge. Southey had arranged for a shorthand report,
so that they might not be lost, as those at the Royal
Institution had been.[5] Portions, in fact, exist of two such
reports; one by a J. Tomalin, who was perhaps Southey's
agent, the other by John Payne Collier, the son of Robinson's
housemate. Collier has the worst of reputations for literary

---

[1] C. 183; G. 221; T. ii. 72, 83, 90; 2 *Gent. Mag.* ix. 580; Morley, 42; O.T. 850,
1027.   [2] Morley, 48.
[3] C. 183; G. 219, 222; T. 149; W. 439, 441; L. 247; Raysor, ii. 46, 221.
[4] Raysor, ii. 211; Morley, 47; Byron, *Letters*, ii. 75, 78, 83, 89.
[5] S. (*W*.), ii. 245.

dishonesty, but his notes agree too closely with other
records to justify any doubt of their genuineness.[1] Some
short notices by Robinson and Collier also appeared in
The Times and *Morning Chronicle*, but John Walter insisted
that anything written in *The Times*, where Coleridge had
hoped for a 'puff', should be 'cold and dry'.[2] From all these
reports most of the characteristic flavour of the lecturer has
naturally evaporated. Robinson, however, attended with
regularity, and supplies a critical comment in his diary and
in letters to Mrs. Clarkson and his brother. He found their
quality very uneven. At times Coleridge reached a level
which was 'all that his friends could wish, his admirers
expect'; but too often he was desultory and digressive and
full of whining apology. At a lecture on *Romeo and Juliet*,
Lamb whispered that Coleridge was giving it in the character
of the Nurse.[3] The Morgans managed to keep him punctual
to his dates, but complained that, though they were constantly laying Shakespeare's plays in his way, he would not
look at them, but only had recourse to his old common-
place book.[4] That is rather an inept criticism. If Coleridge
did not already know enough about Shakespeare for his purpose, he could hardly acquire it by a casual perusal. The
lectures were certainly extempore in form, although Coleridge claims for the first that the reasoning and arrangement
'bore the clearest marks of long premeditation'.[5] And no
doubt they were in part repetitive of those given, less successfully, in 1808. Some fragments of what looks like
material for them exist, and were in part used for the *Literary
Remains*.[6] Any full discussion of the subject-matter is of
course beyond the limits of a biography. The prospectus
promised a course on 'Shakespeare and Milton, in illustration of the Principles of Poetry, and their Applications as
Grounds of Criticism to the most popular Works of later
English Poets, those of the Living included'.[7] This plan was
fairly carried out, although Coleridge's many wanderings
from his professed themes made it necessary to extend the

---

[1] Raysor, ii. 24–198.   [2] G. 221; Raysor, ii. 199–207; Morley, 45, 97.
[3] Raysor, ii. 211–30; Morley, 45, 113–30.
[4] Raysor, ii. 226; Morley, 125.   [5] G. 221.
[6] Raysor, i. 163–256 *passim*.   [7] G. 219; Raysor, ii. 26; Morley, 112.

fifteen lectures already announced to seventeen, which
would, says Robinson, 'gain him *credit* in the City-sense of
the word'; and after all, he once more failed to reach the
living poets.[1] Lady Beaumont had feared that, when he did,
he would make an attack upon Wordsworth, but he repudiated any such intention, and indeed it would not have
been quite like him.[2] His critical integrity was at no time
much affected by his personal relations. In a letter on the
supposed plagiarism of *Christabel* in the *Lay of the Last Minstrel*, which he himself discounted, he describes an episode
which took place at the end of one of the lectures on *Romeo
and Juliet*. A German, who was among his audience, showed
him, and afterwards gave him, a copy of the last part of
A. W. von Schlegel's *Vorlesungen*, which contained a revised
version of lectures on the play delivered at Vienna in 1808,
and pointed out the remarkable resemblances between
Schlegel's views and those just expressed by Coleridge.
'The principles, thought, and the very illustrations are so
nearly the same.' He would have supposed that Coleridge
had heard or read the Vienna lectures, but they were only
just published when he left Germany, and he believed that
he had the only two copies in England. Coleridge said that
he had never heard of the lectures, or read any work of
Schlegel except his translations from Spanish poetry, and a
bystander said that he had heard Coleridge express the same
views on *Romeo and Juliet* in 1808, which was the very year
in which the Vienna lectures were given. The precise extent
of Coleridge's debt to Schlegel as a dramatic critic has
always been matter of controversy. There can be little doubt
that in a later lecture of this course, and afterwards, he made
much use of Schlegel's distinction between the methods of
classic and romantic drama. As regards *Romeo and Juliet*, the
case is not so clear. Coleridge had asked Robinson, just
before the lectures began, to procure Schlegel's *Werke* for
him. Even if he got them, they would not contain the last
part of the *Vorlesungen*. But one point of criticism which was
common to the two writers, the analysis of Romeo's feeling
for Rosaline as being love of being in love, rather than love

---

[1] G. 223; Raysor, ii. 229; Morley, 128.   [2] C. 188; *B.L.* i. 38.

for a woman, had already been made by Schlegel in an earlier
essay on *Romeo and Juliet*, printed in Schiller's *Horen* (1797)
and again in his own *Characteristiken und Kritiken* (1801).[1] In
after life Coleridge protested against a statement by Wordsworth that 'A German critic *first* taught us to think correctly
concerning Shakespeare'.[2]

Lecturing perhaps left little time for social intercourse
during the autumn and winter of 1811. Washington Allston, whom Coleridge had met at Rome, was now in town,
and took a mask of his features, to make a bust. He dined
with Rickman and spent an evening every week or so with
Lamb. Another presage of death, once more in Lamb's
Beaumont and Fletcher, marks one of his visits. But Lamb,
Coleridge thought, was smoking too much, and as a result
drinking spirits too freely. This he attributed to the constant stimulus of Hazlitt's company. Robinson, however,
notes two occasions on which Coleridge himself was so
much overcome by liquor that he was unable to recite
Christabel.[3] Some revival of public interest in *The Friend* now
once more led him to contemplate a reissue of the old numbers, to be followed by a new series. He found publishers
in the firm of John Gale and Thomas Curtis, apparently
the successors of Henry Baldwin. A visit to the north
would be necessary, in order to collect the unstamped
sheets, and wind up affairs with Brown.[4] He can hardly
come, thought Dorothy, when she heard of it, unless he lays
aside his displeasure against William. But Coleridge was
still groaning over 'the never-closing festering wound of
Wordsworth and his family', and recording in his note-book
the suffering felt, 'when all men have seemed to desert us
and the friend of our heart has passed on, with one glance
from his "cold disliking eye".'[5] On 10 February 1812 Coleridge took coach for Liverpool, where he hoped to secure
an engagement to repeat his lectures, but was disappointed.

[1] G. 222; Morley, 96; Raysor, i. xxx, 7, 11; ii. 164, 212, 221, 231, 236; Schlegel,
Werke, vii. 77. Raysor cites A. A. von Helmholtz, *Indebtedness of Coleridge to Schlegel*
(1907).   [2] Raysor, ii. 306.
[3] C. 183; G. 219; W. 439; L. 382; Rickman, 156; Raysor, ii. 33; Morley, 44.
[4] G. 218, 224; T. 149; W. 439; Lippincott, 698; Timperley, 849.
[5] G. 220; *A.P.* 246; W. 441.

On his way through Woodstock he bought a pair of gloves, which he found much dearer than in London. At Oxford the character of the pothouse where the coach pulled up, and its ridiculous appearance with fourteen distinct gaudy pictures painted on it, made him afraid to send for his nephews, lest they should be quizzed by their fellow collegians. A mob of boys hailed the equipage with shouts of 'Lazy Liverpool! Lousy Liverpool', and during the next stage Coleridge had himself experience of the lice, as well as of a would-be pickpocket. Such were the glorious coaching days of Old England. He spent a day at Kendal in order to collect the reprinted *Friends*.[1] Then he drove to Ambleside, and took up his sons to go with him to Keswick. As he passed through Grasmere they naturally thought that he would diverge to the parsonage, to which the Wordsworths had now removed from Allan Bank. But he turned his head aside to conceal his emotion, and to their speechless astonishment drove straight on. Hartley, says his mother went as white as lime when she told him that Wordsworth had a little vexed his father by something he had said to Mr. Montagu, which had been misrepresented.[2] Coleridge was kept longer in the north than he had intended. Brown, who still held Coleridge's type and paper and some of the *Friends*, had taken to drink. He now absconded, and was shortly declared bankrupt. Coleridge was able to recover some of his property, but the type had been treated as stock, and he had to put in his claim as a creditor. Any dividend, he said, should go to Brown. 'Money from the unhappy is a hateful thing!'[3] Snowfalls, moreover, made the roads impassable for coaches, and after leaving Keswick Coleridge had to spend another fortnight at Penrith. At Keswick he had been cheerful and good-natured with his family, and full of hopes, which his wife thought 'airy castles', for a future settlement in London, where they could all live 'in great credit' on his literary work. Never again would he keep a letter from Keswick unopened. 'His promises, poor fellow, are like his Castles—airy nothings.'[4] But he was also in a constant

---

[1] C. 184 (misdated); G. 224-7.
[3] G. 227, 228; R. 26.

[2] M. 7.
[4] M. 7.

'fever of agitation' over the Wordsworth affair, which he
thought would end in 'complete alienation'. He could not
bear to leave the north without seeing them, 'especially Miss
Hutchinson, who has done nothing to offend me'. Dorothy
wrote frequently to Mrs. Coleridge, begging that he would
come over. But this he would not do without an apology
from Wordsworth, which was not forthcoming. He understood indeed that Wordsworth had accepted a version of
the conversation in London, given in error by Montagu,
which differed from his own.

A nuisance! and then a deliberate Liar! O Christ! if I dared after this
crawl to the man, must I not plead guilty to these charges and be a Liar
against my own Soul.

Dorothy, on her side, believed that Coleridge was glad of
an excuse to break with them. Southey did not wonder at
Coleridge's resentment, and thought Wordsworth to blame
for making confidences to a man who talked so freely as
Montagu. It all reads, of course, at this distance of time,
like a quarrel of two silly schoolboys.[1] But in fact it was
only indicative of a rift which had gradually established itself
between two men of common interests, but fundamentally
of very different temper and outlook.

Coleridge was destined never to see Grasmere or Keswick
again. He was back in London by the middle of April, and
again took up his abode with the Morgans, who in the
interval had moved to 71 Berners Street, Soho.[2] He now
felt in no need of narcotic stimulus, and was busy planning
supplemental numbers for *The Friend*, to come out 'during the
flush and fresh breeze of my popularity'. But for these he
badly needed the concluding chapters of Wordsworth's
essay on *Epitaphs*. This was, in the circumstances, a 'delicate
business'. He asked whether Southey could get them out of
Wordsworth. Dorothy hesitated to send them. At any rate
a copy must be taken first. Moreover, Wordsworth was
now in London and Coleridge could ask for them himself.[3]
The idea of continuing *The Friend*, however, fell through,

[1] C. 184; G. 227, 228; M. 7; W. 446; Campbell, 180.
[2] C. 184; G. 224, 229.   [3] C. 186; G. 229, 232; W. 446; Rickman, 161.

and the original series was reissued by itself in the course of the year, with the imprint of Gale and Curtis. Wordsworth had gone up with the rather belated intention of confronting Coleridge with Montagu, and ascertaining what had really been said in Soho. Dorothy hoped that Josiah Wedgwood or some other steady, respectable persons would be present at the interview.[1] Gossip was still flying about. Sharon Turner, the historian, had 'trumpeted abroad' at Longman's table expressions which he attributed to Wordsworth, but which Wordsworth could never have used, or Coleridge himself believe that he used. Wordsworth, wrote Mrs. Clarkson to Robinson, must do something to counteract 'the power of Coleridge's presence and the effect of his eloquence'. A common friend, probably Richard Sharp, sent him on a letter from Coleridge, which left no doubt of his state of mind.[2] Wordsworth approached Coleridge, in the first instance, through Charles Lamb, with his suggestion of a confrontation. Coleridge, also through Lamb, did not reject it, much as he disliked it. But there were things which Wordsworth ought to know, which he could not state before Montagu without disquieting a family slightly known to Wordsworth, and without saying before Montagu what he thought of his wife. This is a little cryptic, but a later letter suggests that there had been some disparagement by Mrs. Montagu of Wordsworth's own family. He wanted, therefore, in the first instance, to transmit to Wordsworth a statement which he had often contemplated sending to Sara Hutchinson, but had been too agitated to do so before he learnt, presumably at Keswick, that all the family at Grasmere were against him. The substance of what Wordsworth had said to Montagu, 'though painfully aggravated,' was true. His complaint was all of '*by* whom it was said, and *to* whom, and *how* and *when*'. And as to the words used, either they were what he averred, or Montagu had misrepresented them, or he himself had lied about them. And if Montagu gave him the lie to his face—'what must be the consequence, unless I am a more abject coward than I have hitherto suspected, I need not say.' Evidently he con-

---

[1] W. 442, 445–7.   [2] C. 188; R. 26; W. 446, *note*.

templated a duel with Montagu.[1] Two days later he wrote
himself to Wordsworth, elaborating what he had said to
Lamb, repudiating responsibility for the spreading of gossip,
and again contemplating the communication of a statement.
But he had now heard, what Lamb had hesitated to tell him
before, for fear of adding 'fuel to the flame', that Wordsworth believed him to have himself invented the words
which he ascribed to Montagu.[2] This letter Wordsworth told
Lamb that he would not open without an assurance that it
contained nothing but a naked report of what Coleridge
believed Montagu to have said, such as he could transmit to
Montagu, and on getting a similar statement from Montagu,
give his own version, and let the matter end there. Coleridge,
however, must cease to make public mention of his supposed injuries. He dropped the idea of a confrontation, for
which there was no fit referee. The statement prepared for
Miss Hutchinson he would not read.[3] Naturally he did not
wish to bring her name into the discussion. In the meantime
Coleridge had for the first time told his full story to Crabb
Robinson, who, to his own life-long and very justifiable
gratification, proved an adroit ambassador. He obtained
permission to repeat to Wordsworth what Coleridge had
said. Wordsworth admitted that he had said he had no
hopes of Coleridge. But he denied that he had ever used
such a phrase as 'rotten drunkard', and did not think that
he had said 'rotting out his entrails by intemperance', although what he did say might have given Montagu that
impression. Nor had he called Coleridge 'a nuisance in his
family', although he might have spoken of particular habits
as a nuisance. These were perhaps fine distinctions. But
Wordsworth accompanied them by the most positive denial
that he had given Montagu any commission whatever to
say anything as from him to Coleridge. He now regretted
that he had spoken at all to so indiscreet a man as Montagu.
This denial seemed to Robinson the one material fact; mere
words could be so easily misinterpreted. He returned to
Coleridge and pressed his view upon him. Coleridge, while
emphatic upon his own love for Wordsworth, was at first

[1] C. 187, 190.   [2] C. 188.   [3] W. 447.

sceptical, but finally agreed to prepare such a short statement as Wordsworth desired. Lamb was not optimistic.
He thought Wordsworth cold. 'It may be so', comments
Robinson, 'healthful coolness is preferable to the heat of
disease.' When he saw Coleridge's statement he thought
that it contained 'the most indubitable internal evidence of
truth'. He took it to Wordsworth, with whom he had a
long conversation, too confidential to be committed to his
diary. He helped Wordsworth to write a reply to Coleridge,
which was, he thought, much facilitated by Wordsworth's
own bad opinion of Montagu's veracity, and mistrust of his
wife. In the reply Wordsworth confirmed what he had said
to Robinson, and expressed his own belief in the sincerity
of Coleridge's statement. He would not inquire further,
unless Coleridge still felt doubts, how the misapprehension
arose. The love and affection between them ought to make
this unnecessary. Robinson left the letter for Coleridge,
who was not at home. Meeting him later on the same day
in company, Coleridge said to him in a half whisper that it
was perfectly satisfactory and that he had immediately sent
an answer. Little of this has been published, but it expressed
both affection and regret. To Southey he affirmed his complete faith in Wordsworth's denial.[1] He and Wordsworth
met several times in the next few days, but not often alone,
and they did not discuss their correspondence. One day,
however, they had a pleasant walk to Hampstead together.
Robinson was flattered by an offer from Wordsworth to
visit any friend to whom he would like to introduce him.[2]
Dorothy bade Wordsworth give Coleridge her love, 'I suppose he will now receive it, though indeed he has acted to
us all (and Sara and I could not possibly have offended him)
as if he intended to insult us.'[3] Mrs. Clarkson could not
have believed that Coleridge could have acted as he had
done, although she knew that he was 'worthless as a friend'.
She, too, seems to have thought that Coleridge had used
her ill, but in what way is not clear.[4] Mrs. Coleridge commented that her husband had now learnt that 'even those

[1] C. 190, 191, 195; Morley, 48, 146–57; R. 28; R. (D.), i. 188, iii. 42; W. 448.
[2] Morley, 156, 157; W. 449.   [3] W. 448.   [4] Morley, 157; R. 29.

very persons who have been the great means of his self-indulgence' were 'as clear-sighted to his failings, & much *less* delicate in speaking of them', than his wife.[1] As far as is known, Wordsworth said nothing to Montagu, to whom he was writing a few months later in affectionate terms.[2]

Coleridge had now formed high hopes of a substantial income from writing and lecturing.[3] He arranged for May a short course at Willis's Rooms, which he thought would draw a more aristocratic audience than Fetter Lane. It was delayed by the assassination of Perceval, which much shocked him, and inspired him with a desire to write on Perceval in the *Courier*. But it ran from 19 May to 5 June, and Wordsworth was able to attend at least part of one lecture before he left town.[4] Little record remains beyond a syllabus and some short notes by Robinson. Coleridge had at first intended to treat of moral subjects, but substituted a comparison of classic and romantic drama, which was probably largely based upon his recent reading of Schlegel. In the last lecture he turned to the subject of jealousy, as handled in *Othello* and the *Winter's Tale*. Financially the enterprise was not a success. Coleridge had hoped to secure high-placed patrons, with the help of Sir Thomas Bernard and Lady Beaumont. But of five hundred half-promised subscribers he only got about fifty, and had to take his revenge in an epigram.[5]

I *dreamt*, that a great Lord had made me a most splendid Promise; awoke and found it as much a delusion, as if the great Lord had really made a Promise.

From June to October Coleridge passes into obscurity. A single letter of 7 August to Stuart probably makes the reason clear enough. He was ill, and had suspected dropsy, but now found it to be only a result of indigestion. A new doctor, Robert Gooch, was attending him, to whom once more he had submitted the whole of his case. Mercury and nitric acid, with a gradual reduction of opiates, would put him right. He was rewriting his play for submission to the

---

[1] M. 7.   [2] W. 463.   [3] W. 446.
[4] C. 185-7, 190-1; G. 224, 230; S. (*W*.), ii. 267; Morley, 130.
[5] C. 189, 191; G. 231, 233; Raysor, ii. 240; Morley, 130.

Haymarket theatre, and also offered Stuart a batch of articles, still to be written, for the *Courier*. Alternatively, could he have a loan for eight days, until the play was finished? Stuart sent him £20.[1] Then, in October, came an unusual stroke of luck. *Osorio*, now rechristened *Remorse*, was submitted, not to the Haymarket, but to Drury Lane, and accepted for early production. Samuel Whitbread, one of the proprietors, and Samuel James Arnold, the manager, were confident of its success.[2] Now began another course of twelve lectures, this time at the Surrey Institution, to an 'evangelical' audience, whose religious opinions he alternately flattered and offended. The syllabus suggests that little new ground was broken. Classicism and romanticism, Shakespeare and Milton, were again the themes. Robinson attended fitfully, and on one occasion slept. His brief notes give the impression that the earlier lectures were of very uneven quality, and as usual often wandered from their subjects. But the later ones redeemed the reputation imperilled at first. Coleridge, thought Robinson, began to recover his lost character among the saints. Coleridge himself was pleased with these, especially as he never once thought of the last until he entered the lecture room.[3] In November came a shock which may long have been anticipated. Josiah Wedgwood wrote to Coleridge that, on account of a change in his circumstances, he now had to pay his share of the annuity granted in 1798 out of capital instead of income, and did not feel able to continue it, unless bound in honour to do so. For this, quite apart from anything Coleridge had or had not done, he seems to have had full justification. It was granted subject to 'the wreck of our fortune', and during the war years the losses of the Wedgwoods had amounted to over £120,000. Coleridge, although for a time incapable of answering through nervous depression, made no protest, but sent a dignified reply, of gratitude for the past, of hope to show some day that he had not wasted the leisure which he had owed to the annuity, and of desire for the restoration

---

[1] G. 232.
[2] C. 192; G. 233; M. 7; R. (*D.*), i. 401; W. 460, 469; S. (*L.*), iv. 10; (*W.*), ii. 315.
[3] C. 193; *Bodl. Montagu MS.* d. 4, f. 104; Raysor, ii. 246; Morley, 132, 134.

of Wedgwood's esteem and friendship. It had been, he said, his intention, if only *The Friend* or his lectures had proved profitable, himself to resign the bounty, and now the acceptance of his play seemed likely to open a way to competence and the opportunity of using the fruits of twenty years' study and observation. To Poole he wrote a little later.

Well, yes it is well!—for I can now be *sure* that I loved him, revered him, and was grateful to him from no selfish feeling. For equally (and may those words be my final condemnation at the last awful day, if I speak not the whole truth), equally do I at this moment love him, and with the same reverential gratitude! To Mr Thomas Wedgwood I felt, doubtless, love; but it was mingled with fear, and constant apprehension of his too exquisite taste in morals. But Josiah! Oh I ever did, and ever shall, love him, as a being so beautifully balanced in mind and heart deserves to be!

Mrs. Coleridge, perhaps, could not be expected to take the matter quite so philosophically. It was her loss, rather than Coleridge's, and she wailed that if Wedgwood had ever seen her children, he would not have had the heart to inflict it.[1]

Remorse was produced on 23 January 1813, and was well received. Coleridge wrote to his wife of the 'unexampled applause' on the first night, of the clapping by the pit which accompanied his entry, and the number of 'unsolicited, unknown yet *predetermined* plauditors', which led a 'malignant' paper to assert that he had collected all the saints from Mile End Turnpike to Tyburn Bar. Mrs. Coleridge was 'much excited, as you may guess', reports Dorothy. Coleridge was not sure that the play would continue to fill the house, but in fact it ran for twenty performances. Some excisions were made after the first night, especially of an episode which had been introduced without Coleridge's knowledge and which he thought 'the lowest depth of the μισητεον'. He 'absolutely had the hiss half way out of my lips and retracted it.' He had never once attended the rehearsal of the last act, 'the bowel-griping cold from the stage floor and weariness from cutting blocks with a razor having always sent me packing homeward before the conclusion of the fourth.' He would have liked other excisions, but gave way,

---

[1] C. 192, 195; G. 233; M. 8; *R.E.S.* vi. 68.

causing the managers to term him 'the Amenable Author'. Lamb contributed a prologue, originally meant for the reopening of Drury Lane after a fire, but rejected, and Coleridge himself an epilogue. Both of these he thought bad. In the preface to a printed version of the play, of which three editions were issued by one Pople, he paid many compliments to the producers and actors, but herein, he says, he made 'a lie edge round the truth as nearly as possible', since the scenes were bad and the acting execrable. Alexander Rae, who did the principal character, Ordonio, was insignificant in person and thin and insufficient in voice. The 'blundering coxcomb' Robert Elliston, who did Alvar, 'by mere dint of voice and self-conceit out-dazzled him'. The preface, as at first issued, also contained a statement of Coleridge's long-standing grudge against Sheridan for his rejection of the play in 1797, but this was omitted from the later editions. The 'dripping' passage had in fact been now cut down to a single phrase—'The weed nods and drips'. Journalistic criticism of the play was reasonably favourable, although Coleridge complained of the 'infernal lies' of *The Times*, and the 'dirty malice' of the *Morning Herald*, and expressed the intention of answering his reviewers in an 'Essay on Dramatic Poetry, relatively to the present State of the Metropolitan Theatres', which he would publish immediately.[1] Robinson put his finger on the weak point of the play when he noted it as Coleridge's great fault that 'he indulges before the public in those metaphysical & philosophical speculations which are becoming only in solitude & with select minds'. And for precisely the same reason *Remorse* always remained a great favourite with Coleridge himself. It expounded 'certain pet abstract notions' of his own. He had tried to express in the conflicting emotions of Ordonio the varying effects of remorse, according as the heart in which it operates is 'gentle' or 'proud and gloomy'.[2] Such subtle psychologizing does not easily get over the footlights, and to the Drury Lane audience *Remorse* can have

---

[1] C. 193 (misdated), 194, 195; G. 234, 236; Rickman, 164; Murray, i. 300; W. 475; Leslie, ii. 32; Michael Kelly, *Reminiscences*, ii. 277; *P.W.* 812; *Osorio* (ed. of 1873); Wise, 82.   [2] Morley, 63, 136; A. p. 51; T.T. 213.

seemed little more than an unusually poetic melodrama. Financially, however, it was Coleridge's nearest approach to a popular success. He reckoned that, with the copyright, it would bring him in £400, 'more than all my literary labours put together; nay thrice as much, subtracting my heavy losses in the "Watchman" and "Friend".' He was able to send his wife £100 and the promise of another £100, which may have somewhat consoled her for the loss of the annuity. And later he hoped to repay her what she had spent on the children.[1] One result of his success which particularly gratified him was the receipt of 'two heart-engendered lines' from Thomas Poole.[2] He had been, he says, 'stung with your unkindness to me in my sore adversity'. He seems to have forgotten that the slight friction over *The Friend* had already been followed by affectionate correspondence. This, however, was not quite recent and he goes on to say—

You perhaps may likewise have heard (*in the Whispering Gallery of the World*) of the year-long difference between me and Wordsworth (compared with the sufferings of which all the former afflictions of my life were less than flea-bites) occasioned (in *great part*) by the wicked folly of the arch-fool Montagu. A reconciliation has taken place, but the *feeling*, which I had previous to that moment, when the (three-fourth) calumny burst, like a thunderstorm from a blue sky, on my soul, after fifteen years of such religious, almost superstitious idolatry and self-sacrifice. Oh, no! no! that, I fear, never can return.

Evidence of the lack of 'feeling' was soon forthcoming. In December 1812 had died Thomas Wordsworth, who had been Coleridge's favourite among the children at Grasmere. Coleridge wrote affectionately to Wordsworth. He could not come down at once, on account, not so much of his lectures, as of the forthcoming rehearsals of his play, on which depended his hopes of leaving town after Christmas, 'and living among you as long as I live'. He offered deep sympathy. 'There is a sense of the word, Love, in which I never felt it but to you and one of your household.' It has been suggested that Wordsworth, annoyed by the reference

---

[1] C. 193, 195; G. 234.
[2] *Addl. MS.* 35343; C. 195; P. ii. 245 ('true' for 'two').

to Sara Hutchinson, sent no reply. Several other letters
reached Grasmere during the next month, all with promises
to come. Dorothy was now thinking of him with her
'wonted affection'.[1] But in March 1813 a series of letters from
Mrs. Clarkson to Robinson tells us that Coleridge had not
after all gone. The Wordsworths had received, through
Morgan, the 'cutting intelligence' that he was going to the
seaside.

After all, what has Coleridge suffered compared with the misery
which he has inflicted. He does not, I know, give pain for the sake of
giving pain. But who does except the Arch fiend?

Mrs. Clarkson abounds in this sense. Coleridge would not
come to see her. She tried to find him at Berners St., but
in vain, and though she liked Mrs. Morgan, thought her
'too young, too idle & too happy' to be a fit medium of
communication. Yet she wanted to know how he managed
himself, and whether any one measured out 'the abominable
drug' to him, and whether he opened his letters from Grasmere. She felt gratitude to the Morgans for their care of
him, but was sure she could not be confidential with them,
especially as Morgan had annoyed her by some criticism of
the women of Grasmere. Finally she saw Coleridge, and
got little hope or comfort out of it. She inclined to think
with Mary Lamb that there was something between him
and the Wordsworths which perhaps made it better that
they should not meet just yet.[2] Dorothy wrote to her on
8 April that she had done all she could.[3]

He will not let himself be served by others. Oh, that the day may
ever come when he will serve himself! Then will his eyes be opened,
and he will see clearly that we have always loved him, do still love him,
and have always loved—not measuring his deserts. I do not now wish
him to come into the North; that is, I do not wish him to do it for the
sake of any wish to gratify us. But if he should do it of himself, I should
be glad as the best sign that he was endeavouring to perform his duties.

It was the last word of an historic friendship.

[1] C. 192; W. 463, 464, 469.   [2] R. 30–2.   [3] W. 478.

XIV

IN THE DEPTHS
March 1813—March 1816

WE do not know whether Coleridge went to the sea-side in the spring of 1813. Early in March a gentle-man in black was found hanging from a tree in Hyde Park. He was moneyless and paperless, but on him was a shirt marked with Coleridge's name. Coleridge read of it in a coffee-house newspaper, and was not surprised. He never travelled without losing a shirt or two. Southey laughed too much to be vexed. No doubt people would say that it was Coleridge himself, but that he was cut down in time, and his friends said it was some one else, to cover up the truth.[1] An entire failure of preserved letters from Coleridge between February and September is probably ominous. At some time this year he came to Salt Hill to tend Allston, who was ill there, and brought with him Dr. Tuthill, one of the doctors whom he later claims to have himself 'tricked'.[2] In August Dorothy heard that the Morgans had 'smashed', and were coming with Coleridge to Keswick.

A melancholy business—coming with them and would not come to see his children! No plans laid for H! I foresee nothing but jealousies and discomforts.

Coleridge, however, did not come. Southey, who visited town in September, met him more than once, and took him to call upon Mme de Staël, who summed up the impressions left upon many by his conversation in the trenchant phrase, 'Pourtant, pour M. Coleridge, il est tout à fait un mono-logue.' Poole also saw him in London. He promised to accompany Southey on his return, but failed him. He must go to Bristol, to give a course of lectures, but would come at Christmas.[3]

By 21 October Coleridge was in fact in Bristol, at the

[1] S. (L.), iv. 24; Leslie, i. 50.　　　　[2] Leslie, i. 33; Allston, 97.
[3] C. 196; W. 486, 490, 492; M. 8; S. (L.), iv. 43; (W.), ii. 327, 332.

White Hart, whence he moved in a few days to 2 Queen's
Square, the abode of his old friend Josiah Wade, who gave
him hospitality for what proved to be a long sojourn.[1] In
addition to the lectures, he was busy, in one of those bursts
of altruism of which he was always capable, with the affairs
of John Morgan. This unfortunate man had succeeded in
wasting a considerable patrimony left him by his father.
Morgan & Sons, and afterwards John Morgan, appear
in London directories from 1801 to 1816 as cheesemongers
at 104 Bishopsgate Street Within, and at 103 were from 1810
to 1817 Brent & Co., tobacconists, of whom the head in
1817 was Matthew Brent, presumably the 'old Mr Brent',
who sent presents to the girls at Keswick in the same year,
and also the father of Morgan's wife and sister-in-law.[2]
Now, in 1813, the cheesemongery business, if not also the
tobacco business, was in trouble. In September Coleridge
described himself as compelled, no doubt for financial
reasons, to sell his library.[3] The Morgans had moved to 19
London Street, Fitzroy Square, and to them Coleridge
wrote several letters from Bristol in October and November.
They were all addressed to the ladies. He wanted them
to settle near Bristol, and hoped that Morgan, when able
to return to them, would resume his original profession
as a lawyer there. Evidently Morgan was in prison for
debt. Meanwhile Coleridge was doing his best to save
the Brent business in Bishopsgate Street, and succeeded in
persuading William Hood and other Bristol friends to
advance money for a settlement with one Lloyd, no doubt
a member of the banking firm, and become Charlotte
Brent's creditors in case of failure. In November Coleridge
contemplated a visit to London, and hoped to bring the
ladies back with him. In December 1813 they were living
at Ashley, between Bath and Box, and here by May 1814
Morgan had joined them.[4]

During October and November Coleridge gave six lectures on Shakespeare and two on Education at Bristol, of

---

[1] G. 237–9; *Rem.* 383; W. 498.
[2] C. 191, 193; S. (*L.*), iv. 361; v. 31; *E.R.* ii. 173; *London P.O. Directory.*
[3] C. 196.   [4] G. 237–42, 246.

which reports are preserved in the *Bristol Gazette*; and concurrently at least two on Milton at Clifton, of which he had
small hopes, and one of which attracted only twelve hearers.
A second Bristol course was advertised for December, but
more than once deferred.[1] Coleridge had been taken ill at
the Greyhound, Bath, on his return from London, and was
attended by Dr. Parry, the father of one of his old companions at Göttingen. It was again opium. To Mrs. Morgan
he wrote,

The Terrors of the Almighty have been around and against me,
and tho' driven up and down for seven dreadful days, by restless Pain,
like a Leopard in a den, yet the anguish and Remorse of mind was worse
than the pain of the whole Body. O I have had a new world opened
to me, in the infinity of my own Spirit! Woe be to me, if this last
warning be not taken.

Later he reproached himself with the cruelty to Mary and
Charlotte involved by his lapse, at a time when they were
themselves ill, and needed his protection. In fact they heard
nothing of him for some months.[2] His illness lasted to the
beginning of April 1814, when his second course of lectures
was again advertised.[3] Apparently he went up to London before giving it, for Cottle tells us, on the authority of a fellow
traveller, that he talked incessantly and amusingly on his
way back until the coach reached Marlborough, and then
discovered that a lady in the coach was the sister of a particular friend of his, and at Bath said that he must diverge
from his journey, and see her safe to her brother's in North
Wales. As a result he was late for his first lecture, which
had to be put off, and even when the adjourned day came,
he had to be hunted up, and taken from his bottle to fulfil his
engagement. Probably Cottle, as usual, is not quite exact.
The lady must, I think, have been Joanna Hutchinson, who
appears to have spent the spring and summer with her brother
in North Wales, and was certainly not unknown to Coleridge.[4]
And in fact the deferred second course of lectures seems
to have begun as advertised on 5 April. There were to have

---

[1] G. 238–42; *Rem.* 352 (a confused account); Raysor, ii. 252–98; Leslie, i. 34.
[2] C. 202; G. 246, 254 (misdated); *Rem.* 351; M. 8; W. 498.
[3] Raysor, ii. 256.   [4] *Rem.* 352 (misdated); W. 504.

been six, four on Milton, one on poetic taste, and one on
Cervantes. Coleridge had been discussing *Don Quixote* at
Salt Hill the year before. But apparently only those on
Milton were in fact given.[1] Another course on the French
Revolution did not get beyond its first lecture.[2] Nothing
is known of a proposed course on Female Education, or
of one on Homer, which Cottle says, probably in error,
was given. Perhaps these two were the same, and the
subject Nausicaa.[3] Coleridge, in fact, was ill again with
erysipelas, once more, no doubt, only a symptom.[4] In the
Milton course he seems to have diverged into a comparison
between Satan and Bonaparte, for the celebration of whose
removal to Elba he designed a great transparency to be
displayed by Wade.[5] A description earlier in the course of
Satan as 'a sceptical Socinian' led to an embittered controversy between the lecturer and his old friend and fellow
Unitarian, John Estlin. Coleridge expressed regret for the
phrase which, however, he thought borne out by passages
in *Paradise Regained*, but Estlin was not mollified, 'raised the
city' against him, and 'behaved downright cruel and brutal'.[6]

The Milton lectures did not even pay the incidental expenses, and Coleridge borrowed £10 from Joseph Cottle,
on the plea that a dirty fellow had threatened to arrest him.[7]
But now Cottle had an unexpected shock. This good-
natured and simple-minded fellow must have been the only
one of Coleridge's friends who did not by this time know
what was the matter with him. The revelation came after
a visit to Hannah More, at which Cottle noticed that
Coleridge's hand shook in lifting a glass of wine. Some one,
to whom he mentioned this, told him that the reason was
opium.[8] His account of what followed is even more than
usually disordered, but can be reconstructed. He formed
the plan of raising among those who wished well to Coleridge
an annuity of £100 or £150, which would be expended on
his maintenance, but not put at his own disposal, until he

---

[1] Raysor, ii. 256; *Rem.* 354, 357; Leslie, i. 36.
[2] Raysor, ii. 258; *Rem.* 357.   [3] Raysor, ii. 258; *Rem.* 354, 357.
[4] *Rem.* 357.   [5] C. 205; Raysor, ii. 257; *Rem.* 355.
[6] G. 244, 245, 247, 251; Estlin, 107; *Rem.* 335, 346 (misplaced).
[7] *Rem.* 357.   [8] *Rem.* 360.

was cured of his habit. Coleridge assented to the plan, but thought it 'one of those Chimeras, which kindness begets upon an unacquaintance with mankind'.[1] The first person whom Cottle approached was Southey, and from Southey he received disconcerting letters in reply. Coleridge had already had such an annuity from the Wedgwoods. The whole trouble lay in opium, which in the quantities taken by Coleridge would in itself consume more than the whole of the sum suggested by Cottle. 'A frightful consumption of *spirits* is added.' The only justification for such a subscription would be the inability of the beneficiary to support himself. This was not the case with Coleridge. He could easily get well-paid work on the *Quarterly* and *Eclectic Reviews*. He had better come to Keswick, raising money for immediate expenses by lectures at Birmingham and Liverpool on the way, and settle down. 'Should you proceed in your intention, my name must not be mentioned.' But if Cottle approached Poole, he should give him Southey's views.[2] Cottle now wrote Coleridge a long and pious appeal to mend his ways, to which Coleridge replied with a full admission of his guilt, into which he had been seduced ignorantly, and which for ten years had caused him indescribable anguish of spirit. His case was 'a derangement, an utter impotence of the *Volition*, and not of the intellectual faculties'. If he had the money, he would gladly place himself in some private madhouse for a time, perhaps that of Dr. Fox.[3] Cottle suggested that Satan was busy with him, but God was greater than Satan. Coleridge should have recourse to prayer. Coleridge answered that he was a Christian, and prayed inwardly to be able to pray, but the power to pray with a faith which would bring a blessing was a gift of God to the elect.[4] Cottle did not think that it was yet a case for a madhouse, but he sent copies of his correspondence to Southey, who repeated his views, and urged a visit to Poole, where new scenes would freshen Coleridge's spirits. He ought to write a play, and thus get means to support Hartley at college. 'From me he shall

[1] *Rem.* 358, 375.   [2] *Rem.* 376, 378; Campbell, 204.
[3] G. 245; *Rem.* 361, 366, 371.   [4] *Rem.* 369.

never hear anything but cheerful encouragement and the language of hope.'[1] Coleridge would not visit Poole. Nor did
he go into an asylum. But Hood persuaded Coleridge to
consult a Dr. Daniel, and on Coleridge's own suggestion
an elderly tradesman, one Hatherfield, was employed as a
keeper, to sleep in his room and accompany him in his
walks. There was a fear of suicide. Coleridge suffered
much, and felt as if he had descended into hell. More than
once he succeeded in 'tricking' Hatherfield, but the doses
of opium were gradually reduced. An attempt to dispense
with them altogether seems to have been abandoned. Coleridge resumed correspondence with Morgan, although conscious that Mary and Charlotte were still sore at his long
neglect of them. Cottle, who had himself fallen ill through
the breaking of a blood-vessel, continued to write letters in
which he suggested that Coleridge was possessed by the
Devil. 'God bless him! he is a well meaning Creature but
a great Fool', Coleridge commented.[2] By the end of May
he was well enough to go to the theatre, where he saw
Charles Mathews in Colman's *Who Wants a Guinea*.[3] But
for the next two months he was still subject to attacks of
erysipelas, due in part to late hours and gin-and-water, indiscreetly permitted by Daniel. He was bothered by the
presence in Bristol of a doleful Mrs. Fermor, a sister of
Lady Beaumont, who required his religious consolations.
He wrote, however, courteously of her to Beaumont, describing himself as 'a forgotten exile from the love of those
whom I most dearly loved'. More than once he thought of
going over to Ashley to see the Morgans, who would be
pleased with the doses of laudanum he should bring. With
them he still hoped, somewhere or other, to renew his
former relations. He could earn six guineas a week, which
would do in a country cottage.[4] On 26 June he wrote his
well-known letter of gratitude and repentance to Wade, in
which he expressed the wish that after his death a 'full and
unqualified narration' of his wretchedness and its cause
might be published as an example to others.[5]

---

[1] *Rem.* 373; Campbell, 204.   [2] C. 198; G. 246-9; *Rem.* 380, 383.
[3] C. 199.   [4] G. 249-52; B. ii. 171; *App.* no. viii.   [5] C. 200.

On 1 August *Remorse* was produced in Bristol, and
Coleridge, in spite of a relapse, went through their parts with
some of the actors.[1] He was now able to attempt some literary
work. Allston was giving an exhibition of his pictures in the
Guildhall, and although Coleridge was now less pleased with
Allston than before, thinking him too narrowly American in
his outlook, he wished if possible to serve him. Allston's
pictures, however, only figure incidentally in the essays
On the Principles of Genial Criticism Concerning the Fine Arts,
which appeared in *Felix Farley's Bristol Journal* during
August and September. His portrait of Coleridge, now in
the National Portrait Gallery, is of this year.[2] Coleridge was
now in communication with Lamb, who incidentally asked
after the Morgans. 'What is gone of that frank-hearted
circle, Morgan and his cos-lettuces? He ate walnuts better
than any man I ever knew.' Later he explained that Morgan
had 'a particular kind of rabbit-like delight in munching salads
with oil without vinegar after dinner—a steady contempla-
tive browsing on them'.[3] And through Lamb Coleridge
learnt from Robinson that John Murray, the publisher,
wanted a translation of Goethe's *Faust*. Lamb, who himself only knew *Faust* at second-hand, advised him to let it
alone. 'How canst thou translate the language of cat-
monkeys?' Coleridge, however, wrote to Murray, offering
to undertake the job.

It is painful, very painful, and even odious to me, to attempt anything
of a literary nature, with any motive of *pecuniary* advantage; but that
I bow to the all-wise Providence, which has made me a *poor* man, and
therefore compelled me by other duties inspiring feelings, to bring
even my Intellect to the Market.

He was 'an idiot at bargaining', but would Murray state
his terms? He must have a complete set of Goethe's works.
Murray offered £100, which Coleridge thought 'humiliat-
ingly low'. But his work had never sold, and he would
accept, subject to rights of reprinting the translation and
adapting it for stage purposes. He had never, in fact, as we

[1]. G. 252; Raysor, ii. 258.
[2] *B.L.* ii. 219; *T.T.* 300; Raysor, ii. 258; *M.L.N.* xliii. 375; C. 202; G. 237, 242,
247, 249–52; *App.* no. vii.   [3] L. 254, 255.

know from his conversations with Robinson, been very much attracted by Goethe, and before long he wrote again to Murray, warning him that, although *Faust* was a work of genius, its fantastic witcheries and general tone of religion and morals would be 'highly obnoxious to the taste and Principles of the present righteous English public'. He offered to do instead a translation of the minor works of Cervantes, which he had just been reading, with an essay on *Don Quixote*, on which he had failed to lecture in the spring, and to add the minor works of Boccaccio. Murray sent no answer, and, although he tried another bookseller, Coleridge found later that some one else was doing Cervantes. To Stuart he complained that Murray had treated him strangely over *Faust*, and wasted some weeks for him.[1] In his heart he was once more contemplating that phantom work on metaphysics and religion which for so many years had floated before his mind. It was now to take the form of a treatise on 'the Logos', or the communicative intelligence in nature and in man, together with a commentary on the Gospel of St. John; and this, indeed, he was ready to put to the press in a large volume. It was still in hand on 12 September, by which time Coleridge, now declared convalescent, had left Bristol, and joined the Morgans in lodgings at Ashley. It was to comprise five treatises, beginning with a study of logic and developing into a defence of the doctrinal articles of the Church, under the general title of *Christianity, the one true Philosophy*. To it would be prefixed an essay on the laws and limits of toleration and liberality, illustrated by fragments of autobiography. Two of his friends had taken upon themselves the risk of printing it at Bristol, in two portly octavos.[2] He had also in hand two satires on *Puff and Slander*, intended as a reply to a review of *Remorse* in the *Quarterly* for April, which was in fact a very fair and not an unfavourable one.[3] And once more he approached Stuart with offers of contributions to the *Courier*, which might include a continuation of *Genial Criticism*, as well as political essays, the latter of which alone appeared in the form of a series of *Letters*

---

[1] C. 201; G. 250, 253, 256; *L.P.* 66; Murray, i. 297, 300; Rogers, i. 191; M. 10; R. (*D.*), i. 395; Morley, 61, 63; T.T. 206.   [2] C. 202; G. 255.   [3] C. 202; G. 289.

to Mr. Justice Fletcher, dealing with the affairs of Ireland, where he thought Jacobinism a danger, and signed as by 'An Irish Protestant'. He was not ashamed, however, once more to dangle the *Character* of Bonaparte. But he had little heart for politics.[1]

> Oh! God! It is very easy to say, Why does not Coleridge do this work and that work? I declare to God, there is nothing I would not do, consistent with my conscience, which was regular labour for a regular revenue. But to write such poetry or such philosophy as I would wish to write, or not to write at all, cannot be done amid distraction and anxiety for the day.

In 1814 Coleridge's son Hartley had turned 17 and was on the point of leaving school. He was full of 'oddities', and his mother and Southey were anxious that he should have the discipline of college. Southey wrote to Coleridge, who made no response, and it became clear that all hopes for Hartley must rest elsewhere. Lady Beaumont, Cottle, and Poole, who was Hartley's godfather, offered contributions, and an application was made to the uncles at Ottery. It perturbed them rather, particularly Edward, whose wife thought that the children should not be brought up as gentlefolks. But they agreed to help. James wrote of Coleridge as 'mad'. Possibly opium or something would remove him to another world. 'What a humbling lesson to all men is Samuel Coleridge.' A fund of £80 was collected, and then, through the good offices of William Hart Coleridge, the son of Luke, and at that time a Student of Christ Church, it was found possible to supplement it by a Postmastership of £50 at Merton. Coleridge seems to have been gratified at the news. Joanna Hutchinson, who walked out from Bath to Ashley, and found him gone, learnt from his landlady that he used to talk to her of his children.[2] He was still at Ashley towards the end of November 1814, but then expected, 'as far as so perplexed a being dare expect anything', to move to the house of a surgeon, by name Page, at Calne in Wiltshire.[3] And at Calne we find him, still with

---

[1] C. 202, 203, 205; *L.P.* 66, 67; S. (*W.*), ii. 383; *O.T.* 677.
[2] M. 8, 9; W. 492, 498, 500, 519, 521; *D.H.* 214; S. (*W.*), ii. 383; *Rem.* 386 (misdated and with interpolations); Campbell, 209.   [3] *L.P.* 67; W. 521; *P.W.* 981.

the Morgans, by March 1815. Here he remained for about
a year. Both at Ashley and at Calne he enjoyed a good deal
of social intercourse, more indeed than Morgan thought was
quite good for him, with neighbouring families. He bought
new black silk stockings to dine with the Marquis of Lans-
downe at Bowood; visited the famous collection of pictures
belonging to Paul Methuen of Corsham; sympathized with
the evangelical principles of Methuen's son Thomas at All
Cannings; and made other clerical acquaintances in William
Money of Whetham, and one Hales of Bromham.[1] For a
time he found 'constant gratification' in the company of
Bowles at Bremhill, but later he complained:

Alas! I injured myself irreparably with him by devoting a fortnight
to the correction of his poems. He took the corrections, but never forgave the corrector.[2]

A particular crony seems to have been Dr. R. H. Brabant of
Devizes, many letters to whom are preserved.[3] Coleridge
took part in a local agitation against the Corn Law of 1815.
He drew up a petition for a meeting in the Calne market-
place, and then, 'mounted on the butchers' table, made a
butcherly speech of an hour long to a very ragged but not
butcherly audience, for by their pale faces few of them
seemed to have had more than a very occasional acquaintance with butchers' meat'. The greed of the country gentlemen at the expense of the poor made him waver in his
support of the Tory ministry, and even to think that Parliamentary Reform was becoming desirable.[4] Hartley spent
his first summer vacation from college with his father at
Calne, and together they saw a performance of *Remorse*
there by a travelling company. Southey had been uneasy
over the probable influence of the father upon the son.
Coleridge, he feared, would lead Hartley 'into all the depths
and mazes of metaphysics', rooting up from his mind all
established principles, and substituting others which would
never serve for the practical purposes of society. Lamb, too,
suggested that it would be good for Hartley to 'go through

[1] C. 206, 207; G. 265; M. 10; W. 521; L.P. 66, 67; *W.R.* xciii. 361, 363; xciv. 12;
Christian Observer (1845), 81, 145.
[2] P. W. Clayden, *Samuel Rogers*, i. 191; *W.R.* xciv. 21.   [3] *W.R.* xciii, xciv.
[4] C. 205; *W.R.* xciii. 344, 347, 354; *Rem.* 389.

a course of matter-of-fact with some sober man after the mysteries'. Could he not spend a week with Poole, before he went back to Oxford?[1]

The year at Calne was one of considerable literary activity. Coleridge's interest had now once more reverted to his *Poems*. He may already have had them in mind during the summer of 1814, when he was reading *Joan of Arc*, to pick out his own contributions, at the request of his friend Hood, and exclaiming at the poverty of Southey's work. Hazlitt says that he criticized this openly in the Bristol Public Library, reciting lines in 'a ridiculous tone (I do not mean his usual tone, but one which he meant should be ridiculous)'.[2] In March 1815 he made an appeal to Cottle. He had collected enough material for one volume, but wanted to complete another, which would include a series of odes, never seen by any, on the sentences of the Lord's Prayer. His work on Christianity was also waiting. But he had to turn off every week to 'some mean subject for the Newspapers'. He was in arrear £25 and it cost him £2 10s. a week to live. He could not do with less, except by alienating himself from all social affections and conversation with persons of the same education. He had remained poor by always having been poor. 'God knows! of the £300 received thro' you *what went to myself*.' Would Cottle take his manuscripts as security, and send him £30 or £40? After recent calumny, he hated the idea of making himself 'a slave to a club of Subscribers to my Poverty'. Cottle, scenting opium, refused, but enclosed £5. This crossed with another letter from Coleridge. He had now bowed his heart down, and asked Hood to form a club. Would Cottle take a reprint of *The Friend*? He was thinking of opening a school in Bristol. 'I cannot, as is feigned of the Nightingale, sing with my breast against a thorn.' Cottle sent another £5. This was the last letter he ever had from Coleridge. Hood and others, one of whom appears to have been J. M. Gutch, an old schoolfellow of Coleridge at Christ's Hospital, now took the manuscripts and lent £45 on them, besides advanc-

---

[1] G. 259; *W.R.* xciii. 358; M. 11; S. (*W.*), ii. 407, 422; L. 272, 274.
[2] Hazlitt, xix. 196; *App.* no. vii.

ing £27 5s. 6d. for the premium on Coleridge's life-policy.
There were to be two volumes, containing both reprints and
unpublished poems; and two prefaces, on the philosophic
and genial criticism of poetry, and on the supernatural in
poetry, in relation to *The Ancient Mariner* and the ballads.[1]
Coleridge's preparations led incidentally to a brief resump-
tion of correspondence with Wordsworth. He wrote to Lady
Beaumont, asking for a copy, which he had lent her, of his
lines on Wordsworth's *Prelude*. Wordsworth took alarm, and
asked him not to publish them, as the *Prelude* itself was not
published, and it would be a 'precursorship of Praise'. He
was still, in spite of Coleridge's silence, 'affectionately' his.
Coleridge replied that he had not decided to publish them, and
should not have done so without consulting Wordsworth.
But he was making a complete collection of his poems, and
wanted this for the purpose, and still more perhaps for the
handwriting, no doubt Sara Hutchinson's, of the only complete copy, which Lady Beaumont had. This led him to a
long and rather critical discussion of Wordsworth's recently
issued *Excursion*. He too ended in affectionate terms. He
had still a preface to write, before he could publish his
volumes.[2] The development of this preface is interesting,
since it was ultimately merged in the *Biographia Literaria*,
as we know it. Evidently it was influenced by Coleridge's
study of the *Excursion*. In July it had become a preface to an
'Autobiographia Literaria, Sketches of my Literary Life and
Opinions, so far as poetry and poetical criticisms are concerned', and was to include a full account of the controversy as to Wordsworth's poems, and 'a disquisition on the
powers of association and on the generic difference between
the Fancy and the Imagination'. He had no doubt that
Wordsworth would be displeased with it.[3] But the 'Autobiographia' had presumably grown out of the 'fragments
of autobiography' which, as we have seen, Coleridge had
intended, some months before, to prefix to his work on
Christianity. This itself was now laid on the shelf, although
not forgotten. By September 1815 it had received the title

---

[1] G. 255, 256; *Rem.* 388, 389; Campbell, 211; M. 10.
[2] C. 205, 206; W. 529a.   [3] *W.R.* xciii. 361.

Logosophia, and had grown from five treatises into six, of which the first would now be 'a philosophical history of philosophy'.[1] Some friction with his backers during the spring seems to have caused Coleridge to write of having 'embrangled myself with some vehement *professors* of friendship, but most indelicate *performers*', with regard to the poems. Possibly the expansion of the preface into a separate volume had caused trouble.[2] But during August and September the copy, both of the *Biographia Literaria* and of a volume of poems, was dispatched to Bristol. In October Coleridge was hoping to arrange for an American edition.[3] The Poems received the title of *Sibylline Leaves*. They consisted almost entirely of reprints, in many cases considerably revised. To *The Ancient Mariner* was added a marginal prose analysis, in some places of singular beauty. Coleridge's contributions to *Joan of Arc*, with the help of the *Visions* written in 1796, became an independent poem under the title of *The Destiny of Nations*. But neither the odes on the Lord's Prayer, which Coleridge was still hoping to write, nor any substantial unpublished poems were forthcoming. Only nine short pieces were new, and among these Coleridge did not after all refrain from including the lines on the *Prelude*, under the title of *To a Gentleman*.[4]

The actual printing of the two volumes was done for Hood and Gutch by John Evans & Co. of Bristol. Some proofs had already reached Coleridge by October 1815. But he had not yet found a London publisher.[5] Bowles had suggested, as far back as March, an attempt to enlist the good offices of Lord Byron, and to Byron Coleridge had written an elaborate letter of self-introduction, which he addressed, he said, 'to your Genius rather than your Rank'. He was very modest about his own literary claims.

A sort of pre-established good will, not unlike that with which the Swan instinctively takes up the weakling cygnet into the Hollow between its wings, I knew I might confidently look for from one who is indeed a Poet; were I but assured that your Lordship had ever thought of me as a fellow-laborer in the same vineyard, and as not otherwise

---

[1] G. 257.   [2] *W.R.* xciii. 344; Campbell, 212.   [3] G. 257–9, 261; *L.P.* 68; M. 11.
[4] *P.W.* 1150; *Christian Observer* (1845), 81, 145.
[5] G. 258, 262; M. 11; Wise, 100.

unworthy your notice. And surely a fellow-laborer I *have* been, and a co-inheritor of the same Bequest, tho' of a smaller portion; and tho' your Lordship's ampler Lot is on the sunny side, while mine has lain upon the North, my *growing* Vines gnawed down by Asses, and my richest and raciest clusters carried off and spoilt by the plundering Fox.

Would Byron let him send the manuscripts of the poems he had in hand, and if he thought well of them recommend them to some respectable publisher? He would rather it were not Longman, who held the copyright of his juvenile volume, which had brought him under the lash of Byron's satire. And with Murray, too, he had had troubles. Ever since he left Germany, he told Byron later, he had been forced in bitterness of soul 'to earn the week's food by the week's labor for the newspapers and the like'. He had even been obliged to write sermons. The tone of obsequious flattery in the first letter is characteristic of Coleridge's usual attitude to men of rank. He had not in fact a high opinion of Byron's poetry.[1] Byron replied that he would do what Coleridge wished, and, being now concerned with the management of Drury Lane, went on to suggest that there was a good opening for tragedy in London. 'We have had nothing to be mentioned in the same breath with *Remorse* for very many years.'[2] This gave a new twist to Coleridge's fancy, and in October he was writing both to Byron and to Stuart about a number of dramatic enterprises. The most important of these was a tragedy, which he hoped would be better than *Remorse*, and could have ready for presentation at Drury Lane after Christmas. But he was also at work upon a dramatic entertainment. He had contemplated revisions of Shakespeare's *Richard II*, and Beaumont and Fletcher's *Pilgrim* and *Beggar's Bush*, but found that he had been anticipated as regards the first two of these. The third, under the title of *The Merchant King or The King and the Beggar*, he could have sent at once, had not a journalistic engagement stood in the way. Also he could consider a pantomime, on a subject from the *Tartarian Tales*; and among his manuscripts were fragments of a tragicomedy on *Love and Loyalty*,

---

[1] G. 256 ('Last' for 'Lash'), 325; *B.L.* ii. 77; *T.T.* 2, 32; Raysor (M.), 285.
[2] Byron, iii. 190.

a dramatic romance called *Laugh Till you Lose Him*, an entertainment, of which the scene lay in Arabia, and a mime or
speaking ballet of *The Three Robbers*.[1] Byron was pleased
with the idea of the tragedy, and told Moore that, if Coleridge
kept his word, Drury Lane would be set up. 'I do think he
only wants a pioneer and a sparkle or two to explode most
gloriously.'[2] Meanwhile, he had received Coleridge's poems,
and apparently asked why *Christabel*, which he had recently
heard recited by Scott, was not included. Coleridge replied
that it was still unfinished and would extend to five books.
He was keeping it to publish alone or with *The Wanderings
of Cain*. He sent Byron a copy. Byron was much impressed,
praised the poem in a note to his *Siege of Corinth*, and
advised Murray to get hold of it. There was some discussion
of Scott's supposed plagiarism, and Byron said that he had
heard Scott speak of Coleridge and of *Christabel*, in particular, with no faint praise.[3] Coleridge was ill during the
greater part of November and December, and when he
recovered, it was not the tragedy, but the dramatic entertainment, henceforward known as *Zapolya*, which he resumed.[4] In January 1816 he complained that Byron had
not answered the most important part of a letter from him,
perhaps as to a possible publisher for his poems. In February, however, though himself in embarrassed circumstances,
Byron sent Coleridge a present of £100. A grant of £20 from
the Literary Fund had also come recently to his relief.[5] The
winter illness was certainly once more the result of opium,
for which Brabant was treating him in March. It gave
rise to a scandal. Coleridge, while staying with William
Money at Whetham, was reported to have sent out his
host's servant to buy him a bottle of brandy. It was no such
thing, he declares; it was only laudanum and gin, for medical
purposes.[6]

Zapolya, Coleridge believed, would be more suitable for
Covent Garden than for Drury Lane. He thought that he
must go to London and arrange for it, and perhaps remain

[1] G. 259, 260; L.P. 68; M.P. xxxiv. 377.　　　[2] Byron, iii. 230; G. 261.
[3] G. 222, 260; Rogers, i. 191; Byron, iii. 228, 245, 246.
[4] G. 263, 265; W.R. xciv. 5.
[5] W.R. xciv. 5; G. 264; Byron, vi. 112.　　　　　　[6] G. 265.

there, although it would be 'a sore heart-wasting' to part with Morgan.[1] Lamb reports him on 9 April 1816 as having been in town about a fortnight.[2]

Nature, who conducts every creature by instinct to its best end, has skilfully directed C. to take up his abode at a Chemist's Laboratory in Norfolk Street. She might as well have sent a Helluo Librorum for cure to the Vatican. God keep him inviolate among the traps and pit-falls. He has done pretty well as yet.

But Lamb was optimistic. Morgan had after all come up with Coleridge, and was attending upon him 'with his un-exampled assiduity and kindness'. But Morgan was once more in financial difficulties, and Coleridge says that his own health suffered from anxiety for his friend. He adopted his usual remedy, collapsed three days after his arrival, and was only pulled through by the wisdom of a new physi-cian, Joseph Adams, and the constant watchfulness of the apothecary.[3]

[1] G. 265; *W.R.* xciv. 5.   [2] L. 286.
[3] G. 266; R. (*D.*), ii. 4; Brandl, 351.

XV

FAIR HAVEN

March 1816—December 1823

ADAMS came to the conclusion that Coleridge's case was not hopeless, but that it was essential that he should place himself for a time under strict medical supervision. Some such measure Coleridge had himself contemplated two years before. He wanted retirement and a garden, and Adams recommended him to James Gillman, then in practice at Moreton House on Highgate Hill. Coleridge called upon Gillman, who immediately fell under the fascination of his conversation, and it was arranged that he should come into residence on the following day. Naturally he did not come until two days later, and in the meantime wrote an elaborate letter, impressing upon Gillman that, although he could not offer any adequate remuneration, he must at least not be suffered to make any addition to his host's family expenses. And he must be treated as one suffering from a specific madness.

You will never *hear* anything but truth from me :—prior habits render it out of my power to tell an untruth, but unless carefully observed, I dare not promise that I should not, with regard to this detested poison, be capable of acting one. No sixty hours have yet past without my having taken laudanum, though for the last week comparatively trifling doses. I have full belief that your anxiety need not be extended beyond the first week, and for the first week I shall not, I must not be permitted to leave your house, unless with you. Delicately or indelicately, this must be done, and both the servants and the assistant must receive absolute commands from you.

On 15 April 1816 Coleridge came, bearing in his hand the proof-sheets of *Christabel*. He looked to a stay, at first of a month, and later of three months, but by the end of the third month he had begun to hope that it would continue indefinitely. And in fact it continued to the end of his life.

Vagrant fancies in 1817 of a return to Keswick, or even a sojourn in Berlin, came to nothing.[1]

Coleridge had now many literary enterprises in hand, which for some weeks, while he was unable to leave Highgate, had to be carried out through the agency of Morgan.[2] John Murray, following Byron's suggestion, had called upon Coleridge in Norfolk St., and offered £80 for the fragment of *Christabel*, and £20 for that of *Kubla Khan*, which Coleridge, who had met Byron since his arrival in town, had just recited to his patron. The two poems, together with *The Pains of Sleep*, duly appeared towards the end of May. Both Lamb and Mrs. Coleridge, probably echoing Southey, regretted the fragmentary publication. But Coleridge says that he only consented to it in order to give the £80 to Morgan, whose necessities had now become clamorous. His statement that *Christabel* 'fell almost dead-born from the Press' seems hardly consistent with the fact that Murray twice reprinted it during the year. But the reviews in the *Examiner* and *Edinburgh Review* were unfavourable, and although the *Quarterly Review* was published by Murray, Gifford would not allow one to appear there.[3] Certainly Murray did not get the profits he had expected. 'I introduce Coleridge and *Christabel*,' wrote Byron to him, 'and Coleridge runs away with your money.' But Byron himself remained an admirer. 'I won't have any one sneer at *Christabel*: it is a fine, wild poem.'[4] Coleridge, in a preface, had declared that, although his poetic powers had been, since 1800, 'in a state of suspended animation', he had had the whole of the tale present to his mind from its first conception, and now hoped during the present year 'to embody in verse the three parts yet to come'. This remained a recurrent dream for several years. Gillman even prints an analysis of the sequel as he understood Coleridge to have planned it. But as to this there can be no certainty. Words-

[1] C. 208; G. 266, 281, 282; Brandl, 351; Gillman, 270; A. W. Gillman, 6; Watson, 51.

[2] G. 266, 268, 269; Brandl, 351.

[3] C. 211; G. 275, 279, 321; Murray, i. 305, 307; Brandl, 351; B.L. ii. 211; M. 13; L. 288; Leigh Hunt, ch. xvi; Campbell, *Poems*, 603; P.W. 213; Wise, 89.

[4] Byron, iii. 367; iv. 31, 37, 54, 99.

worth believed in 1836 that Coleridge had no definite idea
how *Christabel* would end.[1]

The tragedy planned in 1815 was never finished, although
it was still 'on the stocks' during the spring of 1817.[2] But
Zapolya, now described as 'a Christmas Tale', was submitted
to Covent Garden as soon as Coleridge reached London,
and rejected.[3] Coleridge then sent it to Byron for Drury
Lane. But Byron, who left his country for good on 26 April
1816, was no longer a power in the theatre. Douglas
Kinnaird and others, who now controlled the management,
discussed the play with the author, but decided that, although poetical, it was not practicable in its existing form,
and chose instead C. R. Maturin's *Bertram* for their next
production. Coleridge complains that they paid little regard
to Byron's approval, wasted much of his time with irre-
levancies, and talked of his 'damned metaphysics'. It was
suggested that he should recast the play as a melodrama, and
in the meantime publish the original text as a poem, which
would not injure its theatrical chances. How far he attempted
the recast is not clear. A melodrama founded on *Zapolya*,
which was given at the Royal Circus and Surrey Theatre in
1818, may not have been his own work. But he took the
original version to Murray, and offered to prefix the essay
on Dramatic Poetry, which he had originally planned to go
with *Remorse*. This, he thought, would come well from a
successful dramatist. *Remorse* itself was not yet forgotten,
and was revived, to Coleridge's gratification, for Rae's benefit in 1817. Murray gave Coleridge £50 for an edition of
Zapolya, but later allowed Coleridge to repay the amount
and recover the right of publication.[4] *Bertram* was produced
in the autumn of 1816, and Coleridge took his revenge in
the form of a series of critical articles for the *Courier*. How
far these were more than inspired by him is not clear. He
says at one time that he contributed a paragraph to the work

---

[1] C. 214; G. 269, 272, 283; A. 8, 15, p. 50; *T.T.* 268; Gillman, 283, 301; R. (*D.*),
iii. 90; Wordsworth, *Prose Works*, iii. 427; *S.P.* xxxiii. 437.
[2] G. 266, 287; Lippincott, 698, 705; Murray, i. 304.
[3] M. 12, 13; L. 286; R. (*D.*), ii. 4. Both Lamb and Robinson call *Zapolya* in error
a tragedy.
[4] C. 211; G. 266-9, 282, 287; L. 286, 288; Lippincott, 698, 705; Murray, i. 304;
Byron, iv. 171; Hazlitt, xix. 206.

of a friend; at another that they were in great measure dictated by him, but not revised or corrected in style; at a third that they were written by Morgan on thoughts collected from conversations with him.[1]

Coleridge seems at first to have hoped that Murray would become his regular publisher, and that he might be enlisted as a writer in the *Quarterly*. On this probably Gifford interposed a veto. Murray does not seem to have responded to a suggestion by Coleridge for a periodical *Review* of old books. But he offered £200 for a volume of *Rabbinical Tales* on the lines of those in *The Friend*, and with this plan Coleridge played for a year, and then found it beyond his capacity. Murray, on his side, was doubtless discouraged by the poor success of *Christabel*. There was also some misunderstanding about the withdrawal of *Zapolya*. At any rate by March 1817 Coleridge was regretting to Murray 'the change in your mode of thinking respecting me', for which he could not find anything to account in acts or expressions of his own.[2] This was not quite a complete account of the matter, since Coleridge himself had already been for some time in active relations with other publishers. In 1812 the reprinted *Friend* had been issued for him by the firm of Gale & Curtis. The edition was now long exhausted, and Coleridge desired a new one, for which he contemplated a revised text. The firm about this time became, first Gale & Fenner, and then Rest Fenner. But in fact Thomas Curtis, although he had taken orders and nominally discontinued his partnership, was still active in the management of the business, while his brother, Samuel Curtis of Camberwell, was employed as its printer. The firm, however, was of no estimation in the publishing trade. A letter to Gale about *The Friend* was answered by a personal call from Curtis, with whom there was 'talk on solemn questions'. According to Coleridge's own account, much as he appreciated the literary and social relations which he might have at Murray's, he valued still more highly the principles of Gale & Fenner, and preferred 'forming a connection with a religious house'. And with

---

[1] G. 272, 273, 287; *Courier*, 29 Aug., 7, 9, 10, 11 Sept. 1816.
[2] C. 211; G. 271, 275, 282, 350; Murray, i. 304, 305, 307.

Gale & Fenner he made terms, not only for the disposal of
the remaining copies of the original *Friend*, for which he was
to have £60, but also for the revised edition and for the
Sibylline Leaves and *Biographia Literaria*, on the basis of half
profits and an advance of £150. The firm were also to have
the right to publish anything he might write thereafter. And,
as a mark of respect, he also undertook to do for them a
tract on the distresses of the day, in the form of a *Lay Sermon*,
for which he was to have no money, although later he seems
to have regarded himself as entitled to half the profits.[1] But
before the end of September 1816 there were already signs
of friction between the author and his publishers. Neither
the *Sermon* nor the *Biographia* nor the revised *Friend* was yet
to hand, and Gale & Fenner, growing suspicious, refused to
give Coleridge credit for a copy of the old *Friend* which he
wanted to obtain. 'Merciful heavens, Sir, what infamous
calumnies must you have listened to concerning me.' As a
matter of fact, he had been working hard on the *Sermon*, to the
injury of his health, and had to retire to the sea-side at Muddiford in Hampshire for recovery. The scheme for the *Sermon*
had, as usual, grown upon him. There were now to be three
Sermons, addressed respectively to the higher classes, the
higher and middle classes, and the working classes. The first
appeared under the title of *The Statesman's Manual; or The Bible
the Best Guide to Political Skill and Foresight*, before the end of
the year, the second early in 1817, and the third was dropped.[2]
Coleridge was now free for the *Biographia* and *Sibylline Leaves*.
They gave a good deal of trouble before they ultimately
appeared in July and August 1817. There were disputes
with Gutch at Bristol, who, according to Coleridge, had
promised to charge him, as an old schoolfellow, no more
than a sixpence of profit, but now overcharged him both
for the paper and the printing, and in addition vilified him
in letters to Lamb. Gale & Fenner had to put down £28
to redeem the printed sheets from Gutch. There had
been, moreover, much misprinting, and the *Biographia* had

---

[1] G. 249, 273–5, 277, 321, 377; Lippincott, 698, 699.
[2] G. 273–9; *L.P.* 73, 75; *W.R.* xciv. 21; Lippincott, 700; S. (L.), iv. 257; Wise,
92, 94.

exceeded the limits of one volume, but was not long enough
for two. Fresh material had to be hastily assembled. It was
for this purpose that Coleridge had recovered *Zapolya* from
Murray.[1] He did not, however, use it, but substituted the
Letters of Satyrane, which had already appeared in the original
Friend, added the *Courier* articles on *Bertram*, with some changes
and no indication of Morgan's share in them, and wound up
with a final chapter of defence against the critics of his
Christabel, *Zapolya*, and *Statesman's Manual*.[2] It made little
difference to the form of the *Biographia*, which from beginning to end was, in his own words, an 'immethodical miscellany'.[3] This is not the place for detailed criticism of its
profoundly interesting, if often inconclusive and at one
point hastily abandoned, narratives and discussions. But
although Coleridge was largely justified in his claim that,
while ill health and its results had deranged his volition,
they had left his intellectual faculties unaffected, it must be
added that the capacity to shape a book is itself an intellectual
power, and one which he never acquired. Scott advised
Maturin not to answer the criticism of *Bertram*. He was a
favourite with the public and Coleridge had had 'some room
to be spited at the world'.[4] Byron, however, in his exile,
took offence at the attack on Drury Lane. 'He is a shabby
fellow, and I wash my hands of and after him.' Henceforward, while retaining his admiration for *Christabel*, he had
no good word for Coleridge, who, he came to believe, had
joined Southey in accusing him of incest. 'I can believe it, for
I had done him what is called a favour.'[5] Coleridge, on his
side, although he came to think Byron's later poetry 'Satanic',
remained grateful for his praise, and impressed by his person.[6]

If you had seen Lord Byron, you could scarcely disbelieve him—so
beautiful a countenance I scarcely ever saw—his teeth so many station-
ary smiles—his eyes the open portals of the sun—things of light and
for light—and his forehead so ample, and yet so flexible, passing from
marble smoothness into a hundred wreathes and lines and dimples
correspondent to the feelings and sentiments he is uttering.

[1] C. 211, 214; G. 275, 282; Lippincott, 704, 705; *Harvard MS.* 19478·5 F.; Wise,
97, 102.
[2] Campbell, 228, and Shawcross xci are in error in regarding the account in ch. 22
of Wordsworth's poetry as part of the added matter; cf. *B.L.* ii. 131.
[3] *B.L.* i. 64.   [4] Lockhart, iv. 132.   [5] Byron, iv. 171, 272, 484.   [6] T. 169.

It had not been Coleridge's intention to publish *Zapolya* separately, since he wished to add to it *Remorse* and the long-promised essay on dramatic poetry, and perhaps also *Wallenstein* and some translated plays. But the manuscript was with Gale & Fenner, and to his annoyance they put it in type and sent him a proof. Weakly, he says, he allowed the printing to proceed, and in the course of 1817 *Zapolya* appeared.[1] Meanwhile, further trouble with Gale & Fenner was brewing. The firm had in hand an ambitious plan for the publication of an *Encyclopaedia Metropolitana*. Coleridge had taken a leading part in the preliminary discussions, and had drafted a prospectus in conjunction with Stoddart. The scheme commended itself to him, because it was not to be primarily on dictionary lines, but in accordance with what he regarded as a philosophic arrangement of the subject-matter, starting from the Pure Sciences, then taking the Applied Sciences, and lastly the Fine Arts as an intermediate link between the two. The dictionary element was to form a supplement. Some minor modifications subsequently introduced did not altogether please him. Gale & Fenner offered him the editorship at a salary which he understood to be £500 a year. He was to write a preliminary *Treatise on Method*, and to contribute the dictionary, a section on grammar, and apparently another on animal magnetism, which was a subject at that time much in his mind. He accepted, not without a sigh of anguish, since the enterprise, if it succeeded at all, would consume all the years he could expect to live, and oblige him to give up all thought of doing anything of a permanent nature, either as a poet or a philosopher.[2] But he need not have been alarmed. In less than two months after the engagement had been made dissension had broken out between editor and publishers. Gale & Fenner seem to have claimed that the agreed salary was £400. Whatever it was, Coleridge wanted an advance of £300, for which he would pledge his copyrights. They would not give it unless he consented to leave Highgate and live at Camber-

---

[1] C. 211; G. 282 (misdated), 308; Lippincott, 705, 707; Wise, 109.
[2] G. 279, 292; Lippincott, 706, 710; Snyder (M.), vii, x, xiv, xvii; Campbell, 231; Frere, 222; Lowes, 546.

well, where no doubt they thought that Samuel Curtis could keep him up to the mark with copy. This Coleridge absolutely, and wisely, refused to do. He offered a compromise by which he would attend at Paternoster Row two days in the week. But this, after some delay, was not accepted, and evidently he withdrew from the editorship, and would do no more than supply the *Treatise on Method*. Thomas Curtis, whom he had regarded 'not as a mere tradesman, but as a convinced Christian', now became 'a wretch who came to me with every holy name in his mouth, merely to suck my brains'. One John Brown, the author of a book on *The Northern Courts*, called upon him, and told him that the Curtises were spreading calumnies abroad. They said he had cheated Longmans, and Samuel Curtis had often seen him intoxicated with brandy.[1] The first part of the *Encyclopaedia* was issued in January 1818, and was described by Coleridge as 'an infamous catch-penny or rather catch-guinea'. And the *Treatise*, which accompanied it, had been 'so bedeviled, so interpolated and topsy-turvied', that he resolved to publish his own version in a third volume of *The Friend*, to which he had already resolved to add fresh matter. He had, however, great difficulty in securing the return of his manuscript from the publishers, and it is not quite clear whether he ultimately succeeded.[2] The revised *Friend* made its appearance towards the end of 1818.[3] It consisted mainly of the original matter of 1809–10, corrected and arranged in an entirely new order. But into the third volume were introduced three new essays on morals and religion, and eight on method, which in any case are more likely to represent a revision of the *Treatise* than its original form. It has been suggested that Coleridge never got his manuscript back, and was obliged to reconstruct what he had written from the bedevilled text. The differences seem rather too extensive for this. But in any case, it is likely enough that the *Treatise*, as issued with the *Encyclopaedia*, may contain some fragments of Coleridge's writing, which he did not reproduce.[4]

[1] C. 214; G. 289, 290, 293; Lippincott, 707, 708; Brandl, 351; *Forster MS*. 112.
[2] C. 218; G. 292–4; *1 N.Q.* x. 21; Snyder (*M.*), xvi.
[3] *Fr.* xxi; C. 14; G. 277, 279, 282, 289, 292, 299; A. 6.
[4] *Fr.* iii. 51–216; cf. Snyder (*M.*), xvi, xxiii.

Zapolya, the *Biographia*, the *Sermons*, and the revised *Friend*,
all composed within a period of three years, represent Coleridge's most continuous period of literary activity. To these
must be added a translated *Hebrew Dirge*, published in 1817,
and two pamphlets in support of Sir Robert Peel's legislation on behalf of factory children in 1818.[1] Some writing
there was also for the *Courier*, besides the *Bertram* articles.
In 1816 Coleridge was still proposing articles on Catholic
emancipation to Stuart, and in 1818 asking William Mudford,
who had just become the editor, as to the tone of the paper,
and offering a series of 'characters'—to include Bonaparte.[2]
Possibly his editors may again have failed to disinter some of
his work. All that we can be sure of consists of two communications in defence of Southey, whose early *Wat Tyler* had
been exhumed by an enemy, and made the basis of a charge of
apostasy by Coleridge's old acquaintance, William Smith,
M.P. Two others, sent to the *Westminster Review*, were
rejected. Coleridge's handling of the subject was not appreciated at Grasmere. 'Of injudicious defenders he is surely
the Master Leader', wrote Dorothy, and 'He does nothing
in simplicity—and his praise. is to me quite disgusting'.[3] It
need hardly be said that, in addition to what he accomplished, many phantom works, old and new, flitted across
Coleridge's mind at Highgate; the epic on the Destruction
of Jerusalem, *Puff and Slander*, a translation of the odes in
the Bible, lucubrations on Shakespeare in two volumes, a
collection of Hebridean lore, a series of critical letters
entitled *The Reviewer in Exile, or Critic Confined to an Old
Library*, a periodical on German literature, school-books,
musical entertainments.[4] After all, most of us have our
day-dreams.

On the break-down of the editorship Gillman reduced
his charges to Coleridge. A new helper, J. H. Green, undertook to pay his annual insurance premiums.[5] And he turned

[1] C. 220; G. 286, 296; Prideaux, 5; R. (*D.*), ii. 93; Watson, 171; Wise, 111, 117;
P.W. 433.
[2] C. 209, 210; G. 273, 296; *Canterbury Magazine* (1834), 121, (1835), 31; *R.E.S.*
x. 451; Prideaux, 5, 6, 8–16.
[3] *O.T.* 939, 950; W. 588; S. (*W.*), iii. 65.
[4] G. 269, 272, 276, 277, 289, 290; A. 8.   [5] G. 290, 360.

once more to his old resource of lecturing. An impromptu
address to the London Philosophical Society, for which the
subject handed to him was 'The Growth of the Individual
Mind', was in fact on the theme of his *Treatise*.[1] And this
was followed by a long course, under the same auspices, at
Flower de Luce Court, which touched upon topics, including
once more Shakespeare, over the whole range of literature
from the Middle Ages to the Restoration. Coleridge's friends
bestirred themselves in his interest. 'There are particular
reasons just now', wrote Lamb, 'and have been any time for
the last twenty years why he should succeed.' The course,
which ran from January to March 1818, proved more of a
financial success than any other given by Coleridge. Mrs.
Coleridge got a remittance. And it is the one of which, as
regards subjects other than Shakespeare, we have the fullest
record, both in a number of partial contemporary reports
and in the *Literary Remains*, the critical disquisitions in which
are largely pieced together from material prepared for it.
Some other fragments of this have been recovered from
manuscripts.[2] At the end of the course there was a characteristic little *contretemps*. Mrs. Clarkson wrote of it, rather
maliciously, to Robinson.

You heard perhaps what an ungracious leave he took of his
auditory last spring—calling them together to hear a gratuitous lecture,
causing them to be told that he was too ill to meet them, but as soon
as he recovered they should be sure of the Lecture.—Either he never
recovered or he forgot his promise.

Perhaps this lapse may be explained by the fact that internal
dissensions had arisen in the London Philosophical Society,
as a result of which Coleridge resigned his membership.[3] In
December 1818 he tried his fortunes again at the 'Crown and
Anchor' in the Strand, giving up to March 1819 a course on
the History of Philosophy, and concurrently with this two
successive courses on literature. Little is known of the
latter, which do not seem to have broken fresh ground. But
shorthand notes of the philosophical lectures have been

[1] C. 218; G. 285; Gillman, 354; cf. Raysor, ii. 324.
[2] G. 290–5; A. 1; L. 304, 308; M. 14 (misdated); *D.H.* 273; Morley, 137; Gillman, 329; Watson, 81; Raysor, ii. 53, 299–317; (*M.*), 3–227.
[3] Raysor, ii. 307; G. 298.

preserved, and may some day be published. The returns
from these courses were poor, and Mrs. Coleridge had the
disappointment of receiving no remittance.[1] A proposal for
yet another course, at the Russell Institution, seems to have
come to nothing.[2] The 'Crown and Anchor' lectures can
hardly have been over when an unexpected blow fell upon
Coleridge. Rest Fenner became a bankrupt and all the hopes
of half-profits from the sales of *Zapolya*, the *Lay Sermons*, the
Sibylline Leaves, the *Biographia*, and *The Friend* vanished into
thin air. Incidentally it was revealed that false returns had
been made to Coleridge of the number of copies printed and
sold, which were much beyond what Fenner had accounted
for. Moreover the printing-bill for *The Friend* had not been
paid, and Samuel Curtis, whose business was at least nominally independent of the firm, clapped a lien upon the issue.
Coleridge reckoned his lost profits, of which he had perhaps
formed an optimistic estimate, at £1,100 or £1,200, and in
addition he had to borrow £150 to redeem the copyrights
of the books, which he was advised to withdraw from sale.
He still owed the £150 in 1825, although 'thank God, to one
person only'. This was probably Thomas Allsop, a young
business man, who had made Coleridge's acquaintance at
his lectures, and who now came forward with an unexpected gift. Robinson, however, had heard that the amount
of this was £100.[3] It was, presumably, the financial crash
which led Coleridge, about the same time, to look favourably
upon an offer which reached him to become a contributor
to *Blackwood's Magazine*. Less than two years before he had
been pilloried by the *Magazine* in a review of the *Biographia*,
which incidentally revived the old *Anti-Jacobin* charge, now
perhaps more tenable, of having deserted his wife and
children. The authorship is generally attributed to John
Wilson, the Mathetes of *The Friend*, who was believed by
De Quincey to have had a quarrel with Coleridge before he
left Allan Bank. But the evidence is very thin. All we really
know is that Wilson wrote a review, lost it in an ascent of

[1] C. 222; G. 299-301; A. 3, 44; M. 17; Leslie, i. 43; Raysor, ii. 318-24; K. H.
Coburn in *R.E.S.* x. 428.   [2] Gillman, 351; Raysor, ii. 324.
[3] G. 307, 308, 315, 320, 321, 347, 377; A. 4, 32; Brandl, 351; Prideaux, 18;
R. (*D.*), ii. 286; Watson, 82.

Cairngorm, and said that he would try to write another, but could not promise.[1] Coleridge had been so perturbed by the review that he consulted Robinson as to the possibility of prosecuting Blackwood for libel.[2] Later articles in the *Magazine*, however, by Wilson as well as by Lockhart, had treated Coleridge with respect, although not without indulging in the quips and cranks which were an essential feature of the editorial policy.[3] At any rate a mollified Coleridge now had an interview with William Blackwood, and thereafter wrote him a letter in which he promised to set out his own ideas of how a literary review should be conducted. On the assumption that these were accepted, he was prepared to contribute two sheets a month, but for these he should expect more than the common price.[4] Blackwood replied that he could not promise more than ten guineas a sheet, but that the editor might increase this according to the value of the articles.[5] Probably Coleridge thought this not good enough, for during 1819 only two things of his, perhaps not sent by himself, appeared in the *Magazine*, and in the following January Lamb was telling him that why he should refuse twenty guineas a sheet from *Blackwood's* or any other magazine passed his comprehension.[6] In September, however, came a *Letter to Peter Morris M.D. on the Sorts and Uses of Literary Praise*.[7] This caused Coleridge some annoyance. He denied a statement made by John Scott in the *London Magazine* that it was a private letter to the editor of *Blackwood's* and not meant for publication. But he was perturbed by the suggestions of Lamb and of his sons that the description in it of a certain Atticus, who loved to be praised, but not to praise, would be taken for a portrait of Wordsworth.[8] In October 1821 came a very miscellaneous selection from his literary correspondence, and in January 1822 the beginning of a narrative called *The History and Gests of Maximilian*, which got no sequel.[9] He need not have been

---

[1] A. L. Strout (*P.M.L.A.* xlviii), 103; Oliphant, *Blackwoods*, i. 262.
[2] G. 284; Prideaux, 16.   [3] Strout, 106 sqq.   [4] G. 302; Prideaux, 16.
[5] Oliphant, i. 411.   [6] L. 349; *P.W.* 435; Raysor (M.), 269.
[7] T. Ashe, *Miscellanies*, 238 (incomplete).   [8] G. 315; Strout, 116.
[9] G. 321, 322; A. 15, 33; T. 194; Ashe, 244 (incomplete), 261; Oliphant, i. 218; Strout, 117.

afraid that Wordsworth would put on the cap of Atticus, for
Wordsworth had seen articles in *Blackwood's* so infamous that
he would not have it in his house. The ladies of his family
read Coleridge's contributions surreptitiously elsewhere, but
found them so dull and unintelligible that they could hardly
believe them to be his.[1]

The communications to *Blackwood's* cannot have done
much to restore Coleridge's finances, even though they were
accompanied by 'writing MS. sermons for lazy clergymen,
who stipulate that the composition must not be more than
respectable, for fear they should be desired to publish the
visitation sermon'.[2] An impulse to send an article to the
Eclectic Review in support of Queen Caroline, whose cause, in
spite of his dislike for her advocate Brougham, Coleridge had
somewhat unaccountably espoused, was suppressed by Gillman.[3] And early in 1821 Coleridge was on his beam-ends.
He had all the materials for works on Shakespeare, on
Romantic Poetry, on the History of Philosophy, and for a
volume of Letters on the Old and New Testament and the
Doctrine and Principles of the Fathers and the Reformation.

To the completion of these four works I have literally nothing more
to do than *to transcribe*; but, as I before hinted, from so many scraps and
Sibylline leaves, including margins of books and blank pages, that, unfortunately, I must be my own scribe, and not done by myself, they
will all be lost; or perhaps (as has been too often the case already)
furnish feathers for the caps of others; some for this purpose and some
to plume the arrows of detraction, to be let fly against the luckless bird
from whom they had been plucked or moulted.

In addition there was his 'Great Work', and he would
fain finish the *Christabel*, although he could not now, as in
a past 'proud time' hope for the *Hymns* and the epic on
Jerusalem. He was in debt; the *Reviews* were against him.
He had dedicated himself, and was convinced that he had
not been useless in his generation.

But, from circumstances, the *main* portion of my harvest is still on
the ground, ripe indeed, and only waiting, a few for the sickle, but a
large part only for the *sheaving*, and carting, and housing; but from all
this I must turn away, must let them rot as they lie, and be as though

---

[1] W. 620; R. 54, 55.   [2] A. 15.   [3] A. 11, 13; R. (*D.*), ii. 196.

they never had been, for I must go and gather blackberries and earth-
nuts, or pick mushrooms and gild oak-apples for the palates and fancies
of chance customers.

He could see only one remedy, that those who thought well
of his powers and attainments should subscribe for three or
four years to a yearly sum of £200, which would enable him
to devote two-thirds of his time to the four books already
planned and one-third to the 'Great Work' and to *Christabel*, 'and what else the happier hour might inspire'. He consulted young Allsop.

Am I entitled, have I earned *a right* to do this? Can I do it without
moral degradation?: and, lastly, can it be done without loss of
character in the eye of my acquaintance, and of my friends' acquaintance, who may have been informed of the circumstances?

He had already some promises of contributions.[1] That he
did not pursue the scheme is clear from a letter written in
the following August to De Quincey, who, being now in
financial straits himself, had suggested some repayment of
the £300 which he had bestowed on Coleridge in 1807. This
Coleridge had insisted at the time in regarding as a loan.
But now, after some beating about the bush, and recording
a foreboding that he should one day feel his poverty as a
humiliation, he could do no more than detail to De Quincey
his financial history since he came to Highgate as an explanation of his complete inability to raise the money. He
was already in debt to Gillman for £500, and as for himself,
'So help me God! for months past I have not a shilling
in my pocket—nor do I know how or where to procure a
guinea'.[2] Early in 1822 a new scheme occurred to him.
There had been several young men during the last few years
who believed themselves to have benefited by conversation
and correspondence with him. Of such he might form a
class, who would take a two years' course of instruction, and
in return make such remuneration as each might think
proper. Dorothy Wordsworth saw an advertisement to this
effect which he put in the papers. As a beginning he had
enlisted Charles Stutfield, the son of an old Stowey acquaintance, and one John Watson, who attended regularly on

[1] A. 15.   [2] G. 321.

Thursdays.[1] Invitations to lecture came to him from Dublin through John Anster in 1821 and from Leeds in 1823, but neither of these was accepted.[2] Southey heard of him in July 1823 as planning to bring out his Logic and a collection of poems, and to adapt his *Wallenstein* for Edmund Kean to appear in on the stage.[3]

In spite of his troubles, some of which have still to be recounted, Coleridge seems to have been happier at Highgate than he had been for many years before. He was soon on terms of the closest intimacy with James and Maria Gillman. In the husband he found a man of 'strong, fervid, and agile intellect', and in character 'so generous, so high-hearted, and yet so industrious, self-denying, and economic', and in the wife not merely 'a most affectionate and sisterly nurse', but one who came near to embodying his ideal of womanhood. He compared her to Santa Teresa. Gillman took a warm interest in his philosophical speculations, and before long was acting as his amanuensis. By 1821 Coleridge felt that he owed to Gillman 'under God all the health and means of being useful that I possess', and in 1822 he was writing to him as the 'dear Friend, and Brother of my Soul'. The Wordsworths held up their hands when Coleridge suggested that, in view of Gillman's medical skill, it would be well that his daughter Sara should go to Highgate and receive treatment from him. But Mrs. Coleridge was soon referring to 'those good people, the Gilmans', and frequent letters from Mrs. Gillman to her supplemented the paucity of Coleridge's own.[4] Under Gillman's care the use of opium, if not entirely abandoned, was at least reduced to medicinal doses. Coleridge's health was by now permanently broken, and from time to time he had disabling illnesses. He still suffered from nightmares.[5] But he received much benefit from visits to the sea-side, where he renewed his old delight in bathing. That to Muddiford in 1816 was followed by one to Littlehampton in 1817, and in 1820 he was at Walmer.[6] But as a rule Ramsgate was the resort chosen. He was regu-

---

[1] A. 26; L.P. 76; R. 57.   [2] A. 24, 25; G. 332.   [3] S. (L.), v. 140.
[4] C. 210, 231; G. 273, 290, 306, 316, 320; A. 7, 9, 10; W. 628; M. 19.
[5] Gillman, 303.   [6] C. 215-17, 219; Watson, 86.

larly accompanied by the Gillmans, or, if professional duties intervened, at any rate by Mrs. Gillman. Coleridge says that during his first year at Highgate Gillman acquired a nervous aversion, which endured long after there was any reason for it, from any separation between his wife and their patient. He regarded her as 'a sort of talisman'. No doubt there were druggists' shops at Ramsgate.[1] The arrangement gave rise to some scandal, which was reported to Lamb by Coleridge's old schoolfellow Franklin, now a master at Hertford, in 1824. It may have been this which Lockhart revived in 1852.[2]

There were old friends ready to greet Coleridge on his return to town after nearly two years' interval. Lamb, who had pretended that the wanderer was dead in the December before his arrival, soon felt the accustomed fascination.

I think his essentials not touched: he is very bad, but then he wonderfully picks up another day, and his face when he repeats his verses hath its ancient glory, an Archangel a little damaged.

The even tenour of Lamb's own life in the Temple was once more broken.

Coleridge is absent but 4 miles, and the neighborhood of such a man is as exciting as the presence of 50 ordinary Persons. 'Tis enough to be within the whiff and wind of his genius, for us not to possess our souls in quiet.[3]

Before long, however, a little cloud arose. Coleridge had been refused the loan of two books he needed, on a 'slander' that he did not return his borrowings. And this he said was due to Lamb, who had been accusing him for ten years of keeping a volume of Dodsley's *Old Plays*, which he had never had. Robinson had taken the matter up and talked— 'O ye Gods! how he does talk!'—at the Westminster Library and elsewhere. He had convinced Robinson that to him at least the many books borrowed had all been returned. Perhaps Lamb also was now convinced, but a few years later he was again complaining that, when he was out, Coleridge had come to his rooms and abstracted Luther's *Table Talk* and the works of Bonaventura, leaving two devilish gaps

[1] *L.P.* 87.   [2] L. 536; Studies, 67; *R.E.S.* x. 456.   [3] L. 283, 288.

in his third shelf from the top, where he had knocked out two of its eye-teeth. 'You never come but you take away some folio that is part of my existence.'[1] And Coleridge at Highgate was not quite the same thing as Coleridge in London itself. For some time Lamb saw little of him.

> He is an odd person, when he first comes to town he is quite hot upon visiting, and then he turns off and absolutely never comes at all, but seems to forget there are any such people in the world. I made one attempt to visit him (a morning call) at Highgate, but there was something in him or his apothecary which I found so unattractively-repulsing-from any temptation to call again, that I stay away as naturally as a Lover visits.

Lamb could not, of course, refrain from punning on Gillman's name as Killman.[2] Robinson, too, thought that Gillman behaved with rudeness, standing over him and Lamb with an air as if he meant to express, 'Now Gentlemen, it is time for you to go'. They took the hint, and Lamb said he would never call again.[3] It is likely enough that at first Gillman was distrustful of boon companions. Later Lamb found him and his wife more friendly, and though still disliking to see Coleridge in another man's house, as indeed he had done when Coleridge was at Morgan's, often walked up to Highgate on Sundays, which were the only days left him by the East India Office. Robinson, however, was a much rarer visitant.[4] Of Morgan Coleridge was lamenting in January 1818 that he saw too little. This unfortunate man's affairs had gone from bad to worse. He had returned to Calne for a holiday with the Lambs in the autumn of 1816. About the same time an agent employed by him proved a rascal. Coleridge wrote later of faulty acts done by Morgan himself 'in the confused and feverish dream of Embarrassment'. Both the Bishopsgate Street businesses were still running in 1815 and 1816. By 31 August 1817 Morgan's name had been replaced by that of a James Osborne over the cheesemonger's shop. But the tobacconist's still bore that of Matthew Brent, and in October Lamb described Morgan as a gentleman tobacconist. By the end of 1819 he was again under arrest and could not hope to join his wife,

---

[1] G. 267, 271; L. 366.   [2] L. 288, 292, 293.   [3] Morley, 69.
[4] L. 307, 308, 312, 315, 318; Morley 70, 72, 74; R. (D.), ii. 11, 39, 59.

who had been driven to take a post as a charity-school mistress, until an Insolvent Act had been passed. Southey, who remembered invitations to Morgan's mother's table, when he would otherwise have gone without a dinner, promised him an annuity of £10. Lamb did the same. A third contributor remained anonymous. De Quincey, however, records that Morgan sank under his misfortune in prison, and probably by March 1820, and certainly by August 1821, he was dead. By 1819 Brent's name, as well as Morgan's, had gone from Bishopsgate St.[1] Dorothy Wordsworth guessed that Coleridge would not call upon Mrs. Clarkson, and in fact she seems to have dropped out of his life.[2]

Highgate was still little more than a village, where Coleridge could find spiritual refreshment in the midst of gardens and in the umbrageous glades of Caen Wood. It was in a Highgate lane that Leslie first learnt from him to recognize the notes of the nightingale. There was some local society to be had. Families of Milne, Chisholm, Nixon, Williams, Sutton are in the background of Coleridge's letters.[3] And to Ivy Cottage in 1819 came Charles Mathews, the comedian, whose wife was half-sister of Fanny Kelly, later honoured by a proposal of marriage from Charles Lamb. Mathews records the simplicity of Coleridge's character, and the abstraction of mind which led him habitually, after conversing, to attempt leaving the room through a large mirror on the wall. Coleridge describes a dinner at Ivy Cottage, after which Mathews gave a rehearsal of one of his 'At Homes'. On another occasion Lamb made one of his happiest retorts.[4]

Coleridge. Charles Lamb, I believe you never heard me *preach.*
Lamb. I ne-ever heard you do anything *else!*

Gillman's invigilation, after the beginning, was not so strict as to prevent Coleridge from spending an evening or even a night in town; and he was able, from time to time, to dine with Sir George Beaumont in Grosvenor Square,

---

[1] G. 274, 289, 321; Brandl, 351; L. 301, 345; R. (*D.*), ii. 4; De Q. ii. 208; S. (*L.*), iv. 361; v. 31; *Johnstone's Directory* (1817); *London P.O. Directory.* I have not been able to find a *Directory* for 1818.   [2] W. 605.
[3] C. 221, 227, 259; G. 285, 313, 316, 323, 328, 392, 399; A. 17, 25; Leslie, i. 48; *R.E.S.* x. 453; *P.W.* 441, 1009.
[4] C. 227; G. 306; Mathews, i. 188; iii. 197.

Basil Montagu in Bedford Square, Charles Aders in Euston
Square, Daniel Stuart in Harley Street, Thomas Monkhouse
in Gloucester Place, John Hookham Frere at Blake's Hotel,
or Joseph Henry Green in Lincoln's Inn Fields. With Basil
Montagu he was, at least by 1821, on as intimate terms as
if nothing had happened in 1810.[1] And when Montagu published the last volume of his edition of Bacon in 1834, he
wrote in the preface:

One friend the grave has closed over, who cheered me in my task
when I was weary, and better able, from his rich and comprehensive
mind, to detect errors than any man, was always more happy to encourage and to commend. Wise as the serpent, gall-less as the dove,
pious and pure of heart, tender, affectionate and forgiving, this and
more than this I can say, after the trial of forty years, was my friend and
instructor, Samuel Taylor Coleridge.

Thomas Monkhouse, a first cousin of the Hutchinsons,
formerly of Penrith, and now a prosperous business man in
Budge Row, was also an old acquaintance. Frere, the diplo-
matist and Aristophanic scholar, became one of Coleridge's
most generous supporters during the rest of his life. Coleridge regarded him and Sir George Beaumont as exemplify-
ing the finest type of English gentleman, 'as Edmund Spenser
sang, and Sidney realised the idea'.[2] Frere told Coleridge
that Canning and Lord Liverpool thought highly of him,
and Coleridge addressed a long letter to Lord Liverpool, in
which he claimed the patronage and protection of those
who shared his political convictions. Unfortunately, he also
took occasion to criticize the 'mechanic' philosophy of
Locke and his followers, which led the noble lord to note
upon the letter, 'I cannot well understand him'.[3] Green, a
demonstrator at Guy's and St. Thomas's Hospitals, and the
son of a well-to-do family, also showed great liberality to
Coleridge, and became the associate of his metaphysical
studies, in a series of conversations on Sunday mornings,
which soon took the form of dictations by the older man.
In July 1818 Coleridge was absent from Highgate for a
longer period than usual, on a visit to Green's parents at
St. Lawrence near Maldon in Essex, where the pleasures of

[1] G. 319, 383.   [2] G. 299, 370; B. ii. 246; cf. pp. 303, 323.
[3] C. 214; C. D. Yonge, *Life of Liverpool*, ii. 300.

life on a country estate were qualified by a shortage of snuff, the attentions of gnats, and the self-assertiveness of a young Evangelical clergyman. More and more Coleridge felt that he could be well off nowhere away from the Gillmans.[1] It was during a walk with Green at Highgate on 11 April 1819 that he had his only meeting with John Keats. They were as ships that pass in the night. He remembered Keats many years later as 'a loose, slack, not well-dressed youth', who stayed for a minute or two, left him, and then came back to say, 'Let me carry away the memory, Coleridge, of having pressed your hand!' 'There is death in that hand', said Coleridge to Green. A contemporary letter by Keats himself is, perhaps naturally, more detailed, and suggests a longer interview.[2]

Last Sunday I took a walk towards Highgate and in the lane that winds by the side of Lord Mansfield's park I met Mr Green our Demonstrator at Guy's in conversation with Coleridge—I joined them, after inquiring by a look whether it would be agreeable—I walked with him at his alderman-after-dinner pace for near two Miles I suppose. In those two Miles he broached a thousand things—let me see if I can give you a list—Nightingales, Poetry—on Poetical Sensation—Metaphysics— Different genera and species of Dreams—Nightmare—a dream accompanied with a sense of touch—single and double touch—a dream related—first and second consciousness—the difference explained between will and Volition—so many metaphysicians from a want of smoking the second consciousness—Monsters—the Kraken—Mermaids—Southey believes in them—Southey's belief too much diluted —a Ghost story—Good morning—I heard his voice as he came towards me—I heard it as he moved away—I had heard it all the interval —if it may be called so. He was civil enough to ask me to call on him at Highgate.

It does not appear that Coleridge ever met Shelley, but he had been told that shortly before his death Shelley had expressed a deep wish that he could commune with him, 'as the one only being who could resolve or allay the doubts and anxieties that pressed upon his mind'.[3] At Muddiford Coleridge made the acquaintance of Scott's friend William Stuart Rose, who recorded their pacings on the ribbed sea-

[1] C. 221; A. x; cf. pp. 283, 312.
[2] T.T. 195; 2 Cornhill Mag. xlii. 405; Forman, Letters of Keats, 324; cf. Lowes, 269, 345, 581, and the note by Keats of Coleridge's 'vile' voice in a recently discovered sonnet (C. L. Finney, Evolution of Keats' Poetry, 652). [3] A, p. 139.

sands together in his poem of *Gundimore*; and at Littlehampton of Henry Francis Cary, the fame of whose Dante
translation he much furthered by praise in his lectures, and
Charles Augustus Tulk, to whom he endited many letters on
philosophy.[1] Ludwig Tieck, whom he had met in Rome,
came to London during 1817, and an interchange of views
on Shakespeare took place at Highgate. Robinson reports:

> Coleridge was not in his element. His German was not good and his
> English was not free. He feared he should not be understood if he
> talked his best. His eloquence was therefore constrained.[2]

With Thomas Allsop there was much intercourse. Coleridge
adopted a paternal tone, giving the young man good advice,
such as he had already communicated to the world, out of
his own bitter experience, in the *Biographia*, on the desirability of securing a competence before he attempted literature; and when he became engaged, writing an essay on the
ideal of marriage for the benefit of his prospective bride.[3]
Unfortunately he also used his letters to Allsop as a safety-
valve for his own worst moods of resentment against the
persecution of the *Reviews* and the ingratitude of those to
the establishment of whose fame he had devoted the best
years of his life.[4]

The persecution, if it was persecution, was largely due to
William Hazlitt, who had abandoned painting and metaphysics for literary and political journalism, and in 1816 was
employed both by the *Edinburgh Review* and the *Examiner*.
Hazlitt remains one of the glories of English letters, but his
remarkable gifts of acute critical perception and felicitous
phrasing were too often deflected by a moral thwartness
which beset him in all personal matters. The incident which
led to his departure from Keswick in 1803, and which he
himself probably regarded as no more than a trivial esca-
pade, had caused both Wordsworth and Coleridge to shun
his company, although this was rendered difficult by his
continued relations with the more tolerant Lamb, to whom

---

[1] Campbell, 225; C. 215, 216, 219, 229; G. 293; Cary, *Memoirs*, ii. 18, 28;
Watson, 55.
[2] C. 212, 213, 217; G. 280, 281; Morley, 72; R. (*D.*), ii. 54; Watson, 55; Frere, 222.
[3] A. 2, p. 171.   [4] A. 3; cf. p. 300.

Wordsworth had revealed the story in 1814.[1] Doubtless
Hazlitt resented the ostracism. Moreover, he still clung to
the democracy of his youth, and regarded Wordsworth and
Coleridge, whose political views had shifted, as renegades.
In June 1816 he reviewed *Christabel* in the *Examiner*. Most
of his criticism was well balanced enough; he was not blind
to the beauties of the poem. But he took occasion, perhaps
with the idea of revenging himself for Coleridge's attitude
about Keswick, to suggest that there was 'something disgusting at the bottom of his subject'. He notes, however,
that a line, already known to him, had been omitted in
print 'from mere delicacy', although 'absolutely necessary
to the understanding the whole story'. It was the description of Geraldine's side, revealed in bed, as 'Hideous, de-
formed, and pale of hue', and was wanted to show that
Geraldine was 'a witch'.[2] Then in September came, also in the
Examiner, a very definite act of hostility to Coleridge, also in
the form of a review, but a bogus one, of what Hazlitt felt
sure that Coleridge would write in his *Lay Sermon*, then
already announced, but not yet published. It was a masterpiece of malicious irony. Both Lamb and Robinson were
perturbed, although Lamb acutely observed that after all
'a kind of respect shines thro' the disrespect'. This, indeed,
is the case with nearly all of Hazlitt's writings upon Coleridge.
It is in this one that he incidentally describes him as 'fit to
take up the deep pauses of conversation between Cardinals
and Angels'.[3] Coleridge himself referred to the 'slander' on
Christabel in an appendix to the *Statesman's Manual*, but had
probably not then read the anticipatory review. Of this,
however, he wrote bitterly to Hugh James Rose, a young
Cambridge student of his acquaintance, and dwelt on his
own early kindness to Hazlitt, especially in the Keswick
affair, of which 'the Detail outraged Modesty'.

> Hazlitt possesses considerable Talent; but it is diseased by a morbid
> hatred of the Beautiful, and killed by the absence of Imagination, and
> alas! by a wicked Heart of embruted appetites.

[1] Hazlitt, v. 230; xix. 9; W. 505; L. 262, 270; A, p. 117; Howe, 79.
[2] Hazlitt, xix. 32.
[3] Hazlitt, vii. 114; Howe, 210, 211; L. 292.

This is, perhaps, not very penetrating psychology.[1] Then, in the *Edinburgh Review* for September, appeared another criticism of *Christabel*.[2] The authorship of this has been a matter of much controversy.[3] On internal grounds I should not have been inclined to attribute it to Hazlitt. It is a poor bit of writing, and it is difficult to read into it any repetition of the charge of indecency. Robinson read it and merely noted that it was 'a very stupid review'.[4]

Coleridge, however, before he had himself seen it, had been 'assured' that it was Hazlitt's. He spoke of it with moderation to Robinson, but poured forth his woes in letters to Brabant, Murray, and Wrangham, to whom he told once more the Keswick story. Hazlitt, he says, when reproached, had replied, 'Damn him! I hate him, for I am under obligations to him.' And when reminded that he had frequently declared *Christabel* to be the first poem in the language of its size, his only answer was, 'I grumbled part to myself while I was writing, but nothing stings a man so much as making people believe lies of him.' According to Gillman, Hazlitt at some time admitted the authorship, and said that he was compelled to adopt the tone and character of the periodical for which he was writing. Coleridge's grievance was indeed almost as much against Jeffrey, with whom his personal relations had in the past been friendly, as against Hazlitt himself. He would arraign Jeffrey in some public fashion.[5] Meanwhile Hazlitt had returned to the subject of the *Statesman's Manual* in bona fide reviews both for the *Edinburgh* and the *Examiner*, and had found in it language which he could represent as evidence of at least 'potential infidelity'.[6] To the *Examiner* he also wrote a letter, in another vein, which became the germ of his later paper on *My First Acquaintance with Poets*.[7] Minor attacks upon Coleridge, in connexion with the *Wat Tyler* controversy, followed.[8] Coleridge's protest did not take shape until the appearance of the

---

[1] G. 273, 276; Howe, 212; Morley, 70.
[2] *Ed. Review*, xxvii. 58; Hazlitt (ed. Waller and Glover), x. 411.
[3] Howe, 439; 9 *N.Q.* x. 388, 429; xi. 170, 269.   [4] Howe, 211.
[5] C. 211; G. 279; *W.R.* xciv. 21; Howe, 212; Morley, 70.
[6] Hazlitt, xvi. 99.   [7] Hazlitt, vii. 119, 128.
[8] Hazlitt, vii. 176; xix. 196.

Biographia Literaria in July 1817. The earlier pages of this had contained a notice of Jeffrey's visit to Keswick in 1810, when he was 'treated with every hospitable attention by Mr. Southey and myself', and of the critical remarks on 'the School of whining and hypochondriachal poets that haunt the Lakes', which he afterwards endited. And now, in the final sheets, the story was brought up to date. *Christabel* had been assailed in the *Edinburgh* 'with a malignity and a spirit of personal hatred that ought to have injured only the work in which such a tirade appeared: and this review was generally attributed (whether rightly or no I know not) to a man, who both in my presence and in my absence has repeatedly pronounced it the finest poem in the language'. No doubt allowance must be made for 'the necessity of a certain proportion of abuse and ridicule in a Review, in order to make it saleable'. Then came the 'lampoon' on the *Statesman's Manual*, and the selection of its author to review the same task.

Under the single condition, that he should have written what he himself really thought, and have criticized the work as he would have done had its author been indifferent to him, I should have chosen that man myself, both from the vigor and the originality of his mind, and from his particular acuteness in speculative reasoning, before all others.

But the review was no more than a 'rhapsody of predetermined insult'. A long defence against the charge of 'potential infidelity' follows.[1] Jeffrey's answer was once more to commission Hazlitt with a review of the *Biographia*. And to this he himself appended a long note, in which he shows some misapprehension of Coleridge's meaning. Apparently he thought that he was himself being accused of being the critic of *Christabel*. He had never called it the finest poem of its kind, had only heard four or five lines of it beforehand, was disappointed when he saw it in print, and did not review it. As for the hospitality at Keswick, it amounted to a cup of coffee, after which Coleridge dined with him at his inn. He never suborned any one to abuse or extol the *Statesman's Manual*, knew nothing of any lampoon, and entrusted the review to a writer whom he never suspected and did not now suspect of any personal feelings towards

[1] *B.L.* i. 36; ii. 211.

the author.[1] In 1818 Hazlitt, like Coleridge himself, was
lecturing on poetry, and what he then said, and afterwards
printed, about him might almost be regarded as an apology.[2]

> There is no man who has a better right to say what he thinks of him
> than I have. Is there here any dear friend of Caesar? To him I say that
> Brutus's love to Caesar was no less than his. But no matter.

Coleridge had been the only man he ever knew who
answered to the idea of a man of genius, the only one from
whom he ever learnt anything. He recalls the echo of early
conversations.

> That spell is broke; that time is gone for ever; that voice is heard no
> more: but still the recollection comes rushing by with thoughts of
> long-past years, and rings in my ears with never-dying sound.

But in the next year the author of an attack on *Blackwood's*, under the title of *Hypocrisy Unveiled*, described *Christabel* as 'the most obscene Poem in the English Language', and
Coleridge declared that from pure malignity Hazlitt had
spread abroad the report that Geraldine was a man in disguise. This may be doubted, since he had already written
of her as a 'witch'.[3]

Since both Wordsworth and Southey were from time to
time in London, some renewal of relations with Coleridge
at Highgate was inevitable. But these relations were not
very cordial. About July 1817 Coleridge wrote to Southey,
introducing Tieck, and added in a postscript, 'Should this
meet you, *for God's sake*, do let me know of your arrival in
London; it is so very important that I should see you.' And
in August Southey made up his mind to what he thought
would be a 'hateful visit' to Highgate. He was afraid that
Coleridge wanted to return to Greta Hall. In any case he
would talk about animal magnetism, 'and go on from Dan
to Beersheba in his endless loquacity'. In 1819 Coleridge
sent him, in friendly terms, another introduction for George
Ticknor.[4] Of Wordsworth there is rather more to record.
We do not know how Wordsworth took the appearance of

---

[1] *Ed. Review*, xxviii. 488; Hazlitt, xvi. 115; Howe, 238.
[2] Hazlitt, v. 165.   [3] G. 301; Prideaux, 11.
[4] C. 212 (misdated); G. 282, 301; Campbell, 231; S. (T.), ii. 471.

the lines *To a Gentleman* in *Sibylline Leaves*, or the criticism of his poetry in the *Biographia*. Soon after the publication of this, he had not read it all, but had contented himself with 'skimming parts of it'. In December 1817 he was in London, and met Coleridge, 'quite grey haired, and much agitated, but very agreeable on the whole', both at Monkhouse's, where Sara Hutchinson was also of the company, and at Lamb's, where Robinson records that he 'found two parties congregated round the two poets, but Coleridge had a thicker mass than Wordsworth'. Mrs. Clarkson wrote:

> From your report I think it a pity that W. & C. should have met in company. Men of the world have a certain tact by which they regulate their conduct in society & which seems to have been wanted upon the occasion to which you allude. A man of the world in W——s place would have been kind before strangers, cold in private. W——s better nature I have no doubt would make him affectionate in private & only cold before strangers because his whole mind could not be expressed before them.[1]

In July 1820 Wordsworth, then on the point of starting for a continental tour, wrote regretting that illness had prevented an intended visit to Coleridge, and that he had seen so little of him. He hoped to be more lucky on his return. He did in fact walk over from Hampstead to Highgate in the following November.[2] Meanwhile, and for a year or two later, Coleridge's letters, and, in particular, his indiscreet confidences to Allsop, reveal a distinct undercurrent of rancour towards Wordsworth. He seems to have thought that he had been used and then abandoned. Of *The Friend* he wrote in 1816, that 'from the beginning to this very hour nothing but cold water, or what is far worse, very cold praise, had been bestowed upon it by my friends—even by Southey and Wordsworth'.[3] In 1818 he can forgive his open maligners.[4]

> But I have loved with enthusiastic self-oblivion those who have been so well pleased that I should, year after year, flow with a hundred nameless rills into *their* main stream, that they could find nothing but cold praise and effective discouragement of every attempt of mine to roll onward in a distinct current of my own; who *admitted* that the

---

[1] W. 591; R. 43; R. (*D.*), ii. 80; M. 14 (misdated).
[2] W. 641; W. *Memoirs*, ii. 108.   [3] G. 273.   [4] A. 3.

Ancient Mariner, the Christabel, the Remorse, and some pages of the Friend were not without merit, but were abundantly anxious to acquit their judgments of any blindness to the very numerous defects.

That was not his practice. He was indifferent to praise, but craved for sympathy. He would never admit the faults of genius to those who were incapable of feeling its beauties.

If, in one instance, in my literary life, I have appeared to deviate from this rule, it was not till the fame of the writer (which I had been for fourteen years successively toiling like a second Ali to build up) had been established.

In 1820 he professed annoyance at the discovery that the critical Atticus of his letter to *Blackwood's* on literary praise would be taken to refer to Wordsworth, and so the 'coolness' converted into 'a breach'.[1] In 1821 he received with irony a report, probably after a visit of Robinson to the Lakes, that 'the dwellers at Rydal perceived an amendment in me'. In many things, particularly in detestation of '*silent* or suggestive detraction', it would be well for him if he were now as he was at twenty-five.[2] Some outbursts of 1822 are of a different nature, and the events which provoked them are very obscure. In a letter of 30 May, partly relating to Hartley's affairs, Coleridge writes :[3]

This only let me say, that mournful as my experience of Messrs. —— and —— in my own immediate concerns had been, of the latter especially, I was not prepared for their late behaviour, or, to use Anster's words on the occasion, for so 'piteous lowering of human nature', as the contents of M⟨r⟩ W.'s letters were calculated to produce.

On 8 October, describing to Allsop the 'four griping and grasping sorrows' of his life, he says :[4]

The second commenced on the night of my arrival (from Grasmere) in town with M⟨r⟩ and M⟨rs⟩ Montagu, when all the superstructure raised by my idolatrous Fancy during an enthusiastic and self-sacrificing friendship of fifteen years—the fifteen bright and ripe years, the strong summer of my Life—burst like a Bubble! But the Grief did not vanish with it, nor the love which was the stuff and vitality of the grief, though they pined away up to the moment of . . . .'s last total Transfiguration into Baseness; when with £1,200 a year, and just at the moment that the *extraordinary* Bankruptcy of Fenner and Curtis had robbed me of every penny I had been so many years working for, every penny I possessed in

[1] G. 315; cf. p. 286.   [2] A, p. 140.   [3] A. 30.   [4] A. 32.

the world, and involved me in a debt of £150 to boot, he *first* regretted that he was not able to pay a certain bill of mine to his . . . .'s wife's brother, himself, 'never wanted money so much in his life', &c. &c.; and an hour after attempted to extort from me a transfer to himself of all that I could call my own in the world—my books—as the condition of his paying a debt which in *equity* was as much but in honour and gratitude was far more, *his* debt than mine!

The third sorrow, 'included in the second', was clearly the termination of Coleridge's relations with Sara Hutchinson. The name represented by Allsop's first hiatus can hardly be other than 'Wordsworth', and, if the second represents 'brother's', the person intended is one of the banker Lloyds, who were brothers-in-law of Christopher Wordsworth. The mention of the bankruptcy suggests that the conversations referred to took place during one of Wordsworth's visits to London in 1820. Certainly he had not at that time anything like £1,200 a year, but he was complaining of straitness of means, due to the necessity of providing for the education of his sons.[1] Coleridge was negotiating for Morgan with a Lloyd in 1813 and might have given a security for him. The earlier letter printed by Allsop seems to bring Southey, who certainly helped Morgan, into the affair.[2] But we know of no close relations between Wordsworth and Morgan, and in any case it is difficult to see how even Coleridge could suggest that Wordsworth's debt of honour and gratitude to Morgan was greater than his own. Perhaps it does not all matter much, except to the curious. Coleridge was in an abnormal state of mind, even for him, when he wrote these letters, and Allsop tells us that he forgave fully and entirely the unkind conduct of the gentlemen to whom the first referred.[3] In the spring of 1823 Wordsworth was again in London, and the two met at a dinner given by Monkhouse, when no less than three other poets, Lamb, Moore, and Rogers, were present, and Coleridge 'had all the talk'; and again next day at a musical party in the house of Aders, where Coleridge enjoyed the music, while Wordsworth went to sleep.[4] Sara Hutchinson was present on these occasions, and Lamb talked of a joint trip with her

[1] W. 631, 632.   [2] Cf. pp. 260, 291.   [3] A, p. 192.
[4] Morley, 79; R. (D.), i. 393; L. 464; T. Moore, *Journal*, iv. 51.

and Coleridge to Ramsgate. But he was sure that the Gillmans would not allow it. 'I have a malicious knack at cutting of apron strings.'[1] In 1817 and 1820 came visits from Poole, who was pleased with the Gillmans, while Coleridge was moved to thoughts of 'dear, ever fondly remembered Stowey'.[2]

Shortly before he left Calne, Coleridge wrote to his wife for the first time during nearly three years. Other letters, and occasionally a remittance, followed from Highgate. Mrs. Coleridge was now content with her lot. She had long ceased to wish for her husband's presence at Keswick. The separation had, on the whole, been for the best, she thought, although she grieved on her children's account. In November 1822 she paid a visit to Highgate with her daughter Sara.[3] Now, too, Coleridge saw more of his sons. Hartley spent most of his Oxford vacations with him. 'His manners are rather eccentric', wrote his father, 'otherwise he is in head and heart all I ought to wish.' Derwent, long hoped for, came for the first time in the spring of 1820. Coleridge had been writing him letters of advice on his studies, and wishing he could save enough money to send him to Cambridge. This became possible in 1820 through generous gifts from J. H. Frere and others, and Derwent went to St. John's. In the summer of 1821 both brothers were at Highgate, where the kindly Gillman insisted on treating them as his visitors, and cutting off their expenses from Coleridge's account.[4] The first report from Derwent's tutor was good. But later Coleridge came to think that he was wasting his time at Cambridge in dandyism and coxcombry, and had shown ingratitude alike to his father and to those who for his father's sake had helped him, by speaking of himself to neighbours at Highgate as no more than 'a child of charity'. And he makes the rather odd complaint, in view of his own Cambridge life, that Derwent, while neglecting his studies, had taken the lead in a literary club, about old books. 'If

[1] L. 468.

[2] C. 249 (misdated '1830' for '1821'); Addl. MS. 35343, f. 382; G. 313; P. ii. 254, 258, 279.   [3] M. 14, 17–19; W. 691, 694, 695; cf. p. 315.

[4] C. 214, 228; G. 283, 284, 290, 301, 305, 313, 315, 316, 320, 321; A. 7, 8; M. 14, 15, 17, 19; W. 595, 615, 628; Frere, 222.

such things did not dissipate your time and thought, they *dissipate* and *perplex* your character.'[1]

Hartley became the cause of much more grievous trouble. At Merton he met with kindness from his cousin, William Henry, the son of Luke, then a Student of Christ Church, who as a result paid friendly visits to Highgate.[2] He was twice unsuccessful in competing for the Newdigate English Verse Prize, and took a second class in his Final School. In April 1819 he obtained a close Fellowship at Oriel, for which he was eligible through his birth in Gloucestershire. Some tutoring of a young St. Aubyn in the Isle of Wight followed, and in the autumn his year of Probationary Fellowship began.[3] It proved disastrous. Oriel was an outstanding college in Oxford at this date. The Fellows, among whom were Richard Whately, Edward Hawkins, Thomas Arnold, and John Keble, were men of high ideals, both in scholarship and in conduct. They lived much to themselves, in a close and perhaps somewhat austere society. Hartley did not come up to the standard. He did not feel at home in the Common Room and avoided it. He would not dress for dinner and smelt of tobacco. He clung to old companions of his undergraduate days, not all of the highest social standing. There was a girl, called Mary, to whom he was said to be attached. He resented the espionage by the college servants, to which he believed himself to be subjected. He kept late hours. Moreover, he was easily upset by a glass too much of wine. He was even said to have been found lying drunk in the gutter of Oriel Lane. Some warnings which reached him were disregarded, and in May 1820 it was decided by the resident Fellows to propose to a full college meeting in October that his Fellowship should not be continued after the probationary year. To Coleridge the news came 'as a peal of thunder from a cloudless sky'. Both he and the Gillmans had warned Hartley against drink. It was 'the sin of his nature'. He sent Derwent down to Oxford to see his brother, but on learning of the decision by the Fellows, Hartley had bolted. He was

---

[1] G. 323, 327, 328.   [2] C. 214, 228; G. 281, 297, 320, 327; M. 10, 11.
[3] G. 305; M. 17; Griggs, 8, 10, 19, 22, 32, 34, 35.

heard of at Birmingham, and Coleridge thought he might
have fled to Keswick, or perhaps, in some such mad moment
as that of his own 'army-freak', was planning a flight to
America. He was recovered, however, and denied the worst
charges of intoxication. Coleridge accepted the denial and
arranged with Montagu to give Hartley house-room for a
few weeks. He then devoted himself to the composition of
long, excited, and rather incoherent letters to be sent to
Edward Copleston, the Provost of Oriel, before the fateful
meeting of October, after which he had interviews with
Copleston both in Oxford and in London. But he could get
no hope that the Fellowship would be continued, although
the College offered a *solatium* of £300, which was at first
refused, as involving an admission of guilt, but afterwards
accepted. In December there was another exculpatory statement to the Warden of Merton. Hartley put his own case
in letters to Lady Beaumont and to his brother Derwent.
The details of the controversy are matter for his own biography, rather than his father's, but at the best it is clear that
he was ill fitted to be a Fellow of Oriel.[1] At Montagu's
Hartley was set to work on the Principles of Taste and the
Prometheus of Aeschylus.[2] He came and went between London and Highgate, giving some annoyance by a habit of
bringing friends to dinner on Sundays, which were incon-
venient days for Gillman.[3] More than once he vanished
from Montagu's, and found lodgings for himself among
lawyer friends, on one occasion upsetting his father by failing to keep a promised appointment with him.[4] In the
autumn of 1822 he gave way to drink, while in charge of
Derwent during an illness, and Coleridge then began to suspect that in the Oriel affair he had been deceived and made
an accomplice in deceiving others.[5] He now decided to ship
Hartley off to Ambleside as an assistant in Mr. Dawes's
school, and thereafter father and son never met again.[6]

[1] G. 314, 315, 324; A. 9–12 (misdated); M. 20; Griggs, 11–17, 19, 23, and
Appendix; H.C. *Memoir*, lxxxvi, lxxxvii; T. Mozley, *Reminiscences*, i. 85; ii. 411.
[2] G. 316, 317; A. 10, 14.   [3] G. 316; Griggs, 16–20.
[4] G. 319; M. 20, 21; Griggs, 21, 22; A. 32; H.C. *Memoir*, xciii.
[5] C. 231; A. 32; W. 686.
[6] G. 327; H.C. *Memoir*, xciii; W. 691; Griggs, 23.

XVI

THE SAGE OF HIGHGATE

December 1823—July 1834

IN December 1823 Gillman removed from Moreton House
to No. 3 The Grove, still in Highgate, and here Coleridge
was housed, at his own desire, in a study-bedroom attic, with
a view over Caen Wood, which he called his 'garden', and
a parlour below for the reception of his friends.[1] He was
now, although only fifty, already an old man, and acknowledged it in the best poem of his later years.[2]

> Verse, a breeze mid blossoms straying,
> Where Hope clung feeding, like a bee—
> Both were mine! Life went a-maying
>   With Nature, Hope, and Poesy,
>   When I was young!
> When I was young?—Ah, woful When!
> Ah! for the change 'twixt Now and Then!
> This breathing house not built with hands,
> This body that does me grievous wrong,
> O'er aery cliffs and glittering sands,
> How lightly then it flashed along:—
> Like those trim skiffs, unknown of yore,
> On winding lakes and rivers wide,
> That ask no aid of sail or oar,
> That fear no spite of wind or tide!
> Nought cared this body for wind or weather
> When Youth and I lived in't together.
>
> Flowers are lovely; Love is flower-like;
> Friendship is a sheltering tree;
> O! the joys, that came down shower-like,
> Of Friendship, Love, and Liberty,
>   Ere I was old!
>
> Ere I was old? Ah woful Ere,
> Which tells me, Youth's no longer here!
> O Youth! for years so many and sweet,
> 'Tis known, that Thou and I were one.
> I'll think it but a fond conceit—
> It cannot be that Thou art gone!

[1] G. 332, 367; A. 34, p. 46; L.P. 85; A. W. Gillman, 6; Watson, 51.
[2] P.W. 439, 1084.

Thy vesper-bell hath not yet toll'd :—
And thou wert aye a masker bold !
What strange disguise hast now put on,
To make believe, that thou art gone ?
I see these locks in silvery slips,
This drooping gait, this altered size :
But Spring-tide blossoms on thy lips,
And tears take sunshine from thine eyes !
Life is but thought : so think I will
That Youth and I are house-mates still.

Dew-drops are the gems of morning,
But the tears of mournful eve !
Where no hope is, life's a warning
That only serves to make us grieve,
          When we are old.

Coleridge was still young enough in 1828 to take a walk of
twelve miles and lacerate his feet with a pair of tight-heeled
shoes.[1] But there were recurring bouts of erysipelas, rheumatism, and other maladies, leading him occasionally to
thoughts of death, which he took philosophically.[2]

But no more of this ! We must all die of somewhat and ought, as
the Irish Franciscan in a discourse of Final Causes observed—Let us
all thank God and adore his wisdom and goodness in putting Death at
the end of Life and thereby giving us time of repentance.

He was still able to enjoy himself on social occasions. In
1824 he was seen at a dance given by Green, metaphysicizing
in a corner.[3] In 1828 or 1829 he was the life and soul of a
batchelor dinner-party in the lodgings of F. M. Reynolds,
where Lockhart, Theodore Hook, and William Jerdan were
the other guests. Hook improvised a comic song, every line
of which had reference to Coleridge. At this Coleridge was
in the seventh heaven, and responded with some exquisite
recitation and humorous stories of Wordsworth and other
brother bards. There was much claret, until Coleridge said
he could swallow no more, 'unless it were punch'. After
punch, Hook threw his glass through a window. Coleridge
rose 'with the aspect of a benignant patriarch,' and demo-
lished another pane. He was then persuaded to try a fork at

---

[1] L.P. 87.
[2] G. 332, 361–4; A. 34, 36; L.P. 87; Prideaux, 18–20, 22; Watts, i. 288.
[3] Morley, 83; R. (D.), ii. 272.

a wine-glass mounted on a reversed tumbler. Lockhart described 'the roseate face of Coleridge, lit up with animation, his large grey eye beaming, his white hair floating, and his whole frame, as it were, radiating with intense interest, as he poised the fork in his hand, and launched it at the fragile object'. On the way home he expressed the opinion that Hook was as true a genius as Dante.[1] A more sober party was at Sotheby's in 1828, when Scott, whom Coleridge had refrained from calling on some years before, out of delicacy about *Christabel*, was present. Coleridge, after eating his dinner in silence, became eloquent on the Samothracian mysteries, and on the multiple authorship of the *Iliad* which was one of his favourite heresies. 'Zounds, I was never so bethumped with words,' noted Scott.[2] It must be recorded that the complete abstinence from unprescribed opium, imposed upon him when he first arrived at Highgate, was occasionally broken in later years. A tradition to this effect in the Gillman family has been confirmed by the discovery of a number of notes to one Dunn, a chemist in Highgate, which contain orders for the drug, requests for secrecy, and acknowledgements of a debt, which at one time amounted to £26. Against this no value can attach to the statement of a former errand-boy of Gillman's that, although purchases made by him for Coleridge were believed to be of opium, they were really of snuff. The earliest recorded transaction seems to have been in 1821. Another in 1824 is probably connected with a visit to Allsop, which was meant to be of two days, but from which Coleridge had to be retrieved by Gillman, when it had already extended to ten.[3]

In March 1824 Coleridge was elected, largely through the influence of Montagu, as a Royal Associate of the recently chartered Royal Society of Literature. The position carried an annual grant of 100 guineas from the King's Privy Purse and the obligation of reading an annual essay before the Society. He was asked to declare the department which he should be regarded as representing. The proper answer

[1] W. Jerdan, *Autobiography*, iv. 230; *Quarterly Review*, lxxii. 65.
[2] A. 7, 8; T.T. 71, 182; Scott, *Journal*, ii. 164.
[3] G. 337–42 (341 misdated; cf. A. 25), 384; A. 37, p. 68; Watson, 35, 89; A. W. Gillman, 15; E. Blunden (*T.L.S.* 23. x. 1930).

would have been 'Omniscience', but he managed to express
much the same idea in a couple of paragraphs. An essay,
on *The Prometheus of Aeschylus*, was duly delivered on
18 May 1825, but no more followed. Probably the material
prepared for Hartley in 1821 was utilized. Lamb thought
a prize might be awarded, but on that point the original plan
for the Society had been altered. Mrs. Coleridge did not
expect that any part of the royal bounty would be available
for her use.[1] But no doubt it largely relieved Coleridge from
his dependence on advances from publishers and editors.
He resolved to give up writing in the reviews, and never
again to send a sheet to the press before the whole work was
thoroughly revised and corrected.[2] Broadly speaking, these
good intentions were carried out. From time to time he
seems to have felt under some obligation to continue his
contributions to *Blackwood's*, but nothing, beyond one sonnet, actually appeared.[3] In 1825 he contemplated giving
three lectures in support of a scheme for a London University, but this idea too was dropped.[4] Other vagrant fancies
crossed his mind. The most interesting was of an edition of
Shakespeare, to be done in conjunction with Alaric Watts.
It was a task for which, on the textual side at least, his many
Marginalia to the editions of others show him to have been
ill fitted.[5] A fashion of annual table-books, which arose
about 1825, put a little money into the pockets of poets.
Coleridge sent some of his minor verse and prose to Watts
for *The Literary Souvenir*, to F. M. Reynolds for *The Keepsake*,
and to S. C. Hall for *The Amulet*. It would be unprofitable
to go into the complications with editors and publishers
which accompanied these transactions.[6] Meanwhile Coleridge had at last arranged with the publisher William Pickering
for a new edition of his own *Poems*. This made its appearance in 1828, and was fairly comprehensive. It included *The
Ancient Mariner*, *Christabel*, *Kubla Khan*, *The Pains of Sleep*,

---

[1] C. 234, 235, 240; G. 316, 333, 345, 346, 351; L. 565; M. 27; *Constitution and Regulations of R.S.L.* (1823); cf. p. 305. [2] Watson, 106; Prideaux, 18.
[3] Oliphant, i. 413, 414, 416, 419; C. 252; *P.M.L.A.* xlviii. 117; *P.W.* 1180 (text not given). [4] A. 43. [5] G. 257; Watts, i. 243; Raysor, i. 1-160.
[6] G. 375, 377, 379; Watts, i. 288; Maggs, *Cat.* 607/248; *Harvard MS.* 19478·5 F.; *P.W.* 1181.

the *Sibylline Leaves*, *Remorse*, *Zapolya*, *Wallenstein*, and a selection from the *Juvenile Poems*. But in more than one way the edition was a disappointment. Coleridge had not meant to include any unpublished work. With reluctance he had made a few exceptions at Gillman's request. These Pickering, without any sanction from Coleridge or any payment to him, had also put into his annual *The Bijou*, where they were 'infamously incorrect', and remained so, for the want of proper proofs, in the collected edition. And to them he had added a sonnet written by Blanco White to Coleridge, which caused annoyance to its author, as well as to its subject. Moreover, the profits of the edition had been promised by Coleridge to Gillman, towards the discharge of his debt. But Pickering had printed only three hundred copies, which left no profits. A new edition, with many corrections and alterations, appeared in 1829.[1]

In the main, however, Coleridge was able, from 1824 onwards, to devote himself to what he had long considered to be the great task of his life, the defence of Trinitarian Christianity, both as a practical rule for conduct and for politics, and as a necessity of metaphysical thought. The first result was the treatise to which he gave the name of *Aids to Reflection*. This had grown out of an admiration which he had felt, as far back as 1807, for the writings of the Scottish divine Archbishop Robert Leighton of Glasgow.[2] In 1821 he had for the second time approached John Murray, in the hope that he would 'take me and my concerns, past and future, for print and reprint, under his umbrageous foliage'. Murray he found unexpectedly civil and even kind in his manners, and to him he suggested a selection of the *Beauties of Archbishop Leighton*, to be accompanied by a biographical introduction. Murray took to the idea, and provided a copy of Leighton's works.[3] But by the autumn of 1823 there was once more a rift between author and publisher. Coleridge wanted an edition of his *Poems*. Murray hesitated, and finally gave him the greatest offence by the 'insolent' suggestion that it should be overseen by

---

[1] G. 377; M. 32; Watts, i. 288; Myers, *Cat.* 310/114; *P.W.* 1154; Wise, 301.
[2] *Rem.* 314.   [3] A. 16, 33; C. 230, 232; G. 325.

Henry Hart Milman, then a young contributor to the
Quarterly Review. Thereafter Coleridge had no good word
for 'the Man of Albemarle St.'. Every one, he wrote in 1827,
who had had anything to do with him, had had cause for
dissatisfaction. In 1832, with the Milman affair still rankling,
he called him an 'Anthropoid'.[1] Even before the breach of
1823, however, Coleridge was already in negotiation for the
Leighton book with the firm of Taylor & Hessey, and had
given it the title of *Aids to Reflection*.[2] Early in 1824 he declared that he must sit down to it, and he now clearly worked
with some regularity, since, in spite of the need for much
recasting, final proofs were in hand by March 1825.[3] In
May the book was published, with lines from *Cain* in a
foot-note, and Coleridge became busy with sending copies
and explanations to his relations and friends. It is interesting
to note that one copy went to Derwent's friend, Thomas
Babington Macaulay.[4] Coleridge had planned to supplement
the *Aids* by six disquisitions, for which he invented the
pleasing title of *The Grey-headed Passenger: or Conversations on
Shipboard during a Voyage to the Mediterranean*. These, however, never appeared in the form suggested, although one is
probably represented by the posthumous *Confessions of an
Inquiring Spirit*.[5] Unfortunately the *Aids* was not a financial
success. It was, indeed, like all Coleridge's prose writings,
a shapeless production, which must have baffled the easy
reader. A year after its publication he was complaining that
he had not had sufficient interest to get it even mentioned in
the *Reviews*, although he was gratified to learn that it had
been the means of restoring his publisher Taylor to a belief
in Christianity. And in fact it gave him a considerable repute
among a religious public. He notes commendations from
the Bishop of London, William Howley, and from Joseph
Blanco White, the converted Catholic and later sceptic,
who was stirred by it to make his acquaintance.[6] Edward

---

[1] C. 239; G. 331, 365, 370, 391.   [2] G. 330.
[3] C. 238, 239, 240; G. 341, 344, 346, 348–50; A. 40; *M.L.N.* xliv. 302; L. 504;
M. 26, 28; *Bodl. Montagu MS.* d. 17, f. 62.
[4] C. 251; G. 355, 359–61; Snyder (L.), 153; M. 30, 31; L. 565, 569, 583; S.C.
Memoir, i. 30; *P.W.* 285.
[5] G. 348, 349, 352, 359.   [6] C. 251; G. 355, 362, 364.

Irving, then in the first flush of his fame as a London preacher, dedicated to him his orations on *Missionaries*, in admiring terms. Julius Hare thought that the *Aids* showed its author 'the true sovereign' of modern English thought. Frederick Denison Maurice, and for a time John Sterling, felt that to the book they 'owed even their own selves'.[1] These represent what would now be called the 'left' or 'modernist' wing of contemporary religious speculation. A dissentient note from John Henry Newman, of another school, who found in Coleridge 'a liberty of speculation which no Christian can tolerate' and 'conclusions which were often heathen rather than Christian', probably relates to the views on Biblical inspiration expressed in the *Inquiring Spirit*, rather than to the *Aids*.[2] A second edition of the *Aids* was published by Hurst, Chance & Co. in 1831.[3]

Coleridge regarded the *Aids* as no more than the first part of a comprehensive philosophic design.[4] He had here laid stress on his famous distinction between the Reason and the Understanding. But he had still to unfold the nature of the Reason in its metaphysical aspect, and by so doing to arrive at an ultimate justification of the doctrine of the Trinity. This was to be the great achievement of his *Opus Maximum*, on which he had been more or less engaged since 1821.[5] It had then been in preparation for more than twenty years, and its result would be 'a revolution of all that has been called *Philosophy* or Metaphysics in England and France', since the predominance of 'the mechanical system'.[6] It is clearly the same as the *Logosophia* of 1815, although now conceived, not as six treatises, but as two, a preliminary *Logic* and an *Assertion of Religion*, the *Opus Maximum* proper. The former, which was to be 'level with the plainest capacities', seems to have been the subject of Coleridge's dictation to Stutfield and Watson, while the more important work was reserved for Green. By 1825 he thought the *Logic* was complete. A fragment of it, which draws freely upon Kant and Mendelssohn, appears to be preserved among the *Egerton*

[1] D. 256.   [2] *Essays*, i. 268.
[3] Prideaux, 19, 22, 23, 25; Wise, 131.
[4] G. 359.   [5] Cf. p. 287.   [6] A. 15.

MSS.[1] There was still, however, much to do on the *Opus Maximum*. In May 1825 'Christianity true in *Idea*' had been covered, but 'Christianity true in fact' and 'Christianity true in *Act*' lay ahead, and it was to these that Coleridge looked for an advance from the standpoint of the *Aids* to a complete vindication of the doctrine of the Trinity as involved in the Idea of God, and an explanation of the origin of evil.[2] In 1826 he had become doubtful whether any publisher would take either the *Logic* or the *Opus Maximum* during his life-time, but he was still working steadily on the latter in 1827.[3]

The years from 1824 to 1830 were something of an Indian summer in Coleridge's life. The notes of resentment and persecution become more rare in his letters. He was no longer an alien from his kin. There was peace with his wife. Occasionally he wrote to her, although Mrs. Gillman was still the better correspondent. She even took an interest in hearing of his work.[4] It was for others to watch over Hartley's infirmities, but Hartley was seldom out of his head, and still less often off his heart.[5] Derwent gave him some trouble, through unsettled religious views, which his father attributed to the influence of Macaulay and Charles Austin. He would not read for Honours at Cambridge, and would not take Orders. After two years of teaching, however, at Plymouth and Buckfastleigh, he sloughed his larva of scepticism, in Coleridge's phrase, and returned to Cambridge for divinity lectures. Coleridge advised him on his reading, offered to give him a plan for a school-book, and busied himself with the search for a curacy. Ultimately one was found at Helston in Cornwall, and here Derwent married Mary Pridham, with whom Coleridge was much pleased. In 1829 he even thought of taking a journey to Helston.[6] In 1828 he must have been agreeably surprised by a visit from his brother James. They had met in London during 1818, and James had been pleased with his society.[7] His

[1] A. 14, 15, 26, 33; C. 232; G. 346; M. 28; S. (*L.*), v. 140; Snyder (*L.*), 153, and *passim.*　　[2] G. 349; Snyder (*L.*), 153.　　[3] G. 365; White, i. 439.
[4] G. 372; M. 25, 28.　　[5] G. 372.
[6] G. 358–61, 363, 370, 382, 383; M. 22 (misdated), 26, 28–31 (29 misdated), 34.
[7] G. 376; M. 14 (misdated).

brother George was then just dead. Him too he would
gladly have gone to see in his last illness, but had to content
himself with a letter to his nephew George May, in which he
expressed regret for past misunderstandings.[1]

In vain, have I tried to recall any one moment since my quitting the
University, or any one occasion, in which I have either thought, felt,
spoken, or intentionally acted of or in relation to my brother, otherwise than as one who loved in him father and brother in one, and who,
independent of the fraternal relation and the remembrance of his mani-
fold goodness and kindness to me from boyhood to early manhood,
should have chosen him above all I had known as the friend of my
inmost soul.

It reads curiously, in collation with earlier epistolary references to George. Long before this, however, new links with
Ottery had been established through members of the
younger generation in or near London. Of these there were
four, William Hart, the son of Luke, and three sons of
James, Henry Nelson, whose association with his uncle
was destined to be close, John Taylor, who, like Henry,
was pursuing the law, and Edward, a master at Eton.
William's friendly visits to Highgate seem by 1826 to have
come to an end. He was now Bishop of Barbados, and
Coleridge felt aggrieved that he had done nothing to help
Derwent to a curacy. His own church principles, he supposed, were not 'high' enough for William.[2]

I have little doubt, indeed none, that your episcopal Cousin has con-
trived to sigh and look sad or remain intelligibly silent whenever my
name was mentioned—in short, has done everything in his power to
injure me.

Both John and Edward took an interest in Coleridge's
religious and philosophical studies, and to both he wrote
many letters, especially about the *Aids*. He was a little perturbed when John took the editorship of the *Quarterly* in
1824, since he believed it to be the opinion of publishers
that no review could be successful without the help of satire
and sarcasm. A statement by Frere, that he regarded it as
a trust of dignity and importance, modified his view a little,
and he was even himself prepared to become a contributor.

[1] C. 245; G. 373.   [2] C. 240; G. 363, 370; cf. p. 304.

Nevertheless he was relieved when in a year's time John found the post inconsistent with his legal prospects, and resigned it to Lockhart. John, too, he thought, had been remiss in pushing Derwent's fortunes, and the relations between them may have become less close.[1] John's son, however, afterwards the Lord Chief Justice, recalled several meetings with the poet during his childhood in 1827 and 1828.[2] Possibly Coleridge's favourite nephew at this time was Edward, to whom it has been suggested that the *Confessions of an Inquiring Spirit* may originally have been addressed.[3]

Henry Coleridge came to Highgate at the end of 1822, and recorded the first instalment of his uncle's *Table-Talk*. He also fell in love with his cousin Sara and she with him. Apparently they went on together to Ottery with Mrs. Coleridge, who wrote to Poole that both visits had been 'productive of the greatest satisfaction to all parties'. She would have a great deal to tell when they met at Stowey in the spring. A year later her tone was rather different. Sara was then depressed about the affair of which Poole had been given a hint.[4]

The youth *will* persevere, and now affects to think himself ill-used: he now wishes to keep up a correspondence as *Brother & Sister*, she has not replied to the two last letters.

There was some more *Table-Talk* during May and June 1824, which ended with the expression of a doubt by Coleridge as to the desirability of marriage between first cousins. He was prepared, however, to waive it, on the authority of St. Augustine and the Church.[5] At the end of the year Henry, troubled with rheumatism, accompanied his cousin the Bishop on a pastoral voyage, and on his return published an account of it in his *Six Months in the West Indies*, which contains a good deal of observation and common sense, and also a good deal of lightheartedness. He has thoughts of a Eugenia, whom one passage at least must have made it easy to identify.[6]

[1] C. 239, 240, 243; G. 349, 350, 358, 359, 363, 365, 370, 374; T.T. 23.
[2] I.L.N.   [3] C. 233, 240, 243; G. 347, 354–7, 363–7, 370.
[4] S.C. *Memoir*, i. 37, 123, 265; M. 23, 26; W. 694.
[5] T.T. 32.   [6] *Six Months*, 105.

I love a cousin; she is such an exquisite relation, just standing between me and the stranger to my name, drawing upon so many sources
of love and tying them all up with every cord of human affection—
almost my sister ere my wife!

Coleridge was not best pleased with the book, of which one
episode at least seemed to him 'indiscreet and objectionable'.
He was not indeed best pleased with Henry himself at this
time, thinking that he might have done more to influence
the Bishop in favour of Derwent. A letter in which Henry
subscribed himself as his 'dutiful' nephew, he received with
irony. But he declared that he had read the book through
without any suspicion of an attachment between Henry and
Sara, and first learnt of it from Mrs. Gillman in a discussion
about Eugenia.[1] It is a little difficult to reconcile this with
the table talk about first cousins. Perhaps Henry had put
the point to him, and out of a head full of theology he had
not suspected any personal reference. Meanwhile Sara had
been in bad health and bad spirits, and a second visit to her
father had been more than once deferred. Coleridge now
wrote to his wife, and after full explanations gave his
reluctant consent to an engagement, rather than condemn
his daughter to 'a miserable Heart-wasting'. He was still
uneasy about the kinship, and consulted Stuart, presumably
as a man of the world rather than a theologian. Late in 1826
Sara came once more to Highgate, and the *Table-Talk* was
resumed.[2] An early marriage was not, however, possible.
Henry had only just been called to the Bar, and had no
income. It was not until September 1829 that the wedding
took place at Keswick. By June 1830 Henry and Sara had
settled in a small house at Hampstead, not far from Highgate, and here Sara's mother, after her thirty years at
Keswick, joined them.[3]

Coleridge had continued to prove himself a magnet to
old friends. Lamb describes him in 1824 as 'daily trudging
on Highgate Hill and blooming', and again as 'quite blooming' in 1825. Lamb himself was released from the India
House in that year, and was able to get to Highgate more

freely. Gillman he could now think of as Coleridge's 'more than Friend'. Coleridge, in turn, visited him at Islington in 1826 and at Enfield in 1828. An observer records his kiss of affection on Mary's cheek when they parted.[1] Robinson, Lamb's description of whom as 'that Pineapple of a *Crab*' Coleridge quotes with appreciation, was also faithful, until he went abroad for two years in 1829.[2] From Stuart Coleridge had many kindnesses. He had entered a protest at Highgate against Coleridge's claim in the *Biographia Literaria* to have made the fortunes of the *Morning Post*. But personal relations continued. During several years Stuart gave Coleridge gifts of £30 to enable him to take his autumn seaside holiday, and when he omitted to do so, Coleridge was not slow to remind him. Coleridge, on his side, showed anxious gratitude in arranging for the reception of Stuart's daughter Mary at the Grove, for recovery after a period of illness.[3] He had good offices to do in 1828 also for John Morgan's widow and sister-in-law, who had fallen into poverty, and, although he had nothing in his own purse, describes himself as 'trotting about' with a sick heart all day to make up, guinea by guinea, a sum of £20 for them.[4] Of Allsop, who fell into financial embarrassment, apparently through speculation, he seems to have seen little after 1825. There is a probable reference to him early in 1827. 'I am at this moment heart-sick with anguish from the ruin of a Man who loved me as a Father; but whom I had in vain sought to defascinate.' And in 1829 he regretted to Allsop that his own poor health and lack of influential friends made it impossible to help him to an appointment. It is believed that he repaid the gift made by Allsop in 1819.[5] Sir George Beaumont died in 1827, leaving to Mrs. Coleridge £50, but nothing to Coleridge himself. He expressed, however, no sentiment but sorrow for the death. Lamb thought it an injustice. 'If Coleridge was a scamp, Sir George should not

---

[1] G. 347, 377, 379; L. 522, 544, 631, 757, 760; S. Flower, in *Monthly Repository* (1835), 162.   [2] G. 334; Morley, 83; R. (*D.*), ii. 272, 297, 330, 394.
[3] 2 *Gent. Mag.* ix. 491, 577; C. 241; L.P. 77-81, 85-7; cf. p. 123.
[4] G. 381.
[5] G. 370; A. 45; Colbeck, Radford *Cat.* (1935), 28; L. 597, 629, 647, 648, 679, 728, 746, 877, 906, 971; Watson, 82.

have continued as he did, to invite him to dinner.' Lady Beaumont made some amends by leaving Coleridge £50 in 1829.[1] In 1830 died William Hazlitt, in whose later references to Coleridge, although critical of what Hazlitt regarded as his political apostasy, the 'respect' shines more clearly than of old through the 'disrespect'. Coleridge wrote or adapted a rather bitter epigram on him, but expressed a hope 'that a something existed in his bodily organism that in the sight of the All-merciful lessened his responsibility, and the moral imputation of his acts and feelings'.[2] Highgate was cheered by visits from Poole in 1827 and 1829, the last of which stirred Coleridge to a 'character' of Poole in a footnote to his *Constitution of Church and State*. This, which appeared in 1830, was the last work published during his lifetime. The preface records his scepticism as to the results of Catholic Emancipation, which, like Parliamentary Reform, was a bugbear in his later political thought.[3] Southey saw him in 1825 and probably in 1828.[4] Wordsworth was in London early in 1824, and Coleridge criticized his translation of Virgil.[5] If there had been any renewal of friction in 1820, it can have left no traces so late as 1828, for in that year the two poets, with Wordsworth's daughter Dora, took a trip through Belgium, the Rhineland, and Holland together. At Brussels they fell in with one Thomas Colley Grattan, who accompanied them to the field of Waterloo and up the Meuse from Namur to Dinant. Grattan was impressed by Coleridge's personal appearance, his handsome face, pleasing mouth, grey eyes 'full of intelligent softness', cheeks unfurrowed and showing a healthy bloom, full and lazy figure, but not actually stout. His talk was 'not absolutely tiresome, only somewhat drowsy'. There was logic in it, only 'enveloped in clouds'. His delight in rural scenes was noteworthy.

He was in ecstasies at a group of haymakers in a field as we passed. He said the little girls, standing with their rakes, the handles resting on the ground, 'looked like little saints'. Half-a-dozen dust-covered

[1] G. 383, 397; M. 31; W. 790, 791, 869; Leslie, i. 54.
[2] Hazlitt, viii. 183, 251, 294, 314; xi. 28; xvii. 106; xx. 215; W. 942; *P.W.* 962.
[3] G. 385; *Addl. MS.* 35343, f. 388; M. 34, 36; *Church and State*, 102; Wise, 143.
[4] M. 28, 32.   [5] C. 238; A. 37; W. 713.

children going by the roadside, with a garland of roses raised above their heads, threw him into raptures.

On their return to Namur Grattan left them, and they went down to Liége and thence by Spa and Aix-la-Chapelle to Cologne. Here Coleridge wrote two epigrams on the stinks of the city. From Cologne they proceeded up the Rhine to Bingen and down to Nijmegen, stopping in each transit for a week with Mrs. Aders at Godesberg near Bonn. Another diarist, Julian Young, who was also there, gives a lively account of them. He is less complimentary to Coleridge's outward man than Grattan, thinking him like a dissenting minister, in his stockings of lavender-coloured worsted, white starchless neck-cloth tied in a limp bow, and shabby suit of dusky black. Wordsworth, when they were present together, mostly allowed Coleridge to have the talk to himself, but Young observed no manifestation of small jealousy between them, in spite of 'the vanity possessed by each'. Coleridge decried the poetry of Byron and Scott. 'Byron is meteor. Wordsworth, there is a fixed star.' All the literary lights of Bonn were invited to meet them, Niebuhr, Becker, Schlegel. Coleridge and Schlegel praised each other's translations of Schiller and Shakespeare. But to Grattan Coleridge had described Schlegel as 'a consummate coxcomb' Coleridge's German was so bad that Schlegel had to beg him to speak English. The tour, which lasted from 21 June to 7 August, was completed by a round through the chief Dutch cities, and so by Antwerp back to Ostend. A note-book entry shows Coleridge still capable of a piece of delicate phrasing in prose:

The sweet prattle of the chimes—counsellors pleading in the court of Love—then the clock, the solemn sentence of the mighty Judge—long pause between each pregnant, inappellable word, too deeply weighed to be reversed in the High-Justice-Court of Time and Fate. A more richly solemn sound than this eleven o'clock at Antwerp I never heard—dead enough to be opaque as central gold, yet clear enough to be the mountain air.

He had been indisposed more than once during his travels, but on his return found himself much improved in health as the result of them.[1]

[1] C. 247; G. 377, 378; L.P. 87; A.P. 307; P.W. 477; W. 822, 824, 836, 853;

Coleridge's regard for the Gillmans had soon deepened into affection. By 1828 he felt as if he had been a brother in their family for eleven years. And he did his best to repay them. Gillman records his constant humility and gentleness in their house. They had themselves ill health, to which his letters are full of sympathetic references.[1] They were concerned for the future of their children. Coleridge advised the elder son, James, in his studies for Oxford and the Church.[2] For the younger, Henry, he procured an admission to Eton through his nephew Edward, took the boy down himself on entry, and arranged for his removal a year later, when he proved not to be amenable to school discipline.[3] In another way, perhaps, the Gillmans had their reward. The modest abode of a suburban physician became something of a centre for literary London. It is in 1824 that we first hear of regular Thursday evening meetings for tea and talk at the Grove. 'Attic nights' Coleridge calls them. Basil Montagu and Edward Irving seem to have formed a nucleus, but Green and others soon came in. Robinson describes an early occasion, on which Henry Taylor, then a young clerk at the Colonial Office, was present. The discussion turned on Mohammedanism, which Taylor upheld. 'Are you looking for your turban, Sir,' asked Lamb, when the party were collecting their hats. Lamb came occasionally, but preferred the peace of Sunday visits. Other participants were Aders, William Collins, the painter, and Thomas Chalmers. Coleridge wrote to invite Stuart and his old friend George Dyer. By 1825 the gatherings, though not large, were varied.

In addition to a few ladies and pretty lasses, we have seldom more than five or six in company, and these generally of as many professions or pursuits. A few weeks ago we had present, two painters, two poets, one divine, an eminent chemist and naturalist, a major, a naval captain and voyager, a physician, a colonial chief justice, a barrister, and a baronet; and this was the most numerous meeting we ever had.

The conversation, he says, was miscellaneous. Elsewhere,

R. 94-6, 98; T. C. Grattan, *Beaten Paths*, ii. 107; J. C. Young, *Mem. of C. M. Young*, i. 130.
  [1] C. 239; G. 366, 367, 371, 373, 375-7; A. 34, 40; L.P. 78, 79, 85, 87; M. 29; Gillman, x.
  [2] Watson, 126; L.P. 85; Tregaskis, *Cat.* 1009, nos. 103, 107, 108.
  [3] G. 347, 356, 357, 364-7.

however, he admits that '*one*-versazione', rather than '*con*-versazione' would be the more appropriate term.[1] This also was clearly the opinion of Thomas Carlyle, who was introduced by Montagu and Irving. He records his impressions in a letter, which reads like a first sketch from his full-length appreciation of Coleridge in the *Life of John Sterling*.

I have seen many curiosities; not the least of them I reckon Coleridge, the Kantian metaphysician and quondam Lake poet. I will tell you all about our interview when we meet. Figure a fat, flabby, incurvated personage, at once short, rotund, and relaxed, with a watery mouth, a snuffy nose, a pair of strange brown, timid, yet earnest-looking eyes, a high tapering brow, and a great bush of grey hair; and you have some faint idea of Coleridge. He is a kind, good soul, full of religion and affection and poetry and animal magnetism. His cardinal sin is that he wants *will*. He has no resolution. He shrinks from pain or labour in any of its shapes. His very attitude bespeaks this. He never straightens his knee-joints. He stoops with his fat, ill-shapen shoulders, and in walking he does not tread, but shovel and slide. My father would call it 'skluiffing'. He is also always busied to keep, by strong and frequent inhalations, the water of his mouth from overflowing, and his eyes have a look of anxious impotence. He *would* do with all his heart, but he knows he dares not. The conversation of the man is much as I anticipated—a forest of thoughts, some true, many false, more *part* dubious, all of them ingenious in some degree, often in a high degree. But there is no method in his talk: he wanders like a man sailing among many currents, whithersoever his lazy mind directs him; and what is more unpleasant, he preaches, or rather soliloquises. He cannot speak, he can only *tal-k* (so he names it). Hence I found him unprofitable, even tedious; but we parted very good friends, and promising to go back and see him some evening—a promise which I fully intend to keep. I sent him a copy of *Meister* about which we had some friendly talk. I reckon him a man of great and useless genius: a strange, not at all a great man.

Other growls followed. Coleridge is 'sunk inextricably in the depths of putrescent idleness'. And again, 'Coleridge is a mass of richest spices putrefied into a dung-hill. I never hear him *tawlk* without feeling ready to worship him, and toss him in a blanket.' The final portrait itself, with its long indictment of metaphysical word-spinning and its insight into the tragic story of a high endowment with an insufficient will, is too well known for quotation here. Carlyle

[1] C. 241, 246; G. 335, 362; A. 45; Morley, 83, 88; R. (*D.*), ii. 296, 330; T. Chalmers, *Memoirs*, iii. 160; L. 610; Watson, 83.

was not yet an inhabitant of London, and did not see
Coleridge after the beginning of 1825.[1] Sterling himself
first came to Highgate about 1828. For two and three-
quarter hours he was a listener.

> It is painful to observe in Coleridge, that, with all the kindness and
> glorious far-seeing intelligence of his eye, there is a glare in it, a light
> half unearthly, half morbid. It is the glittering eye of the Ancient
> Mariner. His cheek too shows a flush of over-excitement, the red of a
> storm-cloud at sunset.

Sterling remained a disciple to Coleridge's death, but thereafter his intellectual development took another bent.[2] The
Thursdays seem to have been suspended during an illness
of 1829, but may possibly have been resumed later.[3] Edward
Irving, indeed, had proved a disappointment. The simplicity of character, which had originally attracted Coleridge,
had given way under the intoxication of his own eloquence.
He developed strange views on the millennium, and finally
drifted into one of those states of mind in which it is difficult
to distinguish self-delusion from spiritual quackery.[4]

In 1827 Frere, then on the point of departure for a long
residence abroad, had procured for Coleridge from the Earl
of Liverpool the promise of a sinecure as Paymaster to the
Gentleman Pensioners. Coleridge was grateful, although he
did not know what a Gentleman Pensioner might be. Unfortunately both the Earl and Canning, who would have
carried out the promise, died shortly afterwards, and the
sinecure went to another.[5] In 1831, after the accession of
William IV, it was notified to the Royal Associates of the
Society of Literature that the grants made to them out of
the Privy Purse would be discontinued. As Coleridge
picturesquely put it, his poor gold chain of a hundred
links was taken to 'emblazon d'or the black bar across the
Royal Arms of the Fitzclarences'. He made an appeal
through Sotheby to Brougham, the Lord Chancellor, and

---

[1] Carlyle, *Reminiscences*, i. 230, 310; Froude, *Carlyle*, i. 222, 252, 263, 292.
[2] J. C. Hare, *Sterling*, I. xiii–xvi, xlv, cxxviii, cxlii.   [3] M. 34; C. 259.
[4] C. 232, 233, 241, 243, 246, 248; G. 335, 370, 373; A. 43, pp. 111, 129; Brandl,
373; *T.T.* 73, 278; L. 548, 555; R. (*D.*), ii. 267, 394; S.C. *Memoir*, i. 127; *Church and
State*, 166; Oliphant, *Irving*, 92, 97, 110, 290.
[5] G. 371, 372, 383; *L.P.* 83–5; White, i. 439.

others were made on his behalf by Rogers and Lamb to Lord Grey, the First Lord of the Treasury, himself. The Treasury had no control over the Privy Purse. But Grey offered Coleridge a *solatium* in the form of two annual grants of £100. This Coleridge refused. He could accept, he said, 'a public honor and stipend' conferred on him by his Sovereign, but not a private donation from Lord Grey. Meanwhile, there had been public criticism of the King's action, contrary to Coleridge's desire, in the *Englishman's Magazine* and in *The Times*. The matter was closed by a letter from Gillman to *The Times*, announcing Coleridge's decision. An 'insolent letter' Lamb calls it. I do not see any insolence, but Lamb was annoyed that no acknowledgement had been sent to his own intermediary with Lord Grey. 'Poor C. is not to blame, for he is in leading strings.' Later Stuart approached the King himself through his son the Earl of Munster, but only got the reply that the King was a much poorer man than his predecessor, and had to cut down his Privy Purse expenses. Colonel James visited Highgate about this time, and asked for congratulations on an accession to his fortune. 'Brother,' said Coleridge, 'you may at the same time give me your condolence for the loss of my miserable income.' Colonel James did not take the hint, but Coleridge's loss was made up to him by an annual gift from Frere.[1] In 1832 he had a legacy of £300 from Adam Steinmetz, a young man at Highgate, to whom he was much attached. He accepted it with some delicacy, after taking steps to assure himself that Steinmetz was of sound mind.[2] How far he was ever able to discharge his debt to Gillman is uncertain.[3]

The physical improvement due to Coleridge's continental tour was not long maintained, and in 1830 his health may be said to have finally broken down. For three years he spent most of his time in his attic, sometimes, he said, walking about it for seventeen hours a day, but often in bed. His only consolation was that his head remained clear 'like

[1] G. 387; Prideaux, 25; *L.P.* pp. 319, 321; L. 880 ('July' for 'June'); *Englishman's Mag.* (2 June); *The Times* (2; 3, 4, 6 June); S.C. *Memoir*, i. 130; R. (*D.*), iii. 13; *Studies*, 91; *D.H.* 299; W. Scott, *Journal*, ii. 449.
[2] C. 255; M. 40.   [3] A. W. Gillman, 16.

the head of a mountain in blue air and sunshine'.[1] A pathetic letter of gratitude to Mrs. Gillman is probably of 1830.[2]

Wife of the friend who has been more than a brother to me, and who have month after month, yea, hour after hour, for how many successive years, united in yourself the affections and offices of an anxious friend and tender sister to me-ward!

May the Father of Mercies, the God of Health and all Salvation, be your reward for your great and constant love and loving-kindness to me, abiding with you and within you, as the Spirit of guidance, support, and consolation! And may his Grace and gracious Providence bless James and Henry for your sake, and make them a blessing to you and their father! And though weighed down by a heavy presentiment respecting my own sojourn here, I not only hope but have a steadfast faith that God will be your reward, because your love to me from first to last has begun in, and been caused by, what appeared to *you* a translucence of the love of the good, the true, and the beautiful from within me,—as a relic of glory gleaming through the turbid shrine of my mortal imperfections and infirmities, as a Light of Life seen within 'the body of this Death',—because in loving me you loved our Heavenly Father reflected in the gifts and influences of His Holy Spirit!

In 1832 there was certainly another irregular recourse to opium, as a result of which an attempt seems to have been made to dispense even with the medical use of the drug. Coleridge found 'a miracle of grace' in 'a sudden emancipation from a thirty-three years' fearful slavery'.[3] Lamb was affected at receiving from his sick-bed a letter, which apparently contained some reference to their alienation of 1798, and sent a tender reply. To Allsop Lamb wrote:

How you frighted me! Never write again, 'Coleridge is dead', at the end of a line, and tamely come in with 'to his friends' at the beginning of another. Love is quicker, and fear from love, than the transition ocular from Line to Line.[4]

Coleridge's confinement did not prevent him from receiving visitors. Wordsworth saw him several times in the winter of 1830–1, and had long conversations with him. There must have been much to recall. These were their last meetings.[5] Coleridge complained of 'unkind neglect' by Southey, which caused him grief 'wholly and exclusively from my

[1] C. 252, 253, 256; G. 385, 387, 395; M. 35, 39; D.H. 296; Prideaux, 19, 20, 22, 24; Oliphant, *Blackwood*, i. 416, 419; T. ii. 299; W. 909, 926, 949, 961, 962, 1027, 1034; T.T. 184.   [2] C. 250.   [3] C. 254; G. 388–90; Watson, 35.
[4] L. 899, 906; cf. p. 98.   [5] W. 949, 962, 964.

persistent regard for *him*, and *his* better being'.[1] Highgate had by now become something of a place of pilgrimage for such admiring or merely curious strangers as could secure an introduction. Coleridge was ready to receive them graciously. Some even came from America, where an edition of his *Aids*, with an exposition by James Marsh, had given him a repute among a people singularly attracted by religious speculation. An early one was James Fenimore Cooper, whom Coleridge called 'the American Sir Walter'.[2] Some impressions have been handed down to us. In April 1832 H. B. McLellan of Harvard noted his careless dress, venerable locks of white hair, and trembling frame.[3] Later in the same year Robinson brought Walter Savage Landor, who already thought highly of him. 'He was horribly bent, and looked seventy years of age,' says Robinson. 'Landor and he seemed to like each other. Landor spoke in his dashing way, which Coleridge could understand.'[4] Harriet Martineau, probably in 1833, disputed with him as to the value of political economy.[5]

He looked very old, with his rounded shoulders, and drooping head, and excessively thin limbs. His eyes were as wonderful as they were ever represented to be;—light grey, extremely prominent, and actually glittering.

Emerson, in the same year, found 'a short, thick old man, with bright blue eyes and fine clear complexion, leaning on his cane', and taking snuff freely, 'which presently soiled his cravat and neat black suit'. The interview cannot have been a very comfortable one. Coleridge expounded at length the folly and ignorance of Unitarianism, and when Emerson interposed that he had himself been born and bred a Unitarian, merely said, 'Yes, I supposed so', and went on with his discourse.[6]

As I might have foreseen, the visit was rather a spectacle than a conversation, of no use beyond the satisfaction of my curiosity. He was old and preoccupied, and could not bend to a new companion and think with him.

Another late visitor was William Rowan Hamilton, who

---

[1] G. 393; Rickman, 281.   [2] G. 376.   [3] T. ii. 298.
[4] R. 116; R. (*D.*), iii. 13.   [5] *Autobiography*, i. 396.   [6] *English Traits*, ch. i.

only came to know Coleridge in 1832, but was much influenced by him.[1]

It is curious that observers could not agree upon the colour of Coleridge's eyes. To most they were grey, but to Emerson and to an informant of Caroline Fox blue, and to Carlyle brown.[2] During all these later years Henry Coleridge played the part of an affectionate son towards his father-in-law. It is clear from his *Table-Talk* that, whenever his professional duties permitted, he must have been over at Highgate from week to week, and often from day to day, garnering the wealth of reminiscences and reflection that fell from the old man's lips. His ordinary manner, says Henry, was plain and direct enough.[3]

Even when, as sometimes happened, he seemed to ramble from the road, and lose himself in a wilderness of digressions, the truth was, that at that very time he was working out his fore-known conclusion through an almost miraculous logic, the difficulty of which consisted precisely in the very fact of its minuteness and universality. He took so large a scope, that, if he was interrupted before he got to the end, he appeared to have been talking without an object; although, perhaps, a few steps more would have brought you to a point, a retrospect from which would show you the pertinence of all he had been saying. I have heard persons complain that they could get no answer to a question from Coleridge. The truth is, he answered, or meant to answer, so fully, that the querist should have no second question to ask. In nine cases out of ten, he saw the question was short or misdirected; and knew that a mere *yes* or *no* answer could not embrace the truth—that is, the whole truth—and might, very probably, by implication, convey error. Hence that exhaustive, cyclical mode of discoursing in which he frequently indulged; unfit, indeed, for a dinner-table, and too long-breathed for the patience of a chance visiter,—but which, to those who knew for what they came, was the object of their profoundest admiration, as it was the source of their most valuable instruction.

It is, of course, the substance rather than the form of Coleridge's talk that Henry records. Probably habit made it easier for him than for more casual hearers to follow the mental processes which underlay that inexhaustible flow of words. The criticism of Carlyle was perhaps jaundiced, but it has its echoes from others, who were privileged to attend the famous Thursdays. Thomas Chalmers 'caught occa-

[1] C. 253; W. 950, 984, 1012; Hamilton, i. 476, 536-51; ii. 36, 49, 52, 623.
[2] C. Fox, *Journals*, i. 23; Hamilton, ii. 94; cf. pp. 76, 154, 318, 321. [3] *T.T.* xii.

sional glimpses of what he would be at, but mainly he was very far out of all sight and all sympathy'. Irving, however, told him,

> You Scotchman would handle an idea as a butcher handles an ox. For my part, I love to see an idea looming through the mist.[1]

But others, even among those most familiar with Coleridge's mind, shared the sense of bewilderment. Robinson records, after one Thursday:

> It was painful to find myself unable to recall any part of what had so delighted me—i.e. anything which seemed worthy to be noted down. So that I could not but suspect some illusion arising out of the impressive tone and the mystical language of the orator. He talked on for several hours without intermission. . . . His doctrines assume an orthodox air, but to me they are unintelligible.

And after another:

> Coleridge, as usual, very eloquent, but, as usual, nothing remains now in my mind that I can venture to insert here. I never took a note of Coleridge's conversation that was not a *caput mortuum*. But there is a *spirit*, and a glorious spirit too, in what he says at all times.[2]

A visitor to Wordsworth in 1849 tells an amusing story of an evening which his host and Samuel Rogers spent together at Highgate.[3]

> As the two poets walked away together—'I did not altogether understand the latter part of what Coleridge said', was the cautious remark of Rogers. 'I did not understand any of it', was Wordsworth's hasty reply. 'No more did I', exclaimed Rogers, doubtless much relieved.

In the domestic circle itself Sara Coleridge was less fortunate than her husband, and could contribute little to the *Table-Talk*. Henry, she says, could sometimes bring the speaker to earth, but when alone with her, he was almost always 'on the star-paved road, taking in the whole heavens in his circuit'.[4] She can have seen little of him, after the birth of her second child in 1832. Coleridge came over to the christening, and talked much, especially, according to his wife, about Poole, 'as he always does when he speaks of early days'. But thereafter Sara's health broke down,

---

[1] T. Chalmers, *Memoirs*, iii. 160.   [2] R. (*D.*), ii. 296, 330; Morley, 88.
[3] E. Yarnall, *Wordsworth and the Coleridges*, 125.   [4] S.C. *Memoir*, i. 123.

and she long remained in a state of great weakness and despondency.[1]

Coleridge, himself, was better in 1833 than he had been for some years. In June he was able to go with Green and Gillman to a meeting of the British Association at Cambridge, and even to sleep on a bed which was like 'a couple of sacks full of potatoes tied together'. Here he saw his son Derwent, Hamilton, and his old schoolfellow Charles Le Grice, who wrote an account of his sayings in Thirlwall's rooms at Trinity.[2] In July he was once more at Ramsgate, enjoying the company of Lockhart and his wife, a daughter of Walter Scott.[3] He felt ten years younger in spirit, after taking shower-baths of tepid salt water. In the autumn he wrote his own *Epitaph*.[4]

> Stop, Christian passer-by!—Stop, child of God,
> And read with gentle breast. Beneath this sod
> A poet lies, or that which once seem'd he.
> O, lift one thought in prayer for S.T.C.;
> That he who many a year with toil of breath
> Found death in life, may here find life in death!
> Mercy for praise—to be forgiven for fame
> He ask'd, and hoped, through Christ. Do thou the same!

In March 1834 a streak of erysipelas on Coleridge's cheek made him once more anticipate death. 'I should like to see you before I went, if to go I am', he wrote to Green, 'and leave with you the sole Depositorium of my mind and aspirations, which God may suggest to me.'[5] Probably little progress had been made with the *Opus Maximum* since 1827. But he believed the *Logic* to be ready for transcription, with the last part, on the application of the Ideas, which Green had undertaken.[6] He was still, however, to live for some months. Poole came to see him in May, and a little later Sara Hutchinson.[7] In June he wrote an affectionate note to a girl who had sent him a bunch of flowers.

That my sense is from illness become obtuse to the *fragrance* of

---

[1] M. 39-41; W. 961.
[2] R. 134; M. 41; Watson, 89; T.T. 256; Hamilton, ii. 49, 52, 623; Le Grice, *Conversations at Cambridge* (1836).
[3] G. 393; M. 41; *R.E.S.* x. 454.
[4] C. 257; *P.W.* 491.
[5] G. 397; T.T. 333.
[6] C. 258; G. 393; T.T. 147.
[7] P. ii. 294; *Studies*, 228; R. 146.

Flowers, I but little regret, but O! let my eyes be closed when their Beauty is no longer revealed to me, and finds no counterpart in my mind.

The love of flowers was strong upon him during his·years at Highgate.[1] The end came with a sudden attack on 19 July. Henry saw him next day, and brought his blessing to his wife and daughter. They did not go over, and his sons were not sent for, since the doctors thought that family interviews would be too agitating. For a time he would not see even the Gillmans or Green, desiring to be left alone with his Redeemer, and 'to evince in the manner of his death the depth and sincerity of his faith in Christ'. At last he sent for Green, to whom he wished to dictate some final words for the *Opus Maximum*. J. A. Heraud quoted them in a funeral oration at the Russell Institution.

And be thou sure in whatever may be published of my posthumous works to remember that, first of all is the Absolute Good whose self-affirmation is the 'I am', as the eternal reality in itself, and the ground and source of all other reality. And next that in this idea nevertheless a distinctivity is to be carefully preserved, as manifested in the person of the Logos by whom that reality is communicated to all other beings.

Mrs. Gillman, suffering from a broken leg after a fall, was then carried into his room to bid him farewell. Gillman and Green seem to have remained with him to the end.[2] His last act was to write a note asking that provision should be made for Harriet Macklin, a servant who had nursed him tenderly for some years.[3] Half an hour later coma supervened, and he passed away at 6.30 in the morning of 25 July 1834. A granddaughter of Mrs. Gillman reports that a moment later a myrtle which stood in his attic burst into bloom, and filled the chamber with its fragrance. About this there may be a touch of hagiology. But the myrtle had a real existence. Mrs. Gillman gave it to him in 1827, and a sprig from it long flourished at Ottery.[4]

An autopsy was taken at his own request, the report of which, as interpreted by a writer in the *Lancet*, suggests that

[1] C. 221; G. 399; L. 562, *note*; Watson, 52, 112; Mathews, i. 188; *P.W.* 441.
[2] S.C. *Memoir*, i. 109; *Studies*, 225; Watson, 158; G. 395.
[3] G. 400.   [4] C. 244; Watson, 134.

most of his physical sufferings were due to an enlargement
of the heart, perhaps caused by the adhesion of that organ
to the pericardial sac after inflammation of the latter in early
life.[1] Coleridge had made a will, evidently his own composition, in 1829. After notes of his esteem for Wordsworth, Southey, and Frere, gifts to Sara, Derwent's wife
Mary, and the Gillmans, and mourning rings for Lamb,
Montagu, Poole, Wade and his son Lancelot, and Sara
Hutchinson, he left his property, of which there was little
more than the assurance policy, now worth £2,560, and the
publishing rights in his manuscripts and letters to Green, in
trust for his wife and after her his children. By a codicil of
1830 he directed that any share coming to Hartley should
continue to be held in trust for him.[2] Green worked on the
Opus Maximum during the rest of his life, but was unable to
co-ordinate its fragments into any coherent whole, either
by his Hunterian *Orations* of 1840 and 1847, or by his
Spiritual Philosophy of 1865. There are some who still think
that this task may one day be accomplished. The funeral
took place on 2 August. The family were represented by
Henry and Edward Coleridge, the disciples by Green,
Charles Stutfield, and John Sterling, who came from Cambridge for the purpose. Gillman was ill in bed.[3] But the
deepest mourner was Charles Lamb, who could not bring
himself to attend. He was inconsolable.[4]

His great and dear spirit haunts me. . . . Never saw I his likeness,
nor probably the world can see again. I seem to love the house he died
in more passionately than when he lived. . . . What was his mansion is
consecrated to me a chapel.

Southey wrote, rather unkindly, 'He had long been dead
to me', and 'All who were of his blood were in the highest
degree proud of his reputation, but this was their only feeling concerning him'.[5] Wordsworth's voice broke when he
read the news to a friend. Coleridge was 'the most *wonderful*
man that he had ever known'.[6]

---

[1] S.C. *Memoir*, i. 109; *Studies*, 227; Watson, 28; *The Times* (8. vi. 1895); *Lancet*
(15. vi. 1895).   [2] Text in *Poems* (publ. J. T. Cox, 1836, 1838).
[3] S.C. *Memoir*, i. 109; *Studies*, 229.
[4] L. 1008-10; Garrod, 24, from *New Monthly Magazine* (1835); S.C. *Memoir*,
i. 126, 134; Lucas, *Life*, ii. 266.
[5] S. (*W*.), iv. 381.   [6] W. 1070; W. *Memoirs*, ii. 288; Batho, 368.

Although I have seen little of him for the last twenty years, his mind had been habitually present with me, with an accompanying feeling that he was still in the flesh. That frail tie is broken, and I, and most of those who are nearest and dearest to me, must prepare and endeavour to follow him.

Lamb himself died before the year was out, and Wordsworth linked his name with Coleridge's in verse.[1]

> Nor has the rolling year twice measured,
> From sign to sign, its steadfast course,
> Since every mortal power of Coleridge
> Was frozen at its marvellous source;
>
> The rapt One, of the godlike forehead,
> The heaven-eyed creature sleeps in earth:
> And Lamb, the frolic and the gentle,
> Has vanished from his lonely hearth.
>
> Like clouds that rake the mountain-summits,
> Or waves that own no curbing hand,
> How fast has brother followed brother,
> From sunshine to the sunless land!

So Coleridge passed, leaving a handful of golden poems, an emptiness in the heart of a few friends, and a will-o'-the-wisp light for bemused thinkers.

[1] *Extempore effusion upon the Death of James Hogg* (Nov. 1835).

APPENDIX
LETTERS FROM COLERIDGE

I

To GEORGE DYER

[1796, May 29. From Harvard College Library.]

Sunday Evening—

My dear Sir

Last week I was on an affair of business at Stowy, about 50 miles from Bristol—I returned on Saturday Evening—& found that unfortunately Mrs Coleridge had sent the two letters with some other things in a parcel to me at Stowy, the Monday before:— which parcel arrived at Stowy about the time that I arrived at Bristol—I shall receive it on Thursday Morning—& as soon as I receive it, will write you.

How deeply I am affected by your kindness, you will conceive better than I can express.—You have already sent a sum amply sufficient to extricate me from my difficulties, & to provide for my expences till such time as my literary Industry will, I trust, find employment—

Deeply affected and almost agitated with that Gratitude, which, if Philosophy discourage, Nature will more wisely compel, I remain

Your's sincerely & affectionately,
S. T. COLERIDGE.

[*Addressed*]　　George Dyer
　May 29th　　N° 10 Clifford's Inn
　　　　　　　Fleet Street
　　　　　　　London.
[*Stamped*]　　Bristol.

II

To RICHARD WORDSWORTH

[From Dove Cottage. Stutfield, referred to also in C. 249 (misdated 1830 for 1821) and G. 385 of 1830 was the father of Coleridge's amanuensis, Charles Stutfield. A letter of the same date to Poole (*Addl. MS.* 35343 f. 213) is vituperative of Richard Wordsworth.]

Tuesday, Sept. 10, 1799
Exeter.

Dear Wordsworth

The letter by which I received the lottery tickets gave me information that you had not received the shirt &c, & this morning I received your letter to the Express Purpose of the Same— /

I am vexed, as you will easily suppose when I tell you that *within* a week of my arrival at Stowey I sent them directed to you, by Mr Stutfield, a Wine & Brandy Merchant, who happened then to be at Stowey & offered to take the said parcel for me, promising me (with his own Mouth) to deliver the same — — / — This Evening I will write to my Friend Poole who knows Stutfield's address, requesting him immediately on receipt of mine to write to Stutfield —if I do not hear from Stutfield in the course of a decent time certifying that he has performed the promise, the performance of which he has so long & so unjustifiably neglected, Mrs Coleridge will not delay to do (what *she* now wishes)—i.e.— transmit a shirt & cravat, trusting to your goodness for the acceptance of = for =, it not being in my power to preserve absolute Identity — — —

I received this morning a letter from William & was agitated to find that his Health is in a State w̄ch I should deem alarming—

Your's Sincerely
S. T. COLERIDGE.

P.S. Till I hear from Stutfield the very idea of your Shirt will stick more burningly to my Memory than Deianira's Shirt did to Hercules's Skin—altho' I entreat you to look into the Article of Domestic News in the London Papers to see whether or no a Mr Stutfield was found on Hounslow Heath or elsewhere with his throat cut from Ear to Ear—for he *ought* to be dead, as a Moral Being, having promised me that if alive he would not delay to deliver the parcel, the *great importance* of which I happened by a sort of prophetic Presentiment to impress upon him with almost a deathbed Energy & Solemnity—

[*Addressed*] Mr Wordsworth
      Attorney at Law
      Staple's Inn
      Holborn
      London.

III

To SARA HUTCHINSON

[From transcript by Mr. Gordon Wordsworth at Dove Cottage.]

Tuesday, July 27, 1802
(Greta Hall)

My dearest Sara,

If the weather with you be what it is here, our dear Friends must have had a miserable Day yesterday. It rained almost incessantly at Keswick till the late evening, when it fell a deep Calm, & even the Leaves, the very topmost Leaves, of the Poplars & Aspens had Holiday, & like an overworked Boy consumed it in sound sleep. The whole Vale presented a curious Spectacle / the Clouds were scattered by wind & rain in all shapes & heights, above the mountains, on their sides, and low down to their Bases—some masses in the middle of the valley—when the wind & rain dropt down & died, and for two hours all the Clouds, white & fleecy all of them, remained without motion, forming an appearance not very unlike the Moon as seen thro' a telescope. On the mountains directly opposite to our House (in Stoddart's

Tobacco-juice Picture) the Clouds lay in two ridges ⎺⎺⎺⎺⎺⎺⎺ with ⎽⎽⎽⎽⎽⎽⎽

a broad strait road between them, they being the *Walls* of the Road. Blessings on the Mountains! to the Eye & Ear they are always faithful. I have often thought of writing a set of *Play-bills* for the Vale of Keswick—for every day in the Year—announcing each Day the Performance, by his supreme Majesty's Servants, Clouds, Waters, Sun, Moon, Stars, &c. Today the weather is mild, tho' (as Mrs Bancroft informed my wife in a note last week) '*the humid aspect of the general atmosphere is eminently hostile* TO MY FONDLY CHERISHED HOPES'. For I wait only for a truly fine Day to walk off to S. Bees. Best compliments to the River Bee, & if he have any commands to the Saint, his Relative, I shall be happy to communicate the same.

I write now in order to send dear Tom word of Lord Lowther's Farms: [Here follows a list of twelve farms on the Lowther Estate advertised to be let. No. 11 runs: Wastdale Head & Foot with Demmings & its extensive Sheep Heaths.] O! would that No. 11 were as good for *Farmer Tom* as it would be for *Friend Tom*. I know it well; the situation is fine beyond description, 11 miles from Keswick thro' Borrowdale!! Ravenglass is its market Town. I have no doubt the Farm would answer capitally, but for one Thing, the People of England, 'od rabbit 'em! are not stone-eaters; if they were, I dont know a Place in which there is a greater Plenty & variety of that solid & substantial Food. What soft washy pap-like Stuff is a piece of Beef compared with a stout Flint! But there is no persuading People to their own good! So we will have done with it.

As I have been transcribing I must give you a touch out of Warner's "Tour thro the Northern Counties." .P. 14. Vol. 1. "In the walks of Literature &c. &c. Bristol has made & still makes a figure &c. &c. The gigantic Intellect & sublime Genius of *COLERIDGE*, which were here first publicly developed &c. &c. & *Chatterton*, second only to his *Monodist* (see *Coleridge's* monody on the Death of Chatterton) &c. Southey's Muse also poured forth those beautiful &c., and the two *Cottles* have given from *their own Press* works which would add to the fame of any Poets *of the Day!*" Ha! Ha! Ha! even to the fame of Giant *Coleridge*, I suppose. Now isn't this a Proof, that it does not depend altogether on a man's own Prudence whether or no he is to become ridiculous. Vol. 2. p. 100. "The animated, enthusiastic & accomplished *Coleridge*, whose residence at Keswick gives additional charm to its impressive scenery, inspired us with Terror (*a lying Scoundrel!*) while he described the universal Uproar (O! Lord! what a lie) that was awakened thro' the mountains by a sudden Burst of involuntary Laughter in the Heart of the Precipices; an incident, which a kindred Intellect, his Friend & Neighbour at Grasmere, *WORDSWORTH* (whose L.B., exclusively almost of modern compositions, breathes the true, nervous & simple spirit of Poetry) has worked up into the following admirable effusion"— here follows Joanna. Could you believe now that the Rogue made up all this out of my telling him that Wordsworth's Echo (tho' purposely beyond Nature) was yet only an *exaggeration* of what really would happen, for that I myself with John Wordsworth & William had laughed aloud at Stickle Tarn in Langdale, & that the effect was quite enough to justify the Poem from being more extravagant than it was its purpose to be. Whatever I told him the Fellow has murdered in this way—a book fuller of Lies & Inaccuracies & Blunders was, I believe, on my conscience, never published. From foolish men that write Books, Lord deliver me! It has been my Lot to be made a Fool of by Madmen, & represented as a Madman by Fools.

Mrs Coleridge is but poorly—the Children are tolerable. I am but so so; the weather has been my Enemy. O that I may be well & look bonny when you all come to us! dear Hartley. I picked up a parcel of old Books at Wilkinson's which he gave me, among them is an old System of Philosophy by some *Fantastic* or other with a large Print of Sun, Moon, Stars, Birds, Beast & Fishes— with Adam & Eve rising out of a Chaos! Derwent immediately recognized the Horse & Cow. Hos! Cu!—& then putting his finger to Eve's bosom said *Ma! Ma!* Pap. i.e. his Mother's or Mary's Bosom into which he puts his little Hand when he is petting. But I asked Hartley what he thought of it; & he said—

it is very curious! A Sea not in a World, but a World rising out of a Sea!! these were his own unprompted Words & entirely his own idea. "There they all are, Adam & Eve & all! Well! I dare say they all stared at one another finely!!!" This strikes me as a most happy image of the Creation. Yesterday *crazy* Peter Crosthwaite (not the Museum Peter) came into Mr Jackson—(Mrs Wilson & Hartley only were at home). Hartley soon found out that he was crazy, turned pale & trembled, & Mrs Wilson snatched him up & brought him in to us / as soon as he came in he cried aloud in an agony, nor could we appease him for near a quarter of an hour / When I talked to him how foolish it was, Well! says he, you know I am always frightened at things that are not like other things. But, Hartley! said I, you would not be frightened if you were to see a number of new Birds or Beasts or Fishes in a Show / Yes, said he, when I was a little Boy I was frightened at the Monkey & the Dromedary in London (*so he was, poor fellow*! God knows) but now I am not frightened at them— *because they are like themselves.* What do you mean, Hartley? "Dont ask me so many questions, Papa! I cant bear it. I mean, that I am not frightened at men that are like men / a monkey is a monkey, and God made the Dromedary—but Peter is a crazy man—he has had a chain upon him!". / Poor fellow!: when he recovered he spent the whole afternoon in whisking about the Kitchen, & telling Mrs Wilson wild stories of his own extempore composition about mad men & mad animals—all frightful: for tho' he cannot endure the least approximation to a sorrowful story from others all his own are most fantastically tragical.

O dear Sara!—how dearly I love you! Dear Mary! Heaven bless you & send back our dear Friends to you!

S. T. COLERIDGE.

Addressed to Miss S. Hutchinson, Gallow Hill, Wykeham, Malton, Yorkshire.

P.M. Keswick—no date.   G. G. W. Nov. 1930.

IV

To SARA HUTCHINSON

[From transcript by Mr. Gordon Wordsworth at Dove Cottage.]

August 10, 1802. Tuesday Evening

My dearest Sara,

You will this morning, I trust, have received the Letter which I left at the Ambleside Post (the first I came to) on Sunday Evening.

I have half such another, the continuation of my tour, written; but on my arrival yesterday at my home, about 8 o'clock in the evening, I found 7 letter⟨s⟩ for me / I opened none for an hour, I was so overglad to see the children again and the first I opened I was forced to answer directly, which was as much as I could do to save the Post—& today I have been so busy letter-writing, that I have not time to finish the great-Sheet Letter—so must send a short one, briefly to say that I have received your two Letters, one of Monday, Aug. 2. inclosing the 5£, which I read last night, & had better left it alone, as I did 5 others—for it kept me awake longer than I ought to have been—and one this evening.

I am well, & have had a very delightful & feeding Excursion, or rather Circumcursion. When you did not hear from me, & in answer to a letter containing a note, you should surely have concluded, my Darling! that I was not at home; for when do I neglect these things to those I love? other things, & weighty ones, God help me! I neglect in abundance; for instance, two little Boxes, which Dorothy fears (& with abundant Reason) are lost, & which contain, besides my cloathes & several very valuable Books, all my written collections made in Germany, which taken merely in a pecuniary point of view are not worth less than 150£ to me—More rain coming! I broke off writing to look at the Sky—it was exactly 35 minutes after 7, which ⟨was⟩ 4 minutes after the real sun set, & long long after the apparent sun-set behind our hills—& I saw such a sight as I never before saw. / Beyond Bassenthwaite at the end of the view was a Sky of bright yellow-green, but over that & extending all over Bassenthwaite, & almost up to Keswick Church a Cloud-Sky of the deepest most fiery Orange. Bassenthwaite Lake look'd like a Lake of "blood-red Wine"—and the River Greta, in all its winding before our house, & the upper part of the Keswick Lake, were fiery red, even as I once saw the Thames when the huge Albion Mills were burning, amid the shouts of an exulting Mob, but with one foot upon Walla Crag, and the other foot exactly upon Calvert's House at Windy Brow was one great Rainbow, *red* and *all* red, entirely formed by the Clouds. I have now seen all the Rainbows, that I suppose, are possible; the Solar Rainbow, with its many colors, the grey lunar Rainbow, & a fiery red Rainbow, wholly from the clouds after sunset.—

I seem, I know not why, to be beating off all Reference to Dorothy & William, & their Letters. I heard from Sotheby of their meeting (though I did not read his Letter till after I had read yours.) I wish, I wish, they were back! When I think of them in Lodgings at Calais, Goslar comes back upon me, & of Goslar I never think but with dejection. [Two lines erased and illegible.] Tomorrow morning they will leave Calais, if they indeed leave it 10 days after the Date of Dorothy's Letter, so that they will probably be with you, I would fain hope, by Monday next. I saw old Molly yesterday; she was weakly but "mended" from what she had been; the Rheumatic Pain & weakness had left her Back, & gone into her arms. I slept at Bratha on Sunday Night; & did not go on to Grasmere, Tho' I had time enough, & was not over-fatigued; but tho' I have no objection to sleep in a lonely House, I did not like to sleep in *their* lonely House. I called the next day —went into the garden—pulled some Peas, & shelled & drest them, & eat them for my dinner with one rasher of Bacon boiled —but I did not go upstairs, nor indeed any where but the Kitchen. Partly I was very wet & my boots very dirty—& Molly had set the Pride of her Heart upon its niceness—still more, I had small desire to go up!

—It was very kind in you, my Darlings! to send the 5£ (which I have now sent back) but it was not very wise. I could have easily procured 3 or 4£ from Mr Jackson, but I gave up the Residence at S. Bees, because I began to reflect that in the present state of my finances I ought not to *spend* so much money. Thomas Ashburner's call was the *occasion* of my resolve not to go to S. Bees, but my own after reflections were the *Cause*. In the course of my Tour (& I was absent 9 days) I gave away to Bairns & footsore Wayfarers four shillings & some odd pence; & I *spent* nine shillings—sum total £0—13—0—but to this must be added the wear & tear of my Boots, which are gone to be mended; & sixpence for a great knee-patch for my Pantaloons, which will not however be worn an hour the shorter time for the said knee-patch. I have *now no clothes but what are patched at the elbows & knees & in the seat* —& I am determined to wear them *out & out*, & to have none till after Christmas.

Hartley is in good spirits; but he does not look well. Derwent too looks less rosy than usual—for we cannot keep him from the Gooseberries. Hartley says: "He is far overwicked; but its all owing to Adam who did the same thing in Paradise". Derwent can *repeat* all the Letters; & can point out six or seven. O, that you could see his Darling mouth, when he shouts out Q. But notwithstanding his erudition, he is very backward in his Tongue.

Lloyd's children are nice fair Babies, but there is nothing *lovely* in their countenances or manners. I have seldom seen children I was so little inclined to caress—fair & clean, as they were, O how many a cottage Bairn have I kissed or longed to kiss, whose cheeks I could scarce see for the healthy dirt—but these I had no wish to kiss! There is a something in children that makes love flow out upon them, distinct from beauty, & still more distinct from good-behaviour. I cannot say—God knows! that our children are even decently well-behaved, & Hartley is no beauty —& yet it has been the Lot of the two children to be beloved. They are the general Darlings of the whole Town; & wherever they go, Love is their natural Heritage.

Mrs Coleridge is now pretty well.

God bless my darling Sara! & thee, dear Mary. I will finish my long Letter as soon as possible, but for the next 3 or 4 days I shall be exceedingly busy. Write immediately. Kind Remembrances to Tom & Joanna.

Bless you, my Darling!
S. T. COLERIDGE.

I have received a large Wedgewood Jug, & a large cup finely embossed with figures, & thick-rimmed with silver, as a present — — from Lady Rush! with a *kind Note*. I had a shrewd suspicion that I was a favourite.

Inclosed is the £5—5s note.

Note. The 'Circumcursion' extended from the 1st of August to the 9th, and is described at length in the 'great-Sheet Letter' or Letter-Journal written during the course of it to S. H., M. H., D. W., and W. W. (Unpublished, 1930). Addressed to Miss S. Hutchinson, Gallow Hill, Wykeham, Malton, Yorkshire.

P.M. Keswick. No date.   G. G. W. Nov. 1930.

V

To the WORDSWORTHS

[From Dove Cottage.]

Mr. J. C. Mottley's Portsmouth.—

Wednesday Morning, April 4th 1804

My dearest Friends

I have this moment read your Letter, Dorothy's & William's: which I received about an hour ago: for the sight of Dorothy's Handwriting in the directions of your Letter move⟨s⟩ me so deeply, that my heart fails me—I dread the emotion from the opening of it—. O dearest & most revered William! I seem to grow weaker & weaker in my moral feelings, and every thing, that forcibly awakes me to Person & Contingency, strikes fear into me, sinkings and misgivings, alienation from the Spirit of Hope, obscure withdrawings out of Life, and something that you have given to Mortimer I believe in your Tragedy, a wish to retire into stoniness & to stir not, or to be diffused upon the winds & have no individual Existence. But all will become better when once I can sit down, & work: when my Time is my own, I shall be myself again. These Hauntings and Self-desertions are, no doubt, connected with the irritable state of my Bowels & the feebleness of my Stomach; but both they & these, their bodily causes, are exasperated by the rapid Changes, I have undergone—not only from one face to another in an endless detail of Change—; but in the abrupt & violent Transitions from Grasmere and dear you to Liverpool, to London, to Drinkings & Discussings—again from these to compleat quietness at Dunmow—& from Sir G. & Lady Beaumont back again to London Parties— — then a few soothing & comfortable Days, & very instructive ones, with those good & (in a most appropriate sense) *elegant* people in town, & now at Portsmouth, from the quietest House & the most select & innocent conversation in London, & merely to particularize the whole of the contrast, from the House of a truly great Painter, a descendant of Beaumont, the Poet (& glorying in it more than in being, as he likewise is, a descendant of Kings, and one of the 4 or 5 most ancient noble families in Europe) to the company of Sailors & Portsmouth Shop-keepers, many of them good-natured & prompt to serve me, but all of them loose livers & loose talkers, smoking & drinking regularly to intoxication—& I in the midst of them with Oaths & Curses flying about me & whizzing by my ears, like Bullets!—This morning, however, my Captain presented himself to me—he arrived last night, he says that the Leviathan, of 74 guns, which is to convey us, has as yet not received her orders, but probably will have them today, namely orders to sail with the first fair wind; but that the Wind at present (S.W.) is point blank against us, and in an obstinate corner.—The Captain seems a good sea man, and dines here today.—I am at no expence here, except Lodging & Washing— which together does not exceed 13 Shillings a week—I have been 4 days at the Crown, with a private room, one dinner, one Tea, 3 breakfasts, one pint of wine, and one glass of Punch;—&

Mottley *congratulated* me, that I got off so cheap as a guinea & a half including Waiter, Boots, & Chambermaid. The last Landlord payed 10,000£ for the Inn to his Predecessor, besides the Rent to the House-owner, & made so large a fortune in six years, that he has retired & built a grand House 10 miles from Portsmouth, that cost him 8000£, & this present Landlord, paying the same sum for the Trade, is making money, they say, still faster— & there are two other Inns in the Town, the one quite as lucrative, and the other nearly so. —— You will direct all your Letters, in the first instance, to Mr Lambe, India House, London (remember to annex the e)—Lamb will carry them to Mr Rickman, who will have them frank'd to me to Mr J. C. Mottley's, Portsmouth) and Mottley will then forward them to me, not only with far greater regularity, than I should get them by the Post, but entirely free of all expence. He is a sort of agent, I believe, to Sir Alexander Ball, the Governor of the Island. In short, *you* have nothing to do but to direct your Letters Mr Lambe, &c— / & write on a large single Sheet, and send two single Letters rather than one double one.—But of all things I most eagerly wish to have my beloved Dorothy's *Tour* / Southey goes to London a week after his Wife's Confinement, if she do well. He could take it, & Rickman could get it franked; if you made it up in *Letters* (not like your last in *pacquets*, but more in the form & size of a common double Letter) each Letter including the weight of the Seal not to exceed an Ounce & a Half—so as to allow for an envelope & large official Seal. The whole weight allowed to be franked by the Clerks of the H. of Commons is two Ounces—you may therefore exceed the ounce & a half, but take care that no one Letter is so much as an Ounce & 3 quarters.—If however Southey should not go, or you should not have it ready, then send it, exactly in the same *Letter-form*, & in Letters, each *short* of an Ounce & 3 quarters, inclusive of the two Envelopes—directed. 1. S. T. Coleridge, Esqre, Mr J. C. Mottley's, Portsmouth. 2. Inclose this in an Envelope, directed simply, J^{no} Rickman, Esqre. 3. Inclose this in another Cover, & direct it to, The Right Honor^{ble}, The Speaker, Palace Yard, Westminster. N.B. Whatever you do, do not forget the 2nd Cover to Rickman, lest the Speaker should find himself Letter-smuggler to Squire Coleridge: and secondly, send them not all together, nor even day after day; but interpose four or five days between each Letter.— And after this once every month or six weeks, if dear William have written any Verses, more than will go in a single Sheet to

Lambe, you will send an Ounce & 3 quarters to me at Mottley's, under cover to Jn° Rickman, Esqre, under cover to the Speaker. —I hope, you will write once every ten days at least, to Lambe & these with one containing the poetry of six weeks—O dear dear Friends: I love you, even to anguish love you: & I know no difference, I feel no difference, between my Love of little *Sara*, & dear little John. Being equally with me, I could not but love them equally: how could I—the child of the man, for whom I must find another name than *Friend*, if I call any others but him by the name of Friend—the Mary & Dorothy's own Darling— the first *free* Hope of you all!—I mean this merely as a Letter of Instructions & mere Intelligence. Your Letter of this morning, as is too often the case with your Letters was not dated. Take care of this, my dear Friends!—I shall feel need to say, God forgive me! if I suffer any two nights to pass without adding a few Lines to my Journal to you / & if any Vessels leave Malta, & no Letter come to you, the Vessel must be lost. I *hope*, I shall be able to send them free of expence.—J. C. Mottley is a Bookseller, & Proprietor of a successful Provincial Paper—he has a large Business, & supplies several Public offices with Stationery—He has 3 Brothers all high in different public Offices here. To me he has been exceedingly civil, & is now, to oblige me & on my representation, using his utmost Interest to procure a place of 100£ & some thing more, in the Sick & Hurt Office for Mrs Coleridge's Brother. I have almost *expectations* that he will succeed: the person, in whose patronage these places are has *promised* him the first vacancy. Five minutes after I had mentioned to him how anxious I was to get him a place, & how deserving a youth he was, he *wrote* to the gentleman in order that I might see the Answer before my Departure. He had been asking my Advice about one of his own Clerks, a fine young man who had & in a very modest way asked for an increase of Salary. I advised Mottley to advance it somewhat beyond his Request: & to promise him in case of perseverance Industry & Fidelity a small Share in the Business as soon as he was ⟨of⟩ age / He is now between 18 & 19—& the whole of Mottley's Shop Business rests on him for Mottley is a man of *Pleasure* / I grounded my advice on his (Mottley's) character & the necessity, as a measure of Prudence, that he should have some one bound to him by other than common Ties. Mottley stood like one lost in Thought, then said, you are *right*! you are quite in the Right, Sir! I will do it, by God!—Then I mentioned to him poor George Fricker, &c.

Mottley has just been in here: tells me, he has done exactly as I advised him—& left the young man in such agitation of Joy & Gratitude, (in great measure on account of a Mother to whom he is devoted & who is in extreme Distress) that he begged leave to retire to his Lodgings for a couple of Hours . . I have told this Story on account of an anecdote that affected me & will affect you. I told him, says Mottley to me, that it was you in great measure, to whom he was indebted for it—the gentleman, who talked to him about the Lyrical Ballads (The young man happened to be reading the Tintern Abbey, & apparently with due Emotion & an intelligent Face). "As I live, Sir! (replied he to Mottley) I felt I dont know how—as I never felt before, at that man's Face when first he spoke to me."—Curious accidents!— Probably, very probably, that young man will some time or other be one of the richest Tradesmen in Portsmouth / & he himself will not be able to say, how much of it he will have owed to the accident of his reading your Tintern Abbey.—Mottley has a number of excellent qualities about him, but he is a sad loose Liver. Drinks hard, smokes hard, cannot bear to be alone; & tho' exceedingly prosperous, & with a nice sweet-tempered Wife & six fine Children, the two youngest exquisitely beautiful in the petite style, yet nevertheless, alas! alas! addicted to almost promiscuous Intercourse with women of all Classes. At first, he ⟨was⟩ a⟨c⟩tually *astonished* at my principles & practice, but now he evidently looks up to me for them / I never looked or spoke severely or austerely to him / & I have some hopes of him from one circumstance—he did not doubt a moment that I had told him the truth respecting myself.—If you speak of him at all in your Letters mention him by the name of Poecilus (Ποικιλος).— Letters here are sometimes opened by order of Government / & his Brother is high in office. I will send off this lest I should be too late for the Post—S.T.C.

[*Addressed*] Mr Wordsworth
      Grasmere, near
        Ambleside
        Kendal
          Westmoreland.

VI

To WILLIAM WORDSWORTH

[May or June 1808. From Dove Cottage. Parts of the letter were printed by W. Knight, *Life of Wordsworth*, ii. 99. The extracts from Dorothy Wordsworth's Letters are W. 324, 333.]

Saturday night.

At 8 o/clock this evening I received a note from the Longmans' in consequence of one from you to them—I have been hunting for your Sister's Letter, as yet to no purpose; but as I put it up with many others from Grasmere, in some one or other of my repositories, I shall be sure to find it before this can go off to you; & will leave a space for her words concerning the Poem. At present, I can only state how I understood, and what I believe to be the substance of them.

In my re-perusals of the Poem it seemed always to strike on my feeling as well as judgement, that—if there were any serious defect, it consisted of a disproportion of the Accidents to the spiritual Incidents, and closely connected with this, if it be not indeed the same,—that Emily is indeed talked of, and once appears; but neither speaks nor acts in all the first 3 fourths of the Poem: and as the outward Interest of the Poem is in favor of the old man's religious feelings, and the filial Heroism of his band of Sons, it seemed to require Something in order to place the two Protestant Malcontents of the Family in a light, that made them beautiful, as well as virtuous—In short, to express it *far* more strongly than I *mean* or *think* in order, in the present anguish of my spirits, to be able to express it at all, that $\frac{3}{4}$ths of the Work is every thing rather *than* Emily; (*then*) the last almost a separate (& doubtless most exquisite Poem) wholly *of* Emily.—The whole of the Rout and the delivering up of the Family by Francis I never ceased to find not only *comparatively* very heavy, but to me quite obscure, as to Francis's motives. And on the few, to whom within my acquaintance the Poem has been read either by yourself or me (I have, I believe, read it only at the Beaumonts') it produced the same effect.—Now I had conceived two little Incidents, the introduction of which joined to a little abridgement, and lyrical precipitation of the last Half of the third, I had thought would have removed this defect—so Seeming to me—and bring to a finer Balance the *Business* with the *Action* of the Tale. But after my receipt of your Letter concerning Lamb's censures I felt my courage fail—and that what I deemed a harmonizing would disgust you, as a *materialization* of the Plan, & appear to you like *insensibility*—to the power of the history in the mind. Not that I should have shrunk back from the mere fear of giving transient pain & a temporary offence, from the want of sympathy of feeling & coincidence of opinions—I rather envy than blame that deep interest in a production, which is inevitable perhaps, and certainly not dishonorable to such, as feel poetry their calling and their duty, & which no man would find much fault with if the Object, instead of a Poem, were a large Estate or a Title—it appears to me to become a foible then only, when the Poet denies or is unconscious of, its existence.

But I did not deem myself in such a state of mind, as to entitle me to rely on my opinion when opposed to your's—from the heat & bustle of these disgusting Lectures, for which I receive whole Hods full of plaister of Paris—flatteries about as pleasant to me as rancid large Spanish Olives—these on the one side—& permanent hatred, and the most cruel public Insults on the other—& all this to cost me at least sixty £, exclusive of Lodgings, for which I pay either by obligation or by past services or both—/2. the necessity of publishing the substance of my Lecture on national Education in a very enlarged form, in order to obviate the charge made against me, most unprovokedly, in a very large Company, by Sir Harry Englefield of "base cowardice"—& even this was not the severest sentence of his most solemn & yet most wanton attack—3. for the sake of money, I am at the same time employed every spare hour in a complete "*Rifacciomento*", or "*Umarbeitung*", of the *Geist der Zeit*—the work for which poor *Palm* was murdered by Buonaparte / I not only add a long Preface, but throughout by notes or marked Interpolations, joined to softenings, omissions, and the lowering of the dythirambic style prevalent in the original, make almost a new work—It is done at the warm recommendation of His R. Highness, the Duke of Sussex, & will be an exceedingly interesting work—& likely to have a run.—4. In getting out of a boat at Somer⟨s⟩et stairs, the little Boy stirred it, & I half turning round to bid him be still, had the misfortune of falling backward, & struck the back of my head on the very part, on which I fell at Malta; tho' with no great force, as but for one stone I should have broken my fall entirely, tho' at the price of weakening my wrist a little. This produced the whole next day such a shuttle-like motion from the part horizontally to my forehead with such odd confusion, that I was unable to give the Lecture — — & it returns every now and then tho but for a few

seconds, if ever a Thought agitates me or a sudden sound. 5. I
have been sorely vexed in the failure of my plan of increasing my
assurance, after I had procured all the money necessary—this was
partly from want of foresight, in offering the whole at one place,
& that the most Scrupulous & stern office in London—partly,
I had no medical man to refer to who had known me continuedly
for any length of time—I referred, by permission, to Dr. Babbing-
ton—However, after wasting 8 days they declined assuring my
life for the increase proposed—Had I consulted Montague afore-
hand, this probably would not have happened. I had set my heart
& hope upon it: and the refusal made me very melancholy.
6. Among other wicked calumnies, & in addition to my Brother's
Shameful Usage of me, John Wedgewood & his family have
shamefully abused me / A friend of mine asked John Wedgewood
whether he had seen me / he replied 'No! nor ever wish to see
him. He was ungrateful and inattentive to my poor Brother,
Thomas! during his being with him in his sickness.'—I possess
one letter from T.W. that tells a different story.—These have all
conspired to prevent sorer anguish from going to rest, as a slight
Breeze will keep up the working of a ground-swell; and a mere
atom of Dirt occasion wounds to rankle—

From most of these causes I was Suffering, so as not to allow
me any rational confidence in my opinions, when contrary to
yours! which had been formed in calmness and on long reflection;
then I received your Sister's Letter—stating the wish, that I would
give up the thought of proposing the *means* of correction, and
merely point out the things to be corrected—which as they could
be of no great consequence, you might do in a day or two, & the
publication of the Poem, for the immediacy of which she expressed great anxiety, be no longer retarded—assigning a reason.
—Now the merely verbal *alteranda* did appear to *me too* very few,
& trifling—from your letter on L. I concluded that you would
not, from your own opinion, have the Incidents & Action inter-
fered with—& therefore I sent it off—but soon retracted it, in
order to note down the single words & phrases that I disliked in
the books after the two first—as there would be time to receive
your Opinion of them during the printing of the two first, in
which I saw nothing amiss except the one passage we altered
together, & the two Lines which I scratched out, because *you* yourself were *doubtful*; & Mrs Skepper had told me, that *she* had felt
them exactly as *I* did—namely, as interrupting the spirit of the
continuous tranquil motion of the White Doe—However—tho'

Somewhat grieved by your Sister's exceeding anxiety about pecuniary matters—grieved, heaven knows! for your sake and for her's, because I thought it not only a decaying of genial Hope & former light-heartedness, but as a recurrence of fears, which had harrassed you at Race down / Besides, I could not bear to think, that her judgement should be in danger of *warping*, from money-motives in affairs, which concern—if not your *fame*—yet your thereto introductory *reputation*—& which too by expediting or retarding the steady establishment of your classical Rank, would affect, of course, even your average pecuniary gains—. — Indeed before my Fall, &c. &c. &c, I had indulged the Hope that by a division of Labor you would have no occasion to think about—as if I had been to live, with very warm zealous patronage, I was fast ripening a plan which secures from 12 to 20£ a week—(the Prospectus indeed going to the Press, as soon as Mr Sotheby and Sir G. Beaumont had read it.)—However, on the mere possibility of a genial mood coming upon me, in which I should either see the whole *conduct* of the Poem in the light, in which you & she see it; or such a flash of conviction concerning the excellence of *my own* imagined amendment, as would *Settle* me; I wrote out the last 200 lines, or so of the third Book—& then again sent it off, in order that it might be *advertised* as *in* the press, about the time, when I gave my Lecture on your System & Compositions—which will be, God willing! on Friday *after* next—as my first Lecture on Modern Poetry is to be on *next* Tuesday.—I cannot therefore think my "misinterpretation" a very strange one—and, but that—(unless when I am reading it to & for myself) I can not get rid of the Fear, that it will be talked of, as an imitation of Walter Scott—(I having such daily experiences, what people are, & how different their abiding thoughts, if *they have any*, from those which even the worthiest EXPRESS, & I dare say, feel when under the influence of some immediate sympathy—(I therefore did not send the little preface, in which *my* name was, because I knew, that *the Public* are quick-witted in detecting the most hidden thing that can be made a topic of chit-chat Scandal. If every one, who had seen the Xtabel, believed, without the least suspicion of the difference, that the metre was the same as that of the Lay of the last Minstrel, they will & must, of course, think your metre to be the same with that of the L. of the L.M.—and then your referring the metre of a Poem composed since the publication of the L. of the L.M. to a *MS. Poem*, will appear strange and almost *envious*, if the great priority of the MS. to the Publication be not mentioned at the same time—and if it be, it would then, I fear, be deemed *invidious*, and a covert attack on Scott's originality, which for the world I would not, that *you* should be suspected of—I say, *but* for this apprehension, which I am sure is not an *absurd* one, I should most deeply regret the withdrawal of a Poem so peculiarly yours, and beyond any other *in rhyme* illustrative of your characteristic excellences—tho' I may now add, that it being not only sense, but sense that demands thought in the Reader, & will not leave him to a lax free-will, that the metre being—as you observed of your poem in general, rather dramatic than lyric, i.e. not such an arrangement of syllables, not such a metre, as acts a priori and with complete self-subsistence (as the simple anapestic in its smoothest form, or the praise of Bacchus in Dryden's Ode) but depending for it's beauty always, and often for it's metrical existence, on the *sense* and *passion*—I have something like the same suspicion that you entertained concerning Xtabel, how far this would or would not be an obstacle to it's popularity—Lamb & Miss Lamb, who evidently read it—he twice thro', he said—with no genial effort, no exertion from sympathy, are for the very reason that disqualifies them as Judges concerning it's *true merit*, no unfair Specimens of perhaps the majority of readers of Poetry, especially in the perusal of a new Poem, which does not employ the common excitements of lively interest, namely, curiosity, and the terror or pity from unusual external events & Scenes—convent dungeons &c &c—

I beg to be understood solely as referring to *the Public*, not *the People* / according to your own distinctions / and this only for a While—and chiefly influenced by the wish, that two publications should not succeed each other, both failing in their first general Impression—& perhaps in some measure, by comparing it's *chances* of immediate Sale with the almost *certainty* of the great popularity of either Peter Bell, or Margaret, or even the Salisbury Plain /

God forbid, your Sister should ever cease to use her own Eyes and heart, and only her own, in order to know how a Poem *ought* to affect mankind; but we must learn to see with the Eyes of others in order to guess luckily how it *will* affect them—Neither do I *wish* her to learn this; but then I would have her learn to entertain neither warm Hopes or confident expectations concerning Events dependent on minds & hearts BELOW the distinct ken of her Sympathies. Let her only reflect that (even *excluding* the effect of Routs & continued personal gossip, &c &c, yet) the great majority of the modern Buyers of new Poems read at least 20 whole *Novels* of 2, 3, 4, 5 Volumes each, for *one* poem / you have slightly mentioned this in the Preface to the L.B.—but it deserves to be dwelt on at length—

In fine, I did it for the best—the extracts on the next leaf will shew what grounds I had for taking it as granted, that the speedy Publication of the White Doe had been decided on at Grasmere— the first extract shows your Sister's opinion & feeling, for and from herself—and as the next was written since your return, & expresses the same opinion and as I had not received any letter to the contrary from you—nor had any reason to expect one—I coincided with her, that the Speedier the better, & for her reasons /—I was concerned, not at her opinion, but at the anxiety that seemed to have influenced it, from the very beginning.

S. T. COLERIDGE

I assuredly was commissioned by you to retalk the matter over with Longmans'—I did so—and they finally agreed to your own terms, whether £1 or Guineas. As soon as I had revised it in order to be aware of any little verbal inaccuracies, I promised to send it.—They must be in a strange Puzzle; and suppose that you had not authorized me to dispose of the work to them, for this Season.

—Extract from a Letter, Grasmere, March 31.

"This letter is intended for William, tho' I have little hope that he will be in town when it arrives—

We are exceedingly concerned to hear that you, William! have given up all thoughts of publishing your Poem. As to the Outcry against you, I would defy it—what matter, if you get your 100 guineas into your pocket? Besides it is like as if they had run you down, when it is known you have a poem ready for publishing, and keep it back. It is our belief, and that of all who have heard it read, that the *Tale* would bear it up—and without money what *can* we do? New House! new furniture! such a large family! two servants & little Sally! we *cannot* go on so another half year: and as Sally will not be fit for another place, we must take her back again into the old one, and dismiss one of the Servants, and work the flesh *off our poor bones*. Do, dearest William! do pluck up your Courage—overcome your disgust to publishing—It is but a *little trouble*, and all will be over, and we shall be wealthy, and at our ease for one year, at least."

The Italics are as in the original.—I thought, that the difference might be met halfway between you & Mr Longman: that you were quite right in not giving up your poem to be decided by any set of Critics, he chose to appoint—and on the other hand, that as the question was not the intrinsic merit, but the immediate saleability of the article (for remember, it was not for a Copy-right, but an Edition of 1000) that he had a right to have some clue to guide his Calculation / I proposed, that you should leave it with me, & leave me plenipotentiary—you did / I sent for the Gentleman, on whose Judgment Longman most relied, & with whom you had expressed yourself pleased—talked with him, & read near a third of the poem, & explained *sort* & conduct of the whole / the result was, that Longman acceded to your Terms, whatever they were / for the 100£ instead of *Gns* was a mere mistake of mine / . I wrote—you exprest no dissatisfaction / and I, who had pledged my judgement for the probability of the Sale, yet felt no anxiety on that account, but some, lest it should not be immediately Saleable, purely on account of your last two Volumes.—I found the Poem in diction exceedingly correct; but feared concerning the flow of the Interest ab extra / from your letter concerning L, I, tho' agreeing with you fundamentaly, in the general principle, yet deduced that you had made up your mind as to the essentiality of the *Business* bearing this, & no other proportion to the internal Action / from many of the circumstances, annumerated in this Letter, I conscientiously did not dare rely on my own persuasions in my so disturbed state of mind—therefore receiving from Dorothy in a letter written May the first, the following—

"*We are very anxious* that the White Doe should be published *as soon as possible*—if you would simply mention the passages, to which you object, without attempting to alter them, it would be better—&c—Our main reason (I speak in the name of the Females) for wishing that the Poem may be *speedily* published, is that William may get it out of his head; but further we think that it is of the *utmost importance*, that it should come out before the Buz of your Lectures is settled. The alterations, we trust, will not be of a difficult or troublesome kind."

—Now having promised Mr Longman, that I would take the trouble of correcting every Sheet—having found so few & so trifling corrigenda or melioranda, in the language, and submitting my own Judgement to your's, as to the general conduct of the Story, I am at a loss to know—in what way the having sent it to the Press, under the conviction, that any trifling *verbal* defects which might remain after *my* revisal, & which would have been removed by you!, could bear no proportion to the pecuniary advantage of having the poem published before the King's Birthday—how this can deserve that not to me (let that be as nothing; but) not to Montague, or your Brothers, but to the Booksellers you should write to inform them, that I had proceeded without Authority—& so much so, that the poem itself was no longer to be intrusted

[*The rest is missing.*]

VII

To BASIL MONTAGU

[7 January 1809. From Harvard College Library.]

Grasmere, Kendal

My dear Montagu

Many thanks both for your and for Mrs Montagu's Letter—If I were to give way to my private feelings respecting you, this Sheet would leave me no room for business.—What? if in the summer vacations you & Mrs M. came down hither? and left such of the children as might be thought advisable. You seem to Me so certain of rising to the summit of your profession, and I am sure, will do so much good in it, that I dare not let any thing bribe me to consider as good what might have the effect of distracting your attention—Good heaven! you know Mrs Montague —can you suppose there could be an event more delightful in and of itself to me, and to all of us (but I dare boldly say, to me above all) than her residence within a walk of us? The Idea of this and of its accompaniments, and the whole Form of the Objection to it's realization arising at the same moment in my mind, so affected me, when I first read her letter, that I shed tears. But enough of this, at present.

Savage overweening in my simplicity laid a plot for ruining and enslaving me—His intentional neglect concerning the Prospectuses has thrown me back a month—Since then great difficulties have arisen at the Stamp Office—these have been removed —it is declared, that if I adhere to my Prospectus, the work will be considered as a Pamphlet—But still the difficulties respecting the mode of dispersing the Work are increased by this decision— for hitherto two thirds of the Subscribers live in small towns or single Houses, here three, here two, here one—scarce any where a sufficient number to make a parcel per coach feasible—and thro' the country booksellers they would only receive it once a month perhaps—Enormous as the deduction is, I should prefer it's being on one sheet and stamped, from the convenience of sending it per post—But I have confided the whole to Mr Stuart, a man of the most consummate knowledge of the world, and of rich experience in periodical works—and to me as constant, generous, wise, and disinterested friend, as ever man was blest with / I am waiting with great impatience for a Letter from him—and hope, that in a week at last a hundred or more prospectuses will have been sent to you.

William is head, heart, soul, and fingers in the Spanish Business —In the Courier one Essay of his has appeared, signed G.—the second was lost in London, and so was re-written & sent again / I trust, it will have appeared by this time—six more are to follow.

I mean to send you, as soon as it can be transcribed, a most important memorial from Lord Bacon with additions and regular application to the present state of the Church, in relation to the Dissenters in general, but chiefly & prominently to the Evangelical Preachers & Methodists—It is a masterpiece of Wisdom—My additions are about one fourth—exclusive of a short Introduction —Either you or Mrs M. will give it a careful Reading—and if you think as highly of it, and of it's present applicability as I do—of it's necessity, I might say—you may perhaps be able to make a bargain for me with some bookseller.

Among my Books I miss several of the small octavos (Montgomery's Poems &c) all bound a like in a handsome purple — — a huge number of dear Mr Clarkson's History of the Slave Trade Abolition—of which I can dispose of six Copies here—At all events, send the books &c—All here are well excepting dear Sara Hutchinson, whose side is (alarming) painful—& myself, whose Chest and Respiration are distressingly affected— / Dr Beddoes's Death has taken more Hope out of my Life, than any Event I can remember—I have now no confidence in any medical man breathing. It very grievously affected me—indeed at first with a strange and womanish violence of sorrow. He was good and beneficent to all men; but to me he was tender and affectionate —and went out of the way of his ordinary character to shew it—.

But I have many letters of business to write—so, dear Montagu, farewell!—God bless you, & your's,

and your very affectionate Friend,
S. T. COLERIDGE

Saturday night—
P.S. We are miserably off in our Post—this Letter cannot leave Kendal till Tuesday morning— /

On Sunday Night at 10° clock three days posts arrive at Rydale—and the letters in answer cannot be sent off so as to leave Kendal till Wednesday—perhaps Thursday—so that it sometimes takes ten days for the To-and-froage of a Letter from London — — Ambleside & Windermere receive such a *Vast* of Letters, that we think of making an application to the Post Master, Mr Freeling, signed by the Bishop, Llandaff—Sir D. Fleming, &c.—at present we feel this particularly—that character of Prescience & Prophecy which would have belonged to William's Essays, had they been published as soon as written, is in good measure lost by the Delay—

[*Addressed*] Basil Montagu, Esqre
Lincoln's Inn
London

[*Postmarked*] Jan. 12. 1809.

VIII

To JOHN MORGAN

[16 June, 1814. From Harvard College Library.]

My dear Friend

This ugly Complaint in my Leg, which as the Devil is no *Unicorn*, has brought on a Stomach Sickness & a perilously (for good manners, I mean) sudden elimination of the Ingesta after meals, without previous nausea, present effort, or after pain. I tell Daniel, that I have a schirrous Liver: & he laughs at me for my Information. The angry Itching, which I dare not appease except by the continual application of wet Cloths, keeps me awake two thirds of the Night. Pumping on it 5 or six times a day for 5 minutes together.seems to be most effective—but as it vanishes in an instant, so in an instant does it return—& sometimes the convex of the foot, especially about an inch & a half from the Toes, pits hydropically. But Daniel assures me, that it is mere Wind & Weakness, from the rapid Diminution of the poison-dose,—which he has now so reduced, that *he* thinks all my bodily uneasiness *before*, & tranquillity after, taking the modicum, is *Mental*—that I *make up my mind* to be quiet, because there is nothing more to look forward to for 12 hours; and therefore *am* quiet. That there is *much* Truth in this, I cannot doubt; but not to the Extent, Daniel believes. He overlooks an obscure but most important fact of physiology, that in certain cases (more especially in irritable Constitutions convalescing from complaints of Stomach, Liver, or Kidneys) injurious Substances seem to act by pure abstract *Quality*, diminish the *Quantity* as you will. We have an analogous fact in Night Shade, the very smallest conceivable Doses of which appear to produce nearly the same effects as the largest—and this on all animals, on which it has been tried —& with myself 6 grains of Calomel produce the same effect as one, & one as six. If in addition to his natural quickness of eye & mental Intuition, & to his unaffected Good-sense (one proof of which I was delighted to learn, on the occasion of my having written a marginal Note in a book, he lent me (Willan's Synopsis of Cutaneous Complaints edited by Bateman) in which the Author having scouted the idea of Mother-marks, I had written— Ἐπέχω, me nimiâ experientiâ invitum cogente, i.e. I *hesitate* &c. Daniel was quite delighted—I have suffered myself, says he, for some years to be laughed at by my Brother Surgeons, because I will not *lie* for the honor of Philosophy!—In the multitude of Infants, I have help'd, or witnessed, Nature bringing into the World, whose Mothers I had previously attended, I have had such repeated facts, that I hold it presumptuous Pedantry to reject, because our present state of Science is inadequate to explain, them) —if to these I can add (as I am adding) habits of psychological analysis, Daniel will be one of our first men, in the medical Line.

In head & vigor of mind I am not amiss—in disposition to activity much improved—but subject at times to strange Relapses of Disquietude, without apparent cause or occasion—For instance, all Sunday last I was thoroughly *be-belzebubbed*.—Still however, I hope (especially if Daniel should determine on *bandaging* the small of my Right Leg) to be with you by Tea on Friday; but you dare not positively expect me.

I have had long & affecting Conversations with poor dear Allston. As to Sir G.B. I had given *him* up long ago—& nothing has happened of which, as he well remembers, I did not distinctly warn him, except the envious Duplicity of his Countryman, the wretch who *preys* on fair fame by *side Hints*—thence appropriately called Prey-side-Hint—and put on a Protegée, "whom like a young Dove, he could not but warm at his very breast"— "whose goodness was equal to his Science and Genius"—these were the old fratricide's, very words to *me*, verily, *a merry Cain* sort of treating *Abel* Folks (Spelling, avaunt!)—this I did not (God forbid, that I should) anticipate! All else has been better, rather than worse, than I had feared. Allston has not yet learnt all, he will learn, of the excessive meanness of Patrons, of the malignant Envy & Brutality of the Race of Painters!—The first Hour, I was with him after his re-arrival in England, I told him what a Devildom they were all members of—from three Causes, 1. & least, the necessity of Envy for the greater part in the Metropolis—2. from the double competition of Bread & Reputation—3, & chiefly, from vulgar Birth & want of all the Discipline of classical & gentlemanly education—Be assured, if you do not see me on Friday, it will not ⟨be⟩ a want of good will, or the effect of Indolence—your effusions must be therefore not *satirical*, but L E G iac.—

From mine, & Wade's Friend, Hartley, I can procure you gratis the very best *Advice*. He is one of the acutest Attorneys in Bristol, an honest man, & in full practice—and all the rest in the least possible expensive way.

I looked over the 5 first Books of the 1st (Quarto) edition of Joan of Arc yesterday, at Hood's request, in order to mark the lines written by me.—I was really astonished, 1. at the school-boy wretched Allegoric Machinery—2. at the transmogrification of the fanatic Virago into a modern novel-pawing Proselyte of the age of Reason, a Tom Paine in Petticoats, but *so* lovely!—& in love, moreover!—"on her rubied Cheek Hung Pity's crystal gem"! 3. at the utter want of all rhythm in the verse, the monotiny & dead *plumb down* of the Pauses—& the absence of all Bone, Muscle & Sinew in the single Lines.—His Carmen Triumphale! Is he grown silly?—The Courier for the last 2 years has been repeating me with a thousandfold Echo in its leading §§s; & S has bedevilified into vilest Rhyme rhythmless the leading §§s of the Courier.

My best Love to Mary & Charlotte. Repose, and a wineglass of Infusion of Senna with three tea-spoonfuls of Epsom Salts, as soon as she awakes, 3 mornings in one week, will make a *Hebe* of her—or to pay a yet higher compliment—her own prettier Self—In Bristol they will have it, that Mary is handsomer than Charlotte—how provokingly obstinate! S.T.C.

[*Addressed*] J. J. Morgan, Esqre
      Mrs Smith's
        Ashley
          Box
            Bath.

[*Postmarked*] Bristol
16 Ju⟨ne⟩ 181⟨4⟩.

INDEX

S. T. COLERIDGE

II. Works

GENERAL INDEX

PRINTED IN
GREAT BRITAIN
AT THE
UNIVERSITY PRESS
OXFORD
BY
CHARLES BATEY
PRINTER
TO THE
UNIVERSITY